Waltham Forest

Not For Loan

Chartered Institute of Housing

Housing Costs:

Universal Credit and Council Tax Rebates

2023-24

Sam Lister, Martin Ward
and Roger Thwaits

SHELTER

Help with Housing Costs: Guide to Universal Credit and Council Tax Rebates
Sam Lister and Martin Ward, 2014-23
Sam Lister, Martin Ward and Roger Thwaits 2023-24

Sam Lister is policy and practice officer at the Chartered Institute of Housing (email: *sam.lister@cih.org*) and a founding director of Citizens Advice Worcester and Citizens Advice Hereford. He has specialised in housing benefit and social security since 1993.

Martin Ward is an independent consultant and trainer on housing and benefit related matters (e-mail: *mward@knowledgeflow.org.uk*). He has provided consultancy services and training for several national organisations as well as many local authorities and large and small housing providers across the UK since 1982.

Roger Thwaits studies and writes about HB, CTR and UC. He has been involved with these schemes since they began in 1982, 1990 and 2013. At present he is focusing on supported accommodation and how vulnerable people's housing costs are met.

ISBN 978-1-9993510-8-3

Edited and typeset by Davies Communications
(www.daviescomms.com)

Printed by MBA Group Ltd

Chartered Institute of Housing

CIH is a registered charity and not-for-profit organisation. This means that the money we make is put back into the organisation and funds the activities we carry out to support the housing sector.

We have a diverse membership of people who work in both the public and private sectors in 20 countries on five continents across the world. We were granted a Royal Charter in 1984, and our work is governed by our Royal Charter and Byelaws, overseen by the Privy Council. We are also a registered charity, with education at the core of our charitable status. That means we must comply with the requirements of the law relating to charities. The Charity Commissioners regulate our activities in England and Wales and the Office of the Scottish Charity Regulator in Scotland.

England charity number 244067/R and Scotland number SCO40324.

Chartered Institute of Housing
Suites 5 and 6
First Floor, Rowan House
Westwood Way
Coventry
CV4 8HS

Telephone: 024 7685 1700

E-mail: *customer.services@cih.org*

Website: *www.cih.org*

Shelter

Shelter exists to defend the right to a safe home and fight the devastating impact the housing emergency has on people and society. We do this with campaigns, advice and support – and we never give up. We believe that home is everything.

88 Old Street
London
EC1V 9HU

Telephone: 0300 330 1234

Website: *shelter.org.uk*

For online housing advice and access to our emergency helpline, visit *shelter.org.uk/housing_advice*

Shelter, the National Campaign for Homeless People Limited 2023.

Registered charity in England & Wales (263710) and Scotland (SC002327).

Contents

1	Introduction	1
2	Who can get universal credit	9
3	UC claims and benefit unit	25
4	Migration to UC	43
5	Housing costs UC/SMI can meet	63
6	The housing costs element	87
7	The size of your home	109
8	Support for mortgage interest	119
9	Calculating UC	131
10	Income and capital for UC	151
11	UC changes	181
12	UC payments	191
13	UC overpayments	207
14	UC decisions and appeals	221
15	Council tax	241
16	Council tax rebates	255
17	Main CTR and SAR	267
18	CTR decisions and appeals	279
19	Rate rebates	287
20	Migrants and recent arrivals	303
21	EEA nationals	319
Appendix 1	UC/SMI/CTR legislation	339
Appendix 2	Weekly CTR applicable amounts: 2023-24	345
Appendix 3	Selected weekly benefit rates from April 2023	347
Appendix 4	Equivalent footnote references for Scotland and Wales	349
	Index	355

Preface

This guide explains the rules about universal credit and council tax rebates, focusing on help with housing costs. It gives the rules which apply from 6th April 2023, using information available on that date.

We welcome comments and criticisms on the contents of our guide and make every effort to ensure it is accurate. However, the only statement of the law is found in the relevant Acts, regulations, orders and rules (chapter 1).

We are grateful for the help and encouragement of many people who have been essential to the writing and production of this guide.

In particular, we thank Richard Stanier (Shelter) for his invaluable comments and help throughout each year, John Zebedee for the original material, Linda Davies and Peter Singer (editing and production), and staff from the Department for Work and Pensions and the Rent Service.

Sam Lister, Martin Ward and Roger Thwaits

April 2023

List of tables

Table   **Page**

1.1   UC terminology 2
1.2   Households on UC in Great Britain 4
1.3   Summary of UC changes from April 2022 7
2.1   Basic conditions for UC 9
2.2   16/17 year olds: the eligible groups 11
2.3   Students: the UC eligible groups 14
2.4   Work-related requirements: main rules 18
2.5   No work search or availability requirements 19
2.6   National minimum wage from April 2023 21
2.7   Work capability: medical conditions 22
3.1   Backdating UC: qualifying circumstances 32
3.2   UC assessment periods 33
3.3   People who are not non-dependants 40
4.1   Migration to UC dates and transitional element 44
4.2   Your total legacy benefits 54
4.3   Your indicative UC 55
5.1   Which housing costs and when from 64
5.2   Housing costs UC can meet 65
5.3   Supported or temporary accommodation 66
5.4   Care, support or supervision 67
5.5   Liability of renters 69
5.6   Excluded liabilities 76
5.7   Commerciality, contrivance and renters 77
6.1   Social landlords 88
6.2   Housing costs element for social renters 89
6.3   Service charges 95
6.4   Single people under 35: the UC excepted groups 101
6.5   LHA sizes of accommodation 102
6.6   No housing cost contributions 107
7.1   The UC size criteria 110
7.2   What counts as a bedroom: case law 112
8.1   Examples of alternative finance arrangements 120
8.2   Qualifying repairs and improvements 128
9.1   Amount of UC 132
9.2   UC allowances and elements (2023-24) 135
9.3   Carer element and LCW/LCWRA elements 143

Table		Page

9.4   Calculating UC benefit cap reductions 147
9.5   The UC benefit cap: excepted groups 149
10.1   The UC work allowance (2023-24) 153
10.2   Surplus earnings 154
10.3   Self-employed mixed expenses 161
10.4   What counts as unearned income in UC 165
10.5   The monthly amount of student income 168
10.6   Disregarded capital 172
11.1   When changes of circumstances take effect 183
12.1   Alternative payment arrangements 194
12.2   Maximum amount of budgeting advance 197
12.3   Payments to a landlord 198
12.4   Deductions: rent and service charge arrears 2023-24 203
12.5   UC deductions: priority order 205
13.1   Overpaid UC: recovery methods and rent arrears 214
13.2   Recovery of overpayments: maximum deductions from UC (2023-24) 215
14.1   Decisions, revisions and supersessions 226
14.2   When reconsidered decisions take effect 227
14.3   Non-appealable UC decisions 231
14.4   Directions a tribunal can give 236
15.1   Council tax bands 242
15.2   Owner liable not residents 245
15.3   Council tax exempt dwellings 246
15.4   Council tax disregarded persons 249
16.1   Kinds of CTR 255
16.2   Pension age or working age CTR 256
17.1   Main CTR: weekly non-dependant deductions 270
17.2   Main CTR: no non-dependant deductions 271
17.3   Main income disregards in main CTR 277
18.1   Appeals time limits 282
19.1   When UC rate rebates change 294
19.2   HB rate rebates: weekly non-dependant deductions 300
19.3   HB rate rebates: no non-dependant deductions 300
20.1   Migrants: who can get UC/HB/CTR 305
20.2   Simplified immigration law terminology 308
21.1   The European Economic Area (EEA) 324
21.2   Who is an EEA family member 333

Abbreviations

The principal abbreviations used in the guide are given below.

ADM	The DWP's *Advice for decision makers*
BORG	The DWP's *Benefits overpayment recovery guide*
CTC	Child tax credit
CTGM	The DWP's *Council tax guidance manual*
CTR	Council tax rebate
DLA	Disability living allowance
DLUHC	Department for Levelling Up, Housing and Communities
DWP	The Department for Work and Pensions in Great Britain
ESA	Employment and support allowance
ESA(IR)	Income-related employment and support allowance
HB	Housing benefit
HCS	Housing costs element
HMCTS	His Majesty's Courts and Tribunals Service
HMO	House in multiple occupation
HMRC	His Majesty's Revenue and Customs
IS	Income support
JSA	Jobseeker's allowance
JSA(IB)	Income-based jobseeker's allowance
LCW	Limited capability for work
LCWRA	Limited capability for work and work-related activity
LHA	Local housing allowance
MHCLG	Ministry of Housing, Communities and Local Government
OG	The DWP's *UC Operational Guidance*
PIP	Personal independence payment
SAR	Second adult rebate
SDA	Severe disablement allowance
SMI	Support for mortgage interest
SPC	State pension credit (guarantee credit and savings credit)
UC	Universal credit
UK	England, Scotland, Wales and Northern Ireland
WTC	Working tax credit

Key to footnotes

AA	The Social Security Administration Act 1992
art	Article number
CBA	The Social Security Contributions and Benefits Act 1992
C&P	The Universal Credit, Personal Independence Payment, Jobseeker's Allowance and Employment and Support Allowance (Claims and Payments) Regulations 2013, SI No 380
CT(A&E)	The Council Tax (Administration and Enforcement) Regulations 1992, SI No 613
CT(A&E)S	The Council Tax (Administration and Enforcement) (Scotland) Regulations 1992, SI No 1332
CT(ED)	The Council Tax (Exempt Dwellings) Order 1992, SI No 558
CT(LO)	The Council Tax (Liability of Owners) Regulations 1992, SI No 551
CTP	The Council Tax Reduction Schemes (Prescribed Requirements) (England) Regulations 2012, SI No 2885
CT(RD)	The Council Tax (Reductions for Disabilities) Regulations 1992, SI No 554
CTPW	The Council Tax Reduction Scheme and Prescribed Requirements (Wales) Regulations 2013, SI No 3029
CTR	The Council Tax Reduction Schemes (Default Scheme) (England) Regulations 2012, SI No 2886
CTRW	The Council Tax Reduction Schemes (Default Scheme) (Wales) Regulations 2013, SI No 3035
CTS	The Council Tax Reduction (Scotland) Regulations 2021, SSI No 249
CTS66+	The Council Tax Reduction (State Pension Credit) (Scotland) Regulations 2012, SSI No 319
D&A	The Universal Credit, Personal Independence Payment, Jobseeker's Allowance and Employment and Support Allowance (Decisions and Appeals) Regulations 2013, SI No 381
DDO	The Council Tax (Discount Disregards) Order 1992, SI 1992 No 548
DDR	The Council Tax (Additional Provisions for Discount Disregards) Regulations 1992, SI 1992 No 552
EEA	The Immigration (European Economic Area) Regulations 2016, SI No 1052
FTPR	The Tribunal Procedure (First-tier Tribunal) (Social Entitlement Chamber) Rules 2008, SI No 2685

FTSLT	The First-tier Tribunal for Scotland Local Taxation Chamber (Rules of Procedure) Regulations 2022, SSI No 364
HB	The Housing Benefit Regulations 2006, SI No 213
HB66+	The Housing Benefit (Persons who have attained the age for state pension credit) Regulations 2006, SI No 214
IAA99	The Immigration and Asylum Act 1999
LMI	The Loans for Mortgage Interest Regulations 2017, SI No 725
LGFA	The Local Government Finance Act 1992
IAA99	The Immigration and Asylum Act 1999
NIAA	The Social Security Administration (Northern Ireland) Act 1992
NICBA	The Social Security Contributions and Benefits (Northern Ireland) Act 1992
NIC&P	The Universal Credit, Personal Independence Payment, Jobseeker's Allowance and Employment and Support Allowance (Claims and Payments) Regulations (Northern Ireland) 2016, NISR No 220
NID&A	The Universal Credit, Personal Independence Payment, Jobseeker's Allowance and Employment and Support Allowance (Decisions and Appeals) Regulations (Northern Ireland) 2016, NISR No 221
NIHB	The Housing Benefit Regulations (Northern Ireland) 2006, NISR No 405
NIHB66+	The Housing Benefit (Persons who have attained the age for state pension credit) Regulations (Northern Ireland) 2006, NISR No 406
NILMI	The Loans for Mortgage Interest Regulations (Northern Ireland) 2017, NISR No 176
NIOP	The Social Security (Overpayments and Recovery) Regulations (Northern Ireland) 2016, NISR No 224
NISR	Northern Ireland Statutory Rules
NIPOA	The Social Security (Payments on Account of Benefit) Regulations (Northern Ireland) 2016, NISR No 223
NISSO	The Social Security (Northern Ireland) Order 1998, SI No 1506 (NI 10)
NIUC	The Universal Credit Regulations (Northern Ireland) 2016, NISR No 216
NIUCED	The Universal Credit Housing Costs (Executive Determinations) Regulations (Northern Ireland) 2016, NISR No 222
NIUCTP	The Universal Credit (Transitional Provisions) Regulations (Northern Ireland) 2016, NISR No 226
NIWRO	The Welfare Reform (Northern Ireland) Order 2015, SI No 2006 (NI 1)
NIWRWO	The Welfare Reform and Work (Northern Ireland) Order 2016, SI 2016 No 999 (NI 1)

OPR	The Social Security (Overpayments and Recovery) Regulations 2013, SI No 384
para	Paragraph number
POA	The Social Security (Payments on Account of Benefit) Regulations 2013, SI No 383
reg	Regulation number
RO	Rates (Northern Ireland) Order 1977, SI No 2157
RR	The Rate Relief Regulations (Northern Ireland) 2017, NISR No 184
RRHB	The Rate Relief (General) Regulations (Northern Ireland) 2007, NISR No 204
RRHB66+	The Rate Relief (Qualifying Age) Regulations (Northern Ireland) 2007, NISR No 203
RRLPA	The Rate Relief (Lone Pensioner Allowance) Regulations (Northern Ireland) 2008, NISR No 124
s	Section number
sch	Schedule number
SI	Statutory instrument [year and reference number]
SSA	Social Security Act 1998
SSHD	Secretary of State for the Home Department
SSI	Scottish Statutory Instrument
SSWP	Secretary of State for Work and Pensions
TCEA	Tribunals, Courts and Enforcement Act 2007
UC	The Universal Credit Regulations 2013, SI No 376
UCROO	The Rent Officers (Universal Credit Functions) Order 2013, SI No 382
UCTP	The Universal Credit (Transitional Provisions) Regulations 2014, SI No 1230
UTPR	The Tribunal Procedure (Upper Tribunal) Rules 2008, SI No 2698
VTRE	The Valuation Tribunal for England (Council Tax and Rating Appeals) (Procedure) Regulations 2009, No 2269, as amended by SI 2013/465
VTRW	The Valuation Tribunal for Wales Regulations 2010, No 713, as amended by SI 2013/547
WRA	The Welfare Reform Act 2012
WRWA	The Welfare Reform and Work Act 2016

What you can claim

	Working age	Pension age
Renters		
Rent payments	UC	HB
Service charge payments	UC	HB
Renters in supported or temporary accommodation		
Rent payments	HB	HB
Service charge payments	HB	HB
Owners		
Owner occupier payments	SMI	SMI
Service charge payments	UC	SPC
Shared owners		
Owner occupier payments	SMI	SMI
Rent payments	UC	HB
Service charge payments	UC	HB
All		
Living costs	UC	SPC
Council tax (Great Britain)	CTR	CTR
Rates (Northern Ireland)	RR	RR
Other help	DHPs etc	DHPs etc

Volume 1: Guide to Universal Credit and Council Tax Rebates
Universal credit (UC)
Support for mortgage interest (SMI)
Council tax rebate (CTR)
Rate rebate (RR)
Volume 2: Guide to Housing Benefit
Housing benefit (HB)
State pension credit (SPC)
Discretionary housing payments (DHPs)

Chapter 1 **Introduction**

- ■ Universal credit and migration to UC: see paras 1.2-13.
- ■ Council tax reductions and rebates: see paras 1.14-20.
- ■ Using this guide, the law and guidance: see paras 1.21-30.

1.1   Welcome to this guide, which explains the new system of getting help with your housing costs. The guide is used by people claiming benefits, advisers, landlords, mortgage lenders, benefit administrators and appeal tribunals. It gives the rules from April 2023.

UC scheme

1.2   Universal credit (UC) helps meet your living needs if you are working age. For renters, the housing costs element (HCE) helps pay your rent. For owner occupiers, support for mortgage interest (SMI) loans help pay your mortgage interest.

1.3   UC applies throughout the UK and is replacing six legacy benefits including working age housing benefit (HB) in most cases (para 1.12). During the transition to UC, many people continue to receive these legacy benefits, but once the transition is complete, about seven to eight million households are expected to be on UC.

1.4   Table 1.1 gives the main terminology used in UC, table 1.2 gives statistics, and table 1.3 summarises recent and planned changes to UC.

Who can get UC

1.5   If you are working age:

  (a) you can make a claim for UC at any time;

  (b) but there are exceptions for some under 18-year-olds, students, migrants, prisoners and others.

Chapter 2 describes who can get UC and chapter 3 explains how to claim.

1.6   If you are currently getting one or more legacy benefits (para 1.12):

  (a) the DWP will at some point advise you to claim UC, and in this case you can get transitional protection to stop you being worse off;

  (b) you can claim UC before that, but in this case you don't get transitional protection;

  (c) in either case, you can't go back to legacy benefits.

This is called 'migration' and is explained in chapter 4.

Table 1.1 **UC terminology**

Claimant and joint claimant

A claimant is someone who is making a claim for UC or someone who is getting UC. If you are claiming as a couple you are joint claimants.

Working age and pension age

Pension age is 66 or over. Working age is under 66.

Benefit unit

Your benefit unit means you (both of you if you are a couple) and any children and young persons you are responsible for (but not non-dependants).

Extended benefit unit

Your extended benefit unit means your benefit unit and any non-dependants who live in your household.

Couple and single person

You are a couple if you are two people who are married, in a civil partnership, or living together as a couple. You are single if you are not a couple.

Child and young person

A child is someone under 16. A young person is someone aged 16 to 19 who is in secondary education.

Non-dependant

A non-dependant is an adult son, daughter, relative, friend or other adult who lives with you on a non-commercial basis.

Assessment period

UC is assessed on a monthly basis. Your first assessment period begins on the day you claim UC and the following ones start on the same date each month.

Maximum UC

Your maximum UC represents your living needs and is is made up of a standard allowance and other elements you and your benefit unit qualify for. It is compared with your income when your UC is calculated.

Housing costs element

The housing costs element is the part of your maximum UC which is for your rent and service charges. Mortgage interest can be met by DWP loans (SMI).

Housing cost contribution

Each non-dependant you have is normally expected to make a housing cost contribution towards your rent and service charges.

The amount of your UC

1.7   How much UC you get depends on your financial and other circumstances, including whether you have a family, are capable of work, are a carer, and/or have childcare costs. See chapters 9 and 10.

UC and your housing costs

1.8   You can get help towards your rent and service charge payments as part of your UC. This is called a 'housing costs element'. It is less if you have one or more non-dependants. This is explained in chapters 5 to 7.

1.9   You can get support for your mortgage interest (SMI) as a repayable DWP loan. You must be eligible for UC. This is explained in chapters 5 and 8.

Claims, payments and appeals

1.10   You usually claim UC online. If you are claiming as a couple, you make a joint claim. Your claim goes to:

(a)   the DWP (Department for Work and Pensions) in Great Britain;

(b)   the DFC (Department for Communities) in Northern Ireland.

In this guide, references to the DWP include the DFC.

1.11   UC is based on monthly assessment periods, and you are paid at the end of these. Your landlord or mortgage lender can be paid some of your UC. If you think your UC is wrong, you can ask the DWP or DFC to reconsider and appeal to an independent tribunal. The rules about claims, payments, overpayments and appeals are in chapter 3 and 11 to 14.

The legacy benefits

1.12   The legacy benefits UC is replacing are:

(a)   HB for working age claimants (except in supported or temporary accommodation: table 5.3);

(b)   income-based JSA (JSA(IB));

(c)   income-related ESA (ESA(IR));

(d)   income support (IS);

(e)   child tax credit (CTC); and

(f)   working tax credit (WTC).

Other benefits

1.13   The following benefits continue alongside UC:

(a)   state pension credit (SPC);

(b)   HB for pension age claimants;

(c)   HB for people in temporary or supported accommodation (table 5.3);

(d)   discretionary housing payments (DHPs);

(e)   new-style JSA and ESA (previously called JSA(C) and ESA(C));

(f)   PIP, DLA, carer's allowance, child benefit and all other state benefits (appendix 2).

Table 1.2 **Households on UC in Great Britain**

	All households	With housing costs element
November 2017	623,890	315,282
May 2018	837,361	472,416
November 2018	1,265,215	748,288
May 2019	1,820,786	1,126,395
November 2019	2,343,563	1,489,370
May 2020	4,244,571	2,335,451
November 2020	4,886,146	2,721,102
May 2021	4,986,314	2,913,872
November 2021	4,794,506	2,951,875
May 2022	4,714,277	3,016,638
November 2022	4,915,511	3,148,386

■ Source: DWP, Stat-Xplore (https://tinyurl.com/DWPstat-xplore)

Examples: Help with housing costs: UC and CTR

1. A single tenant

A single person rents her home. If she meets the conditions:

■   she can get a UC housing costs element towards her living needs and her rent;

■   she can get CTR towards her council tax.

2. A home owner couple

A couple are buying their home on a mortgage. If they meet the conditions:

■   they can get UC towards their living needs;

■   they can get an SMI loan towards their mortgage interest;

■   they can get CTR towards their council tax.

Council tax reductions and rebates

1.14 Council tax applies in Great Britain (England, Scotland and Wales). It has several kinds of reductions and rebates that you can get whether you are working age or pension age.

Council tax

1.15 Chapter 15 describes:

(a) who gets a council tax bill;

(b) council tax exemptions;

(c) the single person discount.

Council tax rebates

1.16 Chapters 16 and 17 give the details about CTR, including:

(a) CTR if you are on UC;

(b) CTR for other working age and pension age claimants;

(c) variations between England, Scotland and Wales, and between councils in England;

(d) the different kinds of council tax rebate (CTR).

1.17 The family and household terms in CTR are the same as in UC (table 1.1) except:

(a) a claimant is sometimes called an 'applicant';

(b) 'joint claimant' isn't used because in a couple one of you is the claimant for both;

(c) 'family' is used instead of benefit unit.

Claims, awards and appeals

1.18 You claim council tax reductions and rebates from the council that sends your council tax bill.

1.19 CTR is calculated on a weekly basis, and benefit weeks begin on a Monday. Other council tax reductions are awarded for the exact period you qualify for. If you think your CTR or other reduction is wrong, you can ask the council to reconsider and appeal to an independent tribunal. The rules about CTR claims, awards, and appeals are in chapters 16 and 18.

Rate rebates in Northern Ireland

1.20 Northern Ireland has domestic rates instead of council tax. Rate rebates and other reductions are described in chapter 19.

Using this guide

Benefit rules and figures

1.21   The rules in this guide apply from April 2023. The next edition will give the rules from April 2024.

1.22   The UC figures in this guide apply in assessment periods (para 3.38) beginning on or after 6th April 2023.

1.23   The CTR figures apply from 1st April 2023.

UC law and guidance

1.24   In Great Britain the main law about UC is in:

  (a)   the Welfare Reform Act 2012;

  (b)   The Universal Credit Regulations 2013;

  (c)   the Universal Credit (Transitional Provisions) Regulations 2014.

Equivalent law applies in Northern Ireland and appendix 1 gives the full details for both Great Britain and Northern Ireland.

1.25   Government guidance on the UC scheme for DWP staff in Great Britain is the responsibility of the DWP. It is contained in its Advice for Decision Makers (ADM). The DWP also issues circulars to local councils which are published.

CTR law and guidance

1.26   The main law about CTR is in:

  (a)   the Local Government Finance Act 1992;

  (b)   the Local Government Finance Act 2012;

  (c)   various Council Tax Reduction Schemes Regulations for England, Scotland and Wales.

Appendix 1 gives the full details.

1.27   Government guidance on the CTR scheme is the responsibility of the DLUHC (Department for Levelling Up, Housing and Communities) in England, and of the Scottish and Welsh Governments. In England the Council Tax Guidance Manual (CTGM) is produced by the Valuation Tribunal Service.

Case law

1.28   Case law means judgments made:

  (a)   in Great Britain by the Upper Tribunal (formerly the Social Security Commissioners) and the courts (the High Court, Court of Appeal and Supreme Court);

  (b)   in Northern Ireland by the NI Commissioners and the courts.

Case law interprets the law, and is binding on the DWP/DFC, local councils/NIHE and First-tier Tribunals. This guide gives the case law about UC. It also includes case law about HB and other benefits when this applies to UC.

Finding and using the law and guidance

1.29 The law, guidance and case law is available online (as shown in the footnote below). The footnotes throughout this guide show which piece of law applies to particular paragraphs. For CTR they give the law in England, and the law for Scotland and Wales is in Appendix 4.

Abbreviations

1.30 The tables at the front of this guide give:

(a) a list of abbreviations used in the text; and

(b) a key to the abbreviations used in the footnotes.

Table 1.3 **Summary of UC changes from April 2022**

3rd May 2022 SI 2022/449 15th Sep 2022 NISR 2022/202	Nationals from the ECSMA and ESC treaty member states who have limited leave with a 'no public funds' condition are excluded from UC and CTR. Existing awards can continue until entitlement ends.
4th May 2022 SI 2022/448 NISR 2022/172	Payments of local welfare assistance made by councils are disregarded as capital for UC for up to 12 months.
28th Jun 2022	Social Security (Additional Payments) Act 2022 introduces two additional payments amounting to £650 for people on UC, SPC and legacy benefits. These payments are all disregarded for UC (section 8).
25th Jul 2022 SI 2022/752 NISR 2022/194	Technical changes to the regulations governing the migration to UC. Limit on managed migration to 10,000 claims is lifted. DWP discretionary hardship payments for people who lose out from managed migration abolished.
26th Sep 2022 SI 2022/886 SI 2022/223	Administrative earnings threshold revised (para 2.41)– no longer tied to JSA rate (plus £5/£10 per week). Recalibrated to earnings equivalent to 12 hours per week at the National Living Wage for single person or 19 hours per week for a couple.
1st Oct 2022 SI 2022/942 NISR 2022/211	New exceptions to the LHA shared accommodation rate (para 9.20) for victims of domestic abuse and human trafficking.

1.29 UC regulations with amendments and CTR legislation: www.legislation.gov.uk
UC guidance (ADM): www.gov.uk/government/publications/advice-for-decision-making-staff-guide
UC operational guidance (House of Commons Library, Deposited Papers): DEP2022-0860 Universal Credit guidance, 18 October 2022, https://tinyurl.com/DEP2022-0860
CTR guidance (England): www.gov.uk/government/collections/localising-council-tax-support
Upper Tribunal Decisions prior to Jan 2016: https://tinyurl.com/SSDecisions1
Upper Tribunal decisions from Jan 2016 onwards: https://tinyurl.com/SSDecisions2

18th Oct 2022 SI 2022/990 NISR 2022/230	Irish citizens who left Ukraine due to the Russian invasion are exempt from the habitual residence test.
30th Jan 2023 SI 2023/7 NISR 2023/3	Administrative earnings threshold increases for a single person from the equivalent of 12 hours per week at the National Living Wage to 15 hours per week and for a couple from 19 to 24 hours per week.
31st Jan 2023 6th Apr 2023 SI 2023/6 NISR 2023/4	LHA rates frozen during 2023-24 at their April 2020 cash level.
6th Apr 2023 SI 2023/316 SI 2023/335 NISR 2023/43 NISR 2023/42	Benefits up-rating based on September 2022 consumer prices index of 10.1%. Benefit cap levels also uprated for the first time since 2016 by 10.1%.
6th Apr SI 2023/226 NISR 2023/31	UC claimants can apply for SMI after three months instead of nine. Zero earnings rule for SMI abolished so UC claimants can apply for a mortgage interest loan while in work.

Planned changes

September 2023	Start of nationwide phased rollout of the 'in-work progression' offer. Claimants with low earnings will be required to meet with their work coach to help them increase their hours or earnings (HM Treasury, Autumn Statement 2022, CP 751, para 3.7).
2023 – March 2025	Phase one of the revised 'managed migration' programme: claimants with an award of CTC/WTC , JSA(IB), IS or HB only are transferred. During both phases transitional protection applies and claimants living in supported or temporary accommodation continue to get HB.
April 2025 – March 2028	Second (final) phase of UC managed migration programme. Claimants with an award of ESA(IR) (without tax credits) are transferred (HM Treasury, Autumn Statement 2022, CP 751, para 5.15).
April 2026	The work capability assessment and LCWRA element (paras 2.45, 9.32) to be replaced by a health element based on the assessment for PIP (Health and Disability White Paper, 2023).
April 2026 – March 2028	State pension age is gradually rising from 66 to 67.
April 2028	The transfer of pension age claimants from HB to SPC starts, with a new housing element meeting housing costs in a similar way to UC (HM Treasury, Autumn Statement 2022, CP 751, para 5.14).

Chapter 2 **Who can get universal credit**

- Entitlement and age limits: see paras 2.1-13.
- Students: see paras 2.14-19.
- Migrants, prisoners, hospital detainees and religious orders: see paras 2.20-28.
- Presence in the UK: see paras 2.29-35.
- The claimant commitment: see paras 2.36-46.
- Sanctions and hardship payments: see paras 2.47-54.

Entitlement

2.1 To get UC, you must make a claim and meet the basic conditions in table 2.1. You must also meet the financial conditions (paras 9.3-11).

Table 2.1 **Basic conditions for UC**

(a) You must be working age (under 66).

(b) You must be aged 16 or more.

(c) If you are aged 16 or 17 you must be in an eligible group (table 2.2).

(d) If you are a student you must be in an eligible group (table 2.3).

(e) You must not be an excluded migrant (paras 2.20-21).

(f) You must not be a prisoner, hospital detainee or member of a religious order (paras 2.22-28).

(g) You must in most cases be in the UK (para 2.29).

(h) You must accept a claimant commitment if required to do so (para 2.36).

Notes:

- If you are a single person, you must meet all these conditions (para 2.2).
- If you are in a couple, at least one of you must meet all these conditions (paras 2.4).
- If you are severely disabled, see also paras 4.43-46.

T2.1 WRA 4; UC 3(2),(3), Part 2; NIWRO 9; NIUC 3(1),(2), Part 2

UC for single people

2.2   If you are a single person (paras 3.47-48), you must meet all the basic conditions to get UC (table 2.1).

2.3   In this case:

  (a) you make the claim (para 3.2);

  (b) you get the standard allowance for a single person plus any child and other elements you qualify for (para 9.12);

  (c) your own income and capital is taken into account (para 10.2).

UC for couples

2.4   If you are a couple (paras 3.49-51), you can usually get UC as a joint claim couple, but in some cases as a single person (paras 2.5-8). For polygamous marriages, see paras 3.60-61.

Joint claim couples

2.5   To get UC as a joint claim couple, you must:

  (a) both meet all the basic conditions (table 2.1); or

  (b) both meet all those conditions except that (only) one of you is:

    ■ over 66, or

    ■ an excluded student.

2.6   In this case:

  (a) you and your partner both make the UC claim (para 3.3);

  (b) you get the standard allowance for a couple plus any child and other elements you qualify for (para 9.12);

  (c) you and your partner's joint income and capital is taken into account (para 10.2).

In a couple but claiming as a single person

2.7   To get UC as a single person:

  (a) you must both meet all the basic conditions (table 2.1); except that

  (b) your partner (but not you) is:

    ■ a 16/17-year-old who is not in an eligible group, or

    ■ an excluded migrant, or

    ■ a prisoner, hospital detainee or member of a religious order, or

    ■ absent from the UK.

2.2   WRA 1(1),(2), 2(1)(a), 3(1); NIWRO 6(1),(2), 7(1)(a), 8(1)

2.5   WRA 1(1),(2), 2(1)(b), 3(2); UC 3(2); NIWRO 6(1),(2), 7(1)(b), 8(2); NIUC 3(1)

2.7   WRA 1(1),(2), 2(2), 3(1); UC 3(3); NIWRO 6(1),(2), 7(2), 8(1); NIUC 3(2)

2.8   In this case:

(a) only you make the UC claim (para 3.2);

(b) you get the standard allowance for a single person plus any child and other elements you and your benefit unit qualify for (para 9.12);

(c) you and your partner's joint income and capital is taken into account (para 10.2).

Maximum age

2.9   To get UC, you must be working age (under 66) or in a couple at least one of you must be working age. When you reach 66 (or in a couple, both of you do) you can get SPC (para 11.25).

Minimum age

2.10   To get UC you must have reached the minimum age, or in a couple both of you must have reached the minimum age. This is:

(a) 16 if you are in an eligible group in table 2.2; or

(b) 18 in all other cases.

Table 2.2 **16/17 year olds: the eligible groups**

(a) Your benefit unit includes a child or (if you are in a couple) a young person (para 3.62).

(b) You have limited capability for work or for work and work-related activity (paras 2.43-45).

(c) You are within:

  ▪ 11 weeks before your expected date of confinement during pregnancy, or

  ▪ 15 weeks after giving birth (including a still-birth after 24 weeks of pregnancy).

(d) You are a carer and meet the conditions for a carer element (para 9.39), even if you share care (para 9.40).

(e) You are without parental support (para 2.13).

Note: Only (a) and (b) apply to care leavers (paras 2.11-12).

2.9   Pensions Act 1995, sch 4 para 1(6); WRA 4(1)(b),(4); UC 3(2)(a);
         Pensions (Northern Ireland) Order 1995, SI No 3213, sch 2 para 1(7); NIWRO 9(1)(b),(4); NIUC 3(1)(a)

2.10   WRA 4(1)(a),(3); NIWRO 9(1)(a),(3)

T2.2   UC 8(2), 26(3)(b)(ii), 30, sch 4 para 4; NIUC 8(2), 27(3)(b)(ii), 31, sch 4 para 4

16/17-year-old care leavers

2.11   If you are a care leaver aged 16 or 17, you can only get UC if you are in group (a) or (b) in table 2.2. And in these cases your UC only covers your living costs, not your rent or service charges.

2.12   You are a care leaver if:

(a) you were in care (looked after by a local authority) for one or more periods beginning after you reached 14 (in Scotland, following a children's hearing);

(b) one of these periods continued past your 16th birthday; and

(c) the periods totalled at least three months, or (except in Scotland) would have done apart from the fact that on your 16th birthday you were in hospital or detained in an institution under a court order.

But periods of up to one month aren't counted towards the three months if you spent them in respite care and then returned to the care of your parent(s) or the person with parental responsibility for you.

Without parental support

2.13   In table 2.2(e) and table 2.3(f), you are 'without parental support' if you aren't in care but:

(a) you have no parent or guardian (i.e. someone acting in the place of your parent); or

(b) you cannot live with them because:

   ▪ you are estranged from them, or

   ▪ there is a serious risk to your physical or mental health or of significant harm if you did; or

(c) you are living away from them, and they cannot support you financially because they:

   ▪ have a physical or mental impairment, or

   ▪ are detained in custody, or

   ▪ are prohibited from entering or re-entering the UK.

2.11   UC 8(1),(2),(4); NIUC 8(1),(2),(4)

2.12   UC 8(4) definition: 'care leaver'; NIUC 8(4)

2.13   UC a definition: 'looked after by a local authority', 8(1)(g),(3),(4); NIUC 2,8(1)(g),(3),(4)

Students

Who is a student

2.14   You are a student if you are undertaking:

(a) non-advanced education (para 2.15); or

(b) full-time advanced education (para 2.16).

The DWP can treat any other course as falling within (a) or (b) if it is incompatible with the work-related requirements in your claimant commitment (para 2.38).

Non-advanced education

2.15   This means:

(a) education or training up to level 3 (A levels or equivalent) that includes more than 12 hours per week of guided learning during term time;

(b) but not courses provided under an employment contract or government-sponsored work preparation courses.

Full-time advanced education

2.16   This means:

(a) full-time education above level 3 (degree or equivalent); and

(b) any other course for which you get a student loan or grant (para 10.56).

In (a) 'full-time' usually relates to the course description rather than the amount of time the student devotes to it ([2022] UKUT 73 (AAC)).

The period you count as a student

2.17   You count as a student from the day you start the course to the day it ends or you abandon it or are dismissed from it. This:

(a) includes all term-times and vacations within that period; but

(b) doesn't include periods in which:

■   you take time out of your course with the consent of your educational establishment because you are (or have been) ill or caring for someone, and

■   you aren't eligible for a student loan or grant.

2.18   You also count as a student the 31st August after:

(a) your 16th birthday, in all cases; and

(b) your 19th birthday, if you began non-advanced education before that birthday.

2.14   UC 12(1),(1A),(2),(4); NIUC 12(1),(2),(4)

2.15   UC 5(1)(b),(2)-(4), 12(1A),(1B) definition: 'relevant training scheme'; NIUC 6(1)(b),(2)-(4)
        https://www.gov.uk/what-different-qualification-levels-mean

2.16   UC 12(2),(3), 68(7); NIUC 12(2),(3), 68(7)

2.17   UC 13; NIUC 13

2.18   UC 5(1),(2); NIUC 6(1),(2)

Which students can get UC

2.19   Table 2.3 shows which students are eligible for UC. If you are an excluded student (a student not in the table), you can't get UC. And if you are in a couple, you can't get UC if both of you are excluded students. But if only one of you is an excluded student, you can get UC as a joint claim couple (para 2.5).

Table 2.3 **Students: the UC eligible groups**

Non-advanced education and full-time education

(a) Your benefit unit includes a child or young person (para 3.62).

(b) You have a foster child placed with you.

(c) You have reached pension age.

(d) You:

  ■ are on PIP, DLA or (in Scotland) adult or child disability payment, attendance allowance or an equivalent benefit (para 10.54); and

  ■ have limited capability for work (LCW) or for work and work-related activity (LCWRA) (paras 2.43-45); and

  ■ were assessed as having LCW or LCWRA (in your claim for UC or ESA) before you started receiving education (Kays v SSWP).

(e) You transferred to UC as part of managed migration (paras 4.24-26) and since your migration day (para 4.29) you have not:

  ■ changed to a different course;

  ■ become a couple or a single person as described in para 4.51;

  ■ had a reduction in your earned income of the kind in para 4.52;

  ■ had a gap in your UC of longer than three months due to an increase in your earned or unearned income; or

  ■ had a gap in your UC of any length in any other case.

Non-advanced education only

(f) You:

  ■ are aged under 21, or aged 21 and reached that age while on your course; and

  ■ are without parental support (para 2.13).

Note: The details of (e) were different before 25th July 2022.

2.19   WRA 4(1)(d),(6); UC 3(2)(b), 13(4), 14; NIWRO 9(1)(d),(6); NIUC 3(1)(b), 13(4), 14

T2.3   UC 2 definition: 'foster parent', 12(3), 14; UCTP 60; NIUC 2, 12(3), 14; NIUCTP 61
        Kays v SSWP [2022] EWHC 167 (Admin) https://caselaw.nationalarchives.gov.uk/ewhc/admin/2022/167

Migrants, prisoners, detainees and religious orders

Migrants and recent arrivals

2.20   Chapter 20 explains:

(a) who is a migrant (for example this includes many recent arrivals to the UK);

(b) which migrants are eligible for UC and which are excluded.

2.21   If you are an excluded migrant, you can't get UC. But if your partner is an excluded migrant and you are not, you can get UC as a single person (para 2.7).

Prisoners

2.22   You are a 'prisoner' if you are detained in custody (other than hospital: para 2.27). You can't get UC (except as explained in para 2.24). But if your partner is a prisoner and you are not, you can get UC as a single person (para 2.7).

Prisoners on temporary release

2.23   You are a prisoner if you are on temporary release, so the rules in paras 2.22 and 2.24 apply to you.

Single prisoners' housing costs

2.24   You can get a UC housing costs element towards your rent and service charges (para 5.3) for the first six months that you are a prisoner if:

(a) you had already claimed UC before you became a prisoner; and

(b) you were entitled to UC as a single person immediately before you became a prisoner (including a couple claiming as a single person: see para 2.7); and

(c) the calculation of your UC included a UC housing costs element; and

(d) you haven't yet been sentenced or have been sentenced but aren't expected to serve more than six months.

2.25   When you meet the conditions in para 2.24, your UC is recalculated to include just the housing costs element (paras 9.7-8).

2.26   If you are a single prisoner you can only get SMI on a dwelling you occupy as your home (para 5.43). See paras 5.47-51 for details.

Hospital detainees

2.27   You are a hospital detainee if you are serving a sentence of imprisonment detained in hospital. You can't get UC (even for housing costs). But if your partner is a hospital detainee and you are not, you can get UC as a single person (para 2.7).

2.21   WRA 4(1)(c),(5); UC 3(3)(b),(e), 9; NIWRO 9(1)(c),(5); NIUC 3(2)(b),(e),

2.22-23 UC 2 definition: 'prisoner'; NIUC 2

2.24-25 WRA 6(1)(a); 19(1)(b),(2),(3); NIWRO 11(1)(a); NIUC 19(1)(b),(2),(3)

2.27   WRA 6(1)(a); UC 19(1)(c),(4); NIWRO 11(1)(a); NIUC 19(1)(c),(4)

Member of a religious order

2.28   You can't get UC if you are a member of a religious order and are fully maintained by them. But if this applies to your partner and not you, you can get UC as a single person (para 2.7).

Presence in the UK

2.29   This section gives the UC basic conditions about being in the UK. This means Great Britain or Northern Ireland, but not Ireland, the Channel Islands or the Isle of Man.

2.30   To get UC you must be in the UK. This means you must be physically present here. If you are in a couple, and you are in the UK but your partner is not, you can get UC as a single person (para 2.7). Exceptions to this rule are in paras 2.31-35.

Crown servants and HM Forces

2.31   You do not have to be in the UK to get UC if you are absent for the following reasons, nor does your partner if they are accompanying you:

(a)   you are a Crown servant or member of HM Forces; and

(b)   you are posted overseas to perform your duties; and

(c)   immediately before you were posted overseas you were habitually resident in the UK.

Temporary absence abroad: first month

2.32   If you are on UC, you can continue to get UC during a temporary absence from the UK of up to one month (so long as it is not expected to exceed one month) whatever the reason for your absence – for example you could be on holiday.

Temporary absence abroad: a death in the family

2.33   You can then continue to get UC for up to one further month during a temporary absence from the UK, if your absence is in connection with the death of:

(a)   your partner; or

(b)   a child or young person you or your partner are responsible for; or

(c)   a close relative (para 5.38) of you or one of the above.

But this applies only if it is unreasonable to expect you to return within the first month.

Temporary absence abroad: medical treatment etc

2.34   If you are on UC, you can continue to get UC during a temporary absence from the UK of up to six months (so long as it is not expected to exceed six months) if your absence is solely in connection with you:

2.28   WRA 6; UC 19(1)(a); NIWRO 11; NIUC 19(1)(a)

2.30   WRA 4(1)(c); UC 3(3)(b); NIWRO 9(1)(c); NIUC 3(2)(b), 9

2.31   UC 10; NIUC 10

2.32-33 UC 11(1)(a),(b)(i),(2); NIUC 11(1)(a),(b)(i),(2)

2.34   UC 11(1)(a),(b)(ii),(3),(5); NIUC 11(1)(a),(b)(ii),(3),(5)

(a) being treated by (or under the supervision of) a qualified practitioner for an illness or physical or mental impairment; or

(b) undergoing convalescence or care which results from treatment for an illness or physical or mental impairment which you had before you left the UK; or

(c) accompanying your partner or a child or young person you are responsible for, if their absence is for one of the above reasons.

Temporary absences abroad: mariners etc

2.35   If you are on UC, you can continue to get UC during a temporary absence from the UK of up to six months (so long as it is not expected to exceed six months) if you are:

(a) a mariner with a UK contract of employment; or

(b) a continental shelf worker in UK, EU or Norwegian waters.

The claimant commitment

2.36   To get UC you must agree to a claimant commitment, or if you are a joint claim couple you both must. This is a record of:

(a) your work-related requirements (para 2.38);

(b) the sanctions that can apply if you don't meet these requirements (para 2.47); and

(c) your duty to notify changes (para 11.2).

If you don't agree to a claimant commitment, you can't get UC (para 2.1). Or if you fail to accept a change to your claimant commitment during your award, you could be subject to a sanction (para 2.47) ([2022] UKUT 56 (AAC)).

2.37   But you don't have to agree to a claimant commitment if:

(a) you lack the capacity to do so; or

(b) exceptional circumstances make it unreasonable to expect you to do so; or

(c) you are terminally ill (para 9.37).

Work-related requirements

2.38   Your work-related activities can include:

(a) looking for work (the work search requirement);

(b) being available for work (the work availability requirement);

(c) attending an interview with your UC coach (the work-focused interview requirement);

(d) carrying out preparation for work (the work preparation requirement).

Table 2.4 summarises which requirements apply to you, and table 2.5 gives more details.

2.36   WRA 4(1)(e), 14; UC 15; NIWRO 9(1)(e), 19; NIUC 15

2.37   WRA 4(2); UC 16; NIWRO 9(2); NIUC 16

2.38   WRA 13; NIWRO 18

Employed earners

2.39   If you are an employed earner, the rules depend on the amount of your earnings (combined earnings in the case of a couple). If these are:

(a) at or above the conditionality threshold (para 2.40), you don't have to meet any of the work-related requirements; or

(b) below the conditionality threshold but at or above the administrative threshold (para 2.41), you only have to meet the work-focused interview and work preparation requirements; or

(c) below the administrative threshold, you have to meet all the work-related requirements

The conditionality threshold

2.40   The conditionality threshold for a single person is what you would earn for working 35 hours week (30 hours if you are an apprentice) at your rate of the national minimum wage (table 2.6). For a couple it is this amount for each of you. But the DWP can agree a lower number of hours if you have a disability, ill health or caring responsibilities for a child or adult.

Table 2.4 **Work-related requirements: main rules**

Your circumstances	Your work-related requirements
(a) Employed earnings at or above conditionality threshold (para 2.40)	No work-related activities
(b) Employed earnings below conditionality threshold but at or above administrative threshold (para 2.41)	Only work-focused interview/work preparation activities
(c) Employed earnings below administrative threshold	All work-related activities
(d) Gainfully self-employed and subject to minimum income floor (para 2.42)	No work-related activities
(e) With limited capability for work (LCW) (para 2.43)	Only work-focused interview/work preparation activities
(f) With limited capability for work and work-related activity (LCWRA)	No work-related activities
(g) With youngest child aged under one	No work-related activities
(h) With youngest child aged one or two	Only work-focused interview/work preparation activities
(i) With youngest child aged three or over	All work-related activities

Note:
The last three entries apply to lone parents and the lead carer in a couple (para 2.46).

2.40   UC 88(1), 90(2)(b),(3),(4); NIUC 87(1), 89(2)(b),(3),(4)

T 2.4   WRA 19(1),(2), 20-22; UC 90(1), 99(1),(6); NIWRO 24(1),(2), 25-27; NIUC 89(1), 97(1),(14)

Table 2.5 **No work search or availability requirements**

If you are in any of these groups, you don't have to meet the UC work search or availability requirements (para 2.38). But in some cases you have to meet the work-focused interview or work preparation requirements.

Employed earners, self-employed, work capability, temporary inability to work	(a) Your employed earnings are above the administrative threshold (para 2.41). (b) You are gainfully self-employed and the minimum income floor (MIF) applies to you (para 2.42). (c) You have limited capability for work (LCW), or for work and work-related capability (LCWRA) (para 2.43). (d) You are unable to work due to illness (usually no more than 14 days) or you are undertaking agreed work preparation.
Children, fostering, adoption, pregnancy *If you are in a couple, (e), (f) and usually (g) can only apply to one of you: you jointly choose which of you this is*	(e) You are responsible for a child under three years old; or (for up to 12 months) for a child under 16 whose parents can't care for them and who would otherwise be likely to go into local authority care. (f) You are the foster parent of a child under 16 years old. (g) You have adopted a child under 16 years old and it is within 12 months of the date of adoption (or the date 14 days before the expected date of placement if you request the 12 months to begin then), but this does not apply if you are the child's close relative (para 5.38) or foster parent. (h) You are pregnant and it is no more than 11 weeks before your expected date of confinement, or you were pregnant and it is no more than 15 weeks after your baby's birth (including a still-birth after 24 weeks of pregnancy).
Pension age, carers, students, domestic violence	(i) You have reached pension age. (j) You meet the conditions for a UC carer element, or would do so except that you share your caring responsibilities with someone who gets the carer element instead of you (para 9.40), or you do not do so but the DWP agrees you have similar caring responsibilities.

T2.5　(a)　UC 90(1),(2), 99(1),(6); NIUC 89(1),(2), 97(1),(14)　(b)　UC 90(5); NIUC 89(5)
　　　(c)　WRA 19(2)(a), 21(1)(a); NIWRO 24(2)(a), 26(1)(a)　(d)　UC 99(4),(4ZA),(4ZB),(5)(a),(c); NIUC 97(7),(7A),(7B),(11)(a),(c)
　　　(e)　WRA 19(2)(c),(6), 20(1)(a),21(1)(aa); UC 86,91(2)(e),(3);　(f)　UC 2,85,86, 89(1)(f), 91(2)(a)-(d);
　　　　　NWRO 24(2)(c),(6), 25(1)(a), 26(5); NIUC 85,90(2)(e),(3),91　　　NIUC 2,84,85, 88(1)(f), 90(2)(a)-(d)
　　　(g)　UC 89(1)(d),(3); NIUC 88(1)(d),(3)　(h)　UC 89(1)(c); NIUC 88(1)(c)
　　　(i)　UC 89(1)(a); NIUC 88(1)(a)　(j)　WRA 19(2)(b); UC 30, 89(1)(b),(2); NIWRO 24(2)(b); NIUC 31, 88(1)(b),(2)

	(k) You are a student and you fall within eligible group (f) in table 2.3, or you have a student loan or grant (other than a part-time postgraduate master's degree loan) and fall within any of the groups in that table.
	(l) You have been a victim of actual or threatened domestic violence within the past six months from a partner, former partner, or family member you are not (or no longer) living with. A 'family member' includes any close relative (table 5.4(k)). It also includes a grandparent, grandchild, step-brother/sister or brother/sister-in-law or, if any of them are in a couple, their partner. This applies for 13 weeks from when you notify the DWP about it, but only if it has not applied to you during the previous 12 months. It can apply for a further 13 weeks if you are responsible for a child
Treatment abroad, drug/alcohol programmes, emergencies etc, death in the family	(m) You are temporarily absent from GB in connection with treatment, convalescence or care for you, your partner or a child or young person, and you meet the conditions in para 2.34.
	(n) You are in an alcohol or drug dependency treatment programme and have been for no more than six months.
	(o) You temporarily have new or increased child care responsibilities (including when a child is affected by death or violence) or are dealing with a domestic emergency, funeral arrangements etc, and the DWP agrees.
	(p) Your partner, or a child or young person you or your partner are responsible for, or a child of yours (even if not included in your benefit unit) has died within the past six months.
	(q) You are a prisoner claiming UC for housing costs.
Prisoners, court proceedings, police protection, public duties	(r) You are attending a court or tribunal as a party to proceedings or witness.
	(s) You are receiving police protection and have been for no more than six months.
	(t) You are engaged in activities which the DWP agrees amount to a public duty.

T2.5　(k)　UC 68(7), 89(1)(da),(e); NIUC 68(7), 88(1)(e)　　　　(l)　UC 98; NIUC 96
　　　(m)　UC 99(3)(c); NIUC 97(6)(c)　　　　　　　　　　　　(n)　UC 99(3)(e); NIUC 97(6)(e)
　　　(o)　UC 99(4A)-(4C),(5)(b),(5A); NIUC 97(8)-(10),(11)(b),(12)　(p)　UC 99(3)(d); NIUC 97(6)(d)
　　　(q)　UC 99(3)(b); NIUC 97(6)(b)　　　　　　　　　　　　(r)　UC 99(3)(a); NIUC 97(6)(a)
　　　(s)　UC 99(3)(f); NIUC 97(6)(f)　　　　　　　　　　　　(t)　UC 99(3)(g); NIUC 97(6)(g)

Table 2.6 **National minimum wage from April 2023**

	Hourly rate	Weekly rate
(a) You are aged 23 or over	£10.42	£364.70
(b) You are aged 21 or 22	£10.18	£356.30
(c) You are aged 18 to 20	£ 7.49	£262.15
(d) You are aged 16 or 17	£ 5.28	£184.80
(e) You are an apprentice	£ 5.28	£158.40

Note: Rate (a) is also called the 'national living wage'. Rates (a)-(d) are based on 35 hours per week, and rate (e) on 30 hours per week.

The administrative threshold

2.41   Since January 2023, the administrative threshold for a single person it is what you would earn for working 15 hours per week at the 23+ rate of the national minimum wage (even if you are under 23). For a couple it is what you would earn for working 24 hours per week between you at that rate. It is planned to change again to 18 hours per week for a single person and from April 2024 to 18 hours for each partner in a couple [www].

Self-employed earners

2.42   If you are self-employed, you don't have to meet any of the work-related requirements (para 2.38). But if your profit is low, you can be treated as having earnings equal to the minimum income floor (MIF) (paras 10.42-46). The MIF is usually the same as the conditionality threshold (para 2.40).

Limited capability for work

2.43   If your ability to work is limited by ill-health or disability, you may qualify as having:

   (a) 'limited capability for work' (LCW) – in this case you only have to meet the work-focused interview and work preparation requirements; or

   (b) 'limited capability for work and work-related activity' (LCWRA) – in this case you don't have to meet any of the work-related requirements.

In both cases, you also qualify for a UC work allowance allowance (para 10.11) and may qualify for a work capability element in your UC (paras 9.31-32). If your medical condition or capability for work changes, see paras 11.23-24.

T2.6   SI 2015/621, regs 4, 4A; SI 2016/68 reg 3; SI 2023/354 reg 2

2.41   UC 99(1),(6); NIUC 97(1),(14)
         HM Treasury, Spring Budget, HC 1183, para 4.146, https://tinyurl.com/HC-1183

2.42   WRA 19; UC 62(1)-(4), 90(5); NIWRO 24; NIUC 63(1)-(4), 89(5)

2.43   WRA 19(2)(a), 21(1)(a),(2),(3); NIWRO 24(2)(a), 26(1)(a),(2),(3)

2.44   The DWP decides who has LCW or LCWRA as follows:

(a)   if you have one of the medical conditions in table 2.7, you automatically qualify;

(b)   if you were on ESA, SDA, IB or IS when you claimed UC, a decision in that benefit also applies for UC (para 9.38);

(c)   if you reclaim UC after a break of no more than six months, a decision that applied before the break continues to apply after it;

(d)   in any other case, the DWP carries out a work capability assessment (para 2.45).

2.45   To get a work capability assessment (WCA) you have to provide the DWP with a doctor's certificate or other medical evidence. The WCA is points-based and looks at whether you can carry out a fixed list of activities. It is usually carried out by telephone or by inviting you to attend a medical examination. The government plans to replace WCAs with a different system of assessment (table 1.3).

Table 2.7 **Work capability: medical conditions**

You don't have to have a work capability assessment when these apply.

Limited capability for work (LCW)

(a)   You are receiving, or recovering from, treatment for haemodialysis, plasmapheresis or total parietal nutrition.

(b)   You are receiving, or recovering from, in-patient treatment in hospital or similar institution.

(c)   You are prevented from working by law, for reasons relating to possible infection or contamination.

(d)   You have a condition that is life threatening or could cause substantial physical or mental health risk to others.

(e)   You are a joint claim couple, and one of you is over pension age and is entitled to PIP, DLA or adult or child disability payment.

Limited capability for work and work-related activity (LCWRA)

(f)   You are terminally ill (para 9.37).

(g)   You are pregnant and there is a serious risk of damage to you or your baby's health.

(h)   You are receiving chemotherapy or radiotherapy for cancer, or likely to receive it within six months, or recovering from it.

(i)   You are a joint claim couple, and one of you is over pension age and is entitled to:

   ■   the daily living component of PIP or adult disability payment,

   ■   the highest rate of the care component of DLA or child disability payment,

   ■   attendance allowance, or

   ■   armed forces independence payment.

2.44   UC 21(3C), 39(1),(6); UCTP 19-23; C&P 26(5); NIUC 27(7), 40(1),(6); NIUCTP 19-24; NIC&P 25(5)

2.45   UC 39(2)-(5); NIUC 40(2)-(5)

T2.7   UC sch 8, sch 9; NIUC sch 8, sch 9

People with children

2.46   If your youngest child is:

(a)   under the age of one, you don't have to meet any of the work-related requirements (para 2.38);

(b)   aged one or two, you only have to meet the work-focused interview and work preparation requirements.

This applies if you are single. If you are a couple it applies to only one of you (the lead carer) and you choose which of you this is.

Sanctions and hardship payments

Who gets a sanction

2.47   The DWP can impose a sanction that reduces your UC if:

(a)   you don't apply for a vacancy, don't take up a work offer, or don't meet your work-related requirements; or

(b)   you lose work or pay voluntarily or for no good reason; or

(c)   a sanction is transferred from your JSA or ESA to your UC.

But you can't be sanctioned if you have limited capability for work and work-related activity (LCWRA).

The amount of your sanction

2.48   Your sanction equals:

(a)   the whole of your standard allowance (table 9.2) if you are aged 18 or over; but

(b)   40% of your standard allowance if you are aged 16 or 17, or don't have any work-related requirements, or only have to attend a work-focused interview.

There are detailed rules about the length of your sanction [www].

Who gets a hardship payment

2.49   The DWP must award you a hardship payment if:

(a)   your sanction equals the whole of your standard allowance (para 2.48(a));

(b)   you make an application for each hardship period (para 2.51);

(c)   you have met your work-related requirements during the past seven days; and

(d)   the DWP agrees that you are 'in hardship'.

T2.7   UC sch 8-9; NIUC sch 8-9

2.46   WRA 19(6), 20(1)(a), 21(1)(aa); UC 86; NIWRO 24(6), 25(1)(a), 26(1)(aa); NIUC 85

2.47   WRA 26, 27; UC 111(3), 112, sch 11; NIWRO 31, 32; NIUC 108(3), 109, sch 11

2.48   UC 101-105, 111(1),(2); NIUC 98-102, 108(1),(2)

2.49   WRA 28(1); UC 116(1); NIWRO 33(1); NIUC 111(1)

Meaning of hardship

2.50   You are 'in hardship' only if:

(a) your sanction means that you can't meet your and your benefit unit's 'most basic and essential needs' for accommodation, heating, food and/or hygiene; and

(b) you have made 'every effort' to access alternative support, and to stop incurring other expenditure.

The hardship period

2.51   Each hardship payment covers a hardship period that runs from the day you applied (or if later, the day you provided information and evidence) to the day before your next normal monthly payment of UC is due (or if that is seven days or less, to the day before the next but one payment is due).

The amount of the hardship payment

2.52   Your hardship payment equals 60% of the UC you lost (as a result of the sanction) in the last assessment period but one. It is converted on a daily basis to cover the number of days in your hardship period.

Repaying hardship payments

2.53   Hardship payments are recoverable, but you can ask the DWP not to recover them, and the DWP has the discretion to waive recovery (BORG 5.83-85). In practice, the DWP usually recovers them at the 25% rate used for overpayments (table 13.2(a)). This means you are expected to repay them by receiving less UC in the future.

2.54   But you don't have to repay hardship payments during any assessment period in which your earnings (including your partner's if you are claiming UC as a couple) are at least equal to the conditionality earnings threshold (para 2.40). And once you have had this level of earnings for 26 weeks since a sanction last applied to you, they stop being recoverable altogether.

2.50   UC 116(2),(3); NIUC 111(2),(3)

2.51   UC 117; NIUC 112

2.52   UC 118; NIUC 113

2.53   UC 119(1); NIUC 114(1)

2.54   UC 119(2),(3); NIUC 114(2),(3)

Chapter 3 **UC claims and benefit unit**

- ■ Making a claim: see paras 3.1-11.
- ■ How to claim: see paras 3.12-18.
- ■ Information and evidence: see paras 3.19-26.
- ■ Start dates and backdating: see paras 3.27-37.
- ■ Assessment periods and reclaims: see paras 3.38-45.
- ■ Your benefit unit: see paras 3.46-69.
- ■ Non-dependants: see paras 3.70-77.

Making a claim

3.1   You can only get UC if:

  (a) you make a claim for it (paras 3.2-3); or

  (b) you are treated as having claimed it (paras 3.4-7); or

  (c) someone claims it on your behalf (paras 3.8-11).

This chapter gives the rules applying to all UC claims. If you are migrating (transferring) from legacy benefits to UC, see also chapter 4.

Claiming as a single person

3.2   You make your claim yourself if:

  (a) you are a single person (para 2.2); or

  (b) you are in a couple but claiming as a single person (para 2.7); or

  (c) in some cases, you are in a polygamous marriage (para 3.61).

You (or a person claiming on your behalf) must provide information and evidence about your claim. In cases (b) and (c) this includes your partner's circumstances.

Claiming as a couple (joint claimants)

3.3   You make your claim jointly with your partner if:

  (a) you are a joint claim couple (para 2.5); or

  (b) in some cases, you are in a polygamous marriage (para 3.61).

Both of you (or a person claiming on your behalf) must provide information and evidence about your claim.

3.1   AA 1,5; NIAA 1,5

3.2   WRA 2(1)(a),(2); UC 3(3),(4); NIWRO 7(1)(a),(2); NIUC 3(2),(3)

3.3   WRA 2(1)(b),(2); UC 3(4); NIWRO 7(1)(b),(2); NIUC 3(3)

If you should have claimed as a couple or as a single person

3.4   The DWP:

(a) can treat you as having claimed UC as a couple if:

- ◾ you each made a claim as a single person, but
- ◾ the DWP decides you are a couple;

(b) must treat you as having claimed UC as a single person if:

- ◾ you made a claim as a couple, but
- ◾ you are only eligible for UC as a single person (para 2.7).

If you become a couple or a single person

3.5   UC continues without you having to make a new claim when:

(a) you become a couple; and

(b) you or your partner (or both of you) have been getting UC (either as a single person or as a couple with someone else); and

(c) you qualify for UC based on your new circumstances.

This also applies when you are a couple but have (until now) only been eligible for UC as a single person (para 2.7).

3.6   And UC continues without you having to make a new claim when:

(a) you become a single person; and

(b) you have been getting UC as a couple; and

(c) you qualify for UC based on your new circumstances.

This applies whether your relationship has ended or your partner has died. It also applies when you are a couple but are now only eligible as a single person (para 2.7).

3.7   In all these cases (paras 3.5-6), the law treats you as having made a claim. You still have to tell the DWP your new financial and other circumstances (para 3.22).

Attorneys and appointees if you are unable to act

3.8   The following may act on your behalf in connection with your UC:

(a) a person who has ordinary or lasting power of attorney for you ('your attorney'); or

(b) a person who is appointed by a court to act for you – this includes a deputy appointed by the Court of Protection in England or Wales, a judicial factor or other guardian in Scotland, or a controller appointed by the High Court in Northern Ireland.

3.4   C&P 9(1)-(4); NIC&P 8(1)-(4)

3.5-7   C&P 9(6),(8)(a),(10); NIC&P 8(6),(8)(a),(10); SI 2014/2887 reg 5

3.8   General law about incapacity etc

3.9   If you don't have an attorney etc (para 3.8), the DWP can appoint someone to act on your behalf (known as an 'appointee'). The appointee:

(a)   must apply in writing to do this (for example in a letter or online); and

(b)   must either be over 18 years old or a firm or organisation.

They can be someone who already acts on your behalf in connection with HB or a social security benefit. DWP guidance [www] suggests an appointee is appropriate if you have a 'mental incapacity or severe physical disability', but the law does not restrict it to these circumstances.

3.10   Your appointee has all the rights you have in connection with UC, including making a claim, receiving payments, and requesting a reconsideration or appeal. They continue to act on your behalf until:

(a)   they resign their appointment (they must give the DWP one month's written notice); or

(b)   the DWP ends their appointment; or

(c)   the DWP is notified that you now have an attorney etc (para 3.8).

If your partner is unable to act

3.11   If you are claiming UC as a couple and your partner is unable to claim jointly with you, you can make the UC claim yourself on behalf of both of you.

How to claim

3.12   You can make your claim for UC:

(a)   online; or

(b)   by telephone if the DWP agrees to this.

Once you have submitted a claim you may subsequently be asked to provide evidence to confirm information you have given, to attend an interview, and to agree to conditions set out in a claimant commitment (paras 2.36-38). If you don't, your claim will be treated as 'closed' and no action taken on it ([2020] UKUT 109 (AAC)).

Online claims and online journal

3.13   Online claims are made to the DWP [www]. You do this by completing an online application which can take up to 40 minutes. You may be able to get help with claiming from the jobcentre, your local council, or by using the DWPs 'Help to Claim' service which is managed by Citizens Advice [www]. Once your claim is made you are given access to an online journal you can use to communicate with the DWP.

3.9   C&P 2(1) definition: 'writing', 57(1)-(3),(6); UCTP 16; NIC&P 2(1),52(1)-(3),(6); NIUCTP 15
http://tinyurl.com/OG-Appointeesv10
DWP, Becoming an appointee for someone claiming benefits https://tinyurl/Unable-to-Act

3.10   C&P 57(4),(5),(7),(8); NIC&P 52(4),(5),(7),(8)

3.11   C&P 9(5); NIC&P 8(5)

3.12   C&P 8(1),(2), 35; NIC&P 7(1),(2),34

3.13   C&P 8(1), sch 2; NIC&P 7(1), sch 1
www.gov.uk/apply-universal-credit
www.citizensadvice.org.uk/about-us/contact-us/contact-us/help-to-claim/

Telephone claims

3.14   The DWP can agree to accept a telephone claim from particular groups of claimants or in individual cases. If you are not able to go online yourself you can contact an adviser on 0800 328 5644 or text phone 0800 328 1344 between 8am and 6pm, Monday to Friday (closed on bank and public holidays). Note if the call 'ends suddenly it is up to you to call back'.

Completing your claim

3.15   An online claim is properly completed if you use the online claim form and follow the instructions. You must also submit it and log out ([2020] UKUT 108 (AAC)). A telephone claim is properly completed if you provide all the information needed to decide your claim during the call. You may also be required to provide appropriate authentication of your identity and other information, and maintain records of your claim.

Completing a defective claim

3.16   The DWP must tell you if your claim is defective, in other words a claim that doesn't meet the conditions in para 3.15. In these cases:

(a)   if it is an online claim, you should re-submit the claim with the missing information, etc, now included;

(b)   if it is a telephone claim, you need only provide the information, etc, that was missing.

If you do this within one month of when you were first informed that your claim was defective, or longer if the DWP considers it reasonable, your claim counts as having being made on the date you originally made it.

Deciding your claim

3.17   The DWP must decide whether you qualify for UC and send you a notice about this (para 14.5).

Amending or withdrawing a claim

3.18   Before the DWP decides your claim you can:

(a)   amend it: the DWP then decides your claim on the amended basis; or

(b)   withdraw it: the DWP then takes no further action on your claim.

You can amend or withdraw a claim by writing to the DWP (online or in a letter, etc), by telephoning them, or in any other way they agree to.

3.14   C&P 8(2); NIC&P 7(1)

3.15   C&P 8(1),(4), sch 2 para 2; NIC&P 7(1),(4), sch 1 para 2

3.16   C&P 8(3)-(6); NIC&P 7(3)-(6)

3.18   C&P 2(1) definition: 'writing', 30, 31; NIC&P 2(1),29,30

Information and evidence

What you should provide

3.19   You have to provide the DWP with information and evidence about whether you qualify, how much you qualify for, and who it should be paid to. This duty applies:

(a)   when you make a UC claim;

(b)   when your circumstances change; and

(c)   when you are overpaid.

3.20   If you are a couple this applies to both of you, even if you are claiming UC as a single person; and information one of you provides can be given to the other.

The information the DWP needs

3.21   The DWP must tell you what information and evidence it needs, and whether you should provide it online, by telephone, or personally by attending the DWP office. If you are making a claim you should provide the information within one month from when the DWP first requests it, or longer if the DWP considers it reasonable (para 3.16).

3.22   The main things the DWP needs to know are:

(a)   your housing costs (para 5.1);

(b)   your income and capital (para 10.2);

(c)   the people who live with you (paras 3.46, 3.71);

(d)   your national insurance number (para 3.25);

(e)   your child benefit number if you have children or young persons;

(f)   details of your bank or similar account.

Using monthly figures

3.23   UC is a monthly benefit. The 'whole month' approach simplifies administration of UC, and avoids numerous changes to your UC if your circumstances change a lot (paras 3.40-41). UC assessment periods are monthly (para 3.38), as are UC allowances and other figures used in the calculation.

Converting housing costs and income to monthly figures

3.24   For housing costs, employed earnings and unearned income, you can give the DWP monthly, weekly or other non-monthly amounts and the DWP converts them to a monthly figure (paras 6.58 and 10.50). For self-employed earnings, you have to provide monthly figures (para 10.40).

3.19   C&P 37(1)-(3), 38(1)-(3),(6); NIC&P 36(1)-(3), 37(1)-(3)

3.20   WRA 2(1)(b); C&P 37(4),(5); NIWRO 7(1)(b); NIC&P 36(4),(5)

3.21   C&P 35, 37(3), 38(3); NIC&P 34, 36(3), 37(3)

3.23   WRA 7; UC 21(1); NIWRO 12; NIUC 21(1)

3.24   UC 26(1), 54(1), 57(2), 61(2), 71, 73(1), sch 4 para 7, sch 5 para 13
         NIUC 27(1), 53(1), 57(2), 62(2), 71, 73(1), sch 4 para 6, sch 5 para 13

National insurance number

3.25   To get UC, you have to give your national insurance number (NINo) and, if you are claiming as a couple, your partner's:

(a) if you don't know your NINo, you must assist the DWP in finding out what it is; or

(b) if you don't have a NINo, you must apply for one and can usually do this using your UC online account.

An Upper Tribunal has decided that your UC payments (and any advance payments you request) can't be made until a NINo is issued ([2022] UKUT 189 (AAC)), but once a NINo is issued you get your UC arrears back to the date of your UC claim.

Information from a third party

3.26   The DWP can require:

(a) your landlord to provide information and evidence about your rent or related matters;

(b) your childcare provider to supply information and evidence relating to the UC childcare costs element (para 9.47);

(c) a person you are caring for to confirm information relating to the UC carer element (paras 9.39-40);

(d) a pension fund holder to provide information (para 10.70);

(e) a rent officer to provide information (para 6.19).

They have one month to do this, or longer if the DWP considers it reasonable.

UC start dates and backdating

Your UC start date

3.27   Your UC starts on your date of claim (paras 3.28-29) except when you make an advance claim, qualify for backdating, or reclaim within six months (paras 3.30-37, 3.43). There are also exceptions when you migrate to UC (chapter 4). Chapter 12 explains when your UC is paid.

Your UC date of claim

3.28   Your date of claim is:

(a) the date the DWP received your properly completed claim (para 3.15); or

(b) the date the DWP received your defective claim if you then complete it within the time allowed (para 3.16).

3.25   AA 1(1A)-(1C),(4)(za); C&P 5; NIAA 1(1A)-(1C),(4)(za); NIC&P 5

3.26   C&P 37(6),(7), 38(7)-(9), 41; NIC&P 36(6),(7), 37(7)-(9), 38

3.27   C&P 26(1); NIC&P 25(1)

3.28   C&P 10(1)(a),(c),(2); NIC&P 9(1)(a),(c),(2)

3.29   There are two further rules:

  (a) if you receive assistance making an online claim (para 3.13), your date of claim is the day you first notified the DWP of your need for assistance;

  (b) if you phone the DWP to make a claim (para 3.14) but they can't take your call until a later date, your date of claim is the day of the first phone call if the later date is within one month.

Advance claims

3.30   If you do not qualify for UC when you claim but will do so within one month, the date of claim is the day you first qualify. The DWP can agree to apply this rule for particular groups of claimants or individual cases.

3.31   You can also choose to claim UC from a date in the future, for example if you claim in advance of losing a job or some other event. In this case, your date of claim is the day you are claiming from.

Backdating

3.32   'Backdating' means you get UC for a period before you claimed it. UC law calls this 'extending the time limit for claiming'.

3.33   You qualify for backdating if:

  (a) one or more of the circumstances in table 3.1 applies to you; and

  (b) as a result, you 'could not reasonably have been expected to make the claim earlier'.

If you are a joint claim couple (para 2.5), one or more of the circumstances in the table must apply to each of you (and (b) above must apply).

Backdating time limit

3.34   Your UC is backdated to one month before the day you claimed UC, or (if later) the day you first meet the conditions in para 3.33, or (if later) the day you first qualify for UC. For example, if you claim UC on 28th February, it can be backdated to 28th January.

Backdating requests

3.35   Your online UC claim (para 3.13) doesn't have a question about backdating. Your circumstances may make it clear to the DWP that you qualify ([2022] UKUT 332 (AAC)), but it is always advisable to request backdating using your online journal as soon as you make your UC claim. If you don't do it straight away, you can request backdating later ([2022] UKUT 242 (AAC)).

3.29   C&P 2(1) definition 'appropriate office', 10(1)(b),(d),(2); NIC&P 2(1), 9(1)(b),(d)

3.30   C&P 32; NIC&P 31

3.31   C&P 10(1); NIC&P 9(1)

3.32   C&P 26(2); NIC&P 25(2)

3.33   C&P 26(2)(a),(b),(4); NIC&P 25(2),(a),(b),(4)

3.35   C&P 26(2); NIC&P 25(2)

Table 3.1 **Backdating UC: qualifying circumstances**

To qualify for backdating one or more of the following must have meant you could not reasonably have claimed UC earlier.

(a) You were previously on JSA(IB), JSA(C), ESA(IR), ESA(C), IS, HB, CTC or WTC, and you were not told about the ending of that benefit until after it had ended.*

(b) You have a disability.

(c) You had an illness that prevented you from making a claim and you have given the DWP medical evidence that confirms this.

(d) You were unable to make a claim on-line because the official computer system wasn't working.

(e) You were in a couple and the DWP decided not to award you UC (or ended your UC) because your partner didn't accept the claimant commitment, and you are now making a claim as a single person.

* Note: If you are claiming UC because of moving to a new area (para 4.20(f)), you count as being told about your HB ending when your new local council tells you that you can no longer claim HB ([2020] UKUT 309 (AAC)).

Examples: Start dates and backdating

1. A claim

Mason claims UC on 5th May and the DWP decides he qualifies for £375 per month.

- His first assessment period starts on 5th May. He should receive UC of £375 for this assessment period by about 12th June (para 12.10).
- His following assessment periods start on the 5th of each month.

2. Backdating

Kathryn gets a letter from her local council on 9th February saying her HB will end on 14th February. She is blind, and the friend who normally reads her letters to her is away on holiday from 7th to 21st February. He reads the letter to her on 22nd February. She makes an online claim for UC that day and qualifies for UC. She asks the DWP to backdate her UC.

The DWP's decision: The DWP agrees that from 9th February Kathryn meets the conditions for qualifying for backdated UC as follows.

Qualifying circumstances: Her circumstances do not fall within (a) in table 3.1, because the council notified her before her HB ended. But they do fall within (b) in the table, because she has a disability.

Ability to claim earlier: Her blindness, and the unavailability of her friend, meant she could not reasonably have been expected to claim UC earlier.

T3.1(a)   C&P 26(3)(a),(aa); UCTP 2(1) definition: 'existing benefits', 15(2); NIC&P 25(3)(a),(aa); NIUCTP 2(1), 14(2)

T3.1(b)-(e)   C&P 26(3)(b)-(d) and (f)-(g) respectively; NIC&P 25(3)(b)-(f)

Backdating UC if you also claim HB

3.36 People who live in supported or temporary accommodation (STA) need to claim HB as well as UC (paras 5.10, 5.12). Whether to backdate your UC and HB are two separate decisions. But usually, if the DWP backdates your UC, the council is likely to accept there is 'good cause' to backdate your HB to the same date (volume 2 chapter 16).

Backdating UC housing costs if the council refuses you HB

3.37 If you claim UC and HB but the council decides your home doesn't meet the definition of STA, you need to go back to the DWP to ask it to include your housing costs in your UC. The DWP says your housing costs 'will be revised back to the date you originally declared you were living in the accommodation' (Housing benefit guidance for supported housing claims paras 64-68 [www]).

Assessment periods and reclaims

Your assessment periods

3.38 UC is calculated and paid for monthly assessment periods, with different people's assessment periods beginning on different days of the month. Yours are decided as follows:

(a) your first assessment period begins on the day your UC starts (para 3.27);

(b) after that, they begin on the same day of each following month, with adjustments for the ends of months (table 3.2).

Table 3.2 **UC assessment periods**

If your first assessment period starts on the day of the month in column 1, your following assessment periods start on the day of the month in column 2 (a), (b) or (c).

1 – Start of first assessment period	2 – Start of following assessment periods		
	(a) Except February	(b) February not in a leap year	(c) February in a leap year
1st to 28th	Same as 1	Same as 1	Same as 1
29th	29th	27th	28th
30th	30th	27th	28th
31st	Last day (30th or 31st)	28th	29th

3.36   HB 83(12),(12A); NIHB 81(12),(12A)

3.37   D&A 9; NID&A 9
        www.gov.uk/government/publications/housing-benefit-guidance-for-supported-housing-claims

3.38-39 WRA 7; UC 21(1),(2), 21A; NIWRO 12; NIUC 22(1)-(3), 22A

T3.2   UC 21(2); NIUC 22(2)

Assessment periods if your start date changes

3.39   Your UC start date can change due to backdating (para 3.35) or because the DWP used the wrong date. When this happens, the DWP can change the start date of:

(a)   all your assessment periods (so they are still one month); or

(b)   just the first assessment period (so that it is longer or shorter than one month).

In the second case, your UC is calculated on a daily basis.

Assessment periods when your circumstances change

3.40   When your circumstances change, your assessment periods don't change. In most cases (table 11.1):

(a)   your new amount of UC is awarded from the first day of the assessment period in which the change takes place; or

(b)   if you stop qualifying for UC, your UC ends from the first day of that assessment period.

If you become a couple (paras 3.5-7) and each of you previously had different assessment periods, the DWP uses the assessment periods of whichever of you means your UC changes or ends earlier.

End of your UC award

3.41   Your UC continues until:

(a)   you stop qualifying for it (para 11.29); or

(b)   you stop providing the information and evidence showing you qualify (para 11.2).

If you become entitled to UC again within six months, the rules about reclaim periods allow you to get UC without making a full UC claim (paras 3.42-45). If you become entitled to UC again after six months, you have to make a full UC claim (paras 3.27, 3.38).

Six month reclaim periods

3.42   You get a six month reclaim period when:

(a)   you make a claim for UC but you don't qualify because your earnings are too high; or

(b)   you are on UC and it stops because your earnings are too high; or

(c)   you are on UC and it stops for any other reason.

In each case, the reclaim period runs for six assessment periods (six months) starting with the first assessment period in which you don't qualify for UC.

3.43   During your reclaim period:

(a)   you can continue to log in to your online account to report your income and changes in your circumstances;

(b)   the DWP continues to get details of your employed earnings from HMRC (para 10.21);

3.40   UC 21(3),(3A),(3B); D&A sch 1 para 20; NIUC 22(4)-(6); NID&A sch 1 para 20

3.41   WRA 3-6, 7(1); D&A sch 1 para 20; NIWRO 8-11, 12(1); NID&A sch 1 para 20

3.42   UC 21(3C)-(3D); C&P 32A; NIUC 22(7)-(8); NIC&P 31A

3.43   UC 21(3), (3A)-(3D); NIUC 21(4)-(8)

(c)   the DWP carries forward your 'surplus earnings' in some cases (para 10.15);

(d)   your assessment periods continue with the same start dates; and

(e)   if you become (re-)entitled to UC, the DWP treats you as having reclaimed and awards you UC (paras 3.44-45).

Reclaim periods for earnings

3.44   If your reclaim period relates to your earnings (para 3.42(a),(b)):

(a)   you get UC from the first day of the assessment period in which you become entitled to UC; and

(b)   in that assessment period, you get a full month's UC.

You get a new reclaim period every time you stop qualifying for UC due to the level of your earnings. But if you don't qualify for any of the six months, you can't get UC until you make a full UC claim (para 3.45).

Other reclaim periods

3.45   If your reclaim period relates to anything other than earnings (para 3.42(c)):

(a)   you get UC from the day you become entitled to UC; and

(b)   in the assessment period containing that day, your UC is calculated on a daily basis.

For example, if the assessment period is 31 days and there are 12 days from the day you become entitled UC to the end of the assessment period, you get 12/31 of the monthly amount.

Your benefit unit

3.46   The rest of this chapter is about:

(a)   your 'benefit unit' – this means you, your partner, children and young persons (paras 3.47-51); and

(b)   your 'extended benefit unit' – this means all the above, plus non-dependants (para 3.71).

These people can affect your entitlement to UC (para 9.4) and your housing costs element (para 6.60).

Single people

3.47   For UC purposes you are a 'single person' if you are not in a couple.

3.48   If you are a single person, your benefit unit is:

(a)   you; and

(b)   any children or young persons you are responsible for.

3.44   UC 21(3C),(3D), 22A; C&P 26(5), 32A; NIUC 22(7),(8), 24; NIC&P 25(5), 31A

3.45   UC 22A; NIUC 24

3.47   WRA 40; NIWRO 46

3.48   WRA 1(2)(a), 9(1)(a), 10(1); NIWRO 6(2)(a), 14(1)(a), 15(1)

Couples

3.49　For UC purposes you are a 'couple' if you are two people who are members of the same household (para 3.52) and are:

(a)　a married couple or civil partners; or

(b)　living together as a married couple or civil partners (para 3.54).

3.50　If you are claiming UC as a joint claim couple (para 2.5), your benefit unit is:

(a)　both of you; and

(b)　any children or young persons either (or both) of you are responsible for.

3.51　If you are in a couple but claiming UC as a single person (para 2.7), your benefit unit is:

(a)　you; and

(b)　any children or young persons you are responsible for.

Members of the same household

3.52　You are only a couple for UC purposes if you are members of the same household. (This applies to married couples and civil partners as well as couples who are living together: [2014] UKUT 186 (AAC).) You are not a couple if you:

(a)　live in different dwellings and maintain them as separate homes (R(SB) 4/83); or

(b)　live in the same dwelling but lead separate lives rather than living as one household (CIS/072/1994).

And you cannot be a member of two (or more) households at the same time (R(SB) 8/85).

3.53　A 'household' generally means a domestic arrangement involving two or more people who live together as a unit (R(IS) 1/99), even when they have a reasonable level of independence and self-sufficiency (R(SB) 8/85). It requires a settled course of daily living rather than visits from time to time (R(F) 2/81). So if you keep your eating, cooking, food storage, finances (including paying your housing costs), living space and family life separate you are unlikely to be members of the same household.

Living together

3.54　If you are not married or in a civil partnership you are only a couple for UC purposes if you are living together as though you were. This means considering:

(a)　your purpose in living together (Crake and Butterworth v the Supplementary Benefit Commission); and

(b)　if your purpose is unclear, your relationship and living arrangements.

3.49　WRA 39, 40; UC 2 definition: 'partner'; NIWRO 45, 46; NIUC 2

3.50　WRA 1(2)(b), 9(1)(b), 10(1); NIWRO 6(2)(b), 14(1)(b), 15(1)

3.51　WRA 1(2)(a), 2(2), 9(1)(a), 10(1); NIWRO 6(2)(a), 2(2), 14(1)(a), 15(1)

3.52　WRA 39(1)(a),(c); NIWRO 45(1)(a),(c)

3.54　WRA 39(1)(b),(d),(2); NIWRO 45(1)(b),(d),(2); Crake and Butterworth v SBC 21/07/80 QBD 1982 1 ALL ER 498

3.55   The following factors are relevant (Crake case and [2013] UKUT 505 (AAC)):

(a)   whether you share the same household;

(b)   the stability of your relationship;

(c)   your financial arrangement;

(d)   whether you have a sexual relationship;

(e)   whether you share responsibility for a child;

(f)   whether you publicly acknowledge you are a couple;

(g)   the emotional element of your relationship.

The decision should be based on the totality of the evidence, and none of the factors is conclusive in itself ([2017] AACR 10) unless you don't share a household (paras 3.52-53).

3.56   There are many reasons why two people might live in the same household or same dwelling. They might be a couple. But they might be landlord/lady and lodger, house sharers, etc. Even living together for reasons of 'care, companionship and mutual convenience' does not by itself mean you are a couple (R(SB) 35/85).

Ending a relationship

3.57   If you were a couple but your relationship has ended, your shared understanding that it has ended and your actual living arrangement are more important than any shared responsibilities and financial arrangements you still have (CIS/72/1994). But if you remain married or in a civil partnership, a shared understanding may not be enough by itself to show you are no longer a couple (CIS/2900/1998).

If your partner is temporarily absent

3.58   If your partner is temporarily absent from your household you continue to count as a couple, unless their absence exceeds or is expected to exceed six months.

3.59   This means you stop counting as a couple if and when your partner:

(a)   decides not to return or decides to be absent for more than six months (whether they decide this at the beginning of the absence or during it); or

(b)   has been absent for six months

For absences outside the UK see paras 2.29-35.

Polygamous marriages

3.60   For UC purposes you are in a 'polygamous marriage' if you or your husband or wife are married to more than one person under the laws of a country which permits polygamy.

3.55   [2017] AACR 10, was [2016] CSIH 84

3.58   UC 3(6); NIUC 3(5)

3.60   UC 3(5); NIUC 3(4)

3.61   The members of the polygamous marriage who live in your household can get UC as follows:

(a)   the two who were married earliest count as a couple;

(b)   each other person in the marriage counts as a single person.

The earlier rules about entitlement to UC and the benefit unit then apply (paras 3.46-51).

Children and young persons

3.62   Your benefit unit includes the children and young persons:

(a)   you are responsible for, if you are:

   ▪   a single person, or

   ▪   in a couple but claiming UC as a single person;

(b)   you or your partner are responsible for, if you are:

   ▪   in a joint claim couple.

3.63   A 'child' means someone under the age of 16.

3.64   A 'young person' means someone aged 16 or more but under 20 (other than your partner) who:

(a)   is in non-advanced education (para 2.15); and

(b)   is not on UC, ESA, JSA, HB, CTC or WTC.

Responsibility for a child or young person

3.65   For UC purposes you are responsible for a child or young person if he or she:

(a)   normally lives with you (paras 3.66-67); and

(b)   is not a foster child or being looked after by a local authority (para 3.68); and

(c)   is not a prisoner (para 2.22).

3.66   Whether a child or young person 'normally lives with you' is a question of fact and is usually straightforward. For example they could be your son or daughter, adopted by you, a step-child, a grandchild or any other child or young person (whether related to you or not), so long as they normally live with you.

3.67   A child or young person can only be the responsibility of one single person or couple at any one time. If they normally live with two or more single persons or couples, they are the responsibility of the single person or couple with the main responsibility. This is decided taking account of all the circumstances, not just who receives the child benefit or the amount of time spent at each address ([2018] UKUT 44 (AAC)). You can choose ('nominate') who this is to be. But the DWP makes the choice instead if:

3.61   UC 3(4); NIUC 3(3)

3.62   WRA 10(1); NIWRO 15(1)

3.63   WRA 40; NIWRO 46

3.64   WRA 10(5); UC 4(3), 5(1),(5); UCTP 28; NIWRO 15(5); NIUC 4(3), 5(1),(5)

3.65   UC 4(1),(2),(6); NIUC 4(1),(2),(6)

3.67   UC 4(4),(5); NIUC 4(4),(5)

(a) you do not choose or cannot agree; or

(b) your choice does not reflect the arrangements between you.

Fostering, pre-adoption and local authority care

3.68   A child or young person is not included in your benefit unit if he or she:

(a) is placed with you as a foster child (also called 'kinship care'); or

(b) is placed with you prior to adoption (but an adopted child is included in your benefit unit); or

(c) is in local authority care, unless this is a planned short-term break to give you time off from caring for them, or one of a series of such breaks.

If a child or young person is temporarily absent

3.69   If a child or young person you are responsible for is temporarily absent from your household they continue to be included in your benefit unit, unless their absence exceeds or is expected to exceed:

(a) six months if they remain in Great Britain during the absence;

(b) one month if they are outside Great Britain;

(c) one further month if they remain outside Great Britain and this is in connection with the death of their close relative (para 5.38) and it would be unreasonable for them to be expected to return within the first month;

(d) six months if they are outside Great Britain in connection with treatment, convalescence or care which meets the conditions in para 2.34.

Non-dependants

3.70   This section explains who counts as a non-dependant. Non-dependants are part of your extended benefit unit (para 3.46). If you are a renter or shared owner and have one or more non-dependants living with you, this can affect the amount of UC you get for your housing costs (paras 7.8 and 6.60).

Who is a non-dependant

3.71   A 'non-dependant' is anyone who:

(a) normally lives in the accommodation with you; and

(b) is not in any of the groups in table 3.3.

For example, a non-dependant is usually an adult son, daughter, other relative or friend who lives with you on a non-commercial basis, whether they are single or in a couple.

3.68   UC 2 definition: 'looked after by a local authority', 4(6), 4A; NIUC 2, 4(6), 5

3.69   UC 4(7); NIUC 4(7)

3.71   UC sch 4 paras 3, 9(1),(2); NIUC sch 4 paras 3, 8(1),(2)

Table 3.3 **People who are not non-dependants**

(a) You and your partner, whether you are claiming UC as a couple or as a single person.

(b) Any child or young person (para 3.73).

(c) A foster child placed with you or your partner (para 3.68).

(d) A resident landlord/landlady and members of their household.

(e) Anyone who is liable to make payments on a commercial basis on the accommodation including:

- a lodger of yours (paras 3.74-75)

- a joint tenant (you rent the accommodation jointly) (para 3.76)

- a separate tenant of your landlord's (the accommodation is rented out in separate lettings).

(f) A non-dependant of anyone described in (e) above (para 3.77).

'Normally living in the accommodation with you'

3.72   To count as a non-dependant a person must 'normally live in the accommodation with you'. For example:

(a) someone who shares essential living accommodation with you, even if you each have your own bedroom, is likely to count as 'living with you' (CH/542/2006, CH/3656/2005); but

(b) a short-term visitor does not count as 'normally' living with you. Nor does a regular or frequent visitor whose normal home is elsewhere – in the UK or abroad ([2018] UKUT 75 (AAC)). Nor does someone you take in temporarily because they have nowhere else to go (CH/4004/2004), though this may change as time goes by (CH/3935/2007).

Non-dependants and children/young persons

3.73   A child or young person (paras 3.63-64) never counts as a non-dependant, whether you, your partner, anyone else or no-one is responsible for them. The only exception is that a child or young person of a non-dependant counts as a non-dependant (and this can be relevant to the size criteria: para 7.14).

Non-dependants and lodgers

3.74   If you have a lodger who pays you rent on a commercial basis, the lodger does not count as a non-dependant.

T3.3   UC sch 4 paras 3, 9; NIUC sch 4 paras 3, 8

3.73   UC sch 4 para 9(1)(b),(2)(a),(c),(g); NIUC sch 4 para 8(1)(b),(2)(a),(c),(g)

3.74   UC sch 4 para 9(2)(d); NIUC sch 4 para 8(2)(d)

3.75   The difference between a lodger and a non-dependant is as follows:

(a)   a lodger is someone who makes payments to you on a commercial basis (table 5.7(a));

(b)   a non-dependant may or may not pay their way. If they do pay you, it is on a non-commercial basis.

Non-dependants and joint tenants

3.76   If you rent your accommodation jointly, your joint tenants are not your non-dependants. For example, if two sisters, a father and son, three friends (and so on) are joint tenants, they are not non-dependants of each other.

3.77   If you jointly rent your accommodation and there is also a non-dependant living there, the non-dependant is included in the UC claim of only one of the joint tenants, as follows:

(a)   the non-dependant may normally live with only one of the joint tenants. In that case, they are included in the UC claim of only that joint tenant;

(b)   the non-dependant may normally live with more than one of the joint tenants. In that case, once they have been included in the UC claim of one joint tenant they are not included in the UC claim of any of the others.

3.76   UC sch 4 para 9(2)(d); NIUC sch 4 para 8(2)(d)

3.77   UC sch 4 para 9(2)(f); NIUC sch 4 para 8(2)(f)

Chapter 4 **Migration to UC**

- ■ Migration: see paras 4.1-12.
- ■ Voluntary migration: see paras 4.13-17.
- ■ Natural migration: see paras 4.18-23.
- ■ Managed migration (pilot scheme and full scheme): see paras 4.24-35.
- ■ The main UC transitional element and the transitional SDP element: see paras 4.36-52.
- ■ The UC transitional capital disregard: see paras 4.53-56.

Migration

4.1 This chapter describes what happens when you transfer from legacy benefits to UC. This is called 'migration'. It also explains the transitional protection that stops many people being worse off as a result of migration. Table 4.1 summarises the main points.

Kinds of migration

4.2 There are three kinds of migration:

(a) 'voluntary migration' is when you transfer to UC because you choose to claim it (para 4.13);

(b) 'natural migration' is when you transfer because a legacy benefit you were on has ended or you become a couple with someone already on UC (para 4.18);

(c) 'managed migration' is when you transfer because the DWP has sent you a migration notice (para 4.24).

Ending your legacy benefits

4.3 The legacy benefits are HB (except in supported or temporary accommodation), JSA(IB), ESA(IR), IS, CTC and WTC. When you make a claim for UC you can continue to get HB at any time on supported or temporary accommodation (table 5.3). Apart from that:

(a) your legacy benefits stop; and

(b) you can't get legacy benefits in the future; but

(c) you may qualify for transitional protection if you are worse off on UC than on legacy benefits (para 4.36).

These apply even if you claim UC by mistake ([2018] UKUT 306 (AAC)) or withdraw your claim ([2023] UKUT 9 (AAC)).

4.2 WRA 36, sch 6 paras 1, 4; UCTP 7, 8, 44, 46; NIWRO 42, sch 6 paras 1, 4; NIUCTP 5, 6, 45, 47

4.3 WRA 33(1), 36, sch 6; UCTP 5(1),(2)(a), 6A(1),(2), 8(2),(2A),(3), 48-52
NIWRO 39(1), 42, sch 6; NIUCTP 3(1),(2)(a), 4A(1),(2), 6(2),(2A),(3), 49-53

Table 4.1 **Migration to UC dates and transitional element**

Type of migration	(A) Start of UC	(B) End of CTC/WTC	(C) End of HB, JSA(IB)/ESA(IR)/IS	(D) Transitional element
(a) Voluntary migration: you choose to claim UC	Date of UC claim	Day before UC starts	Two weeks after (B)	Only if severely disabled
(b) Natural migration: one of your legacy benefits ends	Date of UC claim	Day before UC starts	Two weeks after (B)	Only if severely disabled
(c) Natural migration: you become a couple with someone on UC	Start of assessment period in which you become a couple	Day before you become a couple	Two weeks after (A)	No
(d) Managed migration: you claim UC by the deadline day	Date of UC claim	Day before UC starts	Two weeks after (B)	Yes
(e) Managed migration: you claim UC after the deadline day but by the final deadline	Deadline day	Day before deadline day	Two weeks after (B)	Yes
(f) Managed migration: you claim UC after the final deadline	Date of UC claim	Day before deadline day	Two weeks after (B)	No
(g) Managed migration: you don't claim UC	Not entitled to UC until you claim it	Day before deadline day	Two weeks after (B)	No

Notes:

■ HB continues in supported or temporary accommodation (table 5.3)

■ UC can be backdated (table 3.1) in all cases except (e) and (g)

■ UC can be postdated in case (d) to fit in with your legacy benefit payments

■ If there is a gap between your legacy benefits and UC, you can get a UC advance (paras 12.22-23)

Reconsiderations and appeals

4.4   If you disagree with a decision about migration or transitional protection you can ask the DWP to reconsider it or appeal to a tribunal (chapter 14).

Two-week HB run-on

4.5   You get a two-week run-on of HB overlapping with the beginning of your UC if:

(a) you are on HB when you make your UC claim, and

(b) you don't live in supported or temporary accommodation (table 5.3).

This is called a 'transitional housing payment' in the law.

Amount of two-week HB run-on

4.6   If your transfer to UC is part of voluntary or natural migration, you get 'maximum HB' during the two-week run-on, regardless of the level of your income. This means your eligible rent minus any non-dependant contributions that apply, calculated by the HB rules in volume 2 (so if you have a rent-free week this appears to mean nil for that week).

4.7   If your transfer to UC is part of managed migration, your HB during the two-week run-on continues at the same amount it is on the first day of the run-on (so no changes of circumstance are taken into account after that first day).

Two-week JSA(IB)/ESA(IR)/IS run-on

4.8   If you are on JSA(IB), ESA(IR) or IS when you make your UC claim, you get a two-week run-on of that benefit overlapping with the beginning of your UC. This is in addition to the HB run-on if you qualify for it (para 4.5).

Transitional protection

4.9   If you transfer to UC as part of voluntary or natural migration, you can get:

(a) the two-week run-ons (para 4.5-8);

(b) the transitional SDP element only if you are severely disabled (para 4.43);

(c) protection for some self-employed people (para 10.43(d)).

4.10   If you transfer to UC as part of managed migration, you can get:

(a) the two-week run-ons (paras 4.5-8);

(b) the main transitional element (para 4.38);

(c) the transitional capital disregard (para 4.53);

(d) protection for some students (table 2.3(e));

(e) protection for some self-employed people (para 10.43(d)).

4.5   UCTP 8(2A), 8A, 46(1)(a); NIUCTP 6(2A), 6A, 47(1)(a)

4.6   UCTP 8A(a); NIUCTP 6A(a)

4.7   UCTP 2(1) – 'notified person', 8A(c); NIUCTP 2(1), 6A(c)

4.8   SI 2019/1152 reg 5(1); UCTP 8B; NISR 2019/152 reg 4(1); NIUCTP 6B

4.9   UCTP 8A, 8B, 63, sch 2 paras 1-4; UC 63(1)(a); NIUCTP 6A, 6B, sch 2 paras 1-4; NIUC 64(1)(a)

4.10   UCTP 2(1) – 'notified person', 44(6), 48, 50(1), 51(1); 60; NIUCTP 2(1), 45(6), 49, 51(1), 52(1), 61

Better or worse off?

4.11   The DWP says ('Completing the move to universal credit' [www]) that migrating to UC can make you better off if:

   (a)   you are working and get HB only, or HB with WTC – this is because a smaller percentage of your earnings is deducted from your UC (table 9.1);

   (b)   you are working but not for enough hours to get WTC;

   (c)   you get ESA because you have LCWRA (para 2.43) but don't get a severe disability premium in your legacy benefits.

You are also likely to be better off on UC if you have a working non-dependant – this is because your housing costs element is reduced by a lower figure (para 6.63).

4.12   The DWP says that migrating to UC can make you worse off if:

   (a)   you are self-employed and the minimum income floor reduces your UC (para 10.43);

   (b)   you have been on CTC since before 5th April 2017 and have more than two children;

   (c)   you get ESA with a severe disability premium or an enhanced disability premium;

   (d)   you get a lower rate disabled child premium or element in your legacy benefits.

You may qualify for transitional protection in these cases (para 4.36) or a discretionary housing payment from your local council (para 6.66).

Voluntary migration

Choosing to claim UC

4.13   'Voluntary migration' is the term used when you transfer to UC because you choose to claim it. You can do this at any time, usually because you are sure you will be better off on UC (paras 4.11-12). However, if you aren't sure, claiming UC is risky because you can't go back (para 4.3).

4.14   In voluntary migration cases:

   (a)   your UC starts on the day you claim UC or the day it is backdated to (table 3.1);

   (b)   your CTC/WTC end on the day before your UC starts;

   (c)   your HB (except in supported or temporary accommodation) and JSA(IB)/ESA(IR)/IS end two weeks later;

   (d)   you are only eligible for a UC transitional element if you are severely disabled (para 4.43).

Choosing to remain on legacy benefits

4.15   If you don't transfer to UC as part of voluntary migration, you can remain on any legacy benefits you are already on until natural or managed migration applies to you.

4.11   https://tinyurl.com/Move-to-UC-2022

4.13   SI 2013/983, art 4; UCTP 6A, 8(1),(2),(2A); NISR 2016/XX, reg X; NIUCTP 4A, 6(1),(2),(2A)

4.14   UCTP 8(2),(2A), 8A, 8B, sch 2 para 3; NIUCTP 6(2),(2A), 6A, 6B, sch 2 para 3

4.15   SI 2013/983, art 4; UCTP 8(2),(2A); NISR 2016/XX, reg X; NIUCTP 6(2),(2A)

4.16 Until then, you can make any further claims you need to for:

(a) HB in supported or temporary accommodation (STA) (table 5.3),

(b) HB in general accommodation only in the situations in para 4.17,

(c) CTC while you are on WTC and vice versa,

(d) CTC or WTC if you were getting it in the previous tax year.

Apart from that, you can't make any further claims for legacy benefits.

4.17 You can only claim HB in general accommodation (accommodation that isn't STA) if:

(a) you (and your partner in a couple) have reached pension age; or

(b) you are in the UC assessment period in which you (or your partner in a couple) reach pension age; or

(c) you are in a couple or polygamous marriage, with one under pension age and one over, and you (the HB claimant):

- reached pension age before 15th May 2019, and

- have been on SPC or HB (as a mixed age couple or polygamous marriage) since before that date; or

(d) you are in a couple or polygamous marriage, with one under pension age and one over, and your partner(s) can't get UC because of being an excluded migrant, absent from the UK, a prisoner, hospital detainee, member of a religious order, or under 18 years old (chapter 2).

In the situation in (d), you can only get HB as if you were a single person.

Natural migration

4.18 'Natural migration' is the term used when you transfer to UC because:

(a) one of your legacy benefits has ended (para 4.19); or

(b) you become a couple with someone already on UC (para 4.22).

Claiming UC when a legacy benefit ends

4.19 If your entitlement to a legacy benefit ends (under the rules for that benefit), you can no longer claim other legacy benefits to replace it. So you have to claim UC (or be worse off), and this causes any other legacy benefits you are on to end (para 4.3).

4.20 For example this happens when:

(a) you lose JSA(IB)/ESA(IR)/IS because of starting work or increasing your hours or earnings;

(b) you lose JSA(IB) because of being unfit for work;

(c) you lose ESA(IR) because of becoming fit for work;

(d) you lose WTC because of ending work or reducing your hours;

4.16   UCTP 6A, 11(1); NIUCTP 4A, 9(1)

4.17   UCTP 6A(3)-(5); NIUCTP 4A(3)-(5)

4.19   SI 2013/983 art 4; UCTP 6A(1), 8(2),(2A); NISR 2016/XX, reg X; NIUCTP 4A(1), 6(2),(2A)

(e) you lose IS because your child reaches age five or you stop being responsible for them;

(f) you lose HB because of moving areas; or

(g) you lose a legacy benefit for other reasons.

4.21 In this case:

(a) your UC starts on the day you claim UC or the day it is backdated to (table 3.1);

(b) your CTC/WTC end on the day before your UC starts;

(c) your HB (except in supported or temporary accommodation) and JSA(IB)/ESA(IR)/IS end two weeks later;

(d) you are only eligible for a UC transitional element if you are severely disabled (para 4.43).

Becoming a couple with someone on UC

4.22 If you become a couple with someone who is already on UC, you become part of their UC claim (para 3.5) and this causes all your legacy benefits to end.

4.23 In this case:

(a) your new joint UC claim begins from the first day of your partner's assessment period in which you became a couple;

(b) your CTC/WTC ends on the day before you become a couple;

(c) your HB (except in supported or temporary accommodation) and JSA(IB)/ESA(IR)/IS end two weeks after your joint UC claim begins;

(d) you aren't eligible for a UC transitional element.

This means it can be up to a month from (a) the date your UC starts to (b) the date your CTC/WTC ends.

Examples: Natural migration to UC

1. Getting a job

Joseph is on JSA(IB) and HB. He gets a new job working 16 hours per week and this means his JSA(IB) ends.

- In the past he could have claimed WTC but he can no longer do so.
- He claims UC so his HB also ends.
- He can't in the future claim any of the legacy benefits.

2. Becoming fit for work

Ava is on ESA(IR), CTC and HB. She becomes fit for work and this means her ESA(IR) ends.

- In the past she could have claimed JSA(IB) but she can no longer do so.
- She claims UC so her CTC and HB also end.
- She can't in the future claim any of the legacy benefits.

4.21   UCTP 8(2),(2A), 8A, 8B, sch 2 para 3; NIUCTP 6(2),(2A), 6A, 6B, sch 2 para 3

4.22   UCTP 7(1),(2); NIUCTP 5(1),(2)

4.23   UC 21(3B); UCTP 5(2)(b)(iii), 7(2),(7), 12A, sch 2 para 2; NIUC 22(6); NIUCTP 3(2)(b)(iii), 5(2),(7), 11, sch 2 para 2

3. Losing a job

Leon is on WTC, CTC and HB. He loses his job and this means his WTC ends.

- In the past he could have claimed JSA(IB), ESA(IR) or IS (depending on his circumstances) but he can no longer do so.
- He claims UC so his CTC and HB also end.
- He can also claim JSA(C) or ESA(C) (depending on his circumstances).
- He can't in the future claim any of the legacy benefits.

4. Moving home to a new job or for other reasons

Evie is on HB. She moves to a new area and this means her HB ends.

- In the past she could have claimed HB in the new area but she can no longer do so.
- She claims UC so if she is on any other legacy benefits they also end.
- She can't in the future claim any legacy benefits.

5. Becoming a couple with someone already on UC

Margaret rents a flat and is on HB. Aaron lives with his parents and is on UC. Aaron moves in with Margaret on 15th July and they become a couple. Aaron's assessment periods begin on the 7th day of each month.

- Margaret becomes a joint claimant with Aaron in his UC claim from 7th July.
- Margaret's HB ends on 20th July (two weeks after 6th July).
- Neither of them can in the future claim any legacy benefits.

Managed migration

4.24 'Managed migration' is the term used when you transfer to UC because the DWP:

(a) sends you a migration notice giving you a deadline to claim UC (para 4.27); and

(b) ends your legacy benefits whether or not you claim UC (paras 4.32-35).

4.25 Managed migration ran as a pilot scheme, sometimes with different rules, from 2019 to 2020. It was introduced in full in 2022, and the DWP plans to accelerate and complete it in two phases:

(a) the first phase, from winter 2023 to March 2025, applies to claimants getting WTC or CTC (with or without any other legacy benefit), JSA(IB) or IS (with or without HB) or HB only;

(b) the second phase, from April 2025 to March 2028, applies to claimants getting ESA(IR) (with or without HB).

4.26 DWP guidance ('Completing the move to universal credit', June 2022) emphasises that some people need support when migrating to UC, encourages people to use independent benefit calculators to check whether they will be better off on UC, and advises those who will be better off to voluntarily migrate (para 4.13) rather than wait for managed migration [www].

4.24 UCTP 44, 46; NIUCTP 45, 47

4.25 HM Treasury, Autumn Statement 2022 (CP 751), para 5.15 https://tinyurl.com/statement2022

4.26 https://tinyurl.com/move-to-uc2022; www.gov.uk/benefits-calculators

Your migration notice

4.27   The DWP sends you a migration notice saying:

    (a)   that your legacy benefits will end and you will need to claim UC instead;

    (b)   what you need to do and what will happen if you don't do it;

    (c)   when your 'deadline day' and 'final deadline' are (para 4.29).

If you are in a couple (or polygamous marriage), the DWP normally sends this to each of you.

What you need to do

4.28   You should claim UC by your deadline day, or at the latest by your final deadline. This ensures that:

    (a)   there is no gap between your legacy benefits and UC, and

    (b)   you get a transitional element if you need it (para 4.38).

Your deadline day and final deadline

4.29   In the rules about migration to UC:

    (a)   your 'deadline day' means the day after your legacy benefits run out. It must be at least three months after your migration notice;

    (b)   your 'final deadline' is one month after your deadline day.

If you claim UC on or before your final deadline, the day before your UC starts is called your 'migration day'.

Extending the deadline day and final deadline

4.30   You (or someone on your behalf) can ask the DWP to extend your deadline day, or the DWP can do this without a request. When your deadline day is extended, so is your final deadline, so it is still one month later.

4.31   There must be a 'good reason' for an extension and the DWP decides this on the merits of each individual case. For example, the DWP is likely to agree to an extension [www] if:

    (a)   you are in hospital or have to go to hospital;

    (b)   you have a mental health condition;

    (c)   you have a disability;

    (d)   you have learning difficulties;

    (e)   you are homeless;

    (f)   you have caring responsibilities; or

    (g)   you have a domestic emergency.

4.27   UCTP 44(1),(2); NIUCTP 45(1),(2)

4.28   UCTP 46, 48; NIUCTP 47, 49

4.29   UCTP 44(3), 46(3),(4), 48, 49; NIUCTP 45(3), 47(3),(4), 49, 50

4.30   UCTP 45; NIUCTP 46

4.31   UCTP 45; NIUCTP 46; Explanatory Memo to the SSAC on the draft Managed Migration Regulations 2018, para 36
       https://tinyurl.com/MM-SSAC-Memo-2018

If you claim UC by the deadline day

4.32   If you claim UC on or before your deadline day:

(a) your UC starts on the day you make your UC claim;

(b) your UC can be backdated for up to one month if you meet the conditions (table 3.1);

(c) your UC can be postdated for up to one month, usually to fit in with your legacy benefit payments;

(d) your CTC/WTC end on the day before your UC starts;

(e) your HB (except in supported or temporary accommodation) and JSA(IB)/ESA(IR)/IS end two weeks later;

(f) you are eligible for the transitional element and capital disregard (paras 4.38, 4.53).

These rules mean there is no gap between your legacy benefits and your UC.

If you claim UC after the deadline day but by the final deadline

4.33   If you claim UC after your deadline day but on or before your final deadline:

(a) your UC starts on your deadline day (it is automatically backdated to that day, and can't be backdated further);

(b) your CTC/WTC end on the day before your deadline day;

(c) your HB (except in supported or temporary accommodation) and JSA(IB)/ESA(IR)/IS end two weeks later;

(d) you are eligible for the transitional element and capital disregard (paras 4.38, 4.53).

These rules mean there is no gap between your legacy benefits and your UC.

If you claim UC after the final deadline

4.34   If you claim UC after your final deadline:

(a) your UC starts on the day you make your UC claim

(b) your UC can be backdated for up to one month if you meet the conditions (table 3.1);

(c) your CTC/WTC end on the day before your deadline day;

(d) your HB (except in supported or temporary accommodation) and JSA(IB)/ESA(IR)/IS end two weeks later;

(e) you aren't eligible for the transitional element or capital disregard.

These rules mean there is a gap between your legacy benefits and your UC.

4.32   UCTP 44(1), 46(1), 48, 49, 50(1), 58; C&P 10, 26; NIUCTP 45(1), 47(1), 49, 50, 51(1), 59; NIC&P 9, 25

4.33   UCTP 46(1),(3), 48, 49, 50(1); NIUCTP 46(1),(3), 49, 50, 51(1)

4.34   UCTP 46(1), 48, 49, 50(1); NIUCTP 47(1), 49, 50, 51(1)

If you become a couple or a single person during migration

4.35   If you become a single person or a couple between getting legacy benefits and claiming UC:

(a)   your legacy benefits end the day before each of you claim UC (whether you both claim UC on the same day or not); but

(b)   you aren't eligible for the transitional element or capital disregard.

Examples: Managed migration to UC

1. UC claim made by the deadline day

James is a single person on JSA(IB) and HB. The DWP issues him a migration notice in February, giving him a deadline day of 14th May. He claims UC (as a single person) on 11th May.

- ■ His UC starts on 11th May (para 4.32).
- ■ The last day of his HB and JSA(IB) is 24th May.
- ■ He is eligible for a UC transitional element if he would otherwise be worse off.

2. UC claim made after the deadline day but by the final deadline

Josie and Andrew are a couple on ESA(IR), CTC and HB. The DWP issues a migration notice in March, giving them a deadline day of 12th June. They claim UC (as a couple) on 24th June.

- ■ Their UC starts on 12th June (para 4.33).
- ■ The last day of their CTC is 11th June.
- ■ The last day of their HB and ESA(IR) is 25th June.
- ■ They are eligible for a UC transitional element if they would otherwise be worse off.

3. UC claim made after the final deadline

Alice is a single person on WTC, CTC and HB. The DWP issues her with a migration notice in January, giving her a deadline day of 7th April. She claims UC (as a single person) on 13th May.

- ■ Her UC starts on 13th May (para 4.34).
- ■ The last day of her CTC and WTC is 6th April.
- ■ The last day of her HB is 20th April.
- ■ She isn't eligible for a UC transitional element.

4.35   UCTP 44(1),(4), 48, 50(2); NIUCTP 45(1),(4), 49, 51(2)

The UC transitional elements

4.36   You may qualify for a transitional element if your UC is lower than your legacy benefits. There are two kinds:

(a)   the 'main transitional element' is for people who transfer to UC as part of managed migration (para 4.24);

(b)   the 'transitional SDP element' is for people who transfer to UC as part of voluntary migration, or natural migration caused by the end of a legacy benefit (para 4.43).

If you qualify, the element is included in your UC calculation (para 9.4).

4.37   The rule in (b) was introduced on 27th January 2021 to avoid discrimination for people whose JSA(IB)/ESA(IR)/IS included a severe disability premium (R (TP, AR & SXC) v SSWP). Since then, the High Court has decided that there is also discrimination for people whose JSA(IB)/ESA(IR)/IS included an enhanced disability premium or whose CTC included a disabled child element (R (TP & AR No 3) v SSWP, AB & F v SSWP), but the DWP hasn't amended the UC rules to take this into account.

The main transitional element

Who qualifies for the main transitional element

4.38   You qualify for a main transitional element if:

(a)   you transferred to UC as part of managed migration (para 4.24);

(b)   you made your UC claim on or before your final deadline (paras 4.32-33);

(c)   your indicative UC is less than your total legacy benefits (para 4.39); and

(d)   your claims for legacy benefits and for UC were as a single person in both cases, or as a couple with the same partner in both cases (including, in the case of UC, a couple claiming as a single person: para 2.7).

Your total legacy benefits and your indicative UC

4.39   In the rules about the main transitional element:

(a)   your 'total legacy benefits' means your legacy benefits as calculated in table 4.2;

(b)   your 'indicative UC' means your UC as calculated in table 4.3.

Both of these are calculated as at the day before your UC starts (in the law called your 'migration day'). They can be slightly different from the actual amounts you receive.

4.36   UCTP 46(4), 48, 50(1)(b), sch 2 paras 1-4; NIUCTP 47(4), 49, 51(1)(b), sch 2 paras 1-4

4.37   R (TP, AR & SXC) v SSWP [2020] EWCA Civ 37 www.bailii.org/ew/cases/EWCA/Civ/2020/37.html
        R (TP & AR No.3) v SSWP, AB & F v SSWP [2022] EWHC 123 (Admin)
        www.bailii.org/ew/cases/EWHC/Admin/2022/123.html

4.38   UCTP 46(4), 48, 50(1)(b), 52(1); NIUCTP 47(4), 49, 51(1)(b), 53(1)

4.39   UCTP 49, 52(1), 53, 54; NIUCTP 50, 53(1), 54, 55

How much main transitional element – first month

4.40   In your first UC assessment period, your main transitional element equals:

(a) the total of your legacy benefits (table 4.2);

(b) minus your indicative UC (table 4.3).

This usually means that your first month's UC (when calculated with the transitional element) equals your total legacy benefits. The same applies to para 4.41.

4.41   If your indicative UC is nil, your transitional element equals the total of your legacy benefits plus your excess income. 'Excess income' means:

(a) 55% of your earned income and 100% of your unearned income (calculated as in chapter 10, and after deducting any disregards and work allowance you qualify for);

(b) minus your maximum UC (para 9.4).

Table 4.2 **Your total legacy benefits**

Your 'total legacy benefits' are used to work out your transitional element when you transfer to UC due to managed migration (paras 4.40-41). In all cases:

- ■ use the following figures as at the day before your UC starts;
- ■ convert them to a monthly amount (as shown in brackets);
- ■ add them together to give your total legacy benefits.

(a) HB

- ■ Use the council's HB figure (x 52÷12), ignoring any adjustments for rent-free periods.
- ■ But exclude HB entirely if you live in supported or temporary accommodation (table 5.3).

(b) JSA(IB), ESA(IR) or IS

- ■ Use the DWP's figure (x 52÷12), and include any amount of JSA(IB)/ESA(IR) that is classified as being JSA(C)/ESA(C).

(c) CTC and/or WTC

- ■ Use HMRC's daily figure (x 365÷12).

(d) Benefit cap and sanctions

- ■ The benefit cap and its exceptions all apply (para 9.51), but ensuring that it is not deducted twice (i.e. not from the HB figure in (a) and from the total).
- ■ Don't make deductions for sanctions etc (para 9.11(b)-(e)).

How much main transitional element – subsequent months

4.42 In your second and subsequent UC assessment periods, your main transitional element stays the same as in paras 4.40-41 unless and until it reduces or ends (para 4.49).

Table 4.3 **Your indicative UC**

Your 'indicative UC' is used to work out your transitional element when you transfer to UC due to managed migration (paras 4.40-41). In all cases:

- use the following figures as at the day before your UC starts;
- convert them to a monthly amount (as shown in brackets);
- use the ordinary rules (paras 9.4-10) to calculate your indicative UC.

(a) Standard allowance and elements

- Use the figures in table 9.2 for these (except as in (c) below).

(b) Children and young persons in your benefit unit

- If you were on CTC, include the same children/young persons as in your CTC.
- Otherwise, use the UC rules to decide who to include.

(c) Childcare costs element

- If you were on WTC, use the WTC childcare costs element (x 52÷12) for this.
- Otherwise, use the UC rules to decide this.

(d) Housing costs element

- Use the UC rules to decide this.

(e) Earned income

- If you were on CTC/WTC, use HMRC's annual figure (x 1÷12), then the DWP decides how much to deduct for tax and national insurance.
- If you were on JSA(IB)/ESA(IR)/IS (but not CTC/WTC), use the DWP's figure (x 52÷12).
- If you were only on HB, use the council's figure (x 52÷12).

(f) Unearned income and capital

- The DWP decides these using information about your legacy benefits from you.
- But if you were on CTC/WTC, any capital over £16,000 is disregarded (para 4.53).

(g) Benefit cap and sanctions

- The benefit cap and its exceptions all apply (para 9.51).
- Don't make deductions for sanctions etc (para 9.11(b)-(e)).

4.42   UCTP 55(2)(b),(c); NIUCTP 56(2)(b),(c)

T4.3   UCTP 49, 54; NIUCTP 50, 55

Example: The main transitional element

Heather is a lone parent aged 38 with a disabled child aged 10. They live in a rented flat. Heather gets JSA(IR) of £84.80 pw. She also gets CTC of £640.40 pcm – which is made up of a family element (£45.40 pcm), a child element (£269.60 pcm) and a disabled child element (£325.40 pcm). And she gets HB of £150.00 pw.

Heather receives a migration notice and claims UC before her deadline day.

- Her transfer to UC is part of managed migration (para 4.24) and she qualifies for the main transitional element.
- In her first UC assessment period, her main transitional element is £231.19 pcm calculated as follows.
- In subsequent UC assessment periods, she will continue to get £231.19 pcm unless or until her main transitional element reduces or ends (paras 4.49-52).

		Monthly figures
(a)	**Total legacy benefits used in this calculation (table 4.2)**	
	JSA(IB) £84.80 x 52÷12	£367.47
	CTC £640.40 ÷ 4 x 52 ÷ 12	£693.77
	HB £150.00 x 52÷12	£650.00
	Total	£1,711.24
(b)	**Indicative UC used in this calculation (table 4.3)**	
	Standard allowance for a single person	£368.74
	Child element (higher rate)	£315.00
	Disabled child addition (lower rate)	£146.31
	Housing costs element	£650.00
	Total	£1,480.05
(c)	**Main transitional element first month (para 4.40)**	
	Total legacy benefits	£1,711.24
	Minus indicative UC	£1,480.05
	Equals amount of main transitional element	£231.19

(Based on Case Study 7 in 'Completing the move to universal credit', DWP, June 2022)

The transitional SDP element

Who qualifies for the transitional SDP element

4.43   You qualify for a transitional SDP element if:

(a) you transferred to UC as part of voluntary migration (paras 4.13), or natural migration caused by the end of a legacy benefit (para 4.19);

(b) you or your partner met the conditions for a severe disability premium in your JSA(IB), ESA(IR) or IS (para 4.45) no more than one month before your UC began;

(c) you or your partner also met those conditions on the day your UC started;

(d) your claims for legacy benefits and for UC were as a single person in both cases, or as a couple with the same partner in both cases (including, in the case of UC, a couple claiming as a single person: para 2.7).

4.44   You must have been getting (or entitled to) a severe disability premium in your JSA(IB), ESA(IR) or IS (para 4.43(b)). Getting the premium in just your HB is not enough, but in this case you may be able to get a discretionary housing payment (para 6.66).

Conditions for a severe disability premium

4.45   You meet the conditions for a severe disability premium if:

(a) you receive one or more of the following disability benefits:

- the daily living component of PIP or (in Scotland) adult disability payment, or

- the middle or highest care rate of the care component of DLA or (in Scotland) child disability payment, or

- attendance allowance, or

- constant attendance allowance paid with an industrial injury or war disablement pension, or

- an armed forces independence payment; and

(b) you have no non-dependants living with you (paras 3.70-77) apart from non-dependants who receive any of the disability benefits in (a), or are (or were within the last 28 weeks) certified as severely sight impaired or blind; and

(c) no-one receives carer's allowance or the carer element of UC for caring for you.

4.46   The severe disability premium has two rates:

(a) single people get the single rate if you meet all the conditions in para 4.43:

(b) couples get the double rate if you both meet all the conditions

(c) couples get the single rate if:

- one of you meets all the conditions, and

- the other meets the first two conditions (para 4.43(a) and (b)) or is certified as severely sight impaired or blind.

4.43-44 UCTP 63, sch 2 paras 3, 7; NIUCTP 64, sch 2 paras 3, 7

4.45-46 UCTP 2(1) – 'severe disability premium'; NIUCTP 2(1)

How much transitional SDP element – first month

4.47　　In your first UC assessment period, your transitional SDP element equals the following fixed amount:

(a) for single people, couples claiming UC as a single person, and couples who were getting the single rate of SDP:

- ■ £132.12 if you receive the LCWRA element in your UC,
- ■ £313.79 if you don't receive the LCWRA element;

(b) for joint claim couples who were getting the double rate of SDP:

- ■ £445.91 whether or not you receive the LCWRA element.

These figures apply to new awards starting on or after 10th April 2023.

How much transitional SDP element – subsequent months

4.48　　In your second and subsequent UC assessment periods, your transitional SDP element stays the same as in para 4.47 unless and until it reduces or ends (para 4.49).

Example: The transitional SDP element

James is a single person aged 53. He lives in a rented flat. He gets JSA(IR) which includes a severe disability premium. He also gets HB.

James moves to a new area. He claims UC at his new address and qualifies for a LCWRA element in his UC.

- ■ His transfer to UC is part of natural migration (para 4.19) and he qualifies for a transitional SDP element (para 4.43).
- ■ In his first UC assessment period, his transitional SDP element is £132.12 pcm (para 4.47).
- ■ In subsequent UC assessment periods, he will continue to get £132.12 pcm unless or until his transitional SDP element reduces or ends (paras 4.49-52).

(Based on Case Study 6 in 'Completing the move to universal credit', DWP, June 2022)

Reduction and end of transitional elements

4.49　　The following rules apply to both the main transitional element and the transitional SDP element.

4.47　　UCTP sch 2 para 5; SI 2023/340 reg 7; NIUCTP sch 2 para 5; NISR 2023/45 reg 7

4.48　　UCTP sch 2 para 6; NIUCTP sch 2 para 6

4.49　　UCTP 55(2), 56, 57, sch 2 para 6; NIUCTP 56(2), 57, 58, sch 2 para 6

Reductions in transitional element

4.50 Each time you are awarded one of the following in your UC (chapter 9), or their amount is up-rated or increased for any other reason, your transitional element reduces by the same amount:

(a) a standard allowance;

(b) a child element;

(c) a disabled child addition;

(d) a work capability element (including an LCWRA element in place of an LCW element);

(e) a carer element;

(f) a housing costs element.

But if you are awarded the childcare costs element (para 9.42), or its amount increases, your transitional element doesn't reduce.

End of transitional element

4.51 Your transitional element ends if and when:

(a) the amount reduces to nil (under the rules in para 4.50); or

(b) you were getting UC as a single person and start claiming as a couple; or

(c) you were getting UC as a couple and start claiming as a single person or as a couple with a different partner; or

(d) your earned income was at or above the administrative earnings threshold (para 2.41) in your first UC assessment period, but is lower than that (or nil) in any three consecutive assessment periods; or

(e) you stop being entitled to UC (para 4.52).

It isn't reinstated except as described in para 4.52.

Gaps in your entitlement to UC

4.52 Your transitional element:

(a) ends as soon as you stop qualifying for UC;

(b) is reinstated after a gap in your UC that is due to an increase in your earned income and is less than three assessment periods;

(c) isn't reinstated after any other gap in your UC.

When the transitional element is reinstated as in (b), its amount is the same as if you had been on UC throughout. This rule can apply any number of times and is particularly important for people who receive non-monthly earnings (paras 10.25-27).

4.50   UCTP 55(2),(4),(5); NIUCTP 56(2),(4),(5)

4.51   UCTP 55(3), 56(2)-(4), 57(1); NIUCTP 56(3), 57(2)-(4), 58(1)

4.52   UCTP 56(2), 57(2); NIUCTP 57(2), 58(2)

The transitional capital disregard

Who qualifies for a transitional capital disregard

4.53   You qualify for a transitional capital disregard if:

(a) you transferred to UC as part of managed migration (para 4.24);

(b) you made your UC claim on or before your final deadline (paras 4.32-33);

(c) on the day before your UC started, you were on CTC or WTC or both and you had capital over £16,000;

(d) your claims for legacy benefits and for UC were as a single person in both cases, or as a couple with the same partner in both cases (including, in the case of UC, a couple claiming as a single person: para 2.7).

How the disregard works

4.54   The disregard applies to all your capital over £16,000. This means that:

(a) your capital doesn't stop you qualifying for UC (para 10.73); and

(b) only the first £16,000 of your capital counts as providing you with an assumed income (para 10.74).

You get this disregard in your actual UC (table 10.6(r)) whether or not you qualify for a transitional element. You also get it when your indicative UC is calculated (table 4.3(f)).

End of transitional capital disregard

4.55   Your transitional capital disregard ends if and when:

(a) your capital reduces below £16,000; or

(b) you were getting UC as a single person and start claiming as a couple; or

(c) you were getting UC as a couple and start claiming as a single person or as a couple with a different partner; or

(d) your earned income was at or above the administrative earnings threshold (para 2.41) in your first UC assessment period, but is lower than that (or nil) in any three consecutive assessment periods; or

(e) you have received UC for 12 successive assessment periods, or (if you have breaks in your UC that are due to an increase in your earned income), for 12 assessment periods not counting the gaps; or

(f) you stop being entitled to UC (para 4.56).

It isn't reinstated except as described in para 4.56.

4.53   UCTP 48, 49, 51; NIUCTP 49, 50, 52

4.54   UCTP 51(2); NIUCTP 52(2)

4.55   UCTP 50(2), 51(3),(4), 56(2)-(4), 57(2); NIUCTP 51(2), 52(3),(4), 57(2)-(4), 58(2)

Gaps in your entitlement to UC

4.56   Your transitional capital disregard:

(a) ends as soon as you stop qualifying for UC;

(b) is reinstated after a gap in your UC that is due to an increase in your income and is less than three assessment periods;

(c) isn't reinstated after any other gap in your UC.

When the transitional capital disregard is reinstated as in (b), its amount is the same as if you had been on UC throughout. This rule can apply any number of times and is particularly important for people who receive non-monthly earnings (paras 10.25-27).

4.56   UCTP 56(2), 57(2); NIUCTP 57(2), 58(2)

Chapter 5 **Housing costs UC/SMI can meet**

- ■ The housing costs UC and SMI can meet: see paras 5.1-9.
- ■ Supported and temporary accommodation: see paras 5.10-13.
- ■ Who is liable or treated as liable for housing costs: see paras 5.14-30.
- ■ Sham, non-commercial, contrived and other excluded liabilities: see paras 5.31-42.
- ■ Occupying your home: see paras 5.43-46.
- ■ Absences, moving home and two homes: see paras 5.47-63.

Who gets help with housing costs

5.1   This chapter explains who can get a UC housing costs element (HCE) and support for mortgage interest (SMI). Table 5.1 summarises the rules and chapters 6-8 explain how much you can get.

The housing costs element / UC towards housing costs

5.2   The housing costs element (HCE) is the part of your UC that is for housing costs. It helps meet rent and service charges and is paid to you or your landlord (paras 9.4, 12.30). In this guide, 'housing costs element' (HCE) and 'UC towards housing costs' mean the same as each other.

Support for mortgage interest

5.3   SMI helps meet mortgage interest and alternative finance payments in relation to your home. It is calculated separately from your UC, is paid directly to your lender and is a loan you are expected to pay back (chapter 8).

The payment, liability and occupation conditions

5.4   For both HCE and SMI, you have to meet:

- (b) the payment condition – this says which housing costs can be met (paras 5.5-13, 5.31-42);
- (c) the liability condition – this says you must have a legal obligation to make payments (paras 5.14-30); and
- (d) the occupation condition – this says you must occupy the accommodation as your home (paras 5.43-63).

5.2   WRA 8(2), 11; UC 25, 26(2)-(4); NIWRO 13(2), 16; NIUC 26, 27(2)-(4)

5.3   WRWA 18(1); LMI 3(1),(2), 16, 17, sch 1 paras 2, 5; NIWRWO 13(1); NILMI 3(1),(2), 16, 17

5.4   WRA 11(3)(a)-(c); UC 25(1)(a)-(c); NIWRA 16(3)(a)-(c); NIUC 26(1)(a)-(c)

Table 5.1 **Which housing costs and when from**

	Housing costs element (HCE)	Support for mortgage interest (SMI)
(a) Renters	You can get an HCE towards your rent and service charges from the beginning of your UC claim	You can't get SMI
(b) Shared owners	You can get an HCE towards your rent and service charges from the beginning of your UC claim	You can get SMI towards your mortgage interest, but only after a waiting period of three months
(c) Owner occupiers	You can get an HCE towards your service charges, but only after a waiting period of three months	You can get SMI towards your mortgage interest, but only after a waiting period of three months

Note: For the waiting period for both HCE and SMI, see paras 8.14-17.

Renters

5.5   If you rent your home (as a social or private renter):

(a) you can get an HCE towards your rent and service charges; but

(b) supported and temporary accommodation and some other special cases are excluded (tables 5.1, 5.2).

You can get an HCE from the beginning of your UC claim. (Note that, unlike in HB, you are included in (a) if you are a Crown tenant.)

Shared owners

5.6   If you are a shared owner (para 5.7):

(a) you can get an HCE towards your rent and service charges; and

(b) you can get SMI towards your mortgage interest and alternative finance payments.

You can get an HCE from the beginning of your UC claim. But you can only get SMI when you have completed a waiting period of three months (paras 8.14-17).

T5.1   UC 25(1),(2), 26(2)-(5), sch 5 para 5; LMI 2(1) – 'qualifying period', 3(1),(2), 8(1)(b), sch 1 paras 2(1), 5(1)
        NIUC 26(1),(2), 27(2)-(5), sch 5 para 5; LMI 2(1), 3(1),(2), 8(1)(b), sch 1 paras 2(1), 5(1)

T5.1   WRA(11)(1),(3); UC 25(2),(4)(a), sch 1 paras 2, 3, 3A, 3B, 7-8, sch 3 para 2;
        NIWRO 16(1),(3); NIUC 26(2),(4)(a), sch 1 paras 2, 3, 4, 4A, 8-9, sch 3 para 1(4)

5.5   UC 25(2)(a),(c), 26(2), sch 1 paras 2, 3, 3A, 3B, 7; NIUC 26(2)(a),(c), 27(2), sch 1 paras 2-4, 4A, 8

5.6   UC 25(2)(a),(c), 26(4),(5), sch 1 paras 2(a), 7; LMI 3(2), sch paras 2(1), 5(1)
        NIUC 26(2)(a),(c), 27(4),(5), sch 1 paras 2(a), 8; NILMI 3(2), sch paras 2(1), 5(1)

Table 5.2 **Housing costs UC can meet**

Housing costs that can be included in your HCE

(a) Payments for a tenancy (para 5.17) – rent and service charges.

(b) Payments for a licence or permission to occupy (para 5.18) – rent and service charges.

(c) Payments by a shared owner – rent and service charges.

(d) Payments by an owner occupier – service charges only.

(e) Payments for a croft and croft land – rent and service charges.

(f) Payments for a charitable housing association almshouse – maintenance and service charges.

(g) Payments for a caravan or mobile home:

- site charges if you are an owner or renter, and

- rent if you are a renter.

(h) Payments for a houseboat, including a narrowboat suitable for permanent residence (R(H) 9/08):

- berthing fees and mooring charges or a continuous cruiser licence ([2020] UKUT 158 (AAC)) if you are an owner or renter, and

- rent if you are a renter.

Housing costs that are excluded from your HCE

(i) Payments for the kinds of supported or temporary accommodation in table 5.3.

(j) Payments for care homes and independent (non-NHS) hospitals.

(k) Payments for probation and bail hostels ('approved premises') – for prisoners who are released or on bail.

(l) Payments for tents or similar moveable structures and related site fees.

(m) Payments of ground rent.

(n) Payments of mesne profits/violent profits (paras 5.19-21).

(o) Any other payments that do not fall within items (a)-(h) above.

Notes

- See paras 5.17-19 for the differences between rent, licence payments and mesne profits. In the rest of the guide, we call all of them 'rent'.

- Mesne/violent profits are not listed as being 'rent' and are excluded because they fall under the rule in (o). (Items (i)-(m) are 'rent' but nevertheless excluded.)

- Chapters 6 and 7 explain the amount that can be met by UC. Chapter 8 covers mortgage and similar payments.

T5.2   UC 25(2)(a),(c), sch 1 paras 2, 3, 3A, 3B; NIUC 26(2)(a),(c) sch 1 paras 2-4, 4A

Table 5.3 **Supported or temporary accommodation**

Supported accommodation

(a) Exempt accommodation (with support provided by or on behalf of your landlord)

- You rent from a non-profit landlord (para 5.11); and
- you receive care, support or supervision (table 5.4); and
- the care, support or supervision is provided by your landlord or by someone on your landlord's behalf.

(b) Managed accommodation (with support provided by someone else)

- You rent from a non-profit landlord; and
- you were admitted to the accommodation to meet a need for care, support or supervision; and
- you receive care, support or supervision.

(c) Domestic violence refuges

- You rent from a non-profit landlord or from a local council; and
- the building (or the part you live in) is wholly or mainly used as non-permanent accommodation for people who have left their home as a result of domestic violence (para 5.11); and
- the accommodation is provided to you for that reason.

(d) Local council hostels

- The building (or the part you live in) is owned or managed by a local council; and
- it provides non-self-contained domestic accommodation with meals or food preparation facilities (and is not a care home or independent hospital); and
- you are provided with care, support or supervision by your landlord, or by someone else (this needn't be on your landlord's behalf).

Temporary accommodation

(e) Temporary accommodation for homeless people

- You rent from a local council or a registered housing association; and
- the accommodation is provided to you by your council because you were homeless or to prevent you becoming homeless.

T5.3　　UC sch 1 paras 3A, 3B; UCTP 5(2)(a), 6(8), 7(5)(a), 8(3), 14(3)
　　　　NIUC sch 1 paras 4, 4A; NIUCTP 3(2)(a), 4(8), 5(5)(a), 6(3), 13(3)

Table 5.4 **Care, support or supervision**

This table explains what counts as care, support or supervision (CSS) in supported accommodation (table 5.3).

Meaning of CSS: Supported accommodation means 'accommodation in which a measure of care, support or supervision is provided to assist the occupants with the practicalities of day-to-day living' and the phrase 'care, support or supervision' has its ordinary English meaning (R(H) 2/07 confirmed in R(S) v Social Security Commissioners and Others).

Availability of CSS: The CSS must be available in reality to the tenant, and there must be a real prospect that they will find the service of use (R(H) 4/09 and [2009] UKUT 109 (AAC)).

Meaning of 'support': 'Support' might well be characterised as 'the giving of advice and assistance to the claimant in coping with the practicalities of [their] life, and in particular [their] occupation of the property' ([2010] AACR 2). It is more than ordinary housing management ([2010] AACR 2).

Continuity of support: The support provided must be ongoing (R(H) 4/09). Help with gaining exemption from the council tax because the tenant is severely mentally impaired is more like a setting up cost and is not enough ([2010] AACR 2).

Need for and provision of 'support': What matters is simply whether support is provided to more than a minimal extent, and it is… implicit that support is not 'provided' unless there is in fact some need for it ([2009] UKUT 150 (AAC)).

Dwellings in a group: A dwelling in a group (e.g. sheltered accommodation) doesn't qualify as supported accommodation just because other dwellings in the group do: CSS must be provided to that particular dwelling (CH/1289/2007).

Amount of CSS: CSS must be more than minimal. An average of ten minutes per tenant per week was not enough (in R(H) 7/07), but three hours per tenant per week might be enough (in CH/1289/2007). Just helping with HB claims and reviews, and carrying out safety and security inspections, was not more than minimal; but 'proactively considering what physical improvements or alterations to the properties could be usefully made' in the case for adaptations for disability could be enough ([2010] AACR 2). In the test of what is or is not minimal it is 'unfortunately inherent… that some landlords may just about scrape over the line… while others will not do so' ([2012] UKUT 52 (AAC)).

When there is no relevant history: In a new development it is necessary to look at what is contemplated ([2009] UKUT 109 (AAC)).

CSS provided by more than one person: Both the landlord and another person or body (e.g. social services) can be providing CSS to the same person, so long as what the landlord is providing is more than minimal (R(H) 7/07).

T5.4   R(S) v Social Security Commissioner and Others [2008] EWHC 3097 Admin and [2009] EWHC 2221 Admin
         www.bailii.org/ew/cases/EWHC/Admin/2008/3097.html
         www.bailii.org/ew/cases/EWHC/Admin/2009/2221.html
         [2010] AACR 2, was [2009] UKUT 107 (AAC)

5.7 You are a 'shared owner':

(a) in England and Wales, if you are buying a percentage of the value of your home (typically 25%, 50% or 75%) on a shared ownership lease;

(b) in Scotland, if you are jointly buying your home with your landlord and have the right to purchase their share.

In each case, you usually pay rent as well, but this is not part of the definition ([2020] UKUT 28 (AAC)).

Owner occupiers

5.8 If you are an owner occupier (para 5.9):

(a) you can get an HCE towards your service charges; and

(b) you can get SMI towards your mortgage interest and alternative finance payments.

You can only get an HCE or SMI when you have completed a waiting period of three months (paras 8.14-17).

5.9 We use 'owner occupier' to mean both freeholders and leaseholders, whether you are paying a mortgage or not, and whether you have service charges or not.

Supported or temporary accommodation

5.10 If you live in the kinds of supported or temporary accommodation in table 5.3, you can't get a UC housing costs element, but you can get HB.

Terminology

5.11 In table 5.3 and throughout this guide:

(a) 'non-profit landlord' means:

- ■ a registered or unregistered housing association,

- ■ a registered charity,

- ■ a voluntary organisation whose activities are carried out not for profit (such as a community interest company or community benefit society), or

- ■ a county council in an area of England that has both district councils and a separate county council;

(b) 'local council' means:

- ■ a district, borough or city council in England, or

- ■ a council in Scotland, Wales or Northern Ireland;

(c) 'care, support or supervision' has its ordinary English meaning (R(H) 2/07): for case law about this see table 5.4 ;

5.7   UC 26(6); NIUC 27(6)

5.8   UC 25(2)(c), 26(3)(c); LMI 3(2), sch paras 2(1), 5(1); NIUC 26(2)(c), 27(3)(c); NILMI 3(2), sch paras 2(1), 5(1)

5.10   UC 25(2), sch 1 paras 3(h),(i), 3A, 3B; UCTP 5(2)(a), 6(8), 7(5)(a), 8(3)
         NIUC 26(2), sch 1 paras 3(e),(ea), 4, 4A; NIUCTP 3(2)(a), 4(8), 5(5)(a), 6(3)

5.11   UC 98(4) – 'domestic violence', sch 1 paras 1 – 'exempt accommodation', 'housing association', 'registered charity', 'voluntary organisation', 3A(6); NIUC 96(5) sch 1 paras 1, 4(6)

(d)   'domestic violence' includes controlling or coercive behaviour, violence, psychological, physical, sexual, emotional, financial or other abuse, regardless of the gender or sexuality of the victim. The domestic violence doesn't have to be from a partner or family member; it can be from others including a neighbour or landlord.

In the law, all the types of supported accommodation (table 5.3(a)-(d)) are called 'specified accommodation'. Accommodation that meets description (a) is also called 'exempt accommodation' – whether or not it also meets one or more of descriptions (b)-(d).

Claiming HB as well as UC

5.12   UC online claim forms have a question about whether your home is supported or temporary accommodation. If it is, you need to claim UC from the DWP (for your living costs) and HB from your local council (for your housing costs). Your UC claim can't be treated as an HB claim (and vice versa), so you need to make two claims and keep track of them separately.

Decisions and appeals

5.13   You have the right to request a reconsideration or an appeal to a tribunal. In practice you should use:

(a)   the HB procedures (volume 2 chapter 20) for requests and appeals about whether your home is supported or temporary accommodation – because the DWP follows your local council's decision about this (DWP, Operational Guidance [www]);

(b)   the UC procedures (chapter 14) for requests and appeals about how much of your rent and service charges are met by UC or any other UC matter.

Table 5.5 **Liability of renters**

(a)   *Liability and letting agreements:* You are liable for rent if your obligation to pay it is legally enforceable – a moral obligation is not enough (R v Rugby HBRB ex parte Harrison). Letting agreements are usually in writing in the form of a contract or of a letter that gives the necessary details. But there is no requirement for this (GM A3.50). An agreement by word of mouth is sufficient to create a legally enforceable liability (R v Poole BC ex parte Ross) except in the (rare) case of tenancies with a fixed term of over three years (Law of Property Act 1925, s54).

(b)   *Sham liability:* If evidence shows that there is no intention to enforce the terms of your letting agreement, this can indicate the agreement is a sham so you aren't liable and can't get UC towards your rent (R(H) 3/03).

(c)   *Your circumstances:* It isn't possible to grant a tenancy to yourself (Rye v Rye). And if you already have the right to occupy your home (e.g. as joint owner) no-one can grant you a letting on it (e.g. another joint owner) so you can't be liable.

5.12-13 DWP, 22/05/22, HB guidance for supported housing claims, page 64, https://tinyurl.com/UCClaim
        UC sch 1 paras 3(h),(i), 3A, 3B; UCTP 5(2)(a), 6(8); D&A 5, 9, 23, 24;
        NIUC sch 1 paras 3(e),(ea), 4, 4A; NIUCTP 3(2)(a), 4(8); NID&A 5, 9, 23, 24
        http://tinyurl.com/OG-Supported-Accomm-2022

(d) *Your landlord's circumstances:* Normally your landlord has a legal interest in the dwelling as an owner or tenant but this is not necessarily the case (CH/2959/2006 Bruton v London and Quadrant HT, Lambeth LBC v Kay).

(e) *If you have an attorney or appointee:* An attorney or appointee (paras 3.8-10) can enter a letting agreement for you thus making you liable for rent – even when your attorney is your landlord ([2013] UKUT 128 (AAC)).

(f) *If you are incapable of understanding your agreement:* If you are legally incapable of understanding your letting agreement (e.g. you are under 18 or have a mental disability), the law can be more complicated. In England and Wales, your letting agreement is likely to be valid so you are liable for rent ([2012] AACR 41). Or if it isn't valid, you are likely to be liable or treated as liable under section 7 of the Mental Capacity Act 2005 or under the common law principle of paying for necessaries ([2012] AACR 41). In Scotland, your liability needs to be decided on a 'transaction by transaction approach' ([2012] AACR 20), and in some cases your letting agreement may not be valid so you aren't liable for rent and can't get UC towards it.

(g) *Non-payment or arrears of rent:* If your landlord is unlikely to evict you if you don't pay, this can be evidence that you are not liable. Most landlords expect to end an agreement if a tenant doesn't pay, and in some cases, arrears may suggest you aren't liable (CH/1849/2007). However, not paying your rent 'even for an extensive period' or paying less than your agreement says (even if your landlord has agreed to this), doesn't without other evidence mean you aren't liable ([2010] UKUT 43 (AAC)).

(h) *If your landlord breaks their own occupation agreement by renting to you:* If by granting your letting your landlord has broken their own occupation agreement on your dwelling (e.g. because it says they mustn't rent it out), your own letting agreement is still valid so you are liable for rent (Governors of Peabody Donation Fund v Higgins) until and unless the landlord's right to occupy is terminated.

(i) *If your landlord breaks the law by renting to you:* A contract (including a tenancy) that is made with knowledge that carrying it out involves a criminal act, is not enforceable (Nayyar v Denton Wilde Sapte). For example, if your home had a prohibition/closing order (Housing Act 2004, s32; Housing (Scotland) Act 1987, s122) on it when your landlord offered you a tenancy. The law is less clear if the order was made after the start of the tenancy and/or in England and Wales the agreement may be varied by a first-tier tribunal (Housing Act 2004, s34). But in some parts of the UK different rules apply if your landlord needs a licence but does not have one – see (j) to (l).

(j) *If your landlord needs a licence for a house in multiple occupation (HMO) in Scotland or Northern Ireland:* It is an offence to let an HMO in Scotland or Northern Ireland without a council licence (Housing (Scotland) Act 2006, s154; Houses in Multiple Occupation (Northern Ireland) Act 2016, s30) so the rule in (i) applies. But in Scotland the council can also make an order to suspend your rent, so your liability is nil (Housing (Scotland) Act 2006, s144(1)).

(k) *If your landlord needs an HMO or other licence in England or Wales or has a banning*

> *order:* In England and Wales if your home should be licensed but isn't, the law says your agreement is enforceable (despite the rule in (i)): Housing and Planning Act 2016, s24, Housing Act 2004, s73. But you can apply to a first-tier tribunal for a rent repayment order, or the council can if your rent was paid by UC (Housing and Planning Act 2016, s43-45; Housing Act 2004, s73). In England, this also applies if your landlord has a banning order (Housing and Planning Act 2016, s40).
>
> (l)   *If your landlord/agent doesn't have a licence to manage property in Wales:* Anyone who carries out private rented property management in Wales must have a management licence from Rent Smart Wales [www]. If your landlord/agent doesn't have one the council can apply for a rent repayment order, or a rent stop order (so your liability is nil) (Housing (Wales) Act 2014, s30, 32).

Liability for housing costs

5.14   To get UC or SMI towards your housing costs:

(a)   your housing costs must be of a type that can be met by UC or SMI (table 5.1);

(b)   you must be liable or treated as liable for them (paras 5.16-30);

(c)   your liability must not be a sham (para 5.32)

(d)   your liability must be commercial (para 5.33);

(e)   your liability must not be contrived (para 5.34);

(f)   your liability must not be excluded for other reasons (paras 5.35-41).

5.15   Meeting these conditions is usually shown by your letting agreement or a letter from your landlord and the answers to questions about your tenancy (renters), or by your mortgage agreement or similar document (owners). You must also meet the financial and other conditions for UC/SMI (chapters 2 and 8).

What liability is

5.16   Liability for housing costs means having a legal obligation to pay them. 'A liability to make payments imposes legally enforceable conditions on the parties to the agreement. If one party breaks the agreement, the other party has the right to go to court to seek redress' (ADM F2081). Further details for renters are in table 5.5.

T5.5   R v Rugby BC HBRB ex parte Harrison (1994) 28 HLR 36 R v Poole BC ex parte Ross 05/05/95 QBD 28 HLR 351
Rye v Rye [1962] AC 496
Bruton v London and Quadrant HT [1999] UKHL 26
Lambeth LBC v Kay [2006] UKHL 10
[2012] AACR 41 was [2012] UKUT 12 (AAC)
[2012] AACR 20 was [2011] UKUT 354 (AAC)
The Governors of Peabody Donation Fund v Higgins 20/06/83 CA 10 HLR 82
Nayyar v Denton Wilde Sapte [2009] EWHC 3218 (QB)
https://www.rentsmart.gov.wales

5.14   WRA 11; UC 25, sch 1 para 3, sch 2 paras 5-10; WRWA 18; LMI 3, sch 1, sch 2 paras 3, 6;
NIWRO 16; NIUC 26, sch 1 para 3, sch 2 paras 5-10; NIWRWO 13; NILMI 3, sch 1, sch 2 paras 3, 6

5.16   WRA 11(1)(3)(b); UC 25(3); WRWA 18(1),(4),(5); LMI 3(1),(2)(b), sch 2 paras 2, 5;
NIWRO 16(1),(3)(b); NIUC 26(3); NIWRWO 13(1),(4),(5); NILMI 3(1)(2)(b), sch 2 paras 2, 5

Examples: Liability for rent

1. In a couple and making a joint claim

Maggie has the tenancy of a rented house. Jack is her partner who lives with her. They make a joint claim for UC.

- ◼ Maggie and Jack can get a UC housing costs element (HCE) towards their rent because one of them is liable (para 5.22(b)).

2. Joint tenants who are not a couple

Dylan and Kyra are friends who rent a house in their joint names. Kyra claims UC.

- ◼ Kyra can get a UC HCE towards her half-share of the rent (paras 5.22(c), 6.11, 8.13).

Tenancies

5.17   A tenancy is often described as a stake in the land. It is a contract that:

(a)   gives you the right to occupy a dwelling and to exclude others from it ('exclusive possession'); and

(b)   requires you to pay rent; and

(c)   is for a length of time that can be established (a 'term certain') – in practice this means that it is either:

- ◼ a 'fixed term tenancy' – this has a fixed period, such as six months or a year, after which it ends unless it is renewed, or

- ◼ a periodic tenancy – this has a repeating period such as weekly or monthly, and can be ended by a notice to quit.

Licences and permission to occupy

5.18   A licence is an agreement that gives you the right to occupy and requires you to pay rent (or a fee) but doesn't give you the right to exclude others. Licences are used in hostels and other accommodation where the landlord (or licensor) can place others in the dwelling and/or require you to move rooms. Social landlords sometimes ask for 'use and occupation payments' for permission to occupy if you are not the tenant/licensee, for example if you remained in the home after the tenant/licensee moved into residential accommodation (para 5.23).

Mesne profits/violent profits

5.19   If your landlord says your tenancy or licence or other legal permission to occupy has ended s/he may ask you to pay mesne profits (in Scotland, violent profits) instead of rent to avoid creating a new tenancy. Mesne profits are a sort of compensation for the landlord's lost rent. The law about when they do and do not arise is complex but the main rules for secure and assured tenants is in paras 5.20-21.

5.20 Mesne profits can arise for secure and assured tenants when your landlord:

(a) says you have stopped occupying the dwelling as your 'only or principal home' and have therefore lost your status as a secure/assured tenant; and

(b) issues you with a notice to quit under common law.

Any payments you make up to the date the notice to quit expires are rent (as the tenant), but after that are mesne profits (as a trespasser).

5.21 But mesne profits don't normally arise for secure/assured tenants when the landlord:

(a) has issued you with a 'notice of seeking possession' under one of the Housing Act(s) grounds (e.g. because you have rent arrears) to end your tenancy; and

(b) applies to the court for a possession order to evict you.

Any payments you make up to and including your eviction date (including those made after the possession order but before the eviction) are rent, not mesne profits.

Who is liable for housing costs

5.22 You are liable for housing costs on your home (and can get UC or SMI towards them) if:

(a) you are single and are solely liable for your housing costs; or

(b) you are in a couple and one or both of you are liable for your housing costs; or

(c) you are single or in a couple and are jointly liable for your housing costs with one or more others (e.g. with relatives or friends in a house share).

In case (c), you usually get UC or SMI towards a share of the housing costs (paras 6.11, 8.13).

Who is treated as liable

5.23 You are treated as liable for housing costs on your home (and can get UC or SMI towards them) if:

(a) you are in a couple but claiming as a single person (para 2.7) and your partner is liable but you are not (para 5.24); or

(b) a young person or child that you or your partner are responsible for is liable (para 5.24); or

(c) someone else is liable but you have to make the payments to continue living there (para 5.25); or

(d) your landlord has agreed you can do work on your home instead of paying (para 5.28); or

(e) you have a rent-free period allowed for in your letting agreement (para 5.30); or

(f) in some cases, you are incapable of managing your affairs (table 5.5).

5.22   UC 25(3), sch 2 para 1, sch 4 paras 24, 35; LMI 3(2)(b),(3); NIUC 26(3), sch 2 para 1, sch 4 paras 23, 34; NILMI 3(2)(b),(3)

5.23   UC 25(3)(a), sch 2 paras 2, 3, 4; LMI 3(2)(b), sch 2 paras 2, 5; NIUC 26(3)(a), sch 2 paras 2, 3, 4; NILMI 3(2)(b), sch 2 paras 2, 5

When your partner, young person or child are liable

5.24 You can get UC or SMI towards housing costs if:

(a) your partner is liable for them, but you aren't – this applies whether you have a joint claim or are claiming as a single person (paras 2.5-8); or

(b) a young person or child is liable for them, but you aren't – this means a young person or child that you or your partner are responsible for (para 3.65).

Unlike in para 5.25, you don't have to satisfy a test of reasonableness.

When someone else is liable but you are paying

5.25 You can get UC or SMI towards housing costs if:

(a) the person who is liable for housing costs on your home isn't paying them; and

(b) you are paying them so you can continue living there; and

(c) it is reasonable to treat you as liable; and

(d) it would be unreasonable to expect you to make other arrangements.

5.26 The person who isn't paying the housing costs could be:

(a) your parent, relative or friend;

(b) your ex-partner (if it is your current partner see para 5.24);

(c) the executor of someone who has died;

(d) a company or other body (R(H) 5/05).

5.27 Your need to make the payments must be caused by the liable person's failure to do so rather than something separate ([2017] UKUT 40 (AAC)); and the DWP can look at whether the liable person would resume making the payments if your claim is unsuccessful ([2016] UKUT 570 (AAC)). It is usually reasonable to treat you as liable for housing costs if the person who isn't paying has gone away permanently or is absent for too long to be able to get UC/SMI (para 5.47), but not if they are excluded from UC/SMI for the reasons in table 5.6 (CSHB/606/2005). In the case of SMI, the DWP can take account of the fact that treating you as liable benefits the person who isn't paying (by paying their mortgage for them) (ADM F2090).

When you do work on your home rather than pay housing costs

5.28 You can get UC towards housing costs if your landlord has agreed not to collect rent from you ('waived the rent') in return for repairs or redecoration work that:

(a) you have carried out on your home; and

(b) the landlord would (or should) have carried out.

5.29 The repairs or redecoration works, and the amount the landlord has agreed not to collect, must be reasonable. This rule applies only to repairs or redecoration.

5.24-25 UC sch 2 para 2; LMI sch 2 paras 2(2), 5(2); NIUC sch 2 para 2; NILMI sch 2 paras 2(2), 5(2)

5.28 UC sch 2 para 3; NIUC sch 2 para 3

5.29 UC sch 2 para 3(b); LMI sch 2 para 5(2)(c); NIUC sch 2 para 3(b); NILMI sch 2 para 5(2)(c)

When you have rent-free or service charge-free periods

5.30   If you are a renter, you can get UC towards housing costs during rent-free or service charge-free periods. This is because all your annual payments in these cases are averaged over a full year (para 6.58).

Excluded liabilities

5.31   You can't get UC or SMI towards your housing costs if your liability is excluded. Table 5.5 summarises all the types of excluded liability.

If you aren't liable or your liability is a sham

5.32   Unless you are treated as liable (para 5.23), you can't get UC or SMI towards your housing costs if:

(a) you aren't liable for them (para 5.16) – in other words, you haven't provided evidence that you have to pay them in order to occupy your home; or

(b) you have a sham (pretended) liability – in other words, you have provided evidence but the arrangements between you and your landlord or mortgage lender show there was no intention to create a genuine liability.

In (a), the burden of proof (para 14.13) falls on you to provide evidence of your liability (para 3.19), but in (b) the burden is on the DWP to show your liability is a sham (R(H) 3/03).

If your liability isn't on a commercial basis

5.33   You can't get UC or SMI towards your housing costs if your liability for them isn't on a commercial basis. In deciding this, the DWP should look at your individual circumstances. The burden of proof (para 14.13) falls on the DWP to show that your liability isn't commercial, not on you to show that it is. Table 5.7 gives a summary of court and tribunal decisions for renters; DWP advice is in ADM F2081-84.

If your liability was contrived to obtain or increase UC/SMI

5.34   You can't get UC or SMI towards your housing costs if your liability for them was contrived to obtain UC/SMI or to increase the amount. The burden of proof (para 14.13) falls on the DWP to show that your liability was contrived, not on you to show that it wasn't. Table 5.7 gives a summary of court and tribunal decisions for renters; DWP advice is in ADM F2140-46.

5.30   UC sch 2 para 4; NIUC sch 2 para 4

5.31   WRA 11(3)(a),(b); WRWA 18(4),(5),(8); UC 25(3), sch 2 paras 5-10; LMI sch 2 paras 3, 6
         NIWRO 16(3)(a),(b); NIWRWO 13(4),(5),(8); NIUC 26(3), sch 2 paras 5-10; NILMI sch 2 paras 3, 6

5.32-33 UC 25(3)(a); LMI 3(1), sch 2 paras 2(1), 5(1); NIUC 26(3)(a); NILMI 3(1), sch 2 paras 2(1), 5(1)

5.34   UC sch 2 para 10; LMI sch 2 para 6(c); NIUC sch 2 para 10; NILMI sch 2 para 6(c)

Table 5.6 **Excluded liabilities**

If any of these apply to you, you can't get UC/SMI towards your housing costs. Further details and exceptions are in paras 5.32-42.

Exclusions for renters and owners

   (a) You aren't in fact liable to make rent or owner-occupier payments, or your liability is sham (para 5.32).

   (b) Your liability for rent or owner-occupier payments isn't on a commercial basis (para 5.33).

   (c) Your liability for rent or owner-occupier payments was contrived in order to obtain UC/SMI towards housing costs or to increase the amount (para 5.34).

   (d) Your liability for rent or owner-occupier payments was increased to recover arrears you owe on your current or former home – in this case only the increase is excluded from UC/SMI (para 5.35).

Further exclusions for renters

   (e) Your landlord is a close relative who lives with you (para 5.36).

   (f) Your landlord is a company and you are, or a relative who lives with you is, an owner or director (para 5.39).

   (g) Your landlord is a trustee of a trust and you are, or a relative who lives with you is, a beneficiary or trustee (para 5.40).

Further exclusions for owners

   (h) Your owner-occupier payments are due to a member of your household (para 5.41).

Examples: Treated as liable for rent

1. When someone else is liable but you are paying

Zubin has the tenancy of a rented flat. Gill is his adult daughter who lives with him and is on UC. Zubin goes abroad for a long period and stops paying rent. The landlord accepts rent from Gill and the DWP agrees this arrangement is reasonable.

   ■   Gill can get a UC housing costs element (HCE) towards the rent (para 5.25).

2. Work carried out instead of paying rent

Spencer is a plumber and moves into a rented flat where the rent is £1,000 per month. The boiler is faulty, and the landlord says that if Spencer repairs it and redecorates the room, he can miss the first monthly payment. Spencer claims UC.

   ■   Spencer can get a UC HCE towards this £1,000 (para 5.28).

T5.6   UC 2 definition: 'close relative', 25(3), sch 2 paras 5-10; LMI sch 2 para 6
       NIUC 2, 26(3), sch 2 paras 5-10; NILMI sch 2 para 6

3. Rent-free periods

Flora has the tenancy of a rented flat where the rent is £200 per week except for four rent-free weeks each year. She claims UC.

- Flora's monthly housing costs element is 48 x £200 ÷ 12 = £800 (para 6.58).

- She can get a UC HCE towards this £800 every month, even when there are rent-free weeks (para 5.30).

Table 5.7 **Commerciality, contrivance and renters**

Commerciality

(a) *What makes a letting commercial:* The primary consideration is about what was agreed between you and your landlord rather than what in fact happens. Not only the financial arrangements between you and your landlord but all the terms of your agreement should be taken into account (R v Sutton LBC ex parte Partridge; ADM F2084). Each case must be considered on its individual facts and is a matter of judgment (R(H) 1/03). It is necessary to consider whether your letting agreement contains terms that are not enforceable in law (CH/2899/2005). The arrangements between you should be at 'arm's length' (R v Sheffield HBRB ex parte Smith).

(b) *Claiming UC and rent arrears:* Claiming UC towards your rent can be evidence that your agreement is commercial ([2020] UKUT 240 (AAC)). If your landlord accepts what you get from UC rather than your contractual rent this doesn't by itself mean your letting is non-commercial (CH/1076/2002), nor does your landlord's failure to chase up arrears or take possession proceedings against you ([2010] UKUT 43 (AAC)).

(c) *Personal and moral considerations:* If your letting is in fact commercial, friendliness and kindness between you and your landlord doesn't make it non-commercial (R v Poole BC ex parte Ross, CH/4854/2003, [2009] UKUT 13 (AAC)). Conversely, if your letting is in fact non-commercial, the fact that it was drawn up in a way that meets your moral or religious beliefs doesn't make it commercial (R(H) 8/04).

(d) *Lettings between family members or friends:* A letting between family members may or may not be commercial. The family arrangement is not decisive by itself. If the letting enables a disabled family members to be cared for more easily, this is not decisive by itself. Each case depends on its individual circumstances (CH/296/2004, CH/1096/2008, CH/2491/2007). For example, a letting of an annexe to a disabled

---

T5.7   UC 25(3), sch 2 para 10; NIUC 26(3), sch 2 para 10
          R v Sutton HBRB ex parte Partridge 04/11/94 QBD 28 HLR 315
          R v Sheffield HBRB ex parte Smith 08/12/94 QBD 28 HLR 36
          R v Poole HBRB ex parte Ross 05/05/95 QBD 28 HLR 351
          R v Solihull MBC ex parte Simpson 03/12/93 QBD 26 HLR 370
          R v Barking and Dagenham HBRB ex parte MacKay [2001] EWHC Admin 234
          R v Sutton HBRB ex parte Keegan 15/05/92 QBD 27 HLR 92
          R v South Gloucestershire HBRB ex parte Dadds 1997 QBD 29 HLR 700
          R v Manchester CC ex parte Baragrove Properties 15/03/91 QBD 23 HLR 337

son was commercial ([2011] UKUT 41 (AAC)), as was a letting by a son to his terminally ill mother (2015] UKUT 565 (AAC)), and a letting to a friend in their time of trouble (CH/1097/2004). See also (j).

(e) *Low rents:* Having a low rent doesn't by itself make your letting non-commercial (2015] UKUT 565 (AAC); ADM F2083).

(f) *Statutory tenancies:* A statutory tenancy is one created by law, usually at the end of a contractual tenancy. This does not make it non-commercial (CH/4081/2004).

(g) *If the circumstances of your letting change:* If your letting was commercial when it began, it can become non-commercial if there is an identifiable reason for this (CH/3497/2005).

Contrivance

(h) *What makes a letting contrived:* Your liability for rent must have been contrived as a way of gaining UC towards your housing costs or increasing its amount. The word 'contrived' implies abuse of the UC scheme (in the sense of taking improper advantage, not necessarily bad faith) and there must be evidence that this was a primary or dominant purpose of the agreement (R v Solihull HBRB ex parte Simpson, CH/39/2007, ADM F2142). The circumstances and intentions of both you and your landlord should be taken into account (R v Barking and Dagenham HBRB ex parte Mackay, R v Sutton HBRB ex parte Keegan).

(i) *If there is no advantage:* Your letting can't be contrived if no advantage is gained by you or your landlord ([2021] UKUT 193 (AAC)).

(j) *Lettings between family members or providing support:* If your landlord is a relation of yours (e.g. your parent) this does not by itself mean your letting is contrived (Solihull case), but your letting may be treated as non-commercial. See also (d).

(k) *High rents and lettings to people on low incomes:* Having a high rent doesn't mean your letting is contrived (R v South Gloucestershire HBRB ex parte Dadds). There is no objection to landlords letting to people on low incomes to make a profit unless their charges and profits show abuse (CH/39/2007, R v Manchester CC ex parte Baragrove Properties). And if you can't afford your rent or know that you will have to claim UC to pay it, this is not evidence that your letting is contrived (Solihull case), though the DWP suggests it could be if you could have avoided this and still been adequately housed (ADM F2145-46).

If your liability is increased to cover your arrears

5.35 This rule only applies if your landlord or mortgage lender:

(a) increases the amount of your rent or owner occupier payments;

(b) does this as a way of recovering arrears you owe from past periods (either on your current home or a former home);

(c) does this on an individual basis (rather than on an across-the-board basis).

In this case, you can't get UC or SMI towards the amount of the increase.

5.35   UC sch 2 para 9; LMI sch 2 para 6(b); NIUC sch 2 para 9; NILMI sch 2 para 6(b)

If you are renting from a close relative who lives with you

5.36   You can't get UC towards your rent (or any services charges you pay with it) if your landlord lives in the accommodation (para 5.37) and is:

(a)   your partner (para 3.49); or

(b)   a young person or child you or your partner are responsible for (para 3.65); or

(c)   a 'close relative' of yours or of anyone in (a) or (b) (para 5.38).

This rule doesn't breach human rights (R(H) 5/06).

5.37   Your landlord 'lives in the accommodation' if you share at least some essential living accommodation (CH/542/2006), even if you have exclusive possession of one of the rooms (CH/3656/2004). Sharing just a kitchen may be enough to count as living in the accommodation (CPC/1446/2008), as may sharing a house but being unable to make use of the shared areas due to disability (CPC/3379/2008).

5.38   A 'close relative' is:

(a)   a parent, parent-in-law or step-parent; or

(b)   a daughter/son, daughter/son-in-law or step-daughter/son; or

(c)   a sister/brother or half-sister/brother ([2016] UKUT 517 (AAC)); or

(d)   the partner of any of these.

It is the legal not the blood relationship that is used (R(SB) 22/87). An adopted child's parents are his or her adoptive parents, and their other children (natural or by adoption) are his or her brothers and sisters.

If your landlord is a company that you or your family is part of

5.39   You can't get UC towards your rent (or any service charges you pay with it) if your landlord is a company and one or more of the following is an owner or director of the company:

(a)   you or your partner (para 3.49); or

(b)   a young person you or your partner are responsible for (para 3.65); or

(c)   anyone who:

- lives with you (para 5.37), and
- is a close relative of yours or of anyone in (a) or (b), (para 5.38).

This rule applies even if you can show that there is a genuine reason for your letting. In most cases, 'owner' means a person who holds at least 10% of the shares in the company (the details are summarised in ADM F2110-17).

5.36   UC sch 2 para 5; NIUC sch 2 para 5

5.38   UC 2 definition: 'close relative'; LMI 2(1); NIUC 2; NILMI 2(1)

5.39   UC sch 2 para 6; NIUC sch 2 para 6

If your landlord is a trust that you or your family is part of

5.40　　You can't get UC towards your rent if your landlord is a trustee of a trust and one or more of the following is a beneficiary or trustee of the trust:

(a)　you or your partner (para 3.49); or

(b)　a young person or child you or your partner are responsible for (para 3.65); or

(c)　anyone who:

- 　lives with you (para 5.37), and
- 　is a close relative of yours or of anyone in (a) or (b), (para 5.38).

This rule applies even if you can show that there is a genuine reason for your letting.

If your owner-occupier payments are due to someone who lives in your household

5.41　　You can't get SMI towards your owner occupier payments if they are due to someone who lives in your household. They could be a family member, friend or anyone else. Living in your household means the same here as in para 3.53.

Decisions and appeals

5.42　　If the DWP refuses you UC or SMI towards your housing costs, it must send you a decision notice explaining this (para 14.6). The notice:

(a)　should give clear findings of fact ([2012] UKUT 333 (AAC));

(b)　should only refuse you UC/SMI if the findings of fact support this – e.g. you haven't provided evidence of your liability;

(c)　should state which reason applies to you – e.g. that although you are liable for housing costs, your liability is non-commercial;

(d)　may have to give more than one reason – e.g. that you aren't liable for housing costs, and even if you are, your liability is contrived;

(e)　shouldn't confuse different reasons – e.g. shouldn't mix up non-liability or sham liability with non-commerciality or contrivance (CSHB/718/2002).

Some of the reasons for refusing UC or SMI can be difficult to distinguish and can overlap (ADM F2144). You can appeal about all of them to the DWP and then to a tribunal (chapter 14).

5.40　　UC sch 2 para 7; NIUC sch 2 para 7

5.41　　LMI sch 2 paras 3, 6(a); NILMI sch 2 paras 3, 6(a)

5.42　　SSA 8, 10, 12(6), 28(3)(k), 39(1A); D&A 7(1),(3), 51; NISSO 9, 11, 13(6), 28(3)(k), 39(1A); NID&A 7(1),(3), 51

Occupying your home

5.43 The general rule is that you can only get UC or SMI towards housing costs on accommodation in the UK which you normally occupy as your home (paras 5.44-46). But there are also rules about absences from home, moving home and getting UC/SMI on two homes. The rest of this chapter gives the rules that apply to UC (in all cases) and to SMI when you are entitled to it due to being on UC. But if you are entitled to SMI due to being on SPC or a legacy benefit, the SMI rules are the same as for HB (volume 2 chapter 3).

Types of accommodation

5.44 Your home can be:

(a) a dwelling – this has the same meaning as in council tax and rates law (paras 15.4, 19.2), for example a house, flat, mobile home, or houseboat; or

(b) part of a dwelling – for example a room in a hostel or in someone else's home.

This includes somewhere converted, such as when two flats have been knocked together to form a single home (R(H) 5/09; CH/1895/2008). It doesn't include business premises or somewhere used only for a holiday.

Your normal home

5.45 Whether you normally occupy accommodation as your home is decided in your and your benefit unit's particular circumstances (CH/2521/2002). It means more than paying housing costs or having the right to live there: it means being physically present – though exceptions can arise (R(H) 9/05). If you have more than one home (in the UK or abroad), only one can be your normal home. This is decided on the facts, including how much time you and your family spend in each of them.

Short-term accommodation

5.46 Your home can be somewhere short-term, e.g. if you move a lot or are staying in a hostel or refuge. But it must be a 'home' in the ordinary sense, and this doesn't normally include night shelters where you have no right to live during the day ([2013] UKUT 65 (AAC)).

5.43   UC 25(4), sch 3 para 1; LMI 3(2)(c), sch 3 para 12; NIUC 26(4), sch 3 para 1; NILMI sch 3 para 12

5.44   UC sch 3 paras 1(4), 2; LMI 2(1) definition: 'dwelling', sch 3 para 12(3); NIUC sch 3 para 1(4); NILMI 2(1)

5.45   UC sch 3 para 1(1)-(3); LMI sch 3 para 12(1),(2); NIUC sch 3 para 1(1)-(3); NILMI sch 3 para 12(1),(2)

Absences from home

5.47 This section explains when you can get UC or SMI during an absence from home. If you are in a couple and your partner is absent, see also paras 3.58-59.

Temporary absences

5.48 You can get UC or SMI on your normal home during an absence if:

(a) your absence is temporary (para 5.49);

(b) it is not expected to exceed the time limit (para 5.50);

(c) it has not yet reached the time limit; and

(d) you remain liable for housing costs on your normal home.

Different rules apply when your home is being repaired (para 5.52) or you are in prison (paras 2.22-24), or you are absent abroad (paras 2.29-35).

Intending to return

5.49 Your absence is temporary if you intend to return to your normal home. This is decided by your own intentions rather than what a relative or official intends for you. But your return must be possible within the time limit. Wanting to return is not enough if your return is in fact impossible (CSHB/405/2005).

Time limits

5.50 The time limit for temporary absences from your normal home is:

(a) 12 months if your absence is due to a fear of violence (para 5.53); or

(b) six months if your absence is for any other reason.

For example, (b) applies if you are on holiday, working away from home, trying out a care home, going to care for (or be cared for by) a relative or friend, in hospital and so on.

5.51 The 12-month time limit also applies to absences from a temporary home you are staying in due to a fear of violence in your normal home (para 5.54).

Example: Going away for work

Robin rents a private flat in Cornwall and is on UC. He gets a live-in job in Berkshire that is expected to last for six months.

- While he is away, Robin can get a UC housing costs element (HCE) towards the rent on his flat for up to six months (para 5.50), and his earnings are included in the UC calculation.

5.47-48 UC sch 3 para 9; LMI sch 3 para 18; NIUC sch 3 para 8; NILMI sch 3 para 18

5.50-51 UC sch 3 paras 6(4), 9; LMI sch 3 paras 15(4), 18; NIUC sch 3 paras 5(4), 8; NILMI sch 3 paras 15(4), 18

Repairs to your normal home

5.52   When you move somewhere temporary because of essential repairs being carried out on your normal home, you can get UC or SMI towards your housing costs on:

(a)   your temporary home if:

- you don't pay housing costs on your normal home (e.g. you live there with relatives or friends or own it outright), or

- the housing costs on your normal home have stopped;

(b)   your normal home in any other case.

Fear of violence

5.53   For UC/SMI purposes, you have a fear of violence if you fear violence towards yourself or a member of your benefit unit (para 3.46) either:

(a)   in your normal home (whoever it would be from); or

(b)   outside your normal home from a person who was your partner but is no longer.

No violence needs to have actually occurred so long as your fear of it is reasonable.

Temporary absence due to fear of violence

5.54   If you leave your normal home due to a fear of violence and intend to return to it, but it is unreasonable to expect you to do so straight away, you can get UC/SMI for up to 12 months towards housing costs on:

(a)   your normal home; or

(b)   the place you are staying; or

(c)   both, if you are liable for housing costs on both.

5.55   But if one or both are supported or temporary accommodation (table 5.3) you can get HB on one and UC/SMI on the other or HB on both for up to 52 weeks.

Example: Fear of violence

Jenny rents a council flat. Her former partner threatens her outside her home. Jenny goes to a refuge and starts action to enable her to return to her flat.

- Jenny can get a UC housing costs element (HCE) towards the rent on both her flat and the refuge for up to 12 months (paras 5.50, 5.53, 5.55).

5.52   UC sch 3 para 3; LMI sch 3 para 13; NIUC sch 3 para 2; NILMI sch 3 para 13

5.53   UC sch 3 para 6(1); LMI sch 3 para 15(1); NIUC sch 3 para 5(1); NILMI sch 3 para 15(1)

5.54   UC sch 3 paras 6(2),(4), 9(3); LMI sch 3 paras 15(2),(4), 18(2); NIUC sch 3 paras 5(2),(4), 8(3); NILMI sch 3 paras 15(2),(4), 18(2)

5.55   UCTP 5(2)(a), 6(8), 8(3); HB 7(6)(a); HB66+ 7(6)(a); NIUCTP 3(2)(a), 4(8), 6(3); NIHB 7(6)(a); NIHB66+ 7(6)(a)

Moving home

5.56   When you move home your UC changes to take account of your new housing costs (for SMI see paras 8.23 and 8.34). The new amount of UC applies from the beginning of the assessment period containing the date of your move (table 11.1). But in some cases, you can get UC or SMI for up to a month before moving in (paras 5.57-59).

Waiting for adaptations for a disability

5.57   You can get UC or SMI towards housing costs on a new home for up to one month before moving in if:

(a)   you are liable for housing costs there;

(b)   you are waiting for it to be adapted to meet your disability needs or those of a member of your benefit unit (para 3.46);

(c)   you or the member of your benefit unit are getting:

■   the daily living component of PIP, or

■   the standard or enhanced rate of the daily living component of Scottish adult disability payment, or

■   the middle or highest rate of the care component of DLA or Scottish child disability payment, or

■   attendance allowance or an equivalent benefit (para 10.54); and

(d)   you have now moved in and your delay in moving was necessary and reasonable.

The adaptations can include furnishing, carpeting and redecorating as well as changes to your new home's fabric or structure (R (Mahmoudi) v Lewisham LBC).

5.58   You can get UC or SMI towards housing costs on both your old and new home for up to one month before moving if:

(a)   you are liable for housing costs on both of them; and

(b)   you meet the other conditions in para 5.57.

Example: Waiting for adaptations

Wolfgang rents a bedsit and is offered the tenancy of a flat nearer work. He takes on the tenancy and moves in three weeks later after adaptations make it suitable for his wheelchair. He is on the daily living component of PIP.

■   Wolfgang can get a UC housing costs element (HCE) towards both the bedsit and the flat for those three weeks (para 5.58). Because assessment periods are monthly, he gets a UC HCE on both rents for the whole of the assessment period in which he becomes liable for rent on the flat (table 11.1(a)).

5.57   UC sch 3 para 7; LMI sch 3 para 16; NIUC sch 3 para 6; NILMI sch 3 para 16
          R (Mahmoudi) v Lewisham CA (2014) www.bailii.org/ew/cases/EWCA/Civ/2014/284.html

5.58   UC sch 3 para 5; LMI sch 3 para 14; NIUC sch 3 para 4; NILMI sch 3 para 14

Waiting to leave hospital or a care home

5.59   You can get UC or SMI towards your housing costs on a new home for up to one month before moving in if:

(a)   you are liable for housing costs there;

(b)   you (or if you are a couple, both of you) are waiting to leave an NHS or independent hospital (or similar institution) or a care home; and

(c)   you have now moved in.

You need to make your claim promptly (para 3.27).

Two homes

5.60   You can get UC towards your housing costs on two homes when:

(a)   you have a large family (para 5.62); or

(b)   you are absent from your normal home due to fear of violence (para 5.54); or

(c)   you are waiting for adaptations for a disability (para 5.57).

You can get SMI on two homes in cases (b) and (c).

5.61   In any other case you can only get UC or SMI on one home (paras 5.45-46).

Large families housed by social landlords

5.62   You can get UC towards your housing costs on two homes (with no time limit) if:

(a)   you were housed in two rented homes by a social landlord (table 6.1) because of the number of children/young persons living with you; and

(b)   you normally occupy them both with the children/young persons you are responsible for.

No similar rule applies for private renters, owner occupiers or shared owners.

Calculating UC for two homes

5.63   When you qualify for UC towards your housing costs on two homes:

(a)   both housing costs elements are included in the UC calculation (para 9.4); but

(b)   deductions for earned income and housing cost contributions are only made once (paras 6.60, 9.8);

(c)   the size criteria (para 6.15) apply to:

■   the combined number of bedrooms in the case of large families (para 5.62), or

■   each home separately in other cases (para 5.60(b) and (c)).

If you qualify for SMI on two homes, the two amounts are added together (para 8.20). For the benefit cap, see table 9.4.

5.59   UC sch 3 para 8; LMI sch 3 para 17; NIUC sch 3 para 7; NILMI sch 3 para 17

5.61   UC sch 3 para 1(2); LMI sch 3 para 12(2); NIUC sch 3 para 1(2); NILMI sch 3 para 12(2)

5.62   UC sch 3 para 4; NIUC sch 3 para 3

5.63   UC sch 4 paras 17-19, 25(3),(4); LMI 10; NIUC sch 4 paras 16-18, 24(3),(4), NILMI 10

Chapter 6 **The housing costs element**

- ■ Who can get a housing costs element: see paras 6.1-6.
- ■ Social renters including under-occupation and high rents: see paras 6.7-22.
- ■ Service charges (for social renters and owner occupiers): see paras 6.23-33.
- ■ Private renters including local housing allowances: see paras 6.34-55.
- ■ Calculating monthly figures: see paras 6.56-58.
- ■ Housing cost contributions from non-dependants: see paras 6.59-65.
- ■ Discretionary housing payments: see paras 6.66-67.

Who can get a housing costs element

6.1   This chapter explains who can get a housing costs element (HCE) and how it is calculated. It applies to renters, shared owners and owner occupiers. The HCE can help you meet your rent and service charges and is part of your UC (para 9.4). If your HCE doesn't meet your full rent, you may be able to get a discretionary housing payment from your local council (para 6.66).

Renters and shared owners

6.2   If you are a renter or shared owner (para 5.7):

(a) you can get an HCE towards your rent and service charges;

(b) your HCE is calculated differently depending on whether you are a social renter or private renter (paras 6.3-4);

(c) your HCE may be reduced for any non-dependants who live with you (para 6.59).

6.3   The rules for social renters are in paras 6.7-33. They apply to all renters and shared owners who rent from a social landlord (table 6.1).

6.4   The rules for private renters are in paras 6.34-55. They apply to all renters and shared owners who rent from anyone else – for example an individual, a lettings agency, a company, a registered charity, or a not-for-profit organisation.

6.2   UC 25(2)(a),(c), 26(2), sch 4 paras 13, 14, 20, 22, 30, 33
         NIUC 26(2)(a),(c), 27(2), sch 4 paras 12, 13, 19, 21, 29, 32

6.3   UC 26(2),(4),(5), sch 4 paras 2 – 'provider of social housing', 30; NIUC 27(2),(4),(5), sch 4 paras 2, 29

6.4   UC 26(2),(4),(5), sch 4 paras 2, 20; NIUC 27(2),(4),(5), sch 4 paras 2, 19

Table 6.1 **Social landlords**

All the following are social landlords (in UC law 'a provider of social housing'). If you rent your home from any of them you are a social renter.

(a) Local authorities and public bodies:

- in England: county, district and parish councils, London boroughs, the City of London and the council of the Isles of Scilly;

- in Wales: county, county borough and community councils;

- in Scotland: the council that issues your council tax bill;

- in Northern Ireland: the Northern Ireland Housing Executive.

(b) Housing associations, trusts, etc:

- in England: registered providers of social housing (i.e. any landlord who is registered with the Regulator of Social Housing: but see note);

- in Wales and Scotland: registered social landlords, i.e. any landlord that is registered with the Scottish or Welsh Government;

- in Northern Ireland: a housing association registered with the DFC.

Note:

Registered providers of social housing can be profit making or non-profit making. You are a social renter if you rent:

- any housing from a non-profit making registered provider; or

- social housing from a profit making registered provider. This means housing let below a market rent (such as part of the Affordable Rent Programme) and shared ownership tenancies.

You are a private renter if you rent other housing from a profit making registered provider.

Owner occupiers

6.5　　If you are an owner occupier (para 5.9):

(a) you can get an HCE towards your service charges (para 6.23);

(b) you have to complete a waiting period before your HCE begins (para 8.14);

(c) your SMI is not reduced for any non-dependants.

Information you need to provide

6.6　　When you claim UC, you need to provide details of your rent and service charges along with evidence such as your letting agreement; or if you can't, the DWP can make an estimate. In practice:

T6.1　　UC 2 – definition: 'local authority', sch 4 para 2 – definition: 'a provider of social housing'; NIUC sch 4 para 2

6.5　　UC 25(2)(c), 26(3), sch 5 paras 5, 9, 13; NIUC 26(2)(c), 27(3), sch 5 paras 5, 9, 13

6.6　　C&P 8(3), 37(2),(6), 38(3),(9); UC sch 4 paras 7, 22, 30, 31, 33, 34
NIC&P 7(3), 36(2),(6), 37(3),(9); NIUC sch 4 paras 6, 21, 29, 30, 32, 33

(a) if you are a social renter, the DWP needs separate figures for rent and services – your landlord can help with this or may give the information to the DWP for you;

(b) if you are a private renter, the DWP needs one figure for rent and services.

If these are due weekly or on any other non-monthly basis, they are converted to a monthly figure (para 6.56).

Social renters: your HCE

6.7   If you are a renter or shared owner and rent from a social landlord (table 6.1) paras 6.8-33 explain how your housing costs element (HCE) is worked out. The rules about this are summarised in table 6.2.

6.8   The amount of your HCE depends on whether you are:

(a) a sole tenant – in other words, you are the only person liable for rent on your home; or

(b) a joint tenant with only your partner and/or a child or young person you are responsible for – in other words, you are all in the same benefit unit; or

(c) a joint tenant with at least one person who is neither your partner nor a child or young person you are responsible for – in other words, you are in different benefit units.

If (a) or (b) applies to you, see paras 6.9-10. If (c) applies to you, see paras 6.11-13.

Table 6.2 **Housing costs element for social renters**

Step 1: Rent and eligible service charges (paras 6.8-10)

Your HCE is the monthly total of your:

- ▪ rent payments (before subtracting any discount: para 6.14); and
- ▪ eligible service charge payments (if any).

But this is reduced if any of the following steps apply to you.

Step 2: Certain joint tenancies (paras 6.11-13)

If you are in a joint tenancy (for example a house-share) and at least one joint tenant is not in your benefit unit, the HCE is split between you and the other joint tenant(s).

Step 3: Reductions for under-occupation (paras 6.15-18)

If your home has more bedrooms than the UC rules say you are entitled to, your HCE is reduced by:

- ▪ 14% if you have one extra bedroom;
- ▪ 25% if you have two or more extra bedrooms.

But this does not apply if Step 2 applies to you.

Step 4: Reductions for high rents (paras 6.19-22)

If the amounts in Step 1 are unreasonably high, they can be referred to the rent officer, and this may mean your HCE is reduced. If this applies to you, this reduction is made before Step 2 or 3.

T6.2   UC sch 4 paras 3, 5, 6, 31, 32A, 34, 35; NIUC sch 4 paras 3, 5, 30, 33, 34

Your HCE: the general rule

6.9   The general rule for social renters is that your HCE is the monthly total of:

(a)   your rent payments; and

(b)   your eligible service charge payments (if any).

See paras 6.23-33 for which service charges are eligible. For how to convert payments to a monthly figure, see para 6.56.

6.10   But your HCE is reduced if you are under-occupying (paras 6.15-18) and/or if your rent or service charge payments are unreasonably high (paras 6.19-22).

Your HCE: joint tenants not in the same benefit unit

6.11   If you have at least one joint tenant who is not in your benefit unit, the general rule in paras 6.9-10 applies to you, with two differences:

(a)   your HCE is your share of the monthly total of rent and eligible service charge payments;

(b)   the rules about under-occupation do not apply to you.

6.12   Your share is worked out as follows:

(a)   start with the monthly total of your rent and eligible service charge payments;

(b)   divide this by the total number of joint tenants (including yourself);

(c)   multiply the result by the number of joint tenants (including yourself) who are in your benefit unit.

The last step is only needed in the kind of situation illustrated in example 4.

6.13   But if the above produces an unreasonable result, the DWP can agree to split the HCE in some other way, taking account of all the circumstances, including how many joint tenants there are and how you actually split your rent and service charges. See example 5.

Rent discounts

6.14   Some social landlords have a rent discount scheme which reduces your rent as a payment incentive (e.g. for prompt payment or online payment). If you get such a discount, and your landlord's scheme is approved by the DWP, the discount is not deducted from your HCE. For example, if your HCE is normally £800 but your rent is reduced by £25 for prompt payment, your HCE is still £800.

6.9   UC sch 4 paras 3, 5, 6, 32A, 34, 35; NIUC sch 4 paras 3, 5, 33, 34

6.11   UC sch 4 para 35(1),(2),(4); NIUC sch 4 para 34(1),(2),(4)

6.12   UC sch 4 paras 2 definition: 'listed persons', 35(4); NIUC sch 4 paras 2, 34(4)

6.13   UC sch 4 para 35(5); NIUC sch 4 para 34(5)

6.14   UC sch 4 para 32A

Examples: The amount of HCE for social renters

In all these examples, the tenants are social renters, the HCE for the dwelling is £600 per month, they are not under-occupying, and the rent is not unreasonably high.

1. **A sole tenant**
   - The tenant's HCE is simply £600 per month.

2. **A couple who are the only joint tenants**
   - Their HCE is simply £600 per month.

3. **Three joint tenants who are not related**
   - Each one's HCE is £200 per month.

4. **Three joint tenants two of whom are a couple**
   - The couple's HCE is £400 per month (two-thirds of £600).
   - The single person's HCE is £200 per month (a third of £600).

5. **A different split of the HCE**
   - The couple in example 4 have one bedroom and have always paid half the rent. The same applies to the single person. The DWP agrees it is reasonable to split the HCE the same way.
   - So the couple's HCE is £300 per month, and so is the single person's.

Social renters: under-occupation

6.15 Your HCE is reduced if you are under-occupying your home. You count as under-occupying if you have more bedrooms in your home than the UC rules say you qualify for. Other rooms (such as living rooms) are not taken into account.

Exceptions

6.16 The rules about under-occupation don't apply to you if:

(a) you have a joint tenant who is not in your benefit unit (para 6.11); or

(b) you are a shared owner (para 5.7); or

(c) you live in sanctuary scheme accommodation (a social housing scheme that enables additional security to be added to your home) and:

- you – or someone who lives with you – have been the victim of actual or threatened domestic violence – this includes controlling or coercive behaviour, violence, psychological, physical, sexual, emotional, financial or other abuse, regardless of your gender or sexuality,

- the actual or threatened violence was from your partner/former partner, or from your or your partner's/former partner's son, daughter, stepchild, grandchild, parent, stepparent, grandparent, sister, brother, aunt, uncle, niece, nephew or first cousin,

---

6.15   UC sch 4 para 36(1); NIUC sch 4 para 35(1)

6.16   UC sch 4 paras 35(4), 36(5),(6); NIUC sch 4 paras 34(4), 35(5),(6)

- that person no longer lives with you – unless they are a young person (para 3.65) and are dependent on you or someone who lives with you, and

- a health care professional, police officer, registered social worker, your employer or trade union representative, or any public, voluntary or charitable organisation gives evidence in their official capacity that you live in sanctuary scheme accommodation, that you contacted them because of being a victim of actual or threatened domestic violence, and that your circumstances are consistent with that.

Size of accommodation

6.17   You qualify for the number of bedrooms allowed by the 'size criteria' taking into account:

(a) the people in your benefit unit and any non-dependants you have; and

(b) your fostering, overnight care, disability and bereavement needs.

The details are in chapter 7.

The amount of the reduction

6.18   Your HCE is reduced by:

(a) 14% if you have one bedroom more than you are entitled to;

(b) 25% if you have two or more bedrooms more than you are entitled to.

See the following examples.

Examples: Reductions for under-occupation

1. **One extra bedroom.**
    Amelia and Owen are social renters who have two children under 10. They rent a three bedroom house and no-one else lives with them. The HCE for the dwelling is £1,000 per month.

    They qualify for two bedrooms, one for themselves and one for the children. Because their home has one bedroom more than this, their HCE is reduced by 14% (£140) to £860 per month.

2. **Two extra bedrooms.**
    Violet is a social renter. She rents a three-bedroom house and no-one else lives with her. The HCE for the dwelling is £1,000 per month.

    She qualifies for one bedroom. Because her home has two bedrooms more than this, her HCE is reduced by 25% (£250) to £750 per month.

For further examples, see chapter 7.

6.17   UC sch 4 paras 8-12; NIUC sch 4 paras 7-11

6.18   UC sch 4 para 36(2)-(4); NIUC sch 4 para 36(2)-(4)

Social renters: unreasonably high rents

6.19   Unless your home is in the Affordable Rent programme, your HCE can be reduced (paras 6.20-22) if the DWP/DFC consider your rent or service charges are 'greater than it is reasonable to meet by way of the [UC] housing costs element'. The DWP says this could happen if your rent is at least £50 per week higher than the LHA figure that would apply if you were a private renter but considering any special circumstances (ADM F3253).

Housing payment determinations in Great Britain

6.20   In Great Britain, if the DWP considers your rent is unreasonable (para 6.19) it asks the rent officer to make a housing payment determination (HPD). The rent officer:

(a) looks at the payments (rent and/or service charges) the DWP has asked them to consider;

(b) can ask the DWP or your landlord for further information about them;

(c) compares what you pay (or in the case of joint tenants what you pay between you) with what a landlord could reasonably be expected to obtain' on accommodation that matches yours (as far as possible) in terms of council area, number of bedrooms, landlord type (table 6.1(a) or (b)) and state of repair;

(d) excludes care, support and supervision, and all other services, in exempt accommodation (table 5.3(a));

(e) excludes care, support and supervision in other kinds of accommodation (table 5.3(b)-(d));

(f) tells the DWP what is a reasonable amount, or confirms what you are paying is reasonable;

(g) must agree that your rent payments are reasonable if your home is in the Affordable Rent programme.

See para 6.53 for HPD redeterminations.

Reductions in Great Britain

6.21   Where the rent officer decides your rent and/or service charge payments are unreasonably high, the DWP:

(a) uses the amount the rent officer says is reasonable (rather than the amount you actually pay) to work out your eligible rent; but

(b) can agree not to do this if it wouldn't be 'appropriate'.

And if the rules about joint tenants or under-occupying your home (paras 6.11-18) also apply to you, they apply after this rule (table 6.2).

Reductions in Northern Ireland

6.22   In Northern Ireland, the DFC decides whether to reduce your HCE by comparing it with what a landlord could reasonably be expected to obtain (para 6.20(c)).

6.19   UCROO sch 2 para 3(c); UC sch 4 paras 3, 32(1),(2); NIUC sch 4 paras 3,31

6.20-21 UCROO 2 – 'service charge payments', 5, sch 2; UC sch 4 para 32; C&P 40; D&A 19(2), 30

6.22   NIUC sch 4 para 31

Service charges (social renters and owners)

6.23   This section is about service charges. It applies if:

(a)   you are a renter or shared owner and rent from a social landlord (table 6.1); or

(b)   you are an owner occupier (para 5.9).

Different rules apply if you are a renter or shared owner and rent from a private landlord (paras 6.36-37).

6.24   For UC purposes:

(a)   services means 'services or facilities for the use or benefit of persons occupying accommodation'; and

(b)   'service charge payments' means:

■   payments for all or part of the costs or charges relating to services or facilities, or

■   amounts which are fairly attributable to the costs or charges relating to available services or facilities.

6.25   Payments which meet the above definition are service charge payments whether they are:

(a)   named in an agreement or not;

(b)   paid in with the other payments you make on your home or separately;

(c)   paid under the agreement under which you occupy your home or under a separate agreement.

Separating rent and service charges

6.26   When you claim UC or move home or your rent changes, you have to give the DWP one figure for your rent and another for the total of your eligible service charges (if any). Your landlord should tell you these or give them to the DWP for you, and the DWP normally accepts the landlord's figures [www]. But in the end it is the law that distinguishes rent from services, and between eligible and ineligible charges ([2009] UKUT 28 (AAC), CH/3528/2006).

6.27   The following are examples of rent rather than service charges:

(a)   maintenance, repairs and insurance;

(b)   management costs;

(c)   council tax when the landlord is liable (para 15.17);

(d)   other normal overheads; and

(e)   associated administrative costs.

6.24   UC sch 1 para 7(1)(a),(b),(2); NIUC sch 1 para 8(1)(a),(b),(2)

6.25   UC sch 1 para 7(4); NIUC sch 1 para 8(4)

6.26   https://tinyurl.com/DWP-SC-Dec19

6.28   UC sch 1 para 8(2)-(6); NIUC sch 1 para 9(2)-(6)

Table 6.3 **Service charges**

Eligible service charges

Categories A to D are listed in the law as being eligible for UC.

Maintaining the general standard of accommodation (Category A)

- External window cleaning on upper floors.
- For owner occupiers and shared owners only, separately identifiable payments for maintenance and/or repairs.

General upkeep of communal areas (Category B)

- Ongoing maintenance and/or cleaning of communal areas.
- Supply of water, fuel or other commodities to communal areas.

'Communal areas' include internal areas, external areas and areas for reasonable facilities such as laundry rooms and children's play areas. DWP guidance (ADM para F2072) says that ground maintenance (e.g. lawn mowing, litter removal and lighting for access areas) and tenant parking (excluding security costs) should be included.

Basic communal services (Category C)

- Provision of basic communal services.
- Ongoing maintenance, cleaning and/or repair in connection with basic communal services.

'Basic communal services' are those available to everyone in the accommodation, such as refuse collection, communal lifts, secure building access and/or TV/wireless aerials for receiving a free service. DWP guidance (ADM paras F2073-74) says that communal telephones (but not call costs) should be included, as should a fair proportion of the staff management and administration costs of providing communal services.

Accommodation-specific charges (Category D)

- Use of essential items in your own home, such as furniture and domestic appliances.

Excluded service charges

The first two items are listed in the law as being excluded from UC. The others are excluded from UC because they do not fall within categories A to D, and are based on DWP guidance (ADM para F2077).

- Food of any kind.
- Medical or personal services of any kind, including personal care.
- Nursing care, emergency alarm systems or individual personal alarms.
- Equipment or adaptations relating to disability or infirmity.
- Counselling, support or intensive housing management.
- Fuel, water or sewerage charges for your own accommodation.

T6.3   UC sch 1 para 8(4),(6); NIUC sch 1 para 9(4),(6)

- Living expenses such as heating, lighting or hot water.
- Cleaning your own accommodation or having your laundry done.
- Gardening in your own garden.
- Recreational facilities or subscription/fee-based TV.
- Transport, permits, licences or maintenance of unadopted roads.
- Any other service or facility not included in categories A to D.

Special cases

The following are listed in the law as being excluded from UC, even if they are for items falling within categories A to D.

- Services or facilities that could be met by public funds (e.g. Supporting People) even if you do not yourself qualify for such help.
- Payments which result in an asset changing hands (e.g. if you pay for furniture but after a period it will become yours).

See also paras 6.31-33.

Example: Service charges for a leaseholder

Harry is a leaseholder and pays the freeholder for service charges which are eligible for UC. Each year (1st April to 31st March) the freeholder sends Harry bills:

- in February for estimated charges for the following financial year; and
- in May for the finalised balance for the preceding financial year.

1. Harry is on UC and meets the conditions for help with his service charges (para 5.4). On 1st April 2021 he sends the DWP the estimated bill for 2021-22. This is £480 for the year, equivalent to £40 per month over 12 months.

- The DWP awards him £40 per month for the 12 months of 1/4/21 to 31/3/22.

2. In May 2021, Harry sends the DWP the finalised bill for 2021-22. This is £60 for the year, equivalent to £5 per month over 12 months.

- The DWP continues to award him £40 per month until 31/3/22.
- It also awards him £5 per month for the 12 months of 1/5/21 to 30/4/22.

3. In February 2022, Harry sends the DWP the estimated bill for 2022-23. This is £516 for the year, equivalent to £43 per month over 12 months.

- The DWP continues to award him £5 per month until 30/4/22.
- It also awards him £43 per month for the 12 months of 1/4/22 to 31/3/23.

4. In May 2022, Harry sends the DWP the finalised balance for 2022-23. This is £48 for the year, equivalent to £4 per month over 12 months.

- The DWP continues to him £43 per month until 31/3/23.
- It also awards him £4 per month for the 12 months from 1/5/22 to 30/4/23.

Example adapted from DMG volume 13 para 78487.

Which service charges are eligible for UC

6.28 A service charge is eligible for UC if it meets all the following conditions:

(a) it is for an eligible service, not an excluded kind (paras 6.29-30);

(b) you have to pay it in order to occupy your home (para 6.31); and

(c) the service and amount are reasonable (paras 6.32-33).

Eligible and excluded services

6.29 Table 6.3 lists the service charges which are eligible for UC, and the kinds of service charges which are excluded from UC.

6.30 If a service charge is 'eligible', this means it is included in your housing costs element (HCE). If it is 'excluded', this means you can't get UC for it.

A condition of occupying your home

6.31 To be eligible for UC, a service charge must be one you have to pay in order to have the right to occupy your home (para 5.16). This does not need to have applied since you moved in so long as, when you agreed to pay it, the alternative was that you could lose your home.

Unreasonable kinds of service charges

6.32 A service charge can be excluded from UC if the services or facilities are of a kind which it is not 'reasonable to provide'. Although the rules about which service charges are eligible are already strict (table 6.3), this rule could, for example, apply to maintaining a luxury item such as a swimming pool (ADM para F2065).

Unreasonably high service charges

6.33 A service charge can be excluded from UC if the costs and charges relating to it are not of a 'reasonable amount'. But:

(a) if you are a social renter or shared owner, the service charge must be referred to the rent officer for a determination (paras 6.19-22). DWP guidance (ADM para F2068) confirms that this means the reasonable part of the amount for the service charge is eligible for UC (and only the unreasonable part is excluded);

(b) if you are an owner-occupier, DWP guidance (ADM para F2066) is that service charges should not be excluded from UC under this rule.

Private renters: your HCE

6.34 If you are a renter or shared owner and rent from a private landlord (para 6.4) paras 6.35-54 explain how your housing costs element (HCE) is worked out.

6.29   UC sch 1 paras 8(4),(6); NIUC sch 1 paras 9(4),(6)

6.31   UC sch 1 para 8(3); NIUC sch 1 para 9(3)

6.32   UC sch 1 para 8(5); NIUC sch 1 para 9(5)

6.33   UC sch 1 para 8(5); NIUC sch 1 para 9(5)

6.35   The amount of your HCE depends on whether you are:

(a) a sole tenant – in other words you are the only person liable for rent on your home; or

(b) a joint tenant with only your partner and/or a child or young person you are responsible for – in other words, you are all in the same benefit unit; or

(c) a joint tenant with at least one person who is neither your partner nor a child or young person you are responsible for – in other words, you are in different benefit units.

If (a) or (b) applies to you, see paras 6.36-37. If (c) applies to you, see paras 6.38-40.

Your HCE: the general rule

6.36   The general rule for private renters is that your HCE equals:

(a) your actual monthly rent (para 6.37); or

(b) if it is lower, the local housing allowance (LHA) figure which applies to you (para 6.43).

Examples: HCE for private renters

In all these examples the tenants are private renters.

1. A sole tenant

■ A sole tenant's actual monthly rent is £900.

■ If her LHA figure is £800, her HCE is £800.

2. A couple who are the only joint tenants

■ Their actual monthly rent is £700.

■ If their LHA figure is £800, their HCE is £700.

3. Three joint tenants who are not related

■ The actually monthly rent for their dwelling is £1,200.

■ So each one's share of it is £400 (⅓ of £1,200).

■ If the LHA figure (for each of them) is £350, each one's HCE is £350.

4. Three joint tenants, two of whom are a couple

■ The couple are claiming UC, but the single person is not.

■ The actual monthly rent for the dwelling is £1,200.

■ So the couple's share is £800 (⅔ of £1,200).

■ If their LHA figure is £1,000, their HCE is £800.

5. A different split of the actual monthly rent

■ The couple in example 4 have the use of three of the four bedrooms (they have children) and have always paid ¾ of the rent. The DWP agrees it is reasonable to split the actual monthly rent the same way.

■ So their share is now £900 (¾ of £1,200).

■ If their LHA figure is £1,000, their HCE is £900.

6.36   UC sch 4 para 22; NIUC sch 4 para 21

Actual monthly rent

6.37   Your actual monthly rent is the monthly total of your:

(a)   rent payments; and

(b)   service charge payments (if any).

See chapter 5 for which rent and service charge payments count. Unlike the rules for social renters, no service charges are excluded. For how to convert payments to a monthly figure, see para 6.56.

Your HCE: joint tenants not in the same benefit unit

6.38   If you have at least one joint tenant who is not in your benefit unit, the actual monthly rent (para 6.37) is split between you and the other joint tenant(s). Your eligible rent equals:

(a)   your share of the actual monthly rent; or

(b)   if it is lower, the LHA figure which applies to you (para 7.18).

6.39   Your share is worked out as follows:

(a)   start with the actual monthly rent on your dwelling;

(b)   divide this by the total number of joint tenants (including yourself);

(c)   multiply the result by the number of joint tenants (including yourself) who are in your benefit unit.

The last step is only needed in the kind of situation illustrated in example 4.

6.40   But if the above would produce an unreasonable result, the DWP can agree to split the actual monthly rent in some other way, taking account of all the circumstances including how many joint tenants there are and how you actually split your rent and eligible service charges. See example 5.

Legal terminology: 'core rent' and 'cap rent'

6.41   UC law and guidance uses these terms:

(a)   'core rent' means your actual monthly rent (or share of it);

(b)   'cap rent' means the LHA figure which applies to you.

6.37   UC sch 4 paras 3, 5, 6, 23, 24; NIUC sch 4 paras 3, 5, 22, 23

6.38   UC sch 4 para 24(1),(2),(4); NIUC sch 4 para 23(1),(2),(4)

6.39   UC sch 4 paras 2 definition: 'listed persons', 24(4); NIUC sch 4 paras 2, 23(4)

6.40   UC sch 4 para 24(5); NIUC sch 4 para 23(5)

Private renters: local housing allowances

6.42   LHAs are figures used in deciding your HCE (paras 6.36 and 6.38). They are set:

(a) in Great Britain by the rent officer, a government employee who is independent of the DWP; or

(b) in Northern Ireland by the Housing Executive (NIHE).

They are monthly figures that apply from April each year (para 6.51) and are published online in late January [www].

Which LHA figure applies to you?

6.43   The LHA figure that applies to you is the one for:

(a) the size of the accommodation you qualify for (para 6.44); and

(b) the area your home is in (para 6.50).

Size of accommodation

6.44   You qualify for the number of bedrooms allowed by the 'size criteria' taking into account:

(a) the people in your benefit unit and any non-dependants you have; and

(b) your fostering, overnight care, disability and bereavement needs.

The details are in table 7.1.

6.45   But for private renters (unlike social renters):

(a) the maximum number of bedrooms is always four; and

(b) there are further rules if you are single and aged under 35 (paras 6.46-47).

Single people under 35

6.46   You qualify for one-bedroom shared accommodation (rather than self-contained) if you are:

(a) a single person, or in a couple but claiming UC as a single person (para 2.7); and

(b) under 35 years old; and

(c) not in any of the excepted groups in table 6.4.

This rule does not amount to unlawful discrimination ([2020] UKUT 285 (AAC)).

6.42   UCR00 4, sch 1; SI 2020/371; NIUCED 4, sch 1; NISR 2020/53
        https://lha-direct.voa.gov.uk/search.aspx
        www.nihe.gov.uk/Housing-Help/Local-Housing-Allowance/Current-LHA-rent-levels

6.43   UC sch 4 para 25(1),(2),(5); NIUC sch 4 para 24(1),(2),(5)

6.45-47 UC sch 4 paras 8, 12, 26, 29; NIUC sch 4 paras 7, 11, 25, 28

6.46   UC sch 4 paras 27, 28(1),(2); NIUC sch 4 paras 26, 27(1),(2)

Table 6.4 **Single people under 35: the UC excepted groups**

Single under-35-year-olds who fall in these excepted groups qualify for one-bedroom self-contained accommodation. Other single under-35-year-olds qualify for one-bedroom shared accommodation.

(a) You have one or more children or young persons in your benefit unit (paras 3.62 and 3.68).

(b) You are a foster parent or have a child placed with you for adoption (para 7.21).

(c) You have one or more non-dependants (paras 3.70-77).

(d) You are in receipt of:

- the middle or highest rate of the care component of DLA or child disability payment, or

- the daily living component of PIP or adult disability payment at the standard or enhanced rate, or

- a benefit equivalent to attendance allowance (para 10.54).

(e) You left care before the age of 18 and are now aged 18 or over but under 25.

(f) You are an ex-offender managed under a multi-agency (MAPPA) agreement because you pose a serious risk of harm to the public.

(g) You are aged 16 or over, and:

- you have occupied one or more hostels for homeless people (para 6.47) for at least three months. This does not need to have been a continuous three months, and it does not need to have been recent; and

- while you were there, you were offered and you accepted support with rehabilitation or resettlement within the community.

(h) You are a victim of domestic violence (para 5.11) that occurred after you reached 16 and was from your partner or former partner, or your or their son, daughter, stepchild, grandchild, parent, stepparent, grandparent, sister, brother, aunt, uncle, niece, nephew or first cousin.

(i) You are a victim of modern slavery and this has been confirmed by a competent authority under the Trafficking Convention of 2005.

Note: Excepted groups (h) and (i) were introduced on 1st October 2022.

T6.4   UC 2 definition: 'attendance allowance', sch 4 paras 28(3),(4), 29; NIUC 2, sch 4 paras 27(3),(4), 28

Hostels for homeless people

6.47   A hostel for homeless people (see table 6.4(g)) means a building that:

(a) provides non-self-contained domestic accommodation, together with meals or adequate food-preparation facilities;

(b) has the main purpose of providing accommodation together with care, support or supervision, in order to assist homeless people to be rehabilitated or resettled;

(c) is either:

   ▪ managed or owned by a social landlord other than a local authority (table 6.1), or

   ▪ run on a non-commercial basis, and wholly or partly funded by a government department or agency or local authority, or

   ▪ managed by a registered charity or non-profit-making voluntary organisation;

(d) is not a care home (in Scotland a care home service) or independent hospital.

How LHA figures are set

6.48   In each April until April 2020, LHA figures were set at the lower of:

(a) the rent at the 30th percentile (para 6.49);

(b) the national maximum (table 6.5).

They have not increased since then, and remain frozen at 2020's levels from April 2023.

Table 6.5 **LHA sizes of accommodation**

Size of accommodation	National monthly maximum
(a) one-bedroom shared accommodation	£1283.96
(b) one-bedroom self-contained accommodation	£1283.96
(c) two-bedroom dwellings	£1589.99
(d) three-bedroom dwellings	£1920.00
(e) four-bedroom dwellings	£2579.98

Notes:

▪ This table only applies to private renters (para 6.42).

▪ See chapter 7 for which size of accommodation applies to you.

▪ Actual LHAs for (a) are usually lower than those for (b) (though the national maximums are the same).

6.47   UC 2 definition: 'local authority', sch 4 para 29(10); NIUC sch 4 para 28(6)

6.48   UCROO sch 1 para 2(2); SI 2023/6 reg 4; NIUCED sch 1 para 2(2); NISR 2023/4 reg 3

T6.5   UCROO sch 1 para 2(2), SI 2020/371; NIUCED sch 1 para 2(2); NISR 2020/53

Examples: LHAs and size of accommodation

All the following are private renters.

1. A single person aged 24

- Unless she is in an excepted group (see table 6.4), she qualifies for the LHA for one-bedroom shared accommodation.

2. A single person aged 58

- He qualifies for the LHA for one-bedroom self-contained accommodation.

3. A couple

- They qualify for the LHA for one-bedroom self-contained accommodation.

4. A couple with a son aged 9 and a daughter aged 7

- The couple qualify for the LHA for a two-bedroom dwelling.

5. The son in example 4 reaches the age of 10

- Because the children are no longer expected to share a bedroom (table 7.1), the couple qualify for the LHA for a three-bedroom dwelling.

6. Three joint tenants who are not related

- They are all under 35 and none of them is in an excepted group (table 6.4). So each one qualifies for the LHA for one-bedroom shared accommodation.

7. Two brothers who are joint tenants

- They are in their 40s, and the daughter of one of them lives with him. So that brother qualifies for the LHA for a two-bedroom dwelling. The other brother qualifies for the LHA for one-bedroom self-contained accommodation.

For further examples about size of accommodation, see chapter 7.

The rent at the 30th percentile

6.49 The rent at the 30th percentile means the highest rent within the bottom 30% of rents in the rent officer's or NIHE's data. This uses actual rents (including eligible service charges) payable during the year ending on the preceding 30th September, on accommodation which:

(a) is rented on an assured tenancy;

(b) is in a reasonable state of repair;

(c) is the correct size (para 6.44);

(d) is in the correct area (para 6.50); and

(e) excludes rents paid by people on UC or HB (to avoid the effect UC/HB could have on rent levels).

The rent officer or NIHE adjust the figures if necessary to ensure that the LHA for a larger category of dwelling isn't lower than the LHA for a smaller one.

6.49   UCROO sch 1 paras 3, 5; NIUCED sch 1 paras 3, 4

LHA areas

6.50   LHA areas are called 'broad rental market areas' (BRMAs) and are defined by postcodes. They are drawn up by the rent officer/NIHE so that:

(a) a 'person could reasonably be expected to live there having regard to facilities and services for the purpose of health, education, recreation, personal banking and shopping, taking into account of the distance by travel, by public and private transport, to and from those facilities and services';

(b) they contain 'residential premises of a variety of types' held as a 'variety of tenancies'; and

(c) they contain 'sufficient privately rented premises' to ensure that the LHA figures 'are representative of the rents that a landlord might reasonably be expected to obtain in that area'.

They can only be changed with the DWP's consent.

When LHA figures and changes take effect

6.51   When LHA figures change (para 6.48) the new figures take effect:

(a) on 6th April; or

(b) if you are already on UC, from the first day of your assessment period ending on or after 6th April.

For example, if your assessment periods begin on the 7th of each month, (b) means your new LHA figure takes effect from 7th March.

6.52   Your LHA figure changes if:

(a) you qualify for a different size of accommodation or move to a new area – this is a change of circumstances (table 11.1); or

(b) the DWP used the wrong figure – this is an official error (paras 14.30-32); or

(c) there was an error setting the LHA figure or areas (paras 6.53-55).

Rent officer redeterminations in Great Britain

6.53   In Great Britain, the rent officer can reconsider and if necessary correct:

(a) any LHA figure or area (para 6.43); or

(b) any housing payment determination (para 6.20).

This is called a redetermination and can be done with or without a request from the DWP. It also seems possible that you (or someone on your behalf) could request a redetermination, but the law doesn't say either way.

6.50   UCROO 3(3),(4); NIUCED 3(3),(4)

6.51   UCROO 4(3),(4); SI 2020/371; SI 2020/397; NIUCED 4(3),(4); NISR 2020/53; NISR 2020/61

6.52   D&A 19(2), 30, sch 1 paras 20, 21, 29; UCROO 6; NID&A 19(2), 30, sch 1 paras 20, 21, 29; NIUCED 5

6.53-54 D&A 19(2), 21, 30, 35(14)

6.54   When a rent officer redetermination means a new figure applies to you:

(a) if it is higher, the DWP's new decision takes effect from when its original decision took effect (or should have) – so you get arrears of UC back to then;

(b) if it is lower, the DWP's new decision takes effect from the first day of the assessment period following the one in which the DWP receives the figure from the rent officer – so you haven't been overpaid UC.

Redeterminations in Northern Ireland

6.55   In Northern Ireland, the NIHE can correct any LHA figure or area, and the DFC can correct any rent determination it has made (para 6.22). The rules in para 6.54 apply in a similar way.

Calculating monthly figures

Converting rent and service charges to a monthly figure

6.56   Because UC is a monthly benefit, rent or service charge payments which are not monthly are converted to a monthly figure:

(a) multiply weekly payments by 52 then divide by 12;

(b) multiply two-weekly payments by 26 then divide by 12;

(c) multiply four-weekly payments by 13 then divide by 12;

(d) multiply three-monthly payments by 4 then divide by 12;

(e) divide annual payments by 12.

6.57   These rules apply to rent and service charges in all cases. They do not apply to SMI for mortgage interest etc (chapter 8). The law gives no specific rule for daily rent payments. But these usually occur only in the types of accommodation where UC cannot be paid towards housing costs (table 5.3).

Rent-free and service charge-free periods

6.58   If you have rent-free or service charge-free periods (periods during which rent or service charges are not payable), first calculate the annual figure as follows:

(a) if your payments are weekly, subtract the number of rent-free weeks from 52, and multiply your weekly payment by the result;

(b) if your payments are two-weekly, subtract the number of rent-free two-weeks from 26, and multiply your two-weekly payment by the result;

(c) if your payments are four-weekly, subtract the number of rent-free four-weeks from 13, and multiply your four-weekly payment by the result;

(d) in any other case, add together all the payments you are liable to make over a 12 month period.

Then divide the result by 12.

6.55   NID&A 19(2), 21, 30, 35(14)

6.56   UC sch 4 para 7(1),(2), sch 5 para 13(1),(3); NIUC sch 4 para 6(1),(2), sch 5 para 13(1),(3)

6.58   UC sch 4 para 7(2)(d),(3),(3A),(4), sch 5 para 13(4),(4A),(5); NIUC sch 4 para 6(2)(d),(3),(4),(5), sch 5 para 13(4),(5),(6)

Housing cost contributions

6.59   This section describes the housing cost contributions which are deducted from your eligible rent to obtain your housing costs element. This applies if you are a renter or a shared owner, but not if you are an owner occupier (paras 6.2-5).

Housing cost contributions and non-dependants

6.60   One housing cost contribution is deducted from your eligible rent for each non-dependant you have. If two non-dependants are a couple, this means two deductions (not one between them).

6.61   A non-dependant is usually an adult son, daughter, other relative or friend who lives with you on a non-commercial basis: for the details see paras 3.70-77. A housing cost contribution can be described as the amount they are expected to contribute towards your housing costs.

The amount of the contribution

6.62   In 2023-24 the monthly amount of the housing cost contribution is £85.73. This figure applies to each non-dependant, no matter what income they have. But see paras 6.64-65 for when no contribution applies at all.

6.63   The UC contribution of £85.73 per month contrasts with the HB figures which vary with the non-dependant's income and can be up to £506 (monthly equivalent).

When no contribution applies

6.64   No housing cost contribution applies for any of the non-dependants in your home if:

  (a) you are a single person (or claiming UC as a single person) and you are in any of the groups in table 6.6(a)-(e); or

  (b) you are a couple and at least one of you is in any of the groups in table 6.6(a)-(e).

6.65   No housing cost contribution applies for any particular non-dependant in your home who is in any of the groups in table 6.6(f)-(o).

Discretionary housing payments

6.66   Your local council can make discretionary housing payments if:

  (a) you are entitled to a UC housing costs element or HB; and

  (b) you 'appear… to require some further financial assistance… in order to meet housing costs'.

6.60   UC sch 4 para 13; NIUC sch 4 para 12

6.62   UC sch 4 para 14(1); NIUC sch 4 para 13(1)

6.64   UC sch 4 para 15(1); NIUC sch 4 para 14(1)

6.65   UC sch 4 para 16(1); NIUC sch 4 para 15(1)

6.66   The Discretionary Financial Assistance Regulations SI 2001 No 1167
         The Discretionary Financial Assistance Regulations (Northern Ireland) 2001 No 216

6.67 This discretion can be used for people on UC whose housing costs element is lower than their actual rent, and for people on HB whose eligible rent is lower than their actual rent (volume 2). It can also be used in UC to mitigate losses caused by migrating from legacy benefits.

Table 6.6 **No housing cost contributions**

Your circumstances

No housing cost contributions apply for any non-dependants in your home if you or your partner are:

- (a) on the daily living component of PIP or adult disability payment at the standard or enhanced rate;
- (b) on the middle or highest rate of the care component of DLA or child disability payment;
- (c) on attendance allowance or an equivalent benefit (para 10.54);
- (d) entitled to (a), (b) or (c) but not receiving it because of being in hospital; or
- (e) certified as severely sight-impaired or blind by an ophthalmologist or have regained your sight in the last 28 weeks).

Non dependant's circumstances

No housing cost contribution applies for any non-dependant who is:

- (f) under 21;
- (g) on SPC;
- (h) responsible for a child under five years old;
- (i) your son, daughter, step-son or step-daughter (or your partner's if you are claiming UC as a couple) and is a member of the armed forces away on operations;
- (j) on the daily living component of PIP or adult disability payment at the standard or enhanced rate;
- (k) on the middle or highest rate of the care component of DLA;
- (l) on attendance allowance or an equivalent benefit (para 10.54);
- (m) entitled to (j), (k) or (l) but not receiving it because of being in hospital;
- (n) on carer's allowance; or
- (o) a prisoner (para 2.22).

Note: There is no housing cost contribution for someone who doesn't 'normally live' with you, even if they may eventually return (paras 3.71-72).

T6.6   UC 2 – 'blind', sch 4 paras 2 – 'member of the armed forces', 15(2), 16(2); NIUC 2, sch 4 paras 2, 14(2), 15(2)

Examples: Housing cost contributions

All figures are monthly. No-one in these examples (except the younger son in example 2) is in any of the groups in table 6.6.

1. One non-dependant

Ewan's eligible rent is £600. He has one non-dependant, his daughter aged 30.

- Eligible rent   £600.00
- Housing cost contribution   – £85.73
- Housing costs element   £514.27

2. Two non-dependants

Rosie's eligible rent is £950. She has two non-dependants, her sons aged 20 and 24.

- Eligible rent   £950.00
- Housing cost contribution (older son only)   – £85.73
- Housing costs element   £864.27

3. Two non-dependants who are a couple

Hazel's eligible rent is £700. She has two non-dependants, her son and daughter-in-law.

- Eligible rent   £700.00
- Two housing cost contributions (2 x £85.73)   – £171.46
- Housing costs element   £528.54

Chapter 7 **The size of your home**

- ■ The size criteria and your housing costs element: see paras 7.1-4.
- ■ The number of bedrooms you qualify for: see paras 7.5-7.
- ■ Who is included: see paras 7.8-18.
- ■ Qualifying for an additional bedroom: see paras 7.19-28.

The size criteria and housing costs element

7.1 This chapter applies to renters and shared owners, but not owner occupiers. It explains what size of home you can get UC towards, and how this affects your UC housing costs element (HCE). We call these rules the 'size criteria'. They are also sometimes called the 'bedroom tax' or the 'spare room subsidy'. They are similar to the rules used in HB (volume 2 chapter 11) but not always identical.

The social renter size criteria

7.2 If you are a renter or shared owner and rent your home from a social landlord (table 6.1):

- (a) the size criteria say how many bedrooms you qualify for (para 7.5 onwards);
- (b) your HCE is reduced if you have more bedrooms than you qualify for (paras 6.15-18);
- (c) whether a particular room is a bedroom can therefore be important (paras 7.6-7).

The private renter size criteria

7.3 If you are a renter or shared owner and rent your home from a private landlord (para 6.4):

- (a) the size criteria say how many bedrooms you qualify for (para 7.5 onwards);
- (b) your HCE is limited to the local housing allowance figure (LHA) which applies to you (paras 6.36-54);
- (c) whether a particular room is a bedroom is not relevant, because your LHA figure is based on how many bedrooms you qualify for, not how many there are in your home.

The size criteria and unlawful discrimination

7.4 The European Court of Human Rights has decided that the size criteria don't unlawfully discriminate against:

- (a) claimants who have a disabled adult child living with them (JD v UK);
- (b) separated parents with shared care of a child (R (Cotton and Others) v SSWP);
- (c) gypsy travellers ([2019] UKUT 43 (AAC)).

7.2   UC 26(2),(4),(5), sch 4 paras 9-12, 33, 34, 36; NIUC 27(2),(4),(5), sch 4 paras 8-11, 32, 33, 35

7.3   UC 26(2),(4),(5), sch 4 paras 9-12, 22, 25-29; NIUC 27(2),(4),(5), sch 4 paras 8-11, 21, 24-28

Other cases resulted in changes to the law so that the size criteria no longer discriminate between adults and children (R (Daly and Others) v SSWP) or against women living in sanctuary schemes (A v UK).

The number of bedrooms you qualify for

7.5 Table 7.1 shows how to work out the number of bedrooms you qualify for. But further rules apply if:

(a) you have a joint tenant who isn't in your benefit unit (para 7.18);

(b) you have had a bereavement (paras 11.27-28);

(c) you rent from a private landlord and are single and under 35 (para 6.46).

And if you rent from a private landlord, the maximum number of bedrooms is always four.

Table 7.1 **The UC size criteria**

The size criteria are based on the occupiers of your home (paras 7.8-18).

General rules

One bedroom is allowed for each of the following:

- yourself, or yourself and your partner if you are claiming UC as a couple;
- each young person aged 16 or over;
- each non-dependant aged 16 or over;
- two children under 16 of the same sex;
- two children under 10 of the same or opposite sex;
- any other child aged under 16.

Children are expected to share bedrooms in whatever way results in the smallest number of bedrooms. See examples 5 and 6.

Additional bedrooms

One or more additional bedrooms can be allowed for:

- a foster parent or if you are waiting to adopt (para 7.21);
- a person who requires overnight care (paras 7.22-24);
- a disabled person who can't share a bedroom (paras 7.25-28).

7.4   JD and A v United Kingdom [2019] ECHR 753 www.bailii.org/eu/cases/ECHR/2019/753.html
       R (Cotton and others) v SSWP [2014] EWHC Admin 3437 www.bailii.org/ew/cases/EWHC/Admin/2014/3437.html
       R (Daly and others) v SSWP [2016] UKSC 58 www.bailii.org/uk/cases/UKSC/2016/58.html

7.5   UC 37, sch 4 paras 8-10, 24, 26-29; NIUC 39, sch 4 paras 7-9, 23, 25-28

T7.1   WRA 40 definition: 'child'; UC sch 4 paras 10, 12; NIWRO 46; NIUC sch 4 paras 9, 11

What counts as a bedroom

7.6 Whether a particular room in your home is a bedroom (rather than a living room, storage room, etc) can be important if you are a social renter (para 7.2). Neither UC law nor DWP guidance (ADM paras F3110-38) define what a bedroom is (but see para 7.7). In practice, the DWP is likely to follow your landlord's description of whether a room is a bedroom (for example in your letting agreement), but you can ask the DWP to reconsider this and appeal to a tribunal if you disagree (chapter 14).

7.7 There have been a number of court and Upper Tribunal decisions about what is a bedroom, and these are summarised in table 7.2.

Examples: How many bedrooms you qualify for

1. A single person who is the only occupier

She qualifies for one bedroom. If she is a private renter under 35, see para 6.46 for whether she qualifies for shared or self-contained accommodation.

2. A couple who are the only occupiers

They qualify for one bedroom.

3. A single person with three children

He has sons aged 15 and 8 and a daughter aged 13. The sons are expected to share a bedroom. So the household qualifies for three bedrooms.

4. The older son in example 3 reaches 16

Now none of the children are expected to share a bedroom. So the household qualifies for four bedrooms.

5. A couple with four children

They have daughters aged 13 and 4 and sons aged 14 and 8. The children are expected to share bedrooms in the way that results in the smallest number of bedrooms (the daughters sharing, and also the sons). The household qualifies for three bedrooms.

6. The couple in example 5 have a baby

The couple now qualify for four bedrooms. No way of sharing bedrooms can result in a lower number.

7. A single person with two non-dependants

The household qualifies for three bedrooms. This is the case even if the non-dependants are a couple: see para 7.14.

Examples including additional bedrooms are later in this chapter.

Table 7.2 **What counts as a bedroom: case law**

Assessing the room.

The Court of Session has held that whether a room is a bedroom is determined by 'an objective assessment of the property as vacant which is not related to the residents or what their actual use or needs might be' ([2017] AACR 41). In the same way, the Court of Appeal has held that the assessment should be 'carried out… in respect of a nominally vacant house' and that 'the characteristics of the particular individuals are irrelevant' ([2019] AACR 27).

The term 'bedroom'.

The term 'bedroom' has its ordinary or familiar English meaning ([2015] AACR 21). The landlord's designation of the room or its description in the building's plans can be of use in borderline cases rather than being conclusive ([2015] AACR 21); [2018] UKUT 180 (AAC)). And a room can stop counting as a bedroom if exceptional circumstances relating to the physical or mental disability of an occupier mean it is now used as a living room ([2015] UKUT 282 (AAC)).

Practical factors.

Factors to be considered include '(a) size, configuration and overall dimensions, (b) access, (c) natural and electric lighting, (d) ventilation, and (e) privacy' taking account of the adults and children referred to in the regulations (paras 7.8-16), and the relationship of the room to the other rooms in the house ([2015] AACR 21], [2018] UKUT 180 (AAC)). So long as the room is accessible, it is not a requirement that the door opens all the way ([2020] UKUT 247 (AAC)). It should be possible to get into bed from within the room, and there should be somewhere to put clothes and a glass of water, for example a bedside cabinet with drawers ([2016] UKUT 164 (AAC); [2017] UKUT 443 (AAC)).

Overcrowding and unfitness.

The overcrowding rules differ from the size criteria, taking into account living rooms as well as bedrooms, but they can sound 'warning bells' that a room with very small dimensions may not be a bedroom ([2015] AACR 21); [2016] UKUT 164 (AAC); [2017] UKUT 443 (AAC)). A room contaminated with asbestos cannot be counted as a bedroom ([2018] UKUT 287 (AAC)).

T7.2   [2017] AACR 41 is SSWP v Glasgow CC and Another [2017] CSIH 35 https://www.bailii.org/scot/cases/ScotCS/2017/[2017]CSIH35.html
       [2019] AACR 37 is SSWP v Hockley [2019] EWCA Civ 1080 https://www.bailii.org/ew/cases/EWCA/Civ/2019/1080.html
       [2015] AACR 21 was [2014] UKUT 525 (AAC)

Who is included

7.8 All the members of your extended benefit unit are taken into account in deciding how many bedrooms you qualify for. This means:

(a) the people in your benefit unit (paras 7.10-13); and

(b) non-dependants (paras 7.14-16).

You can continue to qualify for a bedroom for up to three months for a member of your extended benefit unit who has died (paras 11.27-28). And there are further rules if you qualify for UC on two homes (para 5.63).

7.9 The DWP decides who to include, not (for example) the rent officer. Decisions about this are appealable to a tribunal: [2010] UKUT 79 AAC.

People in your benefit unit

7.10 Your benefit unit is yourself, your partner if you are claiming UC as a couple, and any children or young persons you are responsible for. For more on who is in your benefit unit, see paras 3.46-69. Table 7.1 shows how many bedrooms you qualify for.

7.11 A child or young person is included as an occupier even if the 'two child limit' means they are not included in your maximum UC (paras 9.4 and 9.17). But a child or young person who spends time in more than one home (for example with each parent) can only be included as an occupier in one of these (para 3.67).

If you or your partner are temporarily absent

7.12 If you and/or your partner are temporarily absent, you are included as an occupier during:

(a) an absence from Great Britain which meets the conditions in paras 2.32-35; or

(b) the first six months that you are a prisoner if you meet the conditions in para 2.24.

If a child or young person is temporarily absent

7.13 A child or young person who is temporarily absent is included as an occupier during:

(a) any period they are included in your benefit unit (para 3.69);

(b) the first six months they are in local authority care (para 3.68); or

(c) the first six months they are a prisoner (para 2.22).

But (b) and (c) only apply if they were included in your benefit unit immediately before their absence, and you then qualified for the housing costs element in your award of UC.

7.8   UC sch 4 para 9(1); NIUC sch 4 para 8(1)

7.10   UC sch 4 para 10(1)(a),(b),(d)-(f); NIUC sch 4 para 9(1)(a),(b),(d)-(f)

7.12   UC sch 4 para 11(1),(3); NIUC sch 4 para 10(1),(3)

7.13   UC sch 4 para 11(1),(2); NIUC sch 4 para 10(1),(2)

Non-dependants

7.14   Non-dependants are normally adult sons, daughters or other relatives or friends who live with you on a non-commercial basis. For more on who is a non-dependant, see paras 3.70-77. If you have one or more non-dependants the rules are as follows:

(a)   you are allowed one bedroom for each non-dependant over 16 (table 7.1). This means two bedrooms for two non-dependants over 16 even if they are a couple;

(b)   one bedroom is allowed for each young person over 16 who is the responsibility of a non-dependant (rather than of you or your partner) – because they also count as a non-dependant (para 3.73);

(c)   a child under 16 who is the responsibility of a non-dependant is taken into account as a child in the normal way (table 7.1) (DWP, Freedom of Information request 5103 of 2016 [www]).

If a non-dependant is temporarily absent

7.15   A non-dependant who is temporarily absent is included as an occupier during:

(a)   an absence from Great Britain which meets the conditions in paras 2.32-35; or

(b)   the first six months that they are a prisoner if they meet the conditions in para 2.24; or

(c)   the first six months in any other circumstances so long as their absence is not expected to exceed six months. (For example they could be away studying.)

But these only apply if they were your non-dependant or included in your benefit unit (e.g. as a child or young person) immediately before their absence, and you then qualified for the housing costs element in your UC.

Non-dependants in the armed forces

7.16   A non-dependant who is temporarily absent is included as an occupier if they are:

(a)   your or your partner's son, daughter, step-son, or step-daughter; and

(b)   a member of the armed forces who is away on operations (para 2.31).

There is no time limit to this rule so long as they intend to return. But it only applies if they were your non-dependant or included in your benefit unit (para 7.10) immediately before their absence (whether or not you then qualified for the housing costs element in your UC).

7.14   WRA 40 definition: 'child'; UC sch 4 para 10(1)(c); NIWRO 46; NIUC sch 4 para 9(1)(c)
         https://tinyurl.com/DWP-FOI-5103-2016

7.15   UC sch 4 para 11(1),(4),(5)(a)-(c),(6); NIUC sch 4 para 10(1),(4),(5)(a)-(c),(6)

7.16   UC sch 4 paras 2 definition: 'member of the armed forces', 11(1),(4),(5)(d); NIUC sch 4 paras 2, 10(1),(4),(5)(d)

Other people in your home

7.17 Bedrooms are not allowed for anyone other than those described above (paras 7.8-16). For example they are not allowed for:

(a) your partner if you are in a couple but claiming UC as a single person (para 2.7);

(b) your husbands and wives in a polygamous marriage, other than the one you are claiming UC with (para 3.61);

(c) lodgers of yours;

(d) separate tenants of your landlord (if your accommodation is rented out in separate lettings);

(e) a resident landlord/landlady;

(f) joint tenants who are not in your benefit unit (para 7.18);

(g) non-dependants of any of the above (see also 3.77);

(h) children and young persons for whom any of the above are responsible (but for children of a non-dependant see para 7.14);

(i) foster children (see also para 7.21).

Joint tenants not in the same benefit unit

7.18 The following rules apply if you are in a joint tenancy (for example a house share) and at least one joint tenant is not in your benefit unit:

(a) if you are a private renter, the size criteria apply separately to each single joint tenant or joint tenant couple, so you each have your own LHA figure (para 6.38);

(b) if you are a social renter, the size criteria do not apply to you at all (para 6.16).

Additional bedrooms

7.19 You may qualify for an additional bedroom for any member of your extended benefit unit (para 7.8) who:

(a) is a foster parent or has a child placed with them for adoption (see para 7.21); or

(b) requires overnight care from a non-resident carer (see paras 7.22-24); or

(c) can't share a bedroom due to their disability (see paras 7.25-28).

7.20 You could qualify for one additional bedroom under each of (a) and (b), and two under (c) (one for you/your partner and one for a child). But if you rent from a private landlord, the maximum number of bedrooms (under the general rules in table 7.1 and these rules) is always four.

7.19   UC sch 4 paras 12(9), 26; NIUC sch 4 paras 11, 25

Fostering/kinship and pre-adoption

7.21   You qualify for an additional bedroom if you, or your partner if you are claiming UC as a couple:

(a) are a foster parent (in Scotland a kinship carer) and:

   ▪ have a child placed with you, or

   ▪ are waiting for placement or between placements, but this only applies for up to 12 months in each period in which you don't have a placement; or

(b) have a child placed with you for adoption (unless you are the child's close relative: para 5.38).

Only one additional bedroom is allowed, even if you have more than one child placed with you. But if any child requires overnight care, see paras 7.23-24.

Example: A foster parent

Jasper and Isla are foster parents. They have two sons of their own aged 13 and 11, and two foster daughters aged 12 and 9.

They qualify for one bedroom for themselves, and one for their two sons. Although they do not qualify for a bedroom for the foster daughters under the general rules (table 7.1), they qualify for one additional bedroom as foster parents. So they qualify for three bedrooms in all.

People who require overnight care

7.22   You qualify for an additional bedroom if an occupier of your home (para 7.23):

(a) is in receipt of:

   ▪ the daily living component of PIP or (in Scotland) adult disability payment at the standard or enhanced rate, or

   ▪ the middle or highest rate of the care component of DLA or (in Scotland) child disability payment, or

   ▪ constant attendance allowance or armed forces independence payment paid as part of an industrial injury or war disablement pension; and

(b) is provided with overnight care on a regular basis (para 7.24) by one or more people who stay in your home and are engaged for this purpose, but who do not live with you.

Only one additional bedroom is allowed, even if more than one occupier meets these conditions.

7.23   For this rule, the occupiers of your home are:

(a) the people in your benefit unit (you, your partner, children and young persons: paras 7.10-13); and

(b) non-dependants (paras 7.14-16); and

(c) any child placed with you or your partner as a foster child (or child in kinship care) or prior to adoption (para 7.21).

7.21   UC 2 definition: 'foster parent', 89(3)(a), sch 4 para 12(1)(b),(4),(5),(9); NIUC 2, 88(3)(a), sch 4 para 11(1)(b),(4),(5),(9)

7.22-23 UC sch 4 para 12(A1),(3),(9); NIUC sch 4 para 11(A1),(3),(9)

7.24 It is not necessary for an actual bedroom to be available for your overnight carer(s). And the care does not have to be every night or on the majority of nights; but must be provided regularly –which means 'habitually, customarily or commonly', not just 'on occasion' or 'when needed': [2014] UKUT 325 (AAC).

> ### Example: A person who requires overnight care
>
> Milo and Grace live alone. Milo receives the daily living component of personal independence payment, and a rota of carers stay every night of the week to care for him. At the weekend Grace provides overnight care for him.
>
> They qualify for one bedroom under the general rules (table 7.1), and one additional bedroom because the carers provide regular overnight care. So they qualify for two bedrooms in all.

Disabled people who can't share a bedroom

7.25 You qualify for an additional bedroom for:

(a) you and your partner if you meet the conditions in para 7.26;

(b) a child under 16 in your home who meets the conditions in para 7.27.

You can qualify under (a) or (b) or both.

7.26 You and your partner meet the conditions if:

(a) you are a joint claim couple (para 2.5); and

(b) one or both of you is in receipt of:

- the daily living component of PIP or adult disability payment at the standard or enhanced rate, or

- the middle or highest rate of the care component of DLA or child disability payment; or

- the higher rate of attendance allowance; and

(c) due to your or your partner's disability, you are 'not reasonably able to share a bedroom' with each other.

7.27 A child under 16 meets the conditions if he or she:

(a) is the responsibility of:

- you, or your partner if you are a joint claim couple (paras 3.65-69 and 7.13), or

- a non-dependant who is an occupier of your home; and

(b) is in receipt of the middle or highest rate of the care component of disability living allowance or child disability payment; and

(c) due to his or her disability, is 'not reasonably able to share a room with another child'.

But an additional bedroom is only allowed if this is needed to ensure the child has their own bedroom. (Young persons aren't included because they qualify for their own bedroom under the general rules in table 7.1.)

7.25-27 UC sch 4 paras 1(2) definition: 'joint renter, 12(1)(c),(d),(6),(6A),(8),(9); NIUC sch 4 paras 1(2),11(1)(c),(d),(6),(6A),(8),(9)

7.28   DWP guidance (ADM para F3135) gives examples of a child who 'disrupts the sleep of and may pose a risk to' or 'would significantly disturb the sleep of' another child; but this does not suggest that these are the only two situations in which an additional bedroom can be allowed.

Examples: Disabled people who can't share a bedroom

1.   A couple live alone. One partner is disabled.

     Under the general rules (table 7.1) they qualify for one bedroom. An additional bedroom is needed and allowed, so they qualify for two bedrooms.

2.   A couple have one child aged 14 who is disabled.

     Under the general rules they qualify for two bedrooms. No additional bedroom is needed or allowed.

3.   A single person has two children aged 12 and 10. One child is disabled.

     Under the general rules they qualify for two bedrooms. An additional bedroom is needed and allowed, so they qualify for three bedrooms.

4.   A couple have two children aged eight and six. One partner in the couple is disabled and one child is disabled.

     Under the general rules they qualify for two bedrooms. Two additional bedrooms are needed or allowed, so they qualify for four bedrooms.

Chapter 8 **Support for mortgage interest**

- Who can get SMI: see paras 8.1-17.
- The amount of your SMI: see paras 8.18-26.
- Claims, payments, repayments and appeals: see paras 8.27-38.
- SMI for people on other benefits: see paras 8.39-44.

Who can get support for mortgage interest

8.1 This chapter explains who can get support for mortgage interest (SMI) and how it is calculated. It applies to owner occupiers and shared owners. SMI can help meet your mortgage interest or similar payments, and is paid as a loan that is secured on your home.

8.2 You can get SMI if you have claimed UC, SPC, JSA(IB), ESA(IR) or IS. See paras 8.3-38 if you are on UC and paras 8.39-44 if you are on the other benefits.

SMI if you are on UC

8.3 You can get SMI if:

- (a) you (or your partner) are liable for owner occupier payments on your home (para 8.8);
- (b) you qualify for UC, or you would qualify except that your income is too high (para 8.19);
- (c) you complete a three-month waiting period (para 8.14); and
- (d) you agree to the DWP's loan offer and to a charge on your home (para 8.30).

8.4 If you stop meeting these conditions, your SMI stops (except as in para 8.17).

8.5 If you began the waiting period before 3rd April, the law is unclear (para 8.6). It seems likely that the DWP will start your SMI at the beginning of your first assessment period that includes 3rd July 2023 or, if earlier, when you complete the nine-month waiting period.

Changes to the rules in April 2023

8.6 Before April 2023, you could only get SMI if you had no earned income, and the waiting period was nine months. Changes to the law on 3rd April 2023 allowed you to claim SMI with earned income, and reduced the waiting period to three months, but left some matters unclear (paras 8.5 and 8.19).

8.1   WRWA 18; LMI 3(2), sch 2 paras 2, 5; NIWRWO 13; NILMI 3(2), sch 2 paras 2, 5

8.2   WRWA 18(3); LMI 3(2); NIWRWO 13(3); NILMI 3(2)

8.3   WRWA 18; LMI 2(1) – 'applicable amount', 'qualifying period', 3(2), 5(1), 8(1), 11(1); NIWRWO 13; NILMI 2(1), 3(2), 5(1), 8(1), 11(1)

8.4   LMI 9(2),(3) as amended by SI 2023/226 reg 2(5)(a); NILMI 9(2),(3); NISR 2023/31

8.5   LMI 2(1) – 'qualifying period' as amended by SI 2023/226 reg 2(2); NILMI 2(1); NISR 2023/31

8.6   LMI 2(1) – 'qualifying period', 3(4) as amended/omitted by SI 2023/226 reg 2(2),(3); NILMI 2(1), 3(4); NISR 2023/31

SMI law and guidance

8.7   In Great Britain the law about SMI is in sections 18-20 of the Welfare Reform and Work Act 2016 and the Loans for Mortgage Interest Regulations 2017 (SI 2017/725). DWP guidance is in ADM memo 8/18 [www]. In Northern Ireland the law is in articles 13-15 of the Welfare Reform and Work (Northern Ireland) Order 2016 and the Loans for Mortgage Interest Regulations (Northern Ireland) 2017 (NISR 2017/176).

Owner occupier payments

8.8   'Owner occupier payments' are:

(a) interest on a mortgage or loan secured on your home (para 8.9); and

(b) payments under an alternative finance arrangement (para 8.10).

You only get SMI towards these if you are liable to make the payments on your home (chapter 5). Capital repayments are never included in SMI.

Mortgages and other loans

8.9   You can get SMI towards any mortgage or other loan that is secured on your home. In the case of a loan, this applies even if it was taken out to purchase items other than your home (e.g. a car loan, a loan for home improvements or a loan to pay service charges). If there is more than one mortgage/loan secured on your home, these are added together (up to the capital limit: para 8.20).

Alternative finance arrangements

8.10   You can get SMI towards any 'alternative finance arrangement' that is recognised by UK law and was undertaken to purchase your home (either full ownership or shared ownership). Alternative finance arrangements are defined in Part 10A of the Income Tax Act 2007 (as amended). They are usually designed for religious purposes but can be used by anyone. Although they are structured to avoid the payment or receipt of interest, the lender's return is equivalent to the finance costs of borrowing. Many different types of product are recognised by UK law: the most common examples are in table 8.1.

Table 8.1 **Examples of alternative finance arrangements**

Purchase and resale (Murabaha)

The finance provider buys the home and immediately re-sells it to the home owner at an agreed higher price, payable either in instalments or in one lump sum at a later date.

Diminishing shared ownership (Musharaka)

This is a partnership contract used to purchase a property. The bank and a customer usually both acquire beneficial interests in the asset. The home owner may pay a fee for

---

8.7   https://tinyurl.com/ADMmemo8-18

8.8   LMI 2(1) – 'qualifying loan', 3(2), sch 2 paras 2(1),(2), 5(1)-(3)

8.9   LMI 2(1) definition: 'relevant accommodation', sch 1 para 5(1)(a),(2); NILMI 2(1), sch 1 para 5(1)(a),(2)

8.10   LMI sch 1 para 5(1)(b),(3),(4); NILMI sch 1 para 5(1)(b),(3),(4)

the use of the asset, while also making payments in stages to gradually acquire an increasing share in, and ultimately all, the ownership of the home.

Profit share agency (Mudaraba/Wakala)

The customer deposits money with a finance institution (usually a bank) and either allows the bank to use it or appoints them as their agent to invest it. Any profits made are shared by the bank and the customer as agreed. The customer may pay a fee to the bank for its services.

Investment bonds (Sukuk)

These are similar to corporate bonds or a collective investment scheme. The finance institution provides the money to the customer to acquire the home in return for a share certificate in the ownership of the property. The property is used and managed by the home owner on behalf of the certificate holders.

SMI for owners and shared owners

8.11 If you are an owner occupier or shared owner (paras 5.9, 5.7):

(a) you can get SMI towards your owner occupier payments (para 8.8);

(b) you have to complete a waiting period before your SMI begins (para 8.14);

(c) your SMI is not reduced for any non-dependants.

8.12 You can also get a housing costs element (HCE) towards your service charges if you are an owner occupier, or towards your rent and service charges if you are a shared owner (chapter 6).

Examples: Support for mortgage interest

1. An owner occupier

Anna owns her home and has a mortgage on it. She is on UC and has no other income.

Once she completes her waiting period, she can get loan payments from the DWP towards her mortgage interest.

2. A shared owner couple

Kevin and Lucy are buying their home in a shared ownership scheme. They are on UC and have no other income.

Once they complete their waiting period, they get loan payments from the DWP towards their mortgage interest. And both during and after their waiting period, they can get UC towards their eligible rent and service charges.

8.11   LMI 3(2), 8(1)(b), 11, 12; NILMI 3(2), 8(1)(b), 11, 12

8.12   UC 25(1),(2), 26(3)-(5), sch 5 paras 2, 5; NIUC 26(1),(2), 27(3)-(5), sch 5 paras 2, 5

SMI for joint owners and shared owners

8.13   If you are a joint owner occupier or joint shared owner with someone who is not in your benefit unit, your SMI/HCE is awarded towards a share of your housing costs. The share is decided:

(a) for your SMI, 'by reference to the appropriate proportion of the payments'; and

(b) for your HCE, as described in paras 6.11-13 or 6.38-40.

In practice the shares in (a) and (b) are normally the same.

The three month waiting period

8.14   The waiting period is three consecutive assessment periods (three months), during which time you must meet the conditions in para 8.16.

8.15   The waiting period applies to:

(a) SMI if you are an owner occupier or shared owner; and/or

(b) an HCE towards service charges if you are an owner occupier.

Waiting period conditions

8.16   You meet the waiting period conditions if

(a) you (or your partner) are liable to make owner occupier payments on your home (para 8.8), and either:

(b) you qualify for UC, or you would qualify except that your income is too high; or

(c) you began the waiting period while you were on JSA, ESA or IS and transferred from that benefit to UC with no gap between them longer than one month.

8.17   The following rules also apply:

(a) if you stop meeting the conditions in para 8.16, you have to complete a new waiting period;

(b) if you become a couple or single person during the waiting period, it continues to run;

(c) once you are getting SMI if there is a break in your UC of six months or less, your SMI restarts when your UC restarts without you having to complete a new waiting period.

8.13   UC sch 4 paras 2 – 'listed persons', 24, 35; LMI 3(3); NIUC sch 4 paras 2, 23, 34; NILMI 3(3)

8.14   UC sch 5 para 5; LMI 2(1) – 'qualifying period', 8(1)(b); NIUC sch 5 para 5; NILMI 2(1), 8(1)(b)

8.15   UC sch 5 para 5; LMI 8(1)(b); NIUC sch 5 para 5; NILMI 8(1)(b)

8.16   UC sch 5 para 6; UCTP 29; LMI 21; NIUC sch 5 para 6; NIUCTP 30; NILMI 21

8.17   UC sch 5 paras 5(3), 7; LMI 2(1) – 'claimant', 'joint claimants', 'qualifying period', 8(3), 9(8); NIUC sch 5 paras 5(3),7; NILMI 2(1), 8(3), 9(8)

The amount of your SMI

Calculating your monthly SMI

8.18 Your monthly SMI is calculated as follows:

(a) start with:

- the capital you owe on your mortgage, loan or alternative finance agreement (paras 8.9-10), or
- your share of it if you are a joint owner or joint shared owner (para 8.13), or
- if lower, the capital limit (para 8.20);

(b) multiply by the standard rate of interest (para 8.25);

(c) divide by 12 to give a monthly figure;

(d) if you have a mortgage or loan protection policy, subtract the monthly amount you receive.

Because the calculation uses a standard rate of interest, your SMI is unlikely to match what you actually pay.

Adjusting your SMI if you have income

8.19 If you have unearned income:

(a) first it is deducted from your UC (para 9.8);

(b) then the remainder (if any) is deducted from your SMI.

If you have earned income, 55% of it is deducted from your UC (para 9.8), but the law about the remainder (if any) of that 55% is unclear (para 8.5). It seems likely that the DWP will deduct it from your SMI.

The capital limit

8.20 The capital limit is £200,000 except when it is increased as described in paras 8.21-22. If you qualify for SMI on two homes (para 5.60), the capital limit (and the increase) applies separately to each of them.

Increasing the capital limit for disability adaptations

8.21 The capital limit is increased if:

(a) you, your partner, or a child or young person you are responsible for is getting:

- the daily living component of PIP, or (in Scotland) adult disability payment, or
- the middle or highest rate of the care component of DLA, or
- attendance allowance or equivalent benefit (para 10.54); and

---

8.18   LMI 11(1), 12(1), 14A; NILMI 11(1), 12(1), 14A

8.19   LMI 2(1) – 'applicable amount', 11(1) step 4, 12(1) step 3; UC 22(1), sch 5 para 4; NILMI 2(1), 11(1), 12(1); UC 23(1), sch 5 para 4

8.20   LMI 11(1),(2), 12(1),(2); NILMI 11(1)(2), 12(1),(2)

8.21   LMI 2(1): 'disabled person', 11(3), sch 3 para 14(3); NILMI 2(1), 11(3), sch 3 para 14(3)

(b) you have a mortgage, loan or alternative finance arrangement (paras 8.9-10) which was to pay for adaptations that were necessary to meet that person's disablement needs; and

(c) as a result, the total capital you owe is greater than £200,000.

8.22   In this case, the £200,000 limit applies to capital you owe for anything other than the adaptations. The capital you owe for adaptations is added, even if this takes the total above £200,000.

Example: Calculating SMI

1. Monthly SMI

Marcia is an unemployed home owner who qualifies for UC.

She purchased her home for £140,000 with a £120,000 repayment mortgage from her bank. The term of the loan is 25 years. At the time of her claim she has repaid £20,000 of the outstanding capital. The interest rate currently charged by her bank on her mortgage is 4.00%. Her current mortgage payments are £640.12 per month (including capital and interest).

She has completed her waiting period (para 8.14) and qualifies for SMI. On the date she completes her waiting period the standard rate of interest is 2.09%.

Marcia's loan payments are calculated as follows:

Total outstanding capital (£120,000 – £20,000)	£100,000
Standard rate of interest	2.09%
Annual amount of SMI (2.09% x £100,000)	£2,090
Monthly amount of SMI (£2,090 divided by 12)	£174.17

2. Adjusting SMI for unearned income

Curtis owns his home and has a mortgage on it. He has been on UC for over nine months and gets UC of £334.91 per month and SMI of £50 per month.

He starts to receive unearned income of £355 per month from an annuity. His UC stops because his unearned income exceeds his maximum UC (para 9.4) by £20.09 per month.

Curtis's SMI is reduced by the £20.09 per month 'excess' income, so he now gets SMI of £29.91 per month (para 8.19).

8.22   LMI 11(3); NILMI 11(3)

Changes in the capital you owe

8.23   Once you are entitled to SMI, its amount is recalculated when the amount of capital you owe changes. This applies whether the capital you owe increases (e.g. because you have taken out a new mortgage/loan or alternative finance arrangement) or decreases (e.g. because you have made a capital repayment).

8.24   But the change in your SMI doesn't take effect until the first anniversary date on or after the change in the capital you owe. 'Anniversary dates' are counted from the first day you were entitled to SMI in your UC or JSA(IB), EAS(IR)/IS (paras 8.39-44).

The standard rate of interest

8.25   A standard rate of interest is used to calculate your SMI (para 8.18). This is the average mortgage rate published by the Bank of England. On 22nd March 2023 it was 2.09%.

8.26   The standard rate of interest only changes when the Bank of England publishes an average mortgage rate that differs from it by 0.5% or more. This new standard rate applies in the calculation of SMI from the date six weeks later. At least seven days before that, the DWP must publish the new standard rate online [www], along with the date it will apply from.

Claims, payments, repayments and appeals

How to get SMI

8.27   To get SMI you need to tell the DWP that you are liable for owner occupier payments. You should do this when you claim UC, and/or when the amount of capital you owe changes.

The DWP's offer of SMI

8.28   The DWP should send an offer of SMI to you, of if you are a couple to both of you. This contains:

(a) a summary of the terms and conditions relating to the loan payments;

(b) the fact that there will be a charge (in Scotland, a standard security) on your property (para 8.29); and

(c) details of where to get further information and independent legal and financial advice.

The charge on your home

8.29   If you accept the DWP's offer, the charge (or standard security) on your property will be registered with the Land Registry. You must 'execute' (sign) the relevant documentation about this. If you are a couple who are joint owners (or joint shared owners) both of you must do this (even if you are claiming UC as a single person).

8.23-24 LMI 11(4)-(5), 12(4)-(5); NILMI 11(4)-(5), 12(4)-(5)

8.25   LMI 13(2),(3),(7); NILMI 13(2),(3),(7)

8.26   LMI 13(4)-(6); NILMI 13(4)-(6) www.gov.uk/support-for-mortgage-interest/what-youll-get

8.27   LMI 2(1) 'claimant', 'joint claimant', 'single claimant', 'qualifying benefit', 3(1),(2); NILMI 2(1), 3(1),(2)

8.28   LMI 5, 6; NILMI 5, 6

8.29   LMI 5(2); NILMI 5(2)

Accepting or refusing the offer

8.30   If you accept the DWP's offer, you are awarded SMI once your waiting period is complete (para 8.14). If you refuse it or don't reply to it, you can't get SMI, but:

(a)   if you are an owner occupier, you can get UC towards service charges (para 6.23); or

(b)   if you are a shared owner, you can get UC towards rent and service charges (chapter 6).

If you later change your mind the DWP should send you a new offer.

How the DWP pays your SMI

8.31   The DWP pays your SMI to your lender (the provider of your mortgage, loan or alternative finance agreement), who must use the payments in the following order:

(a)   towards your current interest;

(b)   towards your arrears of interest;

(c)   towards the capital amount you owe;

(d)   towards any other debts you owe the lender.

The DWP doesn't charge the lender for this service. But if your lender isn't approved or chooses not to receive payments, the DWP pays you.

8.32   The DWP makes the payments monthly in arrears. The payment dates don't necessarily match the dates your UC is paid.

Duration of SMI payments

8.33   SMI payments begin when your waiting period is completed (para 8.14) and continue for as long as you meet the conditions (para 8.3).

Moves

8.34   If you move home (while you are on UC or after it has ended) you can transfer the SMI you owe to your new home, so long as:

(a)   you inform the DWP in advance of your plans;

(b)   your solicitors write to the DWP agreeing to transfer the charge on your old home to your new home; and

(c)   the purchase of your new home is completed within 12 weeks of the sale of your old home.

The DWP can agree to pay your solicitor's costs in transferring the charge, and add this to the SMI you owe.

8.30   LMI 4, 5(1), 8(1)(b); UC 26(2)-(5); LMI 4, 5(1), 8(1)(b); NIUC 27(2)-(5)

8.31   LMI 17, sch 4 paras 4, 5; SI 2020/666; NILMI 17, sch 4 paras 4, 5; NISR 2020/125

8.32   LMI 7; NILMI 7

8.33   LMI 8(1)(b), 9(1)-(3); NILMI 8(1)(b), 9(1)-(3)

8.34   LMI 16A

Interest on SMI

8.35 The DWP charges monthly compound interest on the SMI you have received. The interest rate is set for each half year beginning 1st January and 1st July. The DWP uses the most recent weighted average interest rate on conventional gilts published by the Office for Budget Responsibility [www]. On 1st January 2023, the rate was 3.03%.

Voluntary repayments

8.36 You can choose to make repayments of your SMI at any time, so long as each repayment (other than the final one) is at least £100. If you ask for a 'completion statement', the DWP tells you the balance you owe. The statement is valid for 30 days, during which you aren't charged any interest.

Obligatory repayments

8.37 You have to repay your SMI when:

(a) your home is sold, transferred or disposed of (other than to your partner); or

(b) you die (or in the case of a couple, the last of you who owns your home dies).

But you (or your estate) aren't normally required to repay more than the amount your home sold for, unless this was below the market value.

Appeals

8.38 Appeals about your entitlement to loan payments and their amount are dealt with in the same way as UC (chapter 14). You can't appeal about when and how payments are made, but you can ask the DWP to reconsider this.

SMI if you are on SPC, JSA(IB), ESA(IR) or IS

8.39 If you are on SPC, JSA(IB), ESA(IR) or IS (rather than UC) some of the rules are different. The main differences are in paras 8.40-44. If you are on these benefits your SMI is calculated on a weekly instead of a monthly basis. If you transfer from these benefits to UC, see para 8.16.

The payments SMI can meet

8.40 If you are on SPC, JSA(IB), ESA(IR) or IS (rather than UC), you can only get SMI towards interest on a mortgage or loan you took out for one of the following purposes – whether you have carried that purpose out already ([2017] AACR 22) or plan to carry it out within the next six months:

8.35   LMI 15; NILMI 15 https://obr.uk

8.36   LMI 16(8),(9); NILMI 16(6),(7)

8.37   LMI 16(1)-(7); NILMI 16(1)-(5)

8.38   SSA 8(3)(bc): 'relevant benefit', 28(3)(k), 39(1A); NISSO 9(3)(bc), 28(3)(k), 39(1A)

8.39   LMI 3(2); NILMI 3(2)

8.40   LMI sch 1 paras 1, 2(1)-(4); NILMI sch 1 paras 1, 2(1)-(4)
       [2017] AACR 22 was FMcC v DFC [2016] NICom 70

(a)   to purchase your home or increase your equity in it; or

(b)   to pay for qualifying repairs and improvements (table 8.2); or

(c)   to pay off either of the above.

In the case of SPC only, you can also get SMI towards payments under an alternative finance arrangement.

SMI restrictions for new or increased mortgages or loans

8.41   The SMI restrictions in para 8.42 only apply to new or increased mortgages or loans that you took out while:

(a)   you or someone in your family were on SPC, JSA(IB), ESA(IR) or IS; or

(b)   you were in a gap of up to 26 weeks between periods in which (a) applied.

And the restrictions only apply while you are currently on SPC, JSA(IB), ESA(IR) or IS. They never apply while you are on UC.

Table 8.2 **Qualifying repairs and improvements**

If you are on SPC, JSA(IB), ESA(IR) or IS, you can get SMI towards a loan that you took out for any of the following. (If you are on UC, see instead para 8.9.)

Measures to provide

(a)   a bath, shower, wash basin, sink or lavatory, and necessary associated plumbing, including the provision of hot water not connected to a central heating system;

(b)   ventilation and natural lighting;

(c)   drainage facilities;

(d)   facilities for preparing and cooking food;

(e)   insulation;

(f)   electrical lighting and sockets;

(g)   storage facilities for fuel or refuse.

Repairs

(h)   to an existing heating system;

(i)   of unsafe structural defects.

Other improvements

(j)   damp proofing measures;

(k)   measures to make your home better suited to the needs of a disabled person;

(l)   provision of separate sleeping accommodation for two children/young persons of opposite sexes who are aged 10 or over but under 20.

8.41   LMI sch 1 para 3(1)-(4); NILMI sch 1 para 3(1)-(4)

T8.2   LMI sch 1 para 2(5); NILMI sch 1 para 2(5)

8.42   When the restrictions apply (para 8.41), you can only get SMI on the new mortgage/loan or increased part of the mortgage/loan if:

(a)   it was for a new home better suiting the needs of a disabled person; or

(b)   it was for a new home needed to provide separate sleeping accommodation for two children/young persons of opposite sexes aged 10 or over but under 20; or

(c)   it replaced any of the mortgages/loans in para 8.40 – but in this case your SMI is limited to the SMI you got on the mortgage/loan; or

(d)   it was taken out while you were on HB – but in this case your SMI is limited to the amount of your HB plus any housing costs you were getting in your SPC, JSA(IB), ESA(IR) or IS.

Even when your SMI is limited as in (c) or (d), it increases when the standard rate of interest increases (para 8.26).

Income, capital and non-dependants

8.43   If you are on SPC, JSA(IB), ESA(IR) or IS (rather than UC):

(a)   having earned income doesn't by itself stop you getting SMI, but it reduces your SMI in the same way as unearned income (para 8.19);

(b)   the capital limit is usually £100,000 instead of £200,000 (para 8.20), but apart from that the adjustment for disability adaptations applies in the same way (para 8.21);

(c)   your SMI is calculated by dividing the annual interest figure by 52 instead of 12 (paras 8.18, 8.39);

(d)   if you have one or more non-dependants (para 3.70), deductions are made from your SMI – these depend on your and your non-dependant's circumstances and there are several exceptions: the rules are the same as in SPC (volume 2 chapter 22).

Waiting period and SMI run-on

8.44   The other main differences from UC are as follows:

(a)   if you are on SPC, there is no waiting period;

(b)   if you are on JSA(IB), ESA(IR) or IS, the waiting period is 13 consecutive weeks, but after gaps in that benefit of no more than 52 weeks you don't have to complete a fresh waiting period;

(c)   if you are on JSA(IB), ESA(IR) or IS (not UC or SPC), you get a 'run on' of four extra weeks of SMI when you start employment or self-employment, so long as it is for at least 30 hours per week and is expected to last at least five weeks.

8.42   LMI sch 1 para 3(5)-(9); NILMI sch 1 para 3(5)-(9)

8.43   LMI 2(1): 'Modified Rules', 3(4), 11(1) – step 4,(2), 14, sch 1 paras 1-3; NILMI 2(1), 3(4), 11(1),(2), 14, sch 1 paras 1-3

8.44   LMI 2(1): 'qualifying period', 8(1)(b),(c), 9(4)-(6); NILMI 2(1), 8(1)(b),(c), 9(4)-(6)

Chapter 9 **Calculating UC**

- ■ The amount of your UC: see paras 9.1-11.
- ■ The standard allowance, child element and two child limit: see paras 9.12-28.
- ■ The work capability, carer and child costs elements: see paras 9.29-50.
- ■ The benefit cap: see paras 9.51-63.

The amount of your UC

9.1   This chapter explains how your UC is calculated and how your housing costs are taken into account.

9.2   Your UC is assessed for each monthly assessment period of your award. For how monthly assessments can affect your UC, see paras 3.38-42, 6.56-57, 10.21-27 and 10.40-41.

The calculation

9.3   The following steps (paras 9.4-11) give the calculation of UC. Table 9.1 summarises the rules.

Your maximum UC

9.4   Your 'maximum UC' is the total of:

- (a) a standard allowance for your basic living needs, or for both of you if you are a joint claim couple (para 9.14);
- (b) additional amounts (called 'elements') for children and young persons, work capability, carers and childcare costs (paras 9.15-50);
- (c) a housing costs element towards your rent and/or service charges (chapter 6);
- (d) a transitional element if you have migrated from legacy benefits to UC (paras 4.36-52).

See chapter 8 for help with owner occupier housing costs.

Your income and capital

9.5   The amount of UC you qualify for depends on your income and capital. If you are in a couple, your partner's income and capital are included with yours. This is done even if you are in a couple but claiming UC as a single person (para 2.7).

9.4   WRA 1(3), 8(2); NIWRO 6(3), 13(2)

9.5   WRA 5; UC 3(3), 18(2), 22(3); NIWRO 10; NIUC 3(2), 18(2), 23(3)

Table 9.1 **Amount of UC**

Maximum UC
- Standard allowance
- Housing costs element (after deducting any housing cost contributions)
- Other elements if applicable

MINUS

- 100% of unearned income and
- 55% of earned income (after deducting a work allowance if you qualify for one)

EQUALS

Amount of UC

All figures are monthly.

Capital and the capital limit

9.6   If your capital is over £16,000 you do not qualify for UC. See chapter 10 for how your (and your partner's) capital is assessed and which kinds of capital are counted or ignored.

Income and the amount of UC

9.7   If you have no income, you qualify for maximum UC (para 9.4).

9.8   If you have income, you qualify for maximum UC minus:

  (a) the whole of your unearned income; and

  (b) 55% of your earned income (after a work allowance has been deducted if you qualify for one).

See chapter 10 for how your (and your partner's) income is assessed, the work allowance, and which kinds of income are counted or ignored.

Minimum UC

9.9   If you qualify for at least one penny a month you are awarded UC.

T9.1   WRA 5(1)(b),(2)(b), 8(1),(3),(4); UC 22(1), (3); NIWRO 10(1)(b),(2)(b), 13(1),(3),(4); NIUC 23(1), (3)

9.6   WRA 5(1)(a),(2)(a); UC 18(1); NIWRO 10(1)(a),(2)(a); NIUC 18(1)

9.7   WRA 5(1)(b),(2)(b), 8(1)(a); NIWRO 10(1)(b),(2)(b), 13(1)(a)

9.8   WRA 5(1)(b),(2)(b), 8(1),(3),(4); UC 22(1),(3); NIWRO 10(1)(b),(2)(b), 13(1),(3),(4); NIUC 23(1),(3)

9.9   UC 17; NIUC 17

Rounding

9.10 Amounts used in the calculation of UC are rounded to the nearest penny, with halfpennies being rounded upwards.

Other calculation rules

9.11 Your UC can be reduced if:

(a) the 'benefit cap' applies to you (paras 9.51-63);

(b) a sanction applies to you (paras 2.47-54);

(c) an advance of UC is recovered (paras 12.25 and 12.29);

(d) part of your UC is paid to a third party (paras 12.37-59);

(e) an overpayment is recovered (paras 13.10 and 13.21).

Examples: Amount of UC

All figures are monthly and none of the claimants have capital.

1. Single renter aged 23, no income

Sean's eligible rent is £400.

Maximum UC

■ standard allowance	£292.11
■ housing costs element (eligible rent)	£400.00
■ total	£692.11
Amount of Sean's UC	£692.11

2. Couple over 25, renters, two children aged 5 and 7, unearned income only

Polly and Patrick's eligible rent is £1250. Their unearned income is £300 maintenance received by Polly.

Maximum UC

■ standard allowance	£578.82
■ two child elements (£315.00 + £269.58)	£584.58
■ housing costs element (eligible rent)	£1250.00
■ total	£2413.40
Income deduction	
■ unearned income £300 x 100%	– £300.00
Amount of Polly and Patrick's UC	£2113.40

9.10   UC 6(1); NIUC 7(1)

Allowances and elements

9.12   This section explains which UC allowances and elements you qualify for. The ones you qualify for are added together to give your maximum UC (para 9.4).

9.13   Table 9.2 summarises the allowances and elements that have fixed amounts. The housing costs element (chapter 6) and transitional element vary (paras 4.36-52).

Standard allowance

9.14   Everyone qualifies for a standard allowance (table 9.2). You get:

(a) the single rate if you are a single person, or in a couple but claiming UC as a single person (para 2.7). A lower figure applies if you are under 25;

(b) the couple rate if you are a joint claim couple (para 2.5). A lower figure applies if you are both under 25.

Child element

9.15   You qualify for a child element for each child or young person in your benefit unit (paras 3.62-69):

(a) if at least one child/young person was born before 6th April 2017, you get

  ■ the higher rate for one child/young person, and

  ■ the lower rate for each of the others;

(b) otherwise you get the lower rate for each child/young person.

But if you have any children who were born on or after 6th April 2017, you may be affected by the two child limit (para 9.17).

Disabled child addition

9.16   You qualify for the disabled child addition as follows:

(a) you get the higher rate for each child or young person who is:

  ■ entitled to the highest rate of the care component of DLA or (in Scotland) child disability payment, or

  ■ entitled to the enhanced rate of the daily living component of PIP or (in Scotland) adult disability payment, or

  ■ certified as blind or severely sight-impaired by a consultant ophthalmologist;

(b) you get the lower rate for each child or young person who is entitled to DLA, PIP or (in Scotland) a disability payment, but does not meet the conditions in (a).

You get a disabled child addition for every child/young person who meets these conditions, even if the number of your child elements is affected by the two child limit.

9.14   WRA 9; UC 36(1), (3); SI 2021/313 reg 2; NIWRO 14; NIUC 38(1), (3); NISR 2021/67 reg 2

9.15   WRA 10; UC 24(1), 36(1); UCTP 43; NIWRO 15; NIUC 25(1), 38(1)

9.16   WRA 10; UC 2 definition: 'blind', 24(2), 36(1); SI 2021/786; NIWRO 15; NIUC 2, 25(2), 38(1)

Table 9.2 **UC allowances and elements (2023-24)**

	Monthly amount
Standard allowance	
▪ single under 25	£292.11
▪ single aged 25 or over	£368.74
▪ couple both under 25	£458.51
▪ couple at least one aged 25 or over	£578.82
Child element	
▪ higher rate	£315.00
▪ lower rate	£269.58
Disabled child addition	
▪ higher rate	£456.89
▪ lower rate	£146.31
Work capability elements	
▪ LCW element	£146.31
▪ LCWRA element	£390.06
Carer element	£185.86
Childcare costs element	
▪ maximum for one child from April 2023	£646.35
▪ maximum for one child from July 2023	£951.00
▪ maximum for two or more children from April 2023	£1108.04
▪ maximum for two or more children from July 2023	£1630.00

The two child limit

9.17 The 'two child limit' applies to both children and young persons. It only affects you if:

(a) you have more than two children/young persons in your benefit unit (paras 3.62-69); and

(b) at least one of them was born on or after 6th April 2017 (when the two child limit was first introduced).

The Supreme Court decided that the two child limit doesn't amount to unlawful discrimination (SC, CB and Others v SSWP).

T9.2   UC 36(1); SI 2023/316 sch 13; NIUC 38(1); NISR 2023/43 sch 13

9.17   SC, CB and Others v SSWP [2021] SC 26 http://www.bailii.org/uk/cases/UKSC/2021/26.html

How the two child limit works

9.18   If you have one child/young person you get one child element. Or if you have two you get two child elements.

9.19   But if you have three or more, you get a child element for:

(a) each child/young person who has full protection (para 9.20); and

(b) the oldest two other children/young persons (decided by their date of birth, or time of birth for twins, etc); and

(c) any other child/young person who:

■   has third child protection (para 9.21), or

■   was born before 6th April 2017 (para 9.22).

These rules are applied in the order (a),(b),(c) – this is illustrated in the examples.

Full protection

9.20   'Full protection' can apply to any child/young person (whether your first, second, third, etc). The qualifying conditions relate to:

(a) adoption (para 9.23); and

(b) non-parental care (para 9.24).

Third child protection

9.21   'Third child protection' can only apply to your third or subsequent child/young person (counting only those that don't have full protection). The qualifying conditions relate to:

(a) multiple births (twins etc) (para 9.25); or

(b) non-consensual conception (para 9.26).

Born before 6th April 2017

9.22   You get a child element for every child/young person who was born before 6th April 2017, and this continues for as long as they continue to be children/young persons (paras 3.63-64). But the law only refers to third and subsequent children/young persons, because the oldest two get a child element under the ordinary rule (para 9.19).

9.18   UC 24(1); NIUC 25(1)

9.19   UC 24A, 24B; NIUC 25A, 25B

9.20   UC 24A(1)(za); NIUC 25A(1)(za)

9.21   UC 24A(1)(b); NIUC 25A(1)(b); [2018] EWHC 864 (Admin)
         http://www.bailii.org/ew/cases/EWHC/Admin/2018/864.html

9.22   UC 24A(1)(b),(3); NIUC 25A(1)(b),(3)

Adoption

9.23   A child/young person has full protection (para 9.20) if he or she:

(a) is adopted by you or your partner; or

(b) is placed for adoption with you or your partner.

But this doesn't apply if you or your partner are their parent or step-parent (except as in para 9.28). And it doesn't apply to adoptions arranged directly from outside the British Isles.

Examples: The two child limit

The examples use 'child' to include both children and young persons. Except when stated, none of them qualify for full protection or third child protection (paras 9.20-21).

1. Three children all born before 6th April 2017

A single person has three children, all born before 6th April 2017. She gets three child elements as follows.

- First child   Yes (oldest two)
- Second child   Yes (oldest two)
- Third child   Yes (born before 6.4.17)

2. Three children, two born before 6th April 2017

A couple have three children, two born before 6th April 2017. They get two child elements as follows.

- First child   Yes (oldest two)
- Second child   Yes (oldest two)
- Third child   No (not born before 6.4.17)

3. Three children, all born on or after 6th April 2017

A single person has three children, all born on or after 6th April 2017. He gets two child elements as follows.

- First child   Yes (oldest two)
- Second child   Yes (oldest two)
- Third child   No (not born before 6.4.17)

4. Three children, younger two are twins

A couple have three children, all born on or after 6th April 2017. The younger two are twins. They get three child elements as follows.

- First child   Yes (oldest two)
- Second child (older twin)   Yes (oldest two)
- Third child (younger twin)   Yes (third-child protection)

9.23   UC sch 12 paras 1, 3, 6; NIUC sch 12 paras 1, 3, 6

5. Three children, older two are twins

A couple have three children, all born on or after 6th April 2017. The older two are twins. They get two child elements as follows.

- First child (older twin)   Yes (oldest two)
- Second child (younger twin)   Yes (oldest two)
- Third child   No (no third-child protection)

6. Five children, two adopted

A single person has two adopted children, and three other children born after 6th April 2017. He gets four child elements as follows.

- Adopted child   Yes (full protection)
- Adopted child   Yes (full protection)
- First other child   Yes (oldest other two)
- Second other child   Yes (oldest other two)
- Third other child   No (no third-child protection)

7. Adopted child and twins

A couple have one adopted child, and three other children born after 6th April 2017. The youngest two are twins. They get four child elements as follows.

- Adopted child   Yes (full protection)
- First other child   Yes (oldest other two)
- Second other child (older twin)   Yes (oldest other two)
- Third other child (younger twin)   Yes (third-child protection)

Non-parental care

9.24   A child/young person has full protection (para 9.20) if he or she:

(a) is looked after by you or your partner under formal arrangements made (now or before they reached 16) by social services or a court, or confirmed by you or your partner being entitled to guardian's allowance for them; or

(b) is looked after by you or your partner under informal arrangements (made by you or your partner) if they would otherwise be likely to enter local authority care (in practice a social worker will be asked to confirm this); or

(c) is a child whose parent is also a child (under 16) and in your benefit unit (paras 3.62-69) – for example, if you have a 15-year-old daughter with a baby, this means the baby.

But (a) and (b) don't apply if you or your partner are their parent or step-parent.

9.24   UC sch 12 paras 1, 4; NIUC sch 12 paras 1, 4

Multiple births (twins, etc)

9.25 A child/young person has third-child protection (para 9.21) if he or she was born to you or your partner and:

(a) is the second-born of twins, both of whom are in your benefit unit (paras 3.62-69); or

(b) is the second-born or later-born of triplets or a larger multiple birth, counting only those in your benefit unit.

Non-consensual conception

9.26 A child/young person has third-child protection (para 9.21) if he or she was born to you or your partner as a result of non-consensual intercourse with a person who doesn't (or doesn't now) live with you, for example due to rape or controlling or coercive behaviour.

9.27 Because this is an extremely sensitive issue, the DWP accepts evidence (ADM para F1024):

(a) from a third party it has approved for this purpose, normally a health professional, registered social worker or specialist charity; or

(b) that the person has been convicted of a relevant offence; or

(c) that the Criminal Injuries Compensation Board has made a relevant award to you.

Step parents

9.28 The protections in paras 9.23 and 9.25-27 continue if:

(a) you are a step-parent of a child/young person; and

(b) you were previously getting UC as a couple with their parent or adoptive parent; and

(c) you have remained on UC since then with no break longer than six months.

The same applies if you were getting CTC, JSA(IB) or IS within the six months before your UC began.

9.25   UC sch 12 paras 1, 2, 6; NIUC sch 12 paras 1, 2, 6

9.26-27   UC sch 12 paras 1, 5, 6; UCTP 42; NIUC sch 12 paras 1, 5, 6; NIUCTP 43

9.28   UC 2 definition: 'step-parent', sch 12 paras 1, 6; UCTP 41; NIUC 2, sch 12 paras 1, 6; NIUCTP 42

Work capability elements

9.29   There are two work capability elements:

(a)   the LCW element which is only for old cases (para 9.31); and

(b)   the LCWRA element, which is for both current and old cases (para 9.32).

9.30   You can only get one of these elements as follows:

(a)   if you meet the conditions for both elements, you get the LCWRA element;

(b)   if you are a joint claim couple, only one of you has to meet the conditions;

(c)   if you meet the conditions for a carer element see table 9.3.

If you start or stop qualifying for an element, see paras 11.23-24.

LCW element

9.31   You qualify for an LCW element if:

(a)   you have limited capability for work (LCW) (paras 2.43-45);

(b)   you meet the earnings condition (para 9.33);

(c)   you have had LCW or LCWRA since before 3rd April 2017; and

(d)   you made your UC claim:

-   before 3rd April 2017, or

-   when you were on ESA, SDA, IB or IS, if you claimed that benefit before 3rd April 2017.

LCWRA element

9.32   You qualify for an LCWRA element if:

(a)   you have limited capability for work and work-related activity (LCWRA) (paras 2.43-45);

(b)   you meet the earnings condition (para 9.33); and

(c)   either:

-   you complete a waiting period (para 9.35), or

-   you are swapping from an LCW element to an LCWRA element, or

-   you are terminally ill (para 9.37), or

-   you qualify for an LCWRA element because you were on ESA, SDA, IB or IS when you made your UC claim (para 9.38), or getting national insurance credits in their place at that time ([2022] UKUT 117 (AAC)).

Earnings condition

9.33   If you have earnings at or above the 16-hour threshold (para 9.34), you can't get an LCW or LCWRA element unless:

(a)   you are on PIP, DLA, (in Scotland) child or adult disability payment, attendance allowance or an equivalent benefit (para 10.54); or

(b)   you have one of the medical conditions in table 2.7.

9.29-32 WRA 12; UC 27, 36(1); SI 2017/204 sch 2 paras 8-15; NIWRO 17; UC 28, 38(1); SI 2017/146 sch 2 paras 1-5

9.33   UC 41(2),(3); NIUC 42(2),(3)

The 16-hour threshold

9.34 The 16-hour threshold for a single person is what you would earn for working 16 hours per week at the national minimum wage (table 2.6). For a couple it is this amount for each of you.

The LCWRA waiting period

9.35 The LCWRA waiting period is three months beginning with:

(a) the day you first provide medical evidence; or

(b) the day you request an LCWRA element in the situations in para 9.33(a) or (b).

Your LCWRA element is then awarded from the beginning of the assessment period following the one in which the three months end. During the waiting period you don't get an LCWRA element. But if the amount of your income means you would qualify for UC with the LCWRA element and wouldn't qualify without it, you are awarded UC of one penny a month. This is so that you can count as being on UC.

Breaks in your UC

9.36 If you have a break in your UC of no more than six months:

(a) you don't have to complete a new waiting period when you reclaim; but

(b) if your waiting period was incomplete, it continues to run during the break, and after it if necessary.

You only have to start a new waiting period after a break in your UC of more than six months.

Examples: The LCWRA waiting period

1. A new UC claim

John is awarded UC from 26th July, so his assessment periods begin on the 26th of each month. On 19th August, he provides medical evidence and the DWP agrees he qualifies for an LCWRA element.

- His waiting period runs from 19th August to 18th November (three months)
- He is awarded the LCWRA element from 26th November (the first day of his assessment period).

2. A break in UC

Helen is on UC, and her assessment periods begin on the 5th of each month. On 21st September she provides medical evidence and the DWP agrees she qualifies for an LCWRA element. Then her UC stops from the 5th October to 4th February.

- Her waiting period runs from 21st September to 20th December (three months)
- She is awarded the LCWRA element from 5th February.

9.34-36 UC 28; UCTP 19, 20, 20A; NIUC 29; UCTP 19-21

People who are terminally ill

9.37   Being terminally ill means suffering from a progressive disease which is likely to lead to death within 12 months (this was six months until 4th April 2022). No matter how long it takes you to inform the DWP about this, you are awarded the LCWRA element back to when you became terminally ill (para 11.23).

If you are on ESA, SDA, IB or IS when you claimed UC

9.38   ESA assesses capability for work in the same way as UC but uses different terminology. If you were on ESA when you claimed UC:

(a) the ESA 'work-related activity component' converts into an LCW element in your UC;

(b) the ESA 'support component' converts into an LCWRA element in your UC;

(c) if you were in the 13-week 'assessment phase' for the ESA support component, time spent in it counts towards the waiting period for the LCWRA element (which in this case is 13 weeks, not three months).

Similar rules apply if you were on SDA, IB, or IS for disability or incapacity when you claimed UC.

Carer element

9.39   You qualify for the carer element if:

(a) you are the carer of a severely disabled person (they could be someone in your household, including your partner, or someone outside it) and;

(b) you don't receive any earned income for caring for them; and

(c) either

■ you get carer's allowance for this; or

■ you meet the conditions for carer's allowance, or you would do except that your earnings are too high. The main condition is that you are regularly and substantially caring for them for at least 35 hours per week.

If you are claiming UC as a couple and you each meet the above conditions in relation to a different severely disabled person, you get two carer elements (one each). Further rules are in paras 9.40-41.

Shared care

9.40   Only one person can count as the carer for each severely disabled person. This applies to carer's allowance as well as the carer element. If two or more people meet the conditions for carer's allowance and/or the carer element, you choose who is to count as the carer, or if you do not the DWP chooses. So unless you agree to change who counts as the carer, you can't get the carer element if your partner or anyone else gets carer's allowance or the carer element for the severely disabled person.

9.37   UC 2 definition: 'terminally ill', schs 8, 9; SI 2022/260 reg 2; UC 2, schs 8, 9

9.38   UC 40(1); UCTP 19, 20, 20A, 21-27; NIUC 41(1); UCTP 19-28

9.39   WRA 12; UC 29(1)-(3), 30, 36(1); NIWRO 17; NIUC 30(1)-(3), 31, 38(1)

9.40   UC 29(1),(3); NIUC 30(1),(3)

Carer element and work capability elements

9.41 If you are a single person (or claiming UC as a single person) you cannot get a carer element and an LCWRA or LCW element at the same time. You get the element which is worth most. If you are claiming UC as a couple there are limits to getting these at the same time. You get the element (or combination of elements) that is worth most but without making you better off than two single people. Table 9.3 gives the rules about this.

Table 9.3 **Carer element and LCW/LCWRA elements**

This table explains which element(s) you get if you meet the conditions for both an LCW/LCWRA element and a carer element (paras 9.29-40).

Single people who meet the LCWRA condition	■ You get the LCWRA element (but not the carer element).
Single people who meet the LCW condition	■ You get the carer element (but not the LCW element).

Couples who meet the LCWRA condition	■ You get the LCWRA element.
	
	■ You also get one carer element (never two), but only if:
	
	   ■ both of you meet the LCWRA condition and one or both of you meet the carer condition, or
	
	   ■ one of you meets the LCWRA condition and the other one meets the carer condition.

Couples who meet the LCW condition	■ You get two carer elements (but no LCW element) if both of you meet the carer condition. ■ You get one carer element if one of you meets the carer condition. You also get the LCW element, but only if the other one meets the LCW condition.

Childcare costs element

9.42 You qualify for the childcare costs element if you meet:

(a) the work condition (paras 9.43-44); and

(b) the childcare costs condition (paras 9.45-48).

The amount is 85% of your childcare costs up to a fixed limit (paras 9.49-50).

9.41   UC 29(4); NIUC 30(4)

T9.3   UC 29(4); NIUC 30(4)

9.42   WRA 12; UC 31; NIWRO 17; NIUC 32

The work condition

9.43   If you are a single person you meet the work condition if you:

(a) are in paid work (para 10.8); or

(b) have an offer to start paid work in your current or next assessment period; or

(c) ceased paid work in your current or previous assessment period; or

(d) are receiving statutory sick, maternity, paternity or adoption pay or maternity allowance.

9.44   If you are in a couple (even if you are claiming UC as a single person):

(a) both of you must meet the work condition in para 9.43; or

(b) one of you must meet the work condition and the other one must be unable to provide childcare because they:

■ have limited capability for work or for work and work-related activity (para 2.43-45); or

■ meet the conditions for carer's allowance (whether or not they have claimed it), or would do so except that their earnings are too high (see para 9.39), or

■ are temporarily absent from your household (see para 3.58).

The childcare costs condition

9.45   You meet the childcare costs condition if you or your partner (if you are claiming UC as a couple) pay childcare charges for a child or young person you are responsible for. This means:

(a) a child under 16; or

(b) a young person aged 16, but only in the period before the first Monday in September following their 16th birthday.

This applies even if the number of your child elements is affected by the two child limit.

9.46   Childcare charges only count for these purposes if they are to enable you to:

(a) continue in paid work; or

(b) take up paid work, in the situation in para 9.43(b); or

(c) maintain arrangements you had before you left paid work, in the situations in para 9.43(c) and (d).

9.47   In order to count for these purposes, the childcare charges must be paid to:

(a) a registered childminder, childcare agency or equivalent (including an approved childcare provider outside Great Britain); or

(b) an out-of-school-hours (or pre-school age) scheme provided by a school as part of its school activities.

9.48   Childcare provided by the child's 'close relative' (para 5.38) in the child's home, or by the child's foster parent, is not included.

9.43   UC 31(1)(a),(2); NIUC 33(1)(a),(2)
9.44   UC 3(6), 32(1)(b),(2); NIUC 3(5), 33(1)(b),(2)
9.45   UC 33(1)(a), 35(9); NIUC 34(1)(a), 37(6)
9.46   UC 33(1)(b); NIUC 34(1)(b)
9.47-48 UC 35; NIUC 37

The amount of the childcare element

9.49 The amount of your childcare element is:

(a) 85% of the monthly childcare charges you pay (para 9.50); or

(b) the maximum amount in table 9.2 (if that is lower than the 85%).

But any amount of your childcare charges is ignored which: the DWP considers excessive for the extent of your or your partner's paid work; or is met by an employer or any other person; or is met by government payments in connection with any work-related activity or training you are undertaking.

9.50 You can only get a childcare element towards charges that meet the following conditions:

(a) you have paid the charges or are liable for them (R (Salvato) v SSWP); and

(b) the charges are for:

■ childcare provided in your current assessment period – if you paid for it in your current assessment period or in the two preceding months, or

■ childcare provided in a previous assessment period – if you paid for it in your current assessment period; and

(c) you report the charges to the DWP within your current assessment period or the next one (or later in special circumstances: table 11.1).

You can get discretionary help with costs upfront through the DWP's Flexible Support Fund (para 12.27) which will be expanded to a mandatory scheme from summer 2023 [www].

Example: Childcare element and amount of UC

Kate is 29 and has a child of 7. She works and pays a registered childminder £500 a month. Her eligible rent is £800 a month and she has no non-dependants. She has no capital, and her earnings (after deducting the work allowance) are £1500 a month.

Maximum UC

■ Standard allowance	£368.74
■ Child element (higher rate)	£315.00
■ Childcare element (85% of £500)	£425.00
■ Housing costs element (eligible rent)	£800.00
■ Total	£1908.74

Amount of UC

■ Maximum UC	£1908.74
■ Earned income deduction (55% of £1500)	– £825.00
■ Monthly amount of UC	£1083.74

9.49 UC 34, 36(1); NIUC 35, 38(1)

9.50 UC 33(1)(za), 34A; NIUC 34(1)(a), 36; https://tinyurl.com/HC-1183 para 3.53
      R (Salvato) v SSWP [2021] EWHC 102 (Admin) www.bailii.org/ew/cases/EWHC/Admin/2021/102.htm

The UC benefit cap

9.51　This section describes how the 'benefit cap' can reduce your UC so that the total of your UC and other welfare benefits does not exceed a fixed monthly figure.

9.52　If your UC is reduced because of the benefit cap, you may be able to get a discretionary housing payment from your local council or (in Northern Ireland) welfare supplementary payments (volume 1 chapter 23). The Supreme Court has held that the benefit cap does not discriminate unlawfully: R (SG and others) v SSWP; R (DA and others) v SSWP; R (DS and others) v SSWP.

Benefit cap exceptions

9.53　Table 9.4 and paras 9.58-63 give the situations in which the UC benefit cap does not apply.

The amount of the benefit cap

9.54　The annual amount of the benefit cap is as follows:

(a)　if you are a single person (or claiming UC as a single person) and are not responsible for any children or young persons:

- ■　£16,967 in Greater London,
- ■　£14,753 elsewhere;

(b)　if you are a single person and are responsible for at least one child or young person, or a joint claim couple (with or without children/young persons):

- ■　£25,323 in Greater London,
- ■　£22,020 elsewhere.

Greater London means the London boroughs and the City of London.

The amount of the UC reduction

9.55　Table 9.4 shows how the amount of the reduction (if any) is calculated.

How benefits are included in the UC benefit cap

9.56　Table 9.4(a) lists the benefits that are included in the UC benefit cap. For this purpose:

(a)　benefits other than UC are converted to a monthly figure (para 10.50);

(b)　your partner's benefits are included even if you are claiming UC as a single person (para 2.7);

(c)　benefits are counted before any reductions are made for recovering overpayments, administrative penalties, third party deductions or sanctions;

(d)　amounts you don't receive aren't included (whether this is because of the overlapping benefits rules, or in ESA because you are disqualified);

9.52　WRA 96; UC 79; NIWRO 101; NIUC 79
　　　R (SG and others) v SSWP UKSC (2015) www.bailii.org/uk/cases/UKSC/2015/16.html;
　　　R (DA and others) v SSWP [2019] UKSC 21 www.bailii.org/uk/cases/UKSC/2019/21.html

9.54　WRA 96(5A); UC 80A; NIWRO 101(5A); NIUC 80A

(e) if you become a couple while you are on UC, and your new partner is on HB but not UC, their benefits aren't included during the assessment period in which you become a couple;

(f) SMI (chapter 8) and a two-week run-on of IS etc isn't included (para 4.8);

(g) any Scottish or Welsh benefits are disregarded when calculating the cap.

Housing costs and the UC and HB benefit caps

9.57   As well as the UC benefit cap described here, there is also an HB benefit cap (volume 1 chapter 6). For everyone on UC:

(a) only the UC benefit cap applies to you, not the HB benefit cap;

(b) if you get a UC housing costs element (HCE), it is included in the UC benefit cap;

(c) if you get HB in supported or temporary accommodation (table 5.3), it isn't included in the UC benefit cap – and the HB benefit cap doesn't apply to you;

(d) if you qualify for a UC HCE on two homes (para 5.60), (b) applies to them both. Or if you qualify for HB on one, (c) applies to that one and (b) applies to the other.

Table 9.4 **Calculating UC benefit cap reductions**

For each assessment period of one month:

(a) Add together your and your partner's entitlement in that month to:
- universal credit
- child benefit
- new-style JSA or new-style ESA (except the two-week run on: para 4.8)
- maternity allowance
- severe disablement allowance
- bereavement allowance or widowed parent's allowance (but not bereavement support payments).

(b) If you qualify for the UC childcare costs element in that month (para 9.42), subtract its full amount (para 9.49) from the above total. (Otherwise skip this step.)

(c) If the result exceeds the monthly benefit cap (para 9.54) your UC for that month is reduced by the amount of this excess.

Notes:
- See paras 9.56-57 for further rules about step (a).
- Step (b) 'protects' the childcare costs element from the UC benefit cap (even if the amount of your UC is less than your childcare costs element). It is described in a more complicated way in the law, but this table gives the correct result.

9.56   WRA 96(9),(10) – 'welfare benefit'; UC 78(2), 79(1),(2), 80; UCTP 8B, 9; NIWRO 101(7); NIUC 78, 80; NIUCTP 6B, 7

9.57   UC 80(2),(2A); HB 75F(1)(g); NIUC 80(2),(2A); NIHB 73F(1)(j)

T9.4   WRA 96(2),(10) – 'welfare benefit'; UC 78(2), 80(1),(5), 81; NIWRO 101(2),(7); NIUC 78(2), 80(1),(5), 81

Earned income above the 16-hour threshold

9.58   The benefit cap does not apply to you in any assessment period in which you have earned income at or above the 16-hour threshold (para 9.34). This applies whether you are a single person or in a couple (regardless of your age). And if you are in a couple, your partner's earned income is included (even if you are claiming UC as a single person).

The grace period after a reduction in earned income

9.59   The benefit cap does not apply to you during a 'grace period'. You qualify for a grace period if you had earned income at or above the 16-hour threshold (para 9.34) in each of the 12 months before your grace period begins and:

(a)   your earned income reduces below the 16-hour threshold (or ends) while you are on UC; or

(b)   you or your partner (even if you are claiming UC as a single person) ceased paid work (para 10.8) before your entitlement to UC began.

The rules in these cases are in paras 9.60-62.

9.60   If your earned income reduces below the 16-hour threshold (or ends) while you are on UC (para 9.59):

(a)   your grace period starts on the first day of the assessment period in which that happens;

(b)   it lasts for nine months (in other words, nine assessment periods).

9.61   If you or your partner ceased paid work before your entitlement to UC began (para 9.59):

(a)   your grace period starts on the day after you or your partner ceased paid work (if this applies to both you and your partner, use the most recent of these days);

(b)   it lasts nine months – but the benefit cap does not apply to you until the assessment period following the one in which the grace period ends.

9.62   If your entitlement to UC ends before the end of the nine months, your grace period ends when your UC ends.

Receiving certain benefits

9.63   The benefit cap does not apply to you in any assessment period in which you (or your partner if you are claiming UC as a couple) receive one of the benefits in table 9.5.

9.58   UC 6(1A)(za), 82(1)(a),(4),(5); NIUC 7(1A)(za), 82(1)(a),(4),(5)

9.59   WRA 40 definition: 'claimant'; UC 78(2), 82(1)(b),(2)-(4); NIWRO 46; NIUC 78(2), 82(1)(b),(2)-(4)

9.60   UC 82(2)(a); NIUC 82(2)(a)

9.61   UC 82(2)(b); NIUC 82(2)(b)

9.62   UC 82(2); NIUC 82(2)

9.63   UC 83; NIUC 83

Examples: The UC benefit cap and the grace period

1. A reduction in earned income

Aarna has been on UC for over 12 months. She has had earned income at or above the 16-hour threshold throughout that time, so no benefit cap has applied to her (para 9.58). Her assessment periods start on the 23rd of each month. She loses her job on 31st March.

Aarna's grace period (para 9.60) begins on 23rd March and lasts nine months until 22nd December. The benefit cap applies to her from 23rd December.

2. Losing paid work then claiming UC

Ishir has been working for many years with earned income at or above the 16-hour threshold. He loses paid work on 15th January. When he claims UC a few weeks later, he is awarded it from 26th February. So his assessment periods begin on the 26th of each month.

Ishir's grace period (para 9.61) begins on 16th January and lasts nine months until 15th October. The benefit cap applies to him from the first day of his next assessment period, which is 26th October.

Table 9.5 **The UC benefit cap: excepted groups**

(a) You have earned income equal to or above the 16-hour threshold (para 9.34).

(b) You are in a 'grace period' after your income dropped below the 16-hour threshold (paras 9.59-62).

(c) You qualify for:

- the LCWRA element in your UC (para 9.32), or
- the support component in your ESA, or
- the carer element in your UC (para 9.39).

(d) You are in receipt of:

- PIP, DLA or (in Scotland) adult or child disability payment,
- carer's allowance or guardian's allowance,
- attendance allowance or equivalent benefit (para 10.54),
- industrial injuries benefit,
- a war widow's, widower's, or surviving civil partner's pension,
- a war disablement pension,
- a payment under the Armed Forces and Reserve Forces compensation scheme, or
- a payment from a foreign government similar to any of the last three items;

or entitled to any of these, but don't receive it due to being in hospital/care home.

T9.5   UC 82, 83; NIUC 82, 83

(e) You are responsible for a child or young person who is in receipt of:

- PIP, DLA or (in Scotland) adult or child disability payment,
- carer's allowance (young persons only);

or is entitled to any of these, but doesn't receive it due to being in hospital/care home.

Note: If you are claiming UC as a couple, references to 'you' also include your partner.

Chapter 10 **Income and capital for UC**

- General rules about income and capital: see paras 10.1-6.
- Earned income and the work allowance: see paras 10.7-15.
- Employed earnings: see paras 10.16-29.
- Self-employed earnings: see paras 10.30-41.
- The minimum income floor: see paras 10.42-47.
- Unearned income: see paras 10.48-70.
- Capital: see paras 10.71-97.

General rules

10.1 This chapter explains how your income and capital are assessed for UC purposes. It describes which kinds of income and capital are counted and which are 'disregarded' (which means ignored). If you have capital over £16,000 you can't get UC: see para 10.73. Otherwise your income (including assumed income from capital) affects how much UC you get (paras 10.9 and 10.49). For the UC calculations, see paras 9.3-10.

Whose income and capital are taken into account

10.2 The assessment of your UC takes into account:

(a) your income and capital if you are a single person;

(b) your and your partner's income and capital if you are in a couple.

Your partner's income and capital are included with yours even if you are claiming UC as a single person (para 2.8). In this chapter, 'your' income and capital includes the income and capital of your partner.

10.3 When members of a polygamous marriage count as a couple or single person (paras 3.60-61), only the income and capital of that particular couple or single person are included (not the income and capital of others in the polygamous marriage).

Distinguishing capital from income

10.4 The UC regulations do not provide a definition of income or capital, but the distinction is usually straightforward. For example:

(a) capital includes savings, investments and property, but some capital is disregarded;

(b) income includes earnings, maintenance and benefits, but some income is disregarded.

The rest of this chapter gives the rules for all of these.

10.1   WRA s3, 5; UC 18(1); NIWRO 8, 10, NIUC 18(1)

10.2-3   UC 18, 22(1),(3); NIUC 18, 23(1),(3)

10.5   A particular payment you receive might be capital (e.g. an inheritance) or income (e.g. earnings). This depends on 'the true characteristics of the payment in the hands of the recipient', not what the payment is called by the person paying it: Minter v Hull City Council.

10.6   However, a payment of income can turn into capital. For example, if you receive wages, benefits etc monthly, what you have not spent by the end of the month becomes part of your capital: CH/1561/2005.

Earned income

10.7   Your earned income means your income from one or more of the following:

(a)   employment (paras 10.16-29);

(b)   self-employment (paras 10.30-41); and

(c)   any other paid work (para 10.8).

10.8   'Paid work' means work for which payment is made or expected. It includes employment, self-employment and being [paid for a one-off job. It also includes periods on annual leave and other kinds of leave such as sick leave ([2023] UKUT 21 (AAC)). It doesn't include work which is for a charitable or voluntary organisation or as a volunteer, and for which only expenses are paid or expected.

Why earned income is assessed

10.9   Your earned income is taken into account as follows:

(a)   if you qualify for a work allowance (paras 10.11-12):

■   first the work allowance is deducted from your monthly earned income,

■   then your 'maximum UC' is reduced by 55% of the remainder (paras 9.7-8);

(b)   if you don't qualify for a work allowance:

■   your maximum UC is reduced by 55% of your monthly earned income.

10.10   The UC reduction of 55% of earned income is more generous than the reduction in JSA, ESA and IS, which is 100%. This is designed to encourage people to take up employment or become self-employed or increase their earnings.

The work allowance

10.11   You qualify for a work allowance if you or your partner:

(a)   are responsible for at least one child or young person (paras 3.62-69); and/or

(b)   have limited capability for work or for work and work-related activity (para 2.43).

The UC work allowance is deducted from your monthly earned income (para 10.9). It can be described as the monthly amount you are allowed to 'keep' before your earned income affects the amount of your UC.

10.5   Minter v Hull CC 13/10/11 CA (2011) www.bailii.org/ew/cases/EWCA/Civ/2011/1155.html

10.7   UC 52; NIUC 51

10.8   UC 2 definition: 'paid work', 52(a)(iii); NIUC 2 definition: 'paid work', 51(a)(iii)

10.9   UC 22(1),(3); NIUC 23(1),(3)

10.11   UC 22(1)(b),(3); NIUC 23(1)(b),(3)

10.12   The amounts of the work allowance are in table 10.1. These apply whether you are single or in a couple. If you are in a couple they apply to your combined earnings (even if you are claiming UC as a single person: para 2.7).

Table 10.1 **The UC work allowance (2023-24)**

This table applies if you have children/young persons or have limited capability for work (paras 10.11-12).

(a) Lower rate   **£379**

- Renters in general accommodation
- Renters in temporary accommodation (table 5.3(e))
- Shared owners
- Owner occupiers with a housing costs element (para 6.5)

(b) Higher rate   **£631**

- Renters in supported accommodation (table 5.3(a)-(d))
- Owner occupiers with no housing costs element (para 6.5)
- People with no housing costs

Example: Earned income, work allowance and housing costs element

Penny is single, over 25 and has one child. Her monthly eligible rent is £400. Her monthly earned income is £1,035. Deducting her work allowance of £379 gives £656.
Maximum UC:

standard allowance	£368.74
child element (higher rate)	£315.00
housing costs element (eligible rent)	£400.00
total	£1083.74

Deduction for earned income: £656 x 55%   – £360.80

Amount of Penny's UC   £722.94

10.12   UC 22(2); NIUC 23(2)

T10.1   UC 22; UCTP 5A; SI 2023/316 art 33; NIUC 23; NIUCTP 3A; NISR 2023/43 art 33

The six-month reclaim period for earnings

10.13　　You get a six month reclaim period when:

(a) you make a claim for UC that is unsuccessful because your earnings are too high; or

(b) you are on UC and it stops because your earnings are too high.

The rules apply to both employed and self-employed earnings.

10.14　　During the reclaim period, HMRC should continue to give the DWP details of your earnings, or you should give the DWP details of your self-employed earnings; and in situation (b) above the DWP may treat you as having surplus earnings (para 10.15). Then, if your earnings reduce during the reclaim period, the DWP awards you UC without you having to make a full UC claim. But if you don't qualify for any of the six months, you can't get UC unless and until you make a full UC claim. For further details see paras 3.40-41.

Surplus earnings

10.15　　If you stop qualifying for UC because your earnings are too high, your surplus earnings are carried forward as explained in table 10.2. Surplus earnings are only carried forward when your UC stops, not when you make an unsuccessful UC claim (para 10.13). They are never carried forward if you are a recent victim of domestic violence (table 2.5(l)).

Table 10.2 **Surplus earnings**

This table explains how to assess surplus earnings during the six-month review period that follows a break in your UC because your earnings were too high.

(a) Calculate 'surplus earnings' in the first month you don't qualify for UC

- Start with your monthly earned income.
- Deduct the work allowance if you qualify for one (para 10.11).
- Deduct your 'nil UC threshold' (see below).
- Deduct an allowance of £2,500 (this may reduce to £300 in April 2024).
- Any remaining earnings count as surplus earnings.

(b) Carry forward surplus earnings to next month

- Add your surplus earnings to your earned income (if any) in the next month.
- Deduct the work allowance if you qualify for one.
- Calculate UC using the resultant amount (paras 9.4-11) to see whether you now qualify.
- If you do qualify, you are awarded UC (and you no longer have surplus earnings).
- If you don't, repeat steps (a) and (b) until the end of the six-month review period.

10.13　　C&P 32A(1); NIC&P 31A(1)

10.14　　UC 54A(2); C&P 32A(2); NIUC 54(2); NIC&P 31A(2)

10.15　　UC 54A(1),(5); NIUC 54(1),(5)

T10.2　　UC 54A; NIUC 54

(c) The nil UC threshold

- Start with your maximum UC (para 9.4).
- Deduct unearned income (if any).
- Work out how much earned income is needed, so that 55% of it exactly reduces your UC to nil.
- This amount of earned income is your nil UC threshold.

Example: Surplus earnings

Roger is on UC. He has earnings of the same amount every month plus an annual bonus. In a month with no bonus, he qualifies for UC of £123.45. In 2023 his annual bonus is £3,200 after deductions for tax and national insurance.

- He qualifies for an earnings review period (para 10.13) and this involves surplus earnings (para 10.15).
- In the first month, £224.45 of the bonus is needed to reduce his UC to nil, so £2,975.55 of his bonus is unused. Deducting the allowance of £2,500 leaves £475.55 to carry forward as surplus earnings.
- In the second month, £224.45 of the carried forward surplus earnings is needed to reduce his UC to nil, so £251.10 of his bonus is unused. Deducting the allowance of £2,500 leaves nil to carry forward as surplus earnings.
- In the third month, he has no surplus earnings, so he gets UC of £123.45.

Employed earnings

10.16   'Employed earnings' mean your earnings from employment 'under a contract of service' (an employment contract) or 'in an office' (this applies to directors of limited companies, local authority councillors, clergy and others).

Assessment

10.17   Your employed earnings in an assessment period are your total wages or salary paid in that period (para 10.18) minus amounts deducted in that period (para 10.20).

10.16   UC 52(a); NIUC 51(a)

10.17   UC 54(1); NIUC 53(1)

Amounts that are included

10.18   The following are included as your employed earnings:

(a) the amount you are paid as wages or salary;

(b) expenses paid by your employer when they are taxable (e.g. for travel between home and work);

(c) income tax and national insurance refunded by the employer through PAYE or repaid by HMRC ([2023] UKUT 21 (AAC);

(d) statutory sick, maternity, paternity, adoption and parental bereavement pay; and

(e) if you are in a trade dispute, any of the above that you would receive apart from the dispute.

Amounts that aren't included

10.19   The following aren't included as your employed earnings:

(a) earnings you are owed but haven't yet been paid;

(b) expenses paid by your employer when they are not taxable (e.g. for travel between workplaces);

(c) employee benefits (such as free use of your employer's facilities) whether you pay tax on them or not.

Amounts that are deducted

10.20   The following are deducted from your employed earnings:

(a) tax and national insurance contributions;

(b) tax-deductible pension contributions;

(c) tax-deductible donations you make under a payroll giving scheme; and

(d) a work allowance if you qualify for one (table 10.1).

Information needed about employed earnings

10.21   The DWP assesses your employed earnings (and deductions from them) using information your employer provides to HMRC using HMRC's Real Time Information system. The DWP can also:

(a) estimate your earnings if this information is likely to be unreliable, or your employer fails to provide it, or reports your earnings late ([2017] UKUT 347 (AAC));

(b) allow extra time for your employer (or you) to report your earnings in an assessment period in which they reduce;

(c) disregard your earnings in an assessment period in which you stop work – but you can't insist on the DWP doing this ([2015] UKUT 696 (AAC)).

10.18   UC 55(2)-(4),(4A),(5), 56; NIUC 55(2)-(6), 56

10.19   UC 54(1), 55(2); NIUC 53(1), 55(2)

10.20   UC 55(5); NIUC 55(6),(7)

10.21   AA 159D; UC 54, 61; NIAA 159D; NIUC 53, 62

10.22   If the arrangements in para 10.21 aren't in place for some reason, you should report your employed earnings to the DWP each month. The DWP tells you when you need to do this. If you fail to follow the reporting instructions, the DWP can make an estimate or suspend your UC (para 11.31).

The assessment period earnings belong to

10.23   The DWP takes your employed earnings into account (and any deductions) in the assessment period containing the day you receive them, or the day it receives information about them (paras 10.21-22). In each assessment period one payment is usually taken into account if you are paid monthly, but four or five payments are taken into account if you are paid weekly (paras 10.25-27).

Earnings paid for a previous period

10.24   If you receive arrears (e.g. after a pay rise) or any other earnings for work you did in the past, they are taken into account in the assessment period in which you receive them ([2021] UKUT 46 (AAC), [2018] UKUT 332 (AAC)).

Monthly earnings with a shifted pay day

10.25   If payments of your monthly earnings are shifted (e.g. to avoid a weekend or bank holiday) you may receive two payments in the same assessment period. In this case, the DWP should reallocate the shifted payment to ensure only one payment is taken into account in each of your assessment periods (ADM memo 27/20). The DWP doesn't apply the rule automatically, so you normally need to ask it to do so each time this situation arises.

Five weekly pay days in one assessment period

10.26   If you are paid weekly, some assessment periods contain four pay days, and some contain five. In a month with five pay days, this means your UC is lower or nil. If it is nil, you get a six-month earnings review period during which you continue to report your earnings until your UC starts again (para 10.14).

Two four-weekly pay days in one assessment period

10.27   If you are paid four-weekly, one assessment period each year has two pay days, and the other 11 assessment periods have one pay day. The Court of Appeal has decided that this is not irrational (R (Pantellerisco and others) v SSWP).

10.22   UC 54(2), 61(3),(4); NIUC 53(2), 62(3),(4)

10.23   UC 54(1), 61(2),(6); NIUC 53(1), 62(2),(6)

10.24   UC 54(1), 61(2)(a); NIUC 53(1), 62(2)(a)

10.25   UC 61(5); NIUC 62(5)

10.26   UC 54A; C&P 32A; NIUC 54; NIC&P 31A

10.27   R (Pantellerisco and Ors) v SSWP [2021] EWCA Civ 1454
          www.bailii.org/ew/cases/EWCA/Civ/2021/1454.html

Paid less than the going rate

10.28   If you work for less than the going rate for local comparable services or for nothing, you are counted as having earnings equal to the going rate. But this rule doesn't apply when the work is:

(a)   for someone who doesn't have the means to pay; or

(b)   for a charitable or voluntary organisation and it reasonable to provide the services cheaper or free; or

(c)   done in a government training programme.

This rule applies whether you are employed or self-employed, but is less likely to be used if you are self-employed because of the minimum income floor (para 10.42).

Depriving yourself of earnings

10.29   You are counted as having earnings that you have deprived yourself of. 'Depriving yourself' means you arrange to receive lower earnings in order to get UC or to get more UC, or your employer arranges this. This rule applies whether you are employed or self-employed, but is less likely to be used if you are self-employed because of the minimum income floor (para 10.42).

Self-employed earnings

10.30   'Self-employed earnings' (or 'business income') mean earnings from any kind of 'trade, profession or vocation' where you aren't employed by someone else, whether you are a sole trader or in a partnership.

Assessment

10.31   Your self-employed earnings in an assessment period are your total business receipts in that period (para 10.32) minus your expenses and other amounts deducted in that period (para 10.34). But if this is low you can be counted as having earnings equal to the minimum income floor (para 10.42).

Amounts that are included

10.32   The following are included as your self-employed earnings:

(a)   money payments (cash, credit transfers, cheques, etc);

(b)   payments in kind (this means in goods, not money);

(c)   repayments and refunds of income tax and national insurance; and

(d)   the value of assets you sell or stop using for your business (if you earlier claimed them as an expense).

10.28   UC 52(b), 60(3),(4); NIUC 51(b), 61(3),(4)

10.29   UC 52(b), 60(1),(2); NIUC 51(b), 61(1),(2)

10.30   UC 52(a)(ii), 57(1); NIUC 51(a)(ii), 57(1)

10.31   UC 57(2); NIUC 57(2)

10.32   UC 57(4); NIUC 57(3)

If you are liable for VAT, you can choose whether to include VAT in both your income and expenses, or to exclude VAT in both.

Amounts that aren't included

10.33   The following aren't included as your self-employed earnings:

(a)   income you are owed but haven't yet been paid;

(b)   loans and capital payments into your business.

Amounts that are deducted

10.34   The following are deducted from your self-employed earnings:

(a)   allowable business expenses (paras 10.35-36);

(b)   unused losses (para 10.39);

(c)   income tax and national insurance contributions you pay HMRC in respect of your business;

(d)   tax-deductible pension contributions you make in that period (unless these have already been deducted from any employed earnings you have); and

(e)   a work allowance if you qualify for one (table 10.1).

Allowable business expenses

10.35   Business expenses are allowable only if they are:

(a)   'wholly and exclusively incurred' for the purposes of your business; and

(b)   not 'incurred unreasonably' (in other words, they should be reasonably appropriate, necessary and not excessive); and

(c)   not excluded expenses (para 10.37).

Examples of allowable business expenses

10.36   Allowable business expenses include:

(a)   computer, telephone, postage, stationery and delivery costs;

(b)   transport and vehicle costs and hire and leasing charges;

(c)   materials, supplies, stock and protective clothing;

(d)   advertising and subscriptions to trade and professional bodies;

(e)   bank charges, insurance costs, and accountancy and legal fees;

(f)   staff costs and payments to subcontractors;

(g)   premises costs such as rent, rates, cleaning and fuel;

(h)   interest you pay on business loans up to £41 per month.

10.33   UC 57(5); NIUC 57(4)

10.34   UC 22(1)(b), 57(2); NIUC 57(2), 23(1)(b)

10.35   UC 58(1),(2); NIUC 59(1),(2)

Excluded expenses

10.37   The following expenses are not allowable:

(a)   expenditure on non-depreciating assets (e.g. property, shares and investment assets);

(b)   business entertainment;

(c)   money you owe but haven't yet paid.

(d)   capital repayments on loans;

(e)   interest you pay on business loans in excess of £41 per month.

Expenses for mixed purposes

10.38   If you have expenses which are partly for business and partly for private purposes, you can only claim for your business use. Table 10.3 gives the rules for use of a car, your home and business premises. In other cases (e.g. use of a phone) you need to make a calculation or estimate.

Unused losses

10.39   'Unused losses' are allowable business expenses that:

(a)   you incurred during your current UC award, during a break in your UC no longer than six months, or during a UC award prior to such a gap; and

(b)   you haven't yet claimed in your UC.

You can deduct unused loses from your self-employed earnings if you incurred them on or after 11th April 2018.

Information needed about self-employed earnings

10.40   You should report your self-employed earnings (and deductions from them) to the DWP by the end of each assessment period. The DWP tells you when to do this. The DWP can also:

(a)   estimate your earnings if you fail to provide this information, or report it late;

(b)   allow you extra time in an assessment period in which your earnings reduce;

(c)   disregard your earnings in an assessment period in which you stop work – but you can't insist on the DWP doing this ([2015] UKUT 696 (AAC)).

If you fail to follow the reporting instructions, the DWP can make an estimate or suspend your UC (para 11.31).

The assessment period earnings belong to

10.41   The DWP takes your self-employed earnings into account (and any deductions) in the assessment period containing the day you report them.

10.37   UC 58(3),(3A); NIUC 59(3),(4)

10.38   UC 58(1)(b),(4), 59(1); NIUC 59(1)(b),(5), 60(1)

10.39   UC 57A; NIUC 58

10.40   UC 54, 61(1); NIUC 53, 62(1)

10.41   UC 54(1); D&A sch 1 para 22; NIUC 53(1); NID&A sch 1 para 22

Table 10.3 **Self-employed mixed expenses**

If you use a car for your business you can only claim the flat rate allowance in (a) as a business expense; you can't claim any actual expenses for buying or using it. Otherwise, (a) (for other types of vehicle) and (b) and (c) are options; you can choose to use them or can make a calculation of actual business use. All amounts are monthly.

(a) Allowance for business use of a motor vehicle

If you use a motor vehicle for both business and personal purposes, the flat rate allowance for business use depends on your business mileage in the month. It is:

- for a motorcycle, 24p per mile;
- for a car, van or other motor vehicle:
    - 45p per mile for the first 833 miles, plus
    - 25p per mile after that.

(b) Allowance for business use of your home

If you use your home for business purposes, the flat rate allowance for business use depends on the number of hours you spend there on 'income-generating activities' in the month. It is:

- £10 for at least 25 (but not more than 50) hours;
- £18 for more than 50 (but not more than 100) hours;
- £26 for more than 100 hours.

(c) Adjustment for personal use of business premises

This applies to premises you mainly use for business purposes but which you (or you and anyone else) also occupy for personal use. (For example, if your business is running a care home and you live there or stay there.) The flat rate amount is deducted from the total allowable expenses on the premises in the month. It is:

- £350 if one person (you) occupies the premises;
- £500 if two people (including you) do so;
- £650 if three or more people (including you) do so.

The minimum income floor

10.42   This section only applies to people who are self-employed. It explains when you are counted as having earnings equal to the minimum income floor, and how start-up periods work. The High Court has held that the rules about this are not unlawful (Parkin v SSWP).

10.42   R (Parkin) v SSWP [2019] EWHC 2356 (Admin)
            www.bailii.org/ew/cases/EWHC/Admin/2019/2356.html

T10.3   UC 53(1), 59(2)-(4); NIUC 52(1), 60(2)-(4)

Example: Assessing self-employed earnings

Lesley is a self-employed plumber who provides the following information for a particular month. She used her van wholly for business purposes and all her expenses are allowable. So her self-employed earnings are as shown below.

Income received		£2,492
Use of van	£314	
Buying in stock for use in trade	£170	
Payment to sub-contractor	£80	
Telephone, postage, stationery	£76	
Advertising, subscriptions	£42	
Use of home (table 10.3(b))	£18	
Tax/NI paid to HMRC	£68	
Total allowable expenses	£768	
Self-employed earnings		£1,724

Who does the minimum income floor apply to

10.43   The minimum income floor applies if:

(a) you are in 'gainful self-employment' – this means your business is your main employment and is 'organised, developed, regular and carried on in the expectation of profit';

(b) you are required to carry out all the work-related activities in para 2.38;

(c) you are not in a UC start-up period (paras 10.46-47); and

(d) you are not in the first 12 months since you transferred to UC as part of voluntary, natural or managed migration (chapter 4).

How the minimum income floor works

10.44   The minimum income floor works as follows:

(a) if you are a self-employed single person and your monthly earnings are below your minimum income floor (para 10.45), you are counted as having earnings equal to your minimum income floor; or

(b) if you are in a couple, one or both of you are self-employed, and your combined monthly earnings are below your combined minimum income floors, you are counted as having earnings equal to your combined minimum income floors.

In each case, 'monthly earnings' mean earnings from all sources from this and any other employment or self-employment (after deductions for tax and national insurance).

10.43   UC 62(1),(5), 63(1)(a); NIUC 63(1),(6), 64(1)(a)

10.44   UC 62(2),(3); NIUC 63(2),(3)

Amount of the minimum income floor

10.45   Each single person and each partner in a couple has their own minimum income floor. It equals what you would earn for working 35 hours per week at your rate of the national minimum wage (table 2.6). For example, if you are aged 23 or over, it is £364.70 per week (£1,580 per month). But the DWP can agree that a lower number of hours per week (and therefore a lower minimum income floor) applies to you if you have a disability, ill health or caring responsibilities for a child or adult.

The UC start-up period

10.46   You qualify for a UC start-up period if:

(a) you are taking active steps to increase your earnings up to your minimum income floor;

(b) you have not begun a UC start-up period for your type of business at any time before; and

(c) you have not begun a UC start-up period for any other type of business within the past five years.

10.47   Your start-up period lasts for 12 months beginning with the assessment period in which the DWP agrees you are in gainful self-employment (para 10.43(a)). It is brought to an early end if you stop being in gainful self-employment or stop taking steps to increase your earnings.

Unearned income

10.48   Only certain kinds of income count as your 'unearned income'. These are summarised in table 10.4 and further details are in paras 10.51-70. All other kinds of unearned income are disregarded: for some examples see para 10.53.

Why unearned income is assessed

10.49   Your 'maximum UC' is reduced by the whole amount of your unearned income (paras 9.7-8). Unearned income can also affect the amount of SMI you get towards mortgage interest etc (para 8.19).

10.45   UC 62(2),(3), 90(2),(3); NIUC 63(2),(3), 89(2),(3)

10.46   UC 63(1),(2); NIUC 64(1),(2)

10.47   UC 63(1),(3); NIUC 64(1),(3)

10.48   UC 66; NIUC 66

10.49   UC 66(1)(m); NIUC 66(1)(m)

Converting unearned income to a monthly figure

10.50   To obtain the monthly amount of unearned income:

(a) in general cases:

- ▪ multiply weekly payments by 52 then divide by 12,
- ▪ multiply four-weekly payments by 13 then divide by 12,
- ▪ multiply three-monthly payments by four then divide by 12,
- ▪ divide annual payments by 12;

(b) in the case of fluctuating amounts, calculate over any identifiable cycle, or if there isn't one, over three months or whatever period would give a more accurate result;

(c) in assessment periods in which unearned income starts or stops, convert the result of the above on a daily basis to cover just the period it is paid for.

Retirement pension income

10.51   Retirement pension income counts in full as unearned income. This means any kind of state, occupational or personal retirement pension, including any increase for a partner (but for SPC see para 10.53). Periodic payments from the Payment Protection Fund, and foreign state retirement pension, also count in full as unearned income. See also para 10.70.

Social security benefits

10.52   Table 10.4(b) lists the social security benefits which count as unearned income. They count in full, except for amounts you don't get because of the rules about overlapping benefits.

Disregarded benefits, pensions, etc

10.53   Unearned income that is not listed in the UC regulations is disregarded in your UC assessment. Examples of disregarded benefits and similar payments are:

(a) PIP, DLA, (in Scotland) adult or child disability payment, attendance allowance and equivalent benefits (para 10.54);

(b) child benefit and guardian's allowance;

(c) HB, JSA(IB), ESA(IR), IS, SPC, CTC and WTC;

(d) war pensions;

(e) fostering and kinship care payments and local authority cash benefits;

(f) bereavement support payments;

(g) carers allowance supplement paid to a carer in Scotland;

(h) discretionary housing payments (para 6.66) and other cash benefits from your local council;

(i) fuel and cost of living payments paid by or on behalf of the government;

10.50   UC 73; NIUC 73

10.51   UC 66(1)(a),(da),(la),(2), 67; NIUC 66(1)(a),(da),(la),(2), 67

10.52   UC 66(1)(b),(c); NIUC 66(1)(b),(c)

10.53(a)-(i)   UC 66(1); NIUC 66(1); Social Security (Additional Payments) Act 2022 and 2023, s8

(j)   expenses paid to you as a member (or the carer of a member) of a service user group that relates to health, social care, social housing, social security, child support or employment training initiatives.

Statutory sick, maternity, paternity and adoption pay count as employed earnings (para 10.18).

Table 10.4 **What counts as unearned income in UC**

(a)   Retirement pension income (para 10.51)

(b)   The following social security benefits (para 10.52):
   ■   New-style JSA and ESA;
   ■   JSA(C) and ESA(C);
   ■   carer's allowance;
   ■   bereavement allowance (but not bereavement support payments);
   ■   maternity allowance;
   ■   widow's pension;
   ■   widowed mother's allowance;
   ■   widowed partner's allowance;
   ■   industrial injuries benefit;
   ■   severe disablement allowance.

(c)   Payments from a foreign government analogous to any of the above.

(d)   Maintenance from your current or former spouse or civil partner (para 10.55).

(e)   Student income (para 10.56).

(f)   Training allowances (para 10.61).

(g)   Sports Council awards (para 10.62).

(h)   Some insurance payments (para 10.64).

(i)   Income from an annuity (para 10.65).

(j)   Income from a trust (paras 10.81-82).

(k)   Assumed income from capital (para 10.74).

(l)   Capital treated as income (para 10.78).

(m) Some kinds of rental income and other taxable income (paras 10.66-68 and 10.89-90).

10.53(j)   UC 53(2), 55(3)(b); NIUC 52(2), 55(3)(b)

T10.4   UC 66(1)(a)-(m); UCTP 25; NIUC 66(1)(a)-(m); NIUCTP 26

Example: Unearned income and amount of UC

Chris and Terry are in their 30s and have one child aged 10. Chris has new-style JSA of £84.80 a week, which is £368.47 a month. Terry has maintenance of £300 a month. So their monthly unearned income is £668.47. (Child benefit is disregarded.) They have no earnings or capital, and their eligible rent is £400.

Maximum UC:

■ standard allowance	£578.82
■ child element (higher rate)	£315.00
■ housing costs element (eligible rent)	£400.00
■ total	£1,293.82
Deduction for unearned income	– £668.47
Amount of UC	£625.35

Benefits equivalent to attendance allowance

10.54   The following benefits are equivalent to attendance allowance:

(a) increases in industrial injuries benefit for constant attendance or exceptionally severe disablement;

(b) increases in a war disablement pension for attendance, constant attendance or exceptionally severe disablement;

(c) armed forces independence payments; or

(d) payments for attendance under the Personal Injuries (Civilians) scheme.

Armed forces independence payments (AFIPs) are covered separately in the law but are in practice treated the same way as attendance allowance.

Maintenance

10.55   Payments for your or your partner's maintenance (under an agreement or court order) count in full as unearned income, but only if they are paid by your current or former husband, wife or civil partner. All other maintenance (e.g. for a child) is disregarded.

Student income

10.56   If you are in full-time advanced education (para 2.16), student grants and loans count as your unearned income (paras 10.57-60 and table 10.5). If you are in non-advanced education, education maintenance allowances and all other student grants and loans are disregarded. But for training allowances see para 10.61.

10.54   UC 2 definitions: 'attendance allowance', 'war disablement pension'; NIUC 2

10.55   UC 66(1)(d); NIUC 66(1)(d)

10.56   UC 66(1)(e), 68(1),(6); NIUC 66(1)(e), 68(1),(6)

Student loans

10.57   You are counted as having income from a student loan if you receive the loan under a government scheme, or you could obtain one by taking reasonable steps to do so. The amount you are counted as receiving is:

(a)   the maximum amount of student loan you could obtain by taking reasonable steps to do so (including increases for extra weeks); but

(b)   30% of that maximum amount in the case of a postgraduate degree loan; or

(c)   nil in the case of special support loans (for students on means tested benefits).

This applies even if your actual loan has been reduced because you, your partner, your parent or anyone else is expected to contribute to it, or because you have a grant.

Student grants

10.58   You are counted as having income from a student grant if you receive any kind of educational grant or award from government or any other sources.

10.59   If you have income from both a grant and a student loan (paras 10.57-58), only the following parts of the grant (if you receive them) are counted:

(a)   amounts for the maintenance of your partner, child, young person, non-dependant or anyone other than yourself; and

(b)   amounts specified in the grant as being towards your rent payments (but only if they are rent payments which can be met by UC: table 5.2).

The rest of your grant (or all of it if you don't receive either of the above) is disregarded.

10.60   If you have income from a grant but not from a student loan (paras 10.57-58), the whole of your grant is counted except for any amounts included in it for:

(a)   tuition or examination fees;

(b)   any kind of disability you have;

(c)   term-time residential study away from your educational establishment;

(d)   maintaining a home whose costs are not included in your housing costs element and which is not your term-time address;

(e)   the maintenance of anyone not included in your or anyone else's UC award;

(f)   books and equipment;

(g)   travel expenses as a result of your attendance on the course;

(h)   childcare costs.

10.57   UC 68(2),(5),(7), 69; NIUC 68(2),(5),(7), 69

10.58   UC 68(3),(4),(7); NIUC 68(3),(4),(7)

10.59   UC 68(3), sch 1 para 2; NIUC 68(3), sch 1 para 2

10.60   UC 70; NIUC 70

Table 10.5 **The monthly amount of student income**

Your income from a student loan and/or grant (paras 10.56-60) is calculated as follows:

- it is averaged over the number of monthly assessment periods described below;
- then £110 is disregarded in each of those assessment periods.

(a) One year or shorter courses

Average student income:

- from the assessment period in which the course starts;
- to the assessment period before the one in which the course ends.

(b) Two year or longer courses with long vacations

For each year, average student income:

- from the assessment period in which:
    - the course starts (first year), or
    - the previous long vacation ends (other years);
- to the assessment period before the one in which:
    - the following long vacation starts, or
    - the course ends (final year).

(c) Two year or longer courses without long vacations

For each year, average student income:

- from the assessment period in which:
    - the course starts (first year), or
    - the year starts (other years);
- to the assessment period before the one in which:
    - the next year starts, or
    - the course ends (final year).

'Long vacation'

This means the longest vacation in any year, but if it is less than one month you do not count as having long vacations.

T10.5   UC 68(1),(7), 71; NIUC 68(1),(7), 71

Training allowances

10.61   Training allowances count as unearned income only if:

(a) they are paid under a government work programme training scheme; and

(b) they are for your living expenses (para 10.63) or are instead of UC.

Sports Council awards

10.62   Sports Council awards count as unearned income only if they are for your living expenses (para 10.63).

'Living expenses'

10.63   For the above purpose (paras 10.61-62) living expenses mean the cost of food, ordinary clothing or footwear, household fuel, rent, council tax or other housing costs, for yourself, your partner and any child or young person you are responsible for.

Insurance payments

10.64   Insurance payments count as your unearned income only if they are paid under a policy you took out to insure yourself against losing income due to illness, accident or redundancy.

Annuities, trusts, personal injury and compensation

10.65   For the rules about income and capital relating to these, see paras 10.81-85.

Other taxable income

10.66   Other income you have counts as unearned income if it is taxable under Part 5 of the Income Tax (Trading and Other Income) Act 2005, and is not earned income.

10.67   For example, this can include royalties, copyright, patent and similar payments, unless these are part of your self-employed (or employed) earnings.

10.61   UC 66(1)(f); NIUC 66(1)(f)

10.62   UC 66(1)(g); NIUC 66(1)(g)

10.63   UC 66(2); NIUC 66(2)

10.64   UC 66(1)(h); NIUC 66(1)(h)

10.66   UC 66(1)(m); NIUC 66(1)(m)

Rent received from a lodger/sub-tenant in your home

10.68   Because income from a boarder or sub-tenant is not defined as income for UC purposes it is not taken into account as your earned or unearned income (ADM para H5112). But if you are self-employed and renting out rooms as part of your business then this income is taken into account as part of your self-employed earnings. See paras 10.89-90 if you receive rent on property other than your home.

Other unearned income

10.69   The following also count as unearned income:

(a) assumed income from capital (para 10.74);

(b) some instalments or regular payments of capital (para 10.78); and

(c) income available on application (para 10.70).

Income available on application

10.70   You are counted as having unearned income equal to any amount which:

(a) would be available to you if you applied for it; but

(b) you haven't applied for.

This rule can apply to any kind of unearned income (table 10.4) except UK social security benefits. For example, it can apply to personal or occupational pension schemes. If you are over 60 and not on PIP, the DWP can require your pension holder to provide information relevant to this.

Capital

10.71   All of your capital is taken into account unless it is disregarded. Table 10.6 lists all the kinds of disregarded capital. See paras 10.4-6 for how to distinguish capital from income.

10.72   For example your capital includes:

(a) savings (in cash or in a savings account etc);

(b) investments (shares etc);

(c) property (unless it is disregarded: table 10.6); and

(d) lump sum payments you receive (for example an inheritance).

It can also include notional capital (paras 10.91-97).

10.68   UC 66(1); NIUC 66(1)

10.71   UC 46(1); NIUC 46(1)

10.72   UC 72(1); NIUC 72(1)

Why capital is assessed

10.73   Your capital (apart from disregarded capital) is taken into account as follows:

(a) if it is more than £16,000 you are not entitled to UC; otherwise

(b) the first £6,000 is ignored;

(c) the remainder up to £16,000 is counted as providing you with an assumed amount of income (para 10.74).

Assumed income from capital

10.74   The assumed income from your capital is calculated as follows:

(a) from the total amount of your capital (apart from disregarded capital) deduct £6,000;

(b) then divide the remainder by 250;

(c) each £250 (or part of £250) in excess of the £6,000 is treated as producing a monthly income of £4.35;

(d) this gives the monthly amount of your assumed income from capital. It is counted as your unearned income (paras 10.48-49). The law calls it the 'yield' from your capital.

The kinds of capital disregarded in (a) and in para 10.73 are described throughout this chapter. They are the same for both these purposes except in relation to certain annuities and trusts (paras 10.81-82).

Example: Assumed income from capital

Valda has capital, assessed under the rules in this chapter, of £12,085.93.

- The first £6,000 is ignored, leaving £6,085.93.
- Dividing £6,085.93 by £250 (rounded up) gives 25.
- 25 x £4.35 = £108.75.
- Valda's assumed monthly income from capital is £108.75.

10.73   UC 72(1); NIUC 72(1)

10.74   UC 66(1)(k), 72; NIUC 66(1)(k), 72

Table 10.6 **Disregarded capital**

Your home and other premises

In (a) to (e) only one dwelling can be a person's home at any one time. In (a) to (c) there is no time limit.

(a) Your home.

(b) The home of a 'close relative' (para 5.38) who is over 66 or has limited capability for work or for work and work-related activity (para 2.43).

(c) The home of your partner if:

- your relationship has not ended; but

- you live apart (para 3.52), for example, one of you is in residential care.

(d) A home you intend to occupy if:

- you acquired it within the past six months*; or

- you are taking steps to obtain possession of it, and first sought legal advice about this or began proceedings within the past six months*; or

- you are carrying out essential repairs or alterations to make it fit for occupation, and began doing so within the past six months*.

(e) Your former home if you ceased to occupy it because your relationship with your partner has ended, and:

- they are a lone parent and live in it as their home (in this case there is no time limit); or

- you ceased to occupy it within the past six months*.

(f) A home or any other premises you are taking reasonable steps to dispose of, and began doing so within the past six months*.

Business assets

(g) Any assets wholly or mainly used for a business you are carrying on (para 10.32).

(h) Any assets which were wholly or mainly used for a business you ceased within the past six months* if:

- you are taking reasonable steps to dispose of them; or

- you ceased business because of 'incapacity' and reasonably expect to begin again when you recover.

Money in a life insurance, pension or funeral plan scheme

(i) The value of a life insurance policy.

(j) The value of an occupational or personal pension scheme.

(k) The value of a funeral plan contract, if its only purpose is to provide a funeral.

T10.6(a)-(p)   UC sch 10 paras 1 to 16 respectively, also para 1(2) for (a) to (e); NIUC sch 10 paras 1 to 18

T10.6(q)   UC 46(3), sch 10 para 17; NIUC 46(3), sch 10 para 17
                 Social Security (Additional Payments) Act 2022 and 2023, s8

Money held for particular purposes

(l) Money deposited with a housing association as a condition of occupying your home.

(m) Money you received within the past six months*, and which you intend to use to buy a home, if:

- it is the proceeds of the sale of your former home; or
- it is a grant made to you for the sole purpose of buying a home; or
- it was deposited with a housing association.

You should be actively seeking to meet this intention and it must be reasonably likely to be achieved ([2020] UKUT 247 (AAC)).

(n) Money you received under an insurance policy within the past six months* because of loss or damage to your home or personal possessions.

(o) Money you received within the past six months* which:

- is for making essential repairs or alterations to your home or former home: and
- was given to you (as a grant, loan, gift or otherwise) on condition that it is so used.

Benefits and other amounts

(p) A social fund payment you received within the past 12 months.

(q) A payment you received within the past 12 months, if it was:

- paid by social services to avoid taking a child into care or paid by them to a child or young person who is leaving or has left care; or
- paid by a local council to meet anyone's welfare needs relating to old age or disability (for example a community care or direct care payment) apart from any living expenses described in para 10.63; or
- a discretionary hardship payment (para 6.66) or other cash benefit from your local council; or
- a fuel or cost of living payment paid by or on behalf of the government.

(r) A payment of arrears or compensation for late payment of UC or any UK social security benefit that doesn't count as income for UC (e.g. para 10.53(a)-(c)). This disregard lasts for 12 months. It is extended until the end of your current UC award (when this is longer) if the payment:

- was £5,000, or more; and
- was made because of an official error or error of law (para 14.30); and
- was made while you were on UC, or SPC, JSA(IB), ESA(IR), IS, HB, CTC or WTC if your UC began within one month of them ending.

(s) Any payment made to you as a holder of the Victoria Cross or George Cross. There is no time limit.

(t) The additional amount (£2,500 or £3,500) awarded in the first month of bereavement support payments. This disregard lasts for 12 months.

T10.6(r)   UC sch 10 para 18; UCTP 10A, sch 2 para 7; SI 2019/1152 reg 3(8); NIUC sch 10 para 18; NIUCTP 8A, sch 2 para 7

T10.6(s)-(u) UC sch 10 paras 19-24; NIUC sch 10 paras 19-21

(u) Early years assistance, funeral expense assistance, young carer grant or winter heating assistance awarded in Scotland within the past 12 months.

(v) In Northern Ireland an ex-gratia payment made by the Secretary of State to members of families of the disappeared for up to 52 weeks from the date of the payment, or without time limit, a payment under Victims and Survivors Order 2006.

Personal possessions

(w) Your personal possessions. This means any physical assets other than land, property or business assets: R(H) 7/08.

Extending the six-month disregards

*   The DWP can extend any of the six-month disregards in this table if it is reasonable to do so in the circumstances.

Note: See paras 10.83-85 for further disregards relating to personal injury, compensation and independent living payments; and paras 4.53-56 for the transitional capital disregard.

Valuing capital

10.75   Each item of your capital is calculated as follows:

(a) start with its current market or surrender value;

(b) then disregard 10% if selling it would involve costs;

(c) then disregard any debt or charge secured on it.

Jointly held capital

10.76   If you own a capital item jointly with one or more other people, you are assumed to own it in equal shares unless you provide evidence that it should be divided in some other way.

Capital you hold for someone else

10.77   If you hold someone else's capital for them, it does not count as yours. For example, you might be looking after your child's savings for them, or someone you are caring for may have put your name on a joint bank account with them so you can deal with their money for them. It is up to you to provide evidence that the money is not yours, but you do not need to be a formally documented trustee for them ([2010] UKUT 437 (AAC)).

Instalments and regular payments

10.78   Instalments of capital count as capital, except when an instalment would take your capital over £16,000, in which case it counts as unearned income. Other regular payments count as unearned income – for example annuities (para 10.82).

T10.6(w) UC 46(2); NIUC 46(2)

T10.6(*)   UC 48(2); NIUC 48(2)

10.75   UC 49(1); NIUC 49(1)

10.76   UC 47; NIUC 47

10.78   UC 46(1)(a),(3),(4), 66(1)(l); NIUC 46(1)(a),(3), (4), 66(1)(l)

Capital held in a foreign currency

10.79 If you hold capital in a currency other than sterling, any charge or commission for converting it to sterling is disregarded from it.

Capital outside the UK

10.80 The following rules apply if you possess capital in a country outside the UK:

(a) if there is no prohibition in that country against bringing the money to the UK, its market value is the market value in that country;

(b) if there is such a prohibition, its market value is the amount it would raise if it was sold to a willing buyer in the UK.

The rules in paras 10.75-76 and 10.79 then apply.

Annuities and trusts

10.81 An annuity is an investment made with an insurance company which in return pays you a regular amount – for your retirement or for other purposes. A trust is a way of holding capital so that the trustees control it on behalf of one or more beneficiaries. The following annuities and trusts are disregarded in calculating your capital (for all UC purposes):

(a) retirement annuities (table 10.6(j));

(b) annuities and trusts that hold personal injury payments (para 10.83); and

(c) certain government funded trusts (para 10.85).

Income you receive from (a) counts as retirement pension income (para 10.51). Income you receive from (b) or (c) is disregarded (paras 10.83-85).

10.82 For all other annuities and trusts:

(a) their capital value is included when deciding whether your total capital is over £16,000 – and if it is over £16,000 you don't qualify for UC (para 10.73), but if it isn't over £16,000, steps (b) to (d) apply;

(b) payments of income you receive from the annuity or trust count as your unearned income;

(c) if you do receive payments of income, the capital value of the annuity or trust is disregarded when calculating your assumed income from capital (para 10.74);

(d) if you don't receive payments of income, the capital value of the annuity or trust is included when calculating your assumed income from capital.

10.79   UC 49(3); NIUC 49(3)

10.80   UC 49(2); NIUC 49(2)

10.81   UC 66(1)(i),(j), 67(l), 75; NIUC 66(1)(i),(j), 67(l), 75

10.82   UC 72(2); NIUC 72(2)

Personal injury payments

10.83   A personal injury payment means money which was awarded to you, or which you (or someone on your behalf) agreed to, as a consequence of a personal injury you had. Personal injury payments are disregarded in calculating your capital if they:

(a) are held in a trust (other capital in the trust deriving from them is also disregarded);

(b) are administered by a court on your behalf, or can only be used under a court's direction; or

(c) were paid to you within the past 12 months. This may allow time for them to be placed in a trust so that (a) then applies.

10.84   Personal injury payments are disregarded in calculating your unearned income if they are:

(a) income paid to you from a trust whose capital value is disregarded under para 10.83(a) or (b); or

(b) regular payments to you under an agreement or court order; or

(c) payments to you from an annuity which was purchased using a personal injury payment.

Compensation and independent living payments

10.85   Payments from government established or approved schemes and trusts are disregarded in the calculation of both your capital and your income, if the payment:

(a) compensates or supports you if you have variant Creutzfeldt-Jacob disease; or

(b) compensates or supports you after having been infected with contaminated blood products (examples include the former Macfarlane Trust, Eileen Trust, MFET Ltd and the Scottish Infected Blood Support Scheme); or

(c) compensates you because you were interned or suffered forced labour, injury, property loss or loss of a child in the Second World War; or

(d) compensates or supports you because of the terrorist attacks in London on 7th July 2005, 22nd March 2017 or 3rd June 2017 or in Manchester on 22nd May 2017; or

(e) supports you, if you have a disability, to live independently in your home (for example Independent Living Fund payments from your council or ILF Scotland); or

(f) is a Grenfell Tower or Windrush payment or a payment for historic institutional child abuse.

Also disregarded are compensation awarded as a result of the Post Office Horizon scandal, payments made by the National Emergencies Trust or Child Migrants Trust, and new style ESA special payments. If you are the parent, partner, son or daughter of a person in (a) or (b), payments from the trust or scheme to you, or passed on to you by that person (as a payment or inheritance), are disregarded in most circumstances.

10.83-84   UC 75; NIUC 75

10.85   UC 76; NIUC 76

Actual income from capital

10.86   'Actual income from capital' means:

(a)   interest (on a savings account etc);

(b)   dividends (on shares etc);

(c)   rent (on property you rent out); and

(d)   any other 'actual income derived from' your capital.

Paras 10.87-90 give the rules about this.

Income from disregarded capital

10.87   If the capital is disregarded in the assessment of UC (table 10.6), actual income you receive on it counts as your income. It is usually unearned income (para 10.66). But if you are self-employed, income you receive on your business assets is included in your self-employed earnings (para 10.32). For rent see para 10.89.

Income from counted capital

10.88   If the capital is counted in the assessment of UC (para 10.71), actual income you receive on it counts as your capital from the day it is due. For example this applies to interest you receive on (and leave in) a savings account. For rent see para 10.90.

Rent received on disregarded property

10.89   The rule in para 10.87 means that if you receive rent on a property which is disregarded (table 10.6 (b) to (f)), the rent counts as your income. Since it is the taxable amount which is taken into account (para 10.66) the expenses you incur on the property are deducted. For rent from a lodger in your home, see para 10.68.

Rent received on counted property

10.90   The rule in para 10.88 means that if you receive rent on a property which is not disregarded, the rent counts as your capital from the day it is due. But your capital goes down when you pay for expenses you incur on that property. See the example. (If you receive rent from a property business different rules apply: see paras 10.16, 10.30 and 10.95.)

10.86   UC 72(3); NIUC 72(3)

10.88   UC 72(3); NIUC 72(3)

10.89   UC 66(1)(m); NIUC 66(1)(m)

10.90   UC 72(3); NIUC 72(3)

Example: Rent received on a counted property

Leroy owns a house he does not live in. He rents the rooms there to separate tenants through an agency. The house does not fall within any of the capital disregards, and because he has a large mortgage its capital value is not over £16,000 (see para 10.75).

Leroy's income from the rent is taken into account as capital (para 10.90). Each month he receives rent of £900 from which he pays £800 for agency fees, council tax, utility bills and his mortgage. This means his capital goes up by £100 a month.

Notional capital: deprivation

10.91   You are counted as having notional capital if:

(a) you have deprived yourself of capital; and

(b) the purpose of this was to make you entitled to UC or to more UC.

In this case, the amount of your notional capital is the amount you have deprived yourself of.

Notional capital: exceptions

10.92   The rule in para 10.91 does not apply when you spend capital to:

(a) pay off or reduce any debt you owe; or

(b) buy goods or services if this is reasonable in your circumstances.

What deprivation means

10.93   In deciding whether you have deprived yourself of capital, 'the test is one of purpose', and you can only have deprived yourself if obtaining UC formed 'a positive part' of your planning: [2011] UKUT 500 (AAC). If it is clear that you did not (or could not) appreciate what you were doing, or the consequences of it, you cannot count as having deprived yourself: R(H) 1/06. For further examples of how deprivation has been interpreted, see volume 2 chapter 13. For DWP guidance see ADM paras H1795-1846.

How notional capital reduces

10.94   If you are counted as having notional capital (para 10.91), the amount reduces as follows (whether you are on UC or not):

(a) if your notional capital is more than £16,000, it reduces each month by the amount of UC you would qualify for (if any) in that month without the notional capital;

(b) if your notional capital is more than £6,000 (but not more than £16,000), it reduces each month by the assumed amount of income it produces (para 10.74).

10.91   UC 50(1); NIUC 50(1)

10.92   UC 50(2); NIUC 50(2)

10.94   UC 50(3); NIUC 50(3)

Notional capital and earnings: companies

10.95   You are counted as having notional capital and earnings from a company if:

(a) your relationship to the company is analogous to that of a sole owner or partner; and

(b) the company carries on a trade or a property business; and

(c) the company is not an intermediary or managed service company paying you taxable earnings (under Chapter 8 or 9 of Part 2 of the Income Tax (Earnings and Pensions) Act 2003).

10.96   In this case, you are counted as having notional capital equal to the value of the company or your share in it. But the value of company assets used wholly and exclusively for trade purposes is disregarded, and your actual holding in the company is also disregarded. For DWP guidance, see ADM paras H1874-82.

10.97   And you are counted as having notional earnings equal to the income of the company or your share of it. This is calculated using the rules for self-employed earnings (paras 10.30-41). If it is your main employment the rules about the minimum income floor apply, but you don't qualify for a start-up period (paras 10.42-47).

10.95   UC 77(1),(5),(6); NIUC 77(1),(5),(6)

10.96   UC 77(2),(3)(a); NIUC 77(2),(3)(a)

10.97   UC 77(3)(b),(c),(4); NIUC 77(3)(b),(c),(4)

Chapter 11 **UC changes**

- Changes of circumstances: see paras 11.1-10.
- When changes of circumstances take effect: see paras 11.11-29.
- Suspending, restoring and terminating UC: see paras 11.30-41.

Changes of circumstances

11.1　This section explains how your UC changes when there is a change in your or someone else's circumstances. It applies when:

(a) you or someone else report a change; or

(b) the DWP becomes aware of a change without it being reported.

The duty to report changes

11.2　You have a duty to report any change of circumstances which you might reasonably be expected to know could affect:

(a) your continuing entitlement to UC;

(b) the amount of UC awarded; or

(c) the payment of UC.

These are sometimes called 'relevant changes'.

11.3　This duty applies:

(a) to you if you are a single person, or in a couple but getting UC as a single person;

(b) to both of you if you are getting UC as a couple;

(c) to someone acting on your behalf (paras 3.8-10) or receiving UC on your behalf (para 12.6);

(d) to your landlord if part of your UC is paid to them (paras 12.30, 12.37 and 12.48);

(e) to a third party if part of your UC is paid to them (para 12.55).

Kinds of change you should report

11.4　The DWP should explain the kinds of change you need to tell it about. These include moving home, changes in your rent, income or capital and other changes relating to you, your benefit unit, non-dependants, or someone you are caring for.

11.1　D&A 23, sch 1 paras 21, 29; NID&A 23, sch 1 paras 21, 29

11.2　C&P 38(1),(4), D&A 36(9); NIC&P 37(1),(4), NID&A 36(9)

11.3　C&P 38(1),(4),(7),(8), 41; NIC&P 37(1),(4),(7),(8), 38

Kinds of change your landlord should report

11.5   If part of your UC is paid to your landlord, they should report changes that affect how much UC they receive, and whether UC should be paid to them. This includes changes in your rent or when you move home.

How to tell the DWP about changes

11.6   You should normally be able to tell the DWP about changes via your online account if you have one (para 3.13). If you are told not to use that method, you should be given a contact point you can telephone or write to about changes. In Great Britain you may also be able to report births and deaths by using the Tell Us Once service through the local register office or DWP Bereavement Service.

Reporting changes promptly

11.7   You should tell the DWP promptly about changes. If you delay reporting a change that increases your UC, you may get less UC than you could have done (table 11.1(b)).

Information and evidence

11.8   The DWP can ask you (or another person in para 11.3) for information and evidence about a change of circumstances. The rules are the same as when you made a claim (paras 3.19-22). If you fail to provide this the DWP could suspend payments of your UC (para 11.31).

Decisions about changes

11.9   The DWP makes a decision about:

(a)   how the change affects your UC; and

(b)   (if it does) when the change takes effect.

This is called a 'supersession' or (in a few cases) a 'revision'. These terms are explained in table 14.1, but you don't have to use them when you contact the DWP.

Notices and appeals

11.10   The DWP normally sends you a notice about its decision (para 14.6), and if you disagree you can ask for a reconsideration and appeal (paras 14.17 and 14.39). However, some changes don't automatically require a notice, mainly changes in earned income, and in these cases you can request a notice (e.g. in order to appeal: para 14.6).

11.6   C&P 2 definition: 'appropriate office', 38(5), 39, sch 2; NIC&P 2, 37(5), sch 1
          www.gov.uk/after-a-death/organisations-you-need-to-contact-and-tell-us-once

11.8   C&P 38(2),(3); D&A 33(2),(3); NIC&P 37(2),(3) NID&A 33(2),(3)

11.9   SSA 9-10; D&A sch 1 paras 20, 21, 29; NISSO 10-11; NID&A sch 1 paras 20, 21, 29

11.10   SSA 8, 10; NISSO 9, 11; D&A 7; NID&A 7

When changes of circumstances take effect

11.11   This section explains when changes in circumstances take effect (alter your UC). The general rule is that your UC changes from the first day of the assessment period in which the change of circumstances takes place, but there are exceptions for changes that are reported late (paras 11.13-15). Table 11.1 gives a summary.

11.12   There are further rules for becoming a couple or a single person (paras 3.5-6), child care charges (para 9.50), rent increases, capital, earnings, DWP benefits, capability for work, becoming terminally ill, reaching pension age, end of UC and gaps in UC (paras 11.13-29), reconsiderations (para 14.17) and changes to the law (paras 14.34-35).

Changes increasing or reducing your UC

11.13   When a change means you qualify for a new amount of UC, your UC changes from the first day of the assessment period in which the change takes place. But in the case of UC increases, you may not be paid all your arrears unless you (or someone else) report the change within the time limit (para 11.14).

Table 11.1 **When changes of circumstances take effect**

Type of change	When it takes effect
Changes increasing your UC	
(a) Reported to the DWP, or made by the DWP, within the time limit (the end of the assessment period or in some cases later: para 11.15)	The first day of the assessment period (para 3.38) in which the change takes (or took) place
(b) Reported or made outside the time limit	The first day of the assessment period in which the change is reported, or the DWP first takes action to make it (if this is earlier)
Changes reducing or ending your UC	
(c) All cases	The first day of the assessment period in which the change takes (or took) place

Note: This table applies to changes of circumstances.
For the similar rules for reconsidered decisions see table 14.2.

11.11   D&A sch 1 para 20; NID&A sch 1 para 20

11.13   D&A sch 1 para 22; UC 61; NID&A sch 1 para 22, NIUC 62

T11.1   D&A sch 1 paras 20, 21, 29; NID&A sch 1 paras 20, 21, 29

Examples: Changes of circumstances

1. Starting to pay for childcare costs

Abigail is working and getting UC. Her assessment periods begin on the 26th of each month. She starts paying a childminder to look after her son on 6th June and qualifies for more UC because she is entitled to a childcare costs element.

- ■ If she reports this to the DWP by 25th June, she is within the time limit and her UC increases from 26th May.
- ■ If she reports this between 26th June and 25th July and doesn't have special circumstances for her delay, her UC increases from 26th June.

2. An increase in capital

Barney is unemployed and getting UC. His assessment periods begin on the 26th of each month. His capital increases on 6th June and he qualifies for less UC.

- ■ Whenever he reports this to the DWP, his UC reduces from 26th May.
- ■ If the increase in his capital is so great that he no longer qualifies for UC, his UC ends on 25th May.

3. Size of accommodation needed

Desmond is getting UC and his assessment periods begin on the 21st of each month. His daughter moves out on 1st October and he qualifies for less UC because he is no longer entitled to a bedroom for her.

- ■ Whenever he reports this to the DWP, his UC reduces from 21st September.

Time limit for getting your arrears

11.14   A change is reported within the time limit if:

(a) you report it to the DWP by the end of the assessment period in which it takes place; or

(b) you report it up to 12 months later than (a), and the DWP agrees to a request from you to extend the time limit (para 11.15); or

(c) the DWP takes action to make the change by the end of the assessment period in which it takes place.

Extending the time limit

11.15   The DWP extends the time limit for reporting a change by up to 12 months (para 11.14(b)) if:

(a) there are special circumstances why you couldn't report the change earlier; and

(b) it is reasonable to allow you extra time – the longer you take the more compelling your reasons have to be.

Para 14.29 gives examples of special circumstances that are likely to be accepted.

11.14-15   D&A 36; NID&A 36

Rent increases

11.16   Chapter 6 explains how your rent and/or service charges affect your UC. If you report increases within the time limit, your UC increases from the first assessment period in which your payments change (table 11.1). If the DWP delays your increase to a later assessment period (and you didn't delay reporting the increase) you should ask for a reconsideration and (if that fails) appeal (chapter 14).

11.17   You should tell the DWP when your rent or service charges change, and the DWP normally asks you in early April each year to update your housing costs on your online account. When part of your UC is paid to your landlord, both of you have a duty to tell the DWP about changes (paras 11.4-5), though in practice the DWP expects you to do this rather than leave it to your landlord (paras 12.35-36). If you delay reporting a rent increase you could lose UC (table 11.1(b)).

Examples: Rent increases

1. Monthly rent due in advance

Clodagh is getting UC and her assessment periods begin on the 5th of each month. Her rent is due monthly in advance and her payments increase on 1st July (covering the month of 1st to 31st July).

- So long as she reports this on or before 4th July, she is within the time limit and her UC increases from 5th June.

2. Weekly rent due in arrears

Elvira is getting UC and her assessment periods begin on the 19th of each month. Her rent is due weekly in arrears and her payments increase on Saturday 24th July (covering the week of 18th to 24th July).

- So long as she reports this on or before 18th August, she is within the time limit and her UC increases from 19th July.

Changes in capital

11.18   Only changes that take your capital above a multiple of £250 (from £6,000 upwards) affect your UC (para 10.74). If this happens you need to tell the DWP, and your UC changes from the first day of the assessment period in which your capital changes (table 11.1).

Changes in earnings

11.19   If your employed earnings change, the DWP normally receives details from HMRC (paras 10.21-22). But if your self-employed earnings change, you need to tell the DWP (para 10.40). In each case your UC changes from the first day of the assessment period in which your earnings change (table 11.1).

11.20   Whenever you stop getting UC because your earnings increase, you get a six-month review period during which the DWP should award you UC if your earnings reduce again (para 10.13).

11.16   UC sch 4 paras 3, 6; D&A sch 1 paras 20, 21, 29; NID&A sch 1 paras 20, 21, 29; NIUC sch 4 paras 3, 5

11.18   D&A sch 1 paras 20, 21, 29; NID&A sch 1 paras 20, 21, 29

Changes in DWP benefits

11.21   You shouldn't need to tell the DWP (because it knows already) when your entitlement to any DWP benefit starts, stops or changes. This also applies to changes in your partner's, child's or young person's entitlement to a DWP benefit.

11.22   In these cases, your UC changes:

(a) from the first day of your assessment period in which the DWP benefit changes; or

(b) from when your UC began, if this is later.

If this means your UC increases from a date in the past, you are awarded arrears back to then. But if it means your UC reduces or ends from a date in the past, you have been overpaid back to then.

Changes in capability for work

11.23   When you start qualifying for an LCWRA element (para 9.32) your UC changes as described in table 11.1. But if this is because:

(a) the DWP has received new evidence from a health care professional etc; or

(b) the DWP has changed its mind about the need for you to be assessed (para 2.44); or

(c) you have told the DWP you or your partner are terminally ill (para 9.37);

your UC increases (to include the LCWRA element) from the first day of your assessment period in which you began to meet the LCWRA condition (or from when your UC began, if this is later). This rule means you are awarded arrears of UC back to then.

11.24   When you stop qualifying for an LCWRA or LCW element (para 9.31), your UC changes as described in table 11.1. But if you couldn't reasonably have been expected to know that you no longer qualify (or that you should report this to the DWP), your UC reduces (to remove the LCWRA/LCW element) from the first day of your assessment period in which the DWP makes its decision about this. This rule means you haven't been overpaid UC.

Reaching pension age

11.25   You can claim state pension, SPC and HB up to four months or 17 weeks earlier. If you do, they start on the exact day you (or your partner) reach 66, but your UC continue until the end of that assessment period (para 11.26) during which:

(a) your state pension is included as income in your UC (para 10.51);

(b) your UC is disregarded in your HB and SPC; and

(c) your SPC and HB are disregarded in your UC (para 10.53).

11.21-22   D&A 12, 21, sch1 para 31; NID&A 12, 21, sch 1 para 31

11.23   D&A sch 1 paras 23-25, 28, 30; NID&A sch 1 paras 23-25, 28, 30

11.24   D&A 5(2)(c), 23(2), 26(1),(3), 35(9), sch 1 para 28; NID&A 5(2)(c), 23(2), 26(1),(3), 35(9), sch 1 para 28

11.25   SI 1987/1968 regs 4E, 13D, 15; HB66+ 29(1)(j)(zi) 64(11),(12); SI 2002/1792 reg 15(1)(za)
           NISR 1987/465 regs 4D, 13D, 15; NIHB66+ 27(1)(h)(zi), 62(11),(12); NISR 2003/28 reg 15(1)(za)

11.26 If you claim SPC and/or HB in advance of reaching pension age (para 11.25) your UC continues until the end of the assessment period containing that birthday. So you usually get SPC/HB at the same time as UC for up to a month.

Bereavement run-on

11.27 The bereavement run-on delays the impact of a death on your UC. You qualify for a bereavement run-on if one of the following has died:

(a) your partner if you were claiming UC as a couple;

(b) a child or young person you were responsible for;

(c) a person you were caring for, if you qualified for the UC carer element for caring for them (para 9.39); or

(d) a non-dependant.

11.28 In these cases, your maximum UC (para 9.4) is calculated as though the person had not died during:

(a) the assessment period containing the date of the death; and

(b) the next two assessment periods.

But changes in your financial and other circumstances are taken into account in the normal way. The examples illustrate how bereavement run-on works.

Examples: Bereavement run-on

1. Death of a partner

A homeowner couple are on UC and their assessment periods start on the 13th of each month. Their maximum UC includes the LCWRA element for one of them (para 9.32).

The partner who qualifies for the LCWRA element dies on 3rd June.

■ Because of the bereavement run-on, the surviving partner continues to qualify for the LCWRA element up to and including 12th August. But the surviving partner's new financial circumstances are taken into account from 13th May.

2. Death of a non-dependant

A single person renting a housing association flat is on UC and his assessment periods begin on the last day of each month. His mother lives with him (she is his non-dependant) so he qualifies for two-bedroom accommodation in calculating his housing costs element (para 7.8) but his mother is expected to make a housing cost contribution (para 6.60). His mother dies on 3rd June.

■ Because of the bereavement run-on, he continues to qualify for two-bedroom accommodation until 31st August, and a housing cost contribution continues to be deducted until then.

11.26 UCTP 5(2)(c), 6A(3)-(5); D&A sch 1 para 26; NIUCTP 3(2)(c), 4A(3)-(5); NID&A sch 1 para 26

11.27-28 UC 37; NIUC 39

End of UC and gaps in UC

11.29   When a change means you no longer qualify for UC (para 2.1):

(a) you get no UC from the first day of the assessment period in which the change takes place; and

(b) if the change occurred in the past, you have been overpaid (chapter 13).

But if you qualify for UC again within six months, it is usually straightforward to reclaim (paras 3.42-45).

Suspending, restoring and terminating UC

11.30   This section explains how the DWP can suspend, restore or terminate your UC. The general rules about this are in paras 11.31-37, and the rules for appeals cases are in paras 11.38-41.

Suspending UC

11.31   Suspending UC means that all or part of your UC payments is stopped for the time being. The DWP has told its decision-makers that they should always take account of whether hardship will result before doing this (ADM para A4600).

11.32   The DWP can suspend all or part of your UC when:

(a) it doubts whether you meet the conditions of entitlement for UC;

(b) it is considering whether to change a decision about your UC (paras 11.1 and 14.17);

(c) it considers there may be an overpayment of UC; or

(d) you don't appear to live at your last notified address.

The DWP can do this straightaway or first ask for information or evidence (para 11.33).

Information and evidence

11.33   When the DWP requires information or evidence, it must notify you of what it requires and how long you have to provide it. It must allow you at least 14 days and can allow longer. The DWP can then suspend all or part of your UC if you don't:

(a) provide the information or evidence within the time allowed; or

(b) satisfy the DWP within that time that it doesn't exist or is impossible to obtain.

11.29   D&A sch 1 para 20; C&P 32A; UC 54A; NID&A sch 1 para 20; NIC&P 31A; UC 54

11.32   SSA 22; D&A 44(1),(2)(a); NISSO 22, NID&A 43(1),(2)(a)

11.33   SSA 22; D&A 45; NISSO 22, NID&A 44

Restoring UC

11.34   The DWP must restore payments of your UC when it is satisfied that:

(a) UC is properly payable;

(b) there are no outstanding matters to be resolved; and

(c) you have provided any information or evidence it required, or it doesn't exist or is impossible to obtain.

11.35   Restoring UC means paying the UC that was suspended. The payments should be of the same amount as before; but the rules in paras 11.11-29 apply if there has been a change of circumstances or a decision was wrong.

Terminating UC

11.36   The DWP must terminate your UC if:

(a) it suspended payments of your UC in full;

(b) it required you to provide information or evidence;

(c) more than one month has passed since it required this; and

(d) you haven't provided the information or evidence or satisfied the DWP that it doesn't exist or is impossible to obtain.

The DWP can extend the time limit of one month if this is reasonable (ADM para A4631).

11.37   Terminating UC means you don't get any more payments and your entitlement ends. The DWP can only terminate UC on the date it was suspended from ([2020] UKUT 71 (AAC)). If your UC should have stopped from an earlier date the rules in paras 11.11-29 apply. The DWP should notify you when it terminates your UC.

Suspending and restoring UC in appeals cases

11.38   The DWP can suspend all or part of your UC when an appeal is pending against:

(a) a decision of a First-tier Tribunal, Upper Tribunal or court in your own case; or

(b) a decision of an Upper Tribunal or court in another person's case, and it appears to the DWP that the outcome of the appeal could mean your UC should be changed.

11.34   D&A 46(a),(b); NID&A 45(a),(b)

11.36   SSA 23; D&A 47; NISSO 23, NID&A 46

11.38   SSA 21; D&A 44(1),(2)(b),(c); NISSO 21, NID&A 43(1),(2)(b),(c)

11.39   An appeal counts as 'pending' if:

(a) the DWP has requested a statement of reasons from the First-tier Tribunal and is waiting for this; or

(b) the DWP is waiting for a decision from the Upper Tribunal or court; or

(c) the DWP has received the statement of reasons or decision and:

- is considering whether to apply for permission to appeal, or

- has applied for permission to appeal and is waiting for a decision on this, or

- has received permission to appeal and is considering whether to appeal; or

(d) the DWP has made an appeal and it hasn't yet been decided; or

(e) you or the other person (para 11.38) have made an appeal and it hasn't yet been decided.

In cases (a) to (d) the DWP should keep you informed of its plans.

11.40   The DWP must restore payments of your UC when:

(a) it runs out of time to request a statement of reasons, apply for permission to appeal, or appeal; or

(b) it withdraws an application for permission to appeal, or an appeal; or

(c) it is refused permission to appeal and can't take any further steps to obtain it.

But if the DWP needs information or evidence, the rules in paras 11.33-37 apply.

Changing decisions about suspending, restoring or terminating UC

11.41   You can ask the DWP to reconsider a decision about suspending, restoring or terminating your UC (para 14.17). You can then appeal to a tribunal about a decision to terminate your UC or to alter it when it is restored, but not about a decision to suspend your UC or to restore it without altering it (table 14.3).

11.39   SSA 21(3); D&A 44(3)-(5); NISSO 21(3), NID&A 43(3)-(5)

11.40   D&A 46(c),(d); NID&A 45(c),(d)

Chapter 12 **UC payments**

- How and when your UC is paid: see paras 12.1-12.
- Help with budgeting and payments: see paras 12.13-18.
- Advance payments: see paras 12.19-29.
- Payments to landlords towards rent and rent arrears: see paras 12.30-54.
- Payments to third parties towards other debts: see paras 12.55-59.

Getting your UC

How UC is paid

12.1   The general rule is that your UC is paid into a bank, building society or other account. This means the account you told the DWP about (para 3.22).

12.2   If you can't use a bank or similar account, the DWP can agree to pay you through its payment exception service (ADM B1006). This allows you to collect your UC using a payment card or voucher code at any Post Office or PayPoint outlet [www].

Payment to couples

12.3   If you are a couple, your UC can be paid into an account in one name or joint names. If you can't agree about this, the DWP makes the decision.

12.4   The DWP can also change which of you it makes the payment to, or in exceptional circumstances split the payments between you, if this is in your interests (para 12.7).

Payments to an appointee or attorney

12.5   If you are unable to act, you may have an appointee, attorney or similar person acting for you (paras 3.8-11). Your UC can be paid into their account, or a joint account if you have one with them.

Payments to someone on your behalf

12.6   The DWP can pay all or part of your UC to someone on your behalf if this is necessary to protect your interests (para 12.7). For this rule, you don't have to be unable to act and they don't have to be an appointee, attorney, etc. For example, your UC could be paid to a relative or carer if they are managing your UC on your behalf. This rule is also used for rent payments to landlords (para 12.37).

12.1   C&P 46(1); NIC&P 41(1)
12.2   www.gov.uk/payment-exception-service
12.3   C&P 46(1), 47(4),(5); NIC&P 41(1), 42(4),(5)
12.4   C&P 47(6); NIC&P 42(6)
12.5   C&P 46(1), 57; NIC&P 41(1), 52
12.6   C&P 58(1); NIC&P 53(1)

'Your interests'

12.7   In this chapter, 'your interests' means:

(a)   your own interests;

(b)   your partner's interests if you are a couple (even if you are claiming UC as a single person: para 2.7);

(c)   the interests of a child or young person you or your partner are responsible for (para 3.62);

(d)   the interests of a person you get a UC carer element for (para 9.39).

When UC is paid

12.8   Your UC is paid as follows:

(a)   in England and Wales you are paid monthly unless the DWP agrees to twice-monthly payments (para 12.9);

(b)   in Scotland, once you have received your first monthly payment you can choose between monthly and twice-monthly payments thereafter (for guidance see ADM memos 26/17 and 5/18);

(c)   in Northern Ireland, you are paid twice-monthly unless you choose to be paid monthly.

Monthly payments of UC are made in arrears. They should be made within seven days after the end of the assessment period they are for, or as soon as possible after that. If you are paid twice-monthly, you get half your UC on the normal pay day and the other half 15 days later (para 12.14(a)).

12.9   The DWP can agree to pay your UC:

(a)   twice-monthly in England and Wales if you are having problems budgeting and there is risk of financial harm to you or your family;

(b)   four times a month throughout the UK in exceptional circumstances.

See para 12.14(a) for DWP guidance.

Payment of arrears

12.10   You are due arrears of UC when the DWP has paid you too little in the past as a result of an official or other error (tables 11.1 and 14.2). The DWP pays these arrears in instalments if:

(a)   you agree to this, or in the case of a joint claim couple, you both agree; or

(b)   the DWP considers it is necessary for protecting your interests, or in a couple, either of your interests.

Otherwise the DWP pays the arrears in a lump sum. Whichever way the arrears are paid, they are disregarded as capital for at least 12 months (table 10.6(r)).

12.7   C&P 47(6), 58(1); NIC&P 42(6), 53(1)

12.8(a)   C&P 45, 47(1),(2); NIC&P 40, 42(1),(2)

12.8(b)   SSI 2017/227

12.8(c)   NIC&P 42(1)

12.10   UC 47(6A); NIUC 42(6A)

Payments if you die

12.11   If you die, the DWP can pay or distribute your UC to your personal representatives, legatees, next of kin or creditors. If the person is under 16, the DWP makes the payment to someone over 16 who will use it for their well-being. A written application for these payments has to be made within 12 months after your death, or later if the DWP agrees.

Payments due more than a year ago

12.12   You lose the right to any payment of UC that you haven't received within 12 months after it became due. This rule has been confirmed (CDLA/2807/2003), but the period can be extended if you have continuous good cause from a date within the 12 months to when you write requesting the payment (R(S) 2/63).

Help with budgeting and payments

12.13   Monthly UC payments need to be budgeted in the same way as monthly wages from employment. Not everyone finds this easy, and the DWP offers help with budgeting and payments (paras 12.15-17) either when you claim UC or during your UC award. If the DWP doesn't offer this you can request it, or someone on your behalf (paras 3.8-11) or your landlord can (paras 12.34-36).

How UC is paid

12.14   DWP guidance on budgeting and payment includes:

(a) *UC operational guidance*: *Money guidance and alternative payment arrangements* (OG file 095);

(b) *Guidance: Alternative Payment Arrangements* [www].

For other guidance to landlords see para 12.31.

Budgeting support ('Help to Claim' service)

12.15   Citizens Advice and Citizens Advice Scotland are DWP partner organisations and provide help with claiming UC, money advice and alternative payment arrangements (the 'Help to Claim' telephone service) [www]. The DWP is allowed to share information with one of these partners if it is used to provide 'advice, assistance or support' to you.

12.11   C&P 56; NIC&P 51

12.12   C&P 55; NIC&P 50

12.14(a)   House of Commons, Deposited Papers, DEP2022-0860 https://tinyurl.com/DWPMoneyGuidance

12.14(b)   https://tinyurl.com/UC-APA

12.15   The Social Security (Information-sharing in relation to Welfare Services etc) Regulations 2012, No 1483, regs 2 – 'universal support initiative', 5(1)(h), 10(1)(e), 16(d), 17(3)(c) https://www.citizensadvice.org.uk/helptoclaim/

Alternative payment arrangements

12.16   The DWP can provide the following alternative payment arrangements:

(a) changing who UC is paid to if you are a couple (para 12.4);

(b) paying UC to someone on your behalf (paras 12.5-6);

(c) increasing the frequency of UC payments (para 12.9);

(d) making an advance payment when you are waiting for your UC or if you have one-off expenses (paras 12.19-29);

(e) paying part of your UC to your landlord towards rent or rent arrears (paras 12.30-54);

(f) paying part of your UC to a third party towards debts (paras 12.55-59).

If you are having current difficulties, the DWP says paying part of your UC to your landlord takes priority amongst these.

12.17   Table 12.1 lists the factors the DWP takes into account when it is considering alternative payment arrangements. The DWP should tell you when it is considering starting, changing or stopping these so that you can give your views.

Table 12.1 **Alternative payment arrangements**

The DWP takes these factors into account when it considers whether to make payments to your landlord towards your rent (para 12.37) as well as other alternative payment arrangements (para 12.16). See also paras 12.30-36.

Tier 1 factors

These indicate you have a 'highly likely/probable' need for alternative payment arrangements.

(a) you have drug, alcohol or other addiction problems, e.g. gambling.

(b) You have learning difficulties, e.g. with literacy and/or numeracy.

(c) You have severe or multiple debt problems.

(d) You are in supported or temporary accommodation.

(e) You are homeless.

(f) You are a victim of domestic violence or abuse.

(g) You have a mental health condition.

(h) You are currently in rent arrears, e.g. under threat of eviction or repossession.

(i) You are aged 16 or 17 or a care leaver.

(j) You have multiple and complex needs.

T12.1   *DWP Alternative Payment Arrangements,* Annex A, 13th May 2020 https://tinyurl.com/UC-APA

Tier 2 factors

These indicate you have a 'less likely/possible' need for alternative payment arrangements.

(k) Payments are being made from your UC to a third party, e.g. for fines, utility arrears.

(l) You are a refugee or asylum seeker.

(m) You have a history of rent arrears.

(n) You were previously homeless or in supported accommodation.

(o) You have a physical or mental disability.

(p) You have just left prison or hospital.

(q) You are recently bereaved.

(r) You have problems using English.

(s) You are ex-services.

(t) You are not in education, employment or training.

Discretionary housing payments

12.18 You may be able to get a discretionary housing payment from your local council towards your rent [www]. The council can grant these to people on UC with a housing costs element as well as those on HB. These are discretionary so you shouldn't rely on getting a payment. For further details see volume 2 chapter 23.

Advance payments

12.19 You may be able to get:

(a) a UC advance while you are waiting for a payment of your UC (paras 12.22-25);

(b) a budgeting advance if you have one-off expenses while you are on UC (paras 12.26-29).

In the law these are called 'payments on account'.

12.20 The DWP provides guidance on advances [www]. You can apply online, or call the UC helpline or speak to your work coach. You will be expected to explain why you are applying.

12.21 If the DWP agrees to pay you an advance, it must notify you that it will be repayable (paras 12.25 and 12.29), and if you are a couple it must also notify your partner. You can't appeal about an advance, but you can ask the DWP to reconsider (para 14.17).

Who can get a UC advance

12.22   You can get a UC advance:

(a)   while you are waiting for your first payment following a new claim ('new claim advance');

(b)   within one month of you migrating to UC ('benefit transfer advance'); or

(c)   following a change of circumstances that increases your UC ('change of circumstances advance').

If there is a gap between the end of your legacy benefits and the start of your UC, you can get an advance without having to show you are in need. In all other cases you have to show you are in need.

12.23   You are in need if there is serious risk of damage to your or your partner's health and safety, or that of a child or young person you are responsible for. But in practice the DWP treats you as in need for any kind of UC advance if you are unable to manage until your next scheduled payment (Operational Guidance (OG) [www].

12.24   The DWP decides the amount of a UC advance. The maximum amount for a new claim or benefit transfer is the lower of (OG file 006):

(a)   100% of your expected award (para 9.8);

(b)   your capped UC (para 9.51); or

(c)   24 × 25% of your standard allowance (para 12.25).

For changes of circumstance the maximum advance is 50% of the estimated increase in your UC (OG, file 005). Advances are paid within three working days into your bank account or on the same day if you are in immediate need.

12.25   An advance is repayable and can be recovered in the same ways as an overpayment (para 13.36). Most advances are recovered by making deductions from your ongoing UC payments. The maximum repayment period is 24 months for a new claim or six months for a change of circumstances, but in exceptional circumstances your repayments can be delayed for up to three months (new claims) or one month (change of circumstances) (OG files 005, 006).

Who can get a budgeting advance

12.26   A budgeting advance can be towards:

(a)   you or your partner getting employment or self-employment; or

(b)   'intermittent' expenses, e.g. furniture, household equipment, clothing and footwear.

The DWP says it also considers rent and removal expenses when you move home; home improvements, maintenance and security; and funeral expenses.

12.22   POA 12, 13, 14; UCTP 17; NIUCTP 17; NIPOA 12, 13, 14

12.23   https://deposited papers.parliament.uk/depositedpaper/2284726/files

12.24-25   https://tinyurl.com/AdvanceNewClaim
          https://tinyurl.com/AdvanceCoC

12.26   POA 11, 12; NIPOA 11, 12

12.27   The DWP can pay you a budgeting advance if:

(a) you are on UC; and

(b) during the past six months, you haven't earned more than £2,600 if you are a single person or £3,600 if you are a couple; and

(c) you have repaid any previous budgeting advances and are likely to repay this one; and

(d) you have been getting UC, JSA(IB), ESA(IR), IS or SPC for a continuous period of at least six months. (The DWP says it also includes HB in this list.)

But (d) doesn't apply if the advance is to help you start or stay in work (e.g. up-front childcare costs) and you can't get help from the DWP's Flexible Support Fund (FSF). The FSF provides discretionary non-repayable grants to help with work-related expenses (OG file 062). The guidance says it should always be considered before making a budgeting advance (OG file 004).

12.28   The DWP decides the amount of the budgeting advance. This can't be below £100 or above the maximum in table 12.2. The amount you can get is reduced pound for pound by any capital you have above £1,000 (excluding disregarded capital: table 10.6). If this would reduce the amount to below £100, you can't get a budgeting advance.

12.29   A budgeting advance is repayable. The DWP can recover it in the same way as an overpayment (para 13.36) and usually does this by making deductions from your future payments of UC. You have 24 months to complete the repayment, but this can be extended in exceptional circumstances.

Table 12.2 **Maximum amount of budgeting advance**

Your circumstances	Maximum amount of budgeting advance
Single and not responsible for a child or young person	£348
A couple and not responsible for a child or young person	£464
Responsible for a child or young person	£812

12.27   https://tinyurl.com/FlexibleSupport
https://tinyurl.com/Budgeting-Advance

12.28   POA 15, 16; NIPOA 15, 16

12.29   POA 17; NIPOA 17

T12.2   POA 15; NIPOA 15

Payments to landlords

12.30   If you are a renter or a shared owner, part of your UC can be paid to your landlord. This section gives general information about this, and table 12.3 gives a summary. The next sections give the detailed rules about payments towards your:

(a)   rent (paras 12.37-47); and

(b)   rent arrears (paras 12.48-54).

If your landlord has an agent to collect the rent, payments can be made to them, and in this chapter references to a 'landlord' include an agent.

Table 12.3 **Payments to a landlord**

Payments towards your rent, including service charges

These are paid calendar monthly.

(a)   In England and Wales, your UC housing costs element (or possibly more) can be paid to your landlord if this is in your interests: paras 12.43-44.

(b)   In Scotland and Northern Ireland, you can choose to have your UC housing costs element paid to your landlord: paras 12.45-47.

Payments towards rent arrears

These are paid four-weekly.

(c)   Throughout the UK, part of your UC standard allowance can be paid to your landlord if you have rent arrears: paras 12.53-54.

Note: The payments are sometimes called 'deductions' because the amount paid to your landlord is deducted from your UC. If the DWP is making both payments, the different payment intervals can cause landlords difficulties (para 12.48 and see the example towards the end of this chapter).

12.31   The DWP guidance in para 12.14 includes payments to landlords. The following are mainly for landlords:

(a)   *UC and rented housing: guide for landlords*; and

(b)   *Alternative payment arrangements*.

Requests by you or your landlord

12.32   You can ask the DWP to make payments to your landlord towards rent and/or rent arrears, or your landlord can, or the DWP can do this without your request. Payments can be made whether you have a social or a private landlord (paras 12.34-36).

12.31   https://tinyurl.com/UC-landlord-guide
          https://tinyurl.com/UC-APA

T12.3   C&P 58(1), sch 6 para 7; NIC&P 53(1), sch 5 para 7

12.32   C&P 58(1), sch 6 para 7; NIC&P 53(1), sch 5 para 7

Conditions for making landlord payments

12.33   The DWP will only make payments to your landlord if:

(a)   you or your landlord request it; and

(b)   either you have rent arrears that meet the conditions for payment under those grounds (paras 12.38, 12.48) or at least one of the factors in table 12.1 applies to you.

How you can request landlord payments

12.34   You can request payments be made to your landlord for rent and/or rent arrears through your UC journal or you can call the UC helpline (0800 328 5644) or speak to your work coach.

Requests for information and payments by a social landlord

12.35   If you rent your home from a social landlord (table 6.1) the DWP can tell them if you have made a claim for UC or (if you get UC) when your next payment is due, whether it is your first and the amount of your housing costs element (but no more). Social landlords can sign up to be a DWP 'trusted partner' [www] and most do. Being a trusted partner means the DWP accepts your landlord's notice that you meet the criteria for landlord payment (para 12.33) (on trust that they will only request it if you do). Trusted partners can use the DWP landlord portal to request information and/or payment and to verify any rent details you have given [www]. But the DWP doesn't accept rent changes notified through the portal on your behalf (para 11.17).

Requests for information and payments by other landlords

12.36   Any landlord or managing agent (including a social landlord who is not a trusted partner) can request payments using the online service tool [www]. Data protection law does not allow the DWP to share information about you with your landlord unless you are present and/or give your 'explicit consent'. But a landlord who has requested payments can call the UC helpline (para 12.34) to track their application if they can answer some basic security questions about you (see DWP landlord guide: para 12.31).

Payments to your landlord towards rent

When payments are made in England and Wales

12.37   In England and Wales, the DWP can pay part or all of your UC to your landlord towards your rent (including service charges) if this is necessary to protect your interests or those of a family member or someone you are caring for (para 12.7). The DWP calls these 'managed payment to landlord'. They are paid to your landlord (or agent: para 12.30) calendar monthly, to match the calendar monthly payment of your UC.

12.35   The Social Security (Information-sharing in relation to Welfare Services etc.) Regulations 2012, No 1483, regs 2 – 'social landlord', 5(1)(g),(h),(3A), 10(1)(e); Landlord Portal and Trusted Partner Scheme (Nov 2020) https://tinyurl.com/TrustedLL https://tinyurl.com/landlord-portal

12.36   https://directpayment.universal-credit.service.gov.uk

12.37   C&P 58(1)

Requests and disputes in England and Wales

12.38   You can request payments to your landlord or your landlord can (paras 12.32-36). The DWP says (para 12.31(a)) it is likely to make payments if:

(a)   you have at least two months' rent arrears; or

(b)   you have repeatedly underpaid your rent and have at least one month's rent arrears.

Except where your landlord is a trusted partner (para 12.35) the DWP requires evidence of your arrears. If your landlord provides this and you disagree with the amount, the DWP should give you the opportunity to dispute it (ADM D2026-28).

12.39   DWP guidance also says (ADM D2021-23) that:

(a)   payments are likely if:

- ■   you have a history of persistent misspending, and
- ■   you are threatened with eviction or repossession of your home, and
- ■   you have no other suitable means of dealing with the debt;

(b)   payments are not usually made if:

- ■   you agree to clear the debt, or
- ■   there is evidence that you're determined to do so, or
- ■   paying your landlord isn't in your interests.

When (a) applies, payments to your landlord are 'the first priority' over other alternative payment arrangements, 'in order to safeguard your home'. And if the DWP agrees to more frequent UC payments (para 12.9) or to split payments between you and your partner (para 12.4), it 'automatically' makes payments to your landlord.

12.40   If your HB was previously paid to your landlord, the DWP says payments of UC to your landlord must be considered whether or not you have rent arrears, providing [you] continue to meet the Tier 1 and Tier 2 factors in table 12.1. These factors also apply in other UC cases.

12.41   The DWP should tell you and your landlord who it decides to pay, and when it changes who it pays. The importance of this was emphasised in relation to HB in R(H) 1/08 and R(H) 2/08.

12.42   You can't appeal about whether part or all of your UC should be paid to your landlord towards your rent, or about how much the payment should be. But you can ask the DWP to reconsider (para 14.17), use the formal complaints procedure (para 14.72) and in some cases you may be able to apply for a judicial review.

Amounts in England and Wales

12.43   The DWP has discretion about how much to pay your landlord towards your rent. The amount should reflect your interests (para 12.37) or those of a family member or person you are caring for (para 12.7). For example, if your UC is reduced because of a sanction (para 2.47) and you have limited money for food and basic living needs, the amount paid to your landlord could be small or nil. Or if you have other income as well as UC, it could be high.

12.42   D&A sch 3 para 1(n); NID&A sch 3 para 1(n)

12.43-44   C&P 58(1)

12.44   In practice the DWP usually limits payments to the amount of your housing costs element (chapter 6). But the law allows 'part or all' of your UC to be paid to your landlord towards your rent (and this is different from payments towards rent arrears: paras 12.53-54). So in appropriate cases, the DWP could pay more. For example, if your rent is higher than your housing costs element (because of limitations on eligible rent, non-dependants, ineligible services, etc) the DWP could pay your landlord up to the full amount of your rent. Also, if your UC is lower than your housing costs element (because of the level of your income etc) the DWP could pay the whole of your UC to your landlord. For appeals, see paras 12.41-42.

Payments in Scotland and Northern Ireland

12.45   In Scotland, you can choose to have your UC housing costs element paid to your landlord: you don't have to give a reason.

12.46   In Northern Ireland, your UC housing costs element is always paid to your landlord unless you choose to have it paid to you.

12.47   In Scotland and Northern Ireland paras 12.37-44 apply if you have chosen to have your housing costs element paid to you, and/or to questions about whether the DWP can pay more than the housing costs element to your landlord.

Payments to your landlord towards rent arrears

When payments are made

12.48   The DWP can pay part of your UC to your landlord towards your arrears of rent (including service charges) if:

(a)   the rent arrears relate to your current home (para 5.45); and

(b)   your earned income, if you have any, isn't above the UC work allowance (para 12.50); and

(c)   either:

   ▪   you are getting a UC housing costs element on your home, or

   ▪   your home is exempt accommodation (table 5.3(a)) and you are getting HB there.

The DWP calls these 'third party payments'. Unlike other payments, these are paid to your landlord or agent (para 12.30) four-weekly, but with the monthly amount being paid in only 12 of the 13 four-week cycles that occur over the year (table 12.3 and see the example towards the end of this chapter).

12.49   The arrears can be of rent and/or service charges, whether these are eligible for UC or HB or ineligible. And this applies whether or not your rent/services are or were being met by UC or HB.

12.45   SSI 2017/227 reg 4

12.46   NIC&P 53(1)

12.48   C&P 60, sch 6 paras 2, 7; NIC&P 55, sch 5 paras 2, 7

12.49   C&P sch 6 para 7(3),(8); NIC&P sch 5 para 7(3),(8)

12.50   Payments to your landlord towards rent arrears:

(a)   can only begin if your earned income was below the UC work allowance (table 10.1), or you had no earned income, in your previous assessment period;

(b)   must stop if you had earned income above the work allowance in your previous three assessment periods.

If you are a couple, this rule applies to your combined earned income.

Requests and disputes

12.51   You can request payments to your landlord or your landlord can (paras 12.32-36), and in either case the DWP needs evidence of arrears. If your landlord provides this and you disagree with the amount, the DWP should give you the opportunity to dispute it (ADM D2026-28). The DWP should tell you and your landlord when it starts, changes or ends making payments to your landlord.

12.52   You can appeal about whether part of your UC should be paid to your landlord towards rent arrears, and about how much the payments should be.

Amounts

12.53   The DWP decides how much to pay your landlord towards rent arrears. This is based on your UC standard allowance (para 9.14) and whether any other payments to third parties are being made from your UC (paras 12.55-59).

Example: Payments to a landlord

Luke is a single tenant aged 42. He is on UC and qualifies for a standard allowance of £368.74 and a housing costs element of £800.00, totalling £1168.74.

Luke has serious rent arrears. The DWP decides to pay his landlord:

■ the housing costs element towards rent	£800.00
■ 20% of the standard allowance towards rent arrears (table 12.4)	£73.75
■ Total	£873.75

So in each assessment period:

■ Luke gets	£294.99
■ his landlord gets	£873.75
■ Total	£1168.74

But the payments are made separately on a monthly cycle for the rent (£800) and a four-weekly cycle for the rent arrears (£73.75) (paid in 12 out of 13 four-weekly cycles: para 12.48).

12.54   The amount is a percentage of your UC standard allowance:

(a)   it must be at least 10%, regardless of any other third party payments being made from your UC; and

---

12.50   C&P sch 6 para 7(6),(7); NIC&P sch 5 para 7(6),(7)

12.52   SSA 12; NISSO 13

(b) it can be up to 20% as long as the total deductions don't exceed the maximum (para 12.58).

But in Northern Ireland it is always 5%. The amounts for Great Britain are in table 12.4. The amounts are paid on a four-weekly cycle (para 12.48).

Table 12.4
Deductions: rent and service charge arrears 2023-24

Minimum deduction: 10% of UC standard allowance	Rate
Single under 25	£29.21
Single 25 or over	£36.87
Couple both under 25	£45.85
Couple one or both over 25	£57.88
Maximum deduction: 20% of UC standard allowance	**Rate**
Single under 25	£58.42
Single 25 or over	£73.75
Couple both under 25	£91.70
Couple one or both over 25	£115.76

Payments to third parties towards other debts

When payments are made

12.55   The DWP can pay part of your UC to a third party towards debts you owe them, if the debt is for:

(a) owner-occupier payments that aren't met by SMI (chapter 8), for example because they built up when you weren't on UC;

(b) fuel and/or water charges on your home;

(c) council tax and rates on your home;

(d) child maintenance;

(e) a court fine or compensation order;

(f) a refugee integration loan; and

(g) certain qualifying loans made to you by a credit union or similar mutual organisation.

The DWP calls these 'third party payments', and says they are only used when 'other avenues of recovery have been exhausted'.

12.54   C&P sch 6 paras 4, 7(5); NIC&P sch 5 paras 4, 7(5)

T12.4   C&P sch 6 para 7(5)

12.55   C&P 60, sch 6 paras 1, 3(2), 6-12; NIC&P 55, sch 5 paras 1, 6-12

12.56   The limits on your earned income are the same as for rent arrears payments (paras 12.50, 12.53-54). Requests and disputes are also dealt with in a similar way (paras 12.51-52).

Amounts

12.57   For each debt, the DWP can pay up to 5% of your UC standard allowance (para 9.14). In the case of fuel, it can also agree to pay your ongoing charges.

Maximum third party deductions

12.58   The total amount deducted from your UC towards rent arrears (para 12.48) and other third party debts (para 12.55) is limited as follows:

(a)   the DWP can't pay towards more than three debts at any one time – when necessary, priority is given to rent arrears and owner-occupier payments, then fuel and water;

(b)   DWP policy sets the maximum at 25% of your UC standard allowance except as described for rent arrears in para 12.54;

(c)   the payments from your UC must leave you with at least 1p of your UC.

These limits don't apply to sanctions (para 2.47) or the recovery of overpayments (para 13.36).

12.59   Table 12.5 gives the overall priority for all deductions that can be made from UC.

12.57-58   C&P sch 6 paras 3, 4, 5; NIC&P sch 5 paras 3, 4, 5

Table 12.5 **UC deductions: priority order**

General deductions

   (a) UC fraud penalties (para 13.58)

   (b) Sanctions (para 2.47)

   (c) UC or other DWP benefit advance (para 12.22(a),(c))

   (d) UC benefit transfer advance (para 12.22(b))

   (e) Budgeting advance (para 12.26).

Third party debts and other deductions

   (f) owner occupier service charge payments*

   (g) rent and service charges arrears at the minimum rate* (para 12.54(a))

   (h) fuel*

   (i) council tax/domestic rates arrears*

   (j) fines and compensation orders (minimum rate)

   (k) water charges*

   (l) legacy benefit advances (SF budgeting loan)

   (m) recovery of hardship payments (para 2.53)

   (n) HB and other DWP benefits administrative penalties (para 13.58)

   (o) HB, tax credits and other DWP benefits fraud overpayments

   (p) HB and other DWP benefits civil penalties

   (q) HB and other DWP benefits other overpayments

   (r) repayment of refugee integration loans*

   (s) repayment of eligible loans (credit unions etc)*

   (t) rent arrears at the higher rate (para 12.54(b))

   (u) fines and compensation orders at the higher rate.

* A maximum of three of these deductions can be made at any one time (para 12.58(a)).

T12.5   C&P sch 6 para 5; NIC&P sch 5 para 5

Chapter 13 **UC overpayments**

- ■ What is an overpayment: see paras 13.1-9.
- ■ Recoverability: see paras 13.10-14.
- ■ The amount of an overpayment: see paras 13.15-21.
- ■ Who overpayments can be recovered from: see paras 13.22-35.
- ■ Methods of recovery: see paras 13.36-51.
- ■ Fraud and penalties: see paras 13.52-63.

What is an overpayment

13.1   If you are paid more UC than you are entitled to, this is an overpayment. It is also an overpayment if more UC is paid for you to someone else (e.g. your landlord) than you were entitled to. DWP guidance is in the Benefits overpayment recovery guide (BORG) [www].

13.2   Overpayments usually arise when a decision about your UC was wrong due to:

(a) claimant error – you or your partner gave the DWP the wrong information, failed to give relevant information or were late telling the DWP about a change in your circumstances;

(b) landlord or third-party error – your landlord, employer or someone else gave the DWP the wrong information or failed to give relevant information;

(c) official error – the DWP made a mistake or was late acting on information;

(d) no-one's fault – you have received a benefit or other income for a period in the past.

13.3   Overpayments can also arise when a decision about your UC was correct but there was a payment hiccup – for example the DWP made the same payment twice.

Decisions and notices

13.4   For all UC overpayments the DWP should make the following decisions and send you a notice about them (paras 13.5-7):

(a) an entitlement decision (except for the overpayments in para 13.3); and

(b) an overpayment decision.

Entitlement notices

13.5   An entitlement notice gives the new details about your UC entitlement (para 14.6). It corrects the original wrong decision. Or if the overpayment stretches back over two or more original decisions, it should correct each one. Corrections are also called 'revisions' and 'supersessions' (table 14.1).

13.1-3   AA 71ZB(1)(a),(3),(5); NIAA 69ZB(1)(a),(3),(5)
         www.gov.uk/government/publications/benefit-overpayment-recovery-staff-guide

13.6   The DWP advises that the entitlement decision should clearly revise or supersede the original decision, or each of the original decisions (ADM D1032-33). If there is an appeal the tribunal will expect evidence of this (R (IS) 2/96). Failure to do this means the overpayment decision has no force or effect (ADM D1035).

Overpayment notices

13.7   An overpayment notice should tell you:

  (a)   that there has been an overpayment;

  (b)   the cause of the overpayment;

  (c)   whether the overpayment is recoverable;

  (d)   who the overpayment is recoverable from;

  (e)   the overpayment period;

  (f)   the amount that is recoverable;

  (g)   how the overpayment was calculated;

  (h)   in most cases the reasons for the above.

Items (d) to (f) are listed in UC law; the other items are from DWP guidance (BORG 3.8). If an overpayment is recoverable from more than one person (para 13.27), the notice should name both and be sent to both (CH/3622/2005; R(H) 6/06).

Reconsiderations and appeals

13.8   You can ask the DWP to reconsider any matter relating to an overpayment (para 14.17), for example:

  (a)   whether you have been overpaid;

  (b)   the amount of the overpayment;

  (c)   whether the overpayment is recoverable;

  (d)   who it should be recovered from;

  (e)   the method of recovery.

13.9   You can appeal to a tribunal (para 14.39) about:

  (a)   whether you have been overpaid and/or the amount of the overpayment, so long as your appeal is based on:

     ■   the DWP's entitlement decision (para 13.5) – if you are successful this reduces the overpayment, or

     ■   the amount that can or should be deducted under the rules about diminishing notional capital or moving home (paras 13.17-19 and 13.30); or

  (b)   who an overpayment should be recovered from (para 13.22); or

  (c)   the method of recovery (para 13.36).

But you can't appeal to a tribunal about whether an overpayment is recoverable (para 13.10) or the method of recovery (para 13.36). And you can't appeal about the cause of an overpayment because this is irrelevant to the matters in (a) and (b): [2018] UKUT 332 (AAC).

13.6   AA 71ZB(3); NIAA 69ZB(3)

13.9   D&A sch 3; NID&A sch 3

Recoverability

13.10   All overpayments of UC are recoverable (so long as they have been properly decided: para 13.6). This is the case even if they were due to official error ([2018] UKUT 323 (AAC) [www]) or no-one's fault.

13.11   The DWP's policy is to recover overpayments when it can (BORG 2.2), but it has discretion to waive them (paras 13.12-14). If you request a reconsideration of the overpayment, or appeal about it, the DWP doesn't normally suspend recovery (BORG 4.6, 4.13). But if you are unable to repay an overpayment or have debt problems, you, an adviser or your local council can ask the DWP to suspend recovery temporarily under the DWP's 'Breathing Space' debt relief scheme (BORG para 5.4).

Waiving overpayments and the discretion not to recover

13.12   The High Court has recently emphasised (K v SSWP) that the DWP:

(a)   is not obliged to recover overpayments;

(b)   can waive overpayments (in other words, not recover them);

(c)   must consider a request from you or your adviser to waive an overpayment without insisting that you make your request in a particular way or use particular words;

(d)   must consider a request to waive an overpayment on any reasonable grounds;

(e)   must publish its Decision Maker's Guide to Waiver, which contains guidance to its staff about their power to waive overpayments. (At the time of writing this has not been published.)

13.13   The DWP has said it considers waiving an overpayment when recovery would be detrimental to your or your family's health or welfare, or not in the public interest (BORG para 8.3). The High Court's decision means that it must consider this in a wider range of situations.

13.14   You can ask the DWP to waive recovery using your UC journal. If your reasons are financial, you should give full details of your household income and expenditure. If they are health-related, you should say how having to repay the overpayment would affect your health and include supporting evidence from a medical practitioner or hospital.

The amount of an overpayment

13.15   The amount of an overpayment for a particular period is:

(a)   the amount that was actually paid for that period;

(b)   minus the amount you were entitled to for that period.

13.10   LP v SSWP (UC) [2018] UKUT 332 (AAC)
        www.bailii.org/uk/cases/UKUT/AAC/2018/332.html

13.11   https://tinyurl.com/DWPBORG

13.12   K v SSWP [2023] EWHC 233 (Admin)
        https://www.bailii.org/ew/cases/EWHC/Admin/2023/233.html

13.15   AA 71ZB(1); NIAA 69ZB(1); D&A 21, 35; NID&A 21, 35

13.16   The amount of an overpayment can be reduced:

(a)   when the overpayment relates to capital (para 13.17);

(b)   when there are benefits you have claimed but haven't yet been awarded (para 13.20);

(c)   when the overpayment relates to moving home (para 13.30).

But unlike the 'underlying entitlement' rules in HB (volume 2 chapter 19), it can't be reduced by the amount of any benefits you haven't actually claimed (BORG 3.25).

Diminishing capital

13.17   An overpayment is recalculated if:

(a)   it occurred because of an error about your capital (no matter who caused the error); and

(b)   the overpayment period is over three months.

13.18   At the end of the first three months of the overpayment period:

(a)   the DWP treats your capital as reduced by the amount overpaid during those three months; and

(b)   this reduced capital figure is used to calculate the overpayment after that.

At the end of each subsequent three months of the overpayment, the DWP repeats (a) and (b).

13.19   This rule reduces the overpayment in some cases. It reflects the fact that if you had received less UC (due to the capital being taken into account) you might have used some of it to meet your living and housing costs (BORG 3·30-32).

Example: Diminishing capital

Richie is getting UC of £1,000 per month based on having no income or capital. The DWP later finds he had undeclared capital of £18,000 throughout his time on UC.

His overpayment is calculated as follows:

- ■ For the first three months he doesn't qualify for UC (para 10.73). So, his overpayment is £1,000 per month. For three months this is £3,000

- ■ His capital is then treated as reduced by £3,000 to £15,000. This gives him an assumed income of £156.60 (para 10.56) which reduces his UC entitlement to £843.40 per month.

- ■ For the second three months his overpayment is (£1,000 − £843.40 =) £156.60 per month. For three months this is £469.80.

- ■ His capital is then treated as reduced by £469.80 to £14,530.20, and his UC entitlement is recalculated. This procedure is repeated at the end of each complete three months of his overpayment period.

13.17-19   OPR 7; NIOPR 7

The award of another DWP benefit

13.20   Your UC can be adjusted if:

(a) you are awarded another DWP benefit for a past period; and

(b) this reduces your entitlement to UC for that period (because the other benefit counts as income for UC purposes).

In this case, the DWP can treat part of the UC you were paid as having been for the other benefit. This rule prevents an overpayment arising.

Example: The award of another DWP benefit

Lyra is getting UC of £600 per month. Later she is awarded industrial injuries disablement benefit (IIDB) of £41.52 per week for the entire period she has been on UC, and this is taken into account as income of £179.92 per month (table 10.4 and para 10.52).

The DWP decides to treat £179.92 per month of the UC she has been paid as though it was IIDB. So, she does not get her IIDB arrears but she has not been overpaid.

Other amounts treated as overpayments

13.21   The DWP can recover the following in the same way as it recovers UC overpayments:

(a) UC hardship payments (para 2.49) and UC payments on account (para 12.25) if you are no longer on UC;

(b) penalties and court costs relating to overpayments (paras 13.52-63);

(c) overpayments of most other DWP benefits (a full list is in BORG appendix 1).

Who overpayments can be recovered from

The general rule

13.22   Unless any of the other rules in this section apply, an overpayment is recoverable from you (the claimant).

13.23   For example, this applies to overpayments relating to your income or capital, or your personal, family or household details. But for overpayments towards housing costs, rent arrears or other debts, see paras 13.28-35.

Couples

13.24   When you are claiming UC as a couple (para 2.4) and an overpayment was paid to one or both of you, it is recoverable from you or your partner. If you separate, the DWP says the amount you owe is split equally between you (BORG para 2.22).

13.20   AA 71ZF; NIAA 69ZF; OPR 6; NIOPR 6

13.21   AA 71ZG, 71ZH; NIAA 69ZG, 69ZH; OPR 3; NIOPR 3

13.22   AA 71ZB(2), OPR 4; NIAA 69ZB(2), NIOPR 4

13.24   AA 71ZB(6); NIAA 69ZB(6)

Appointees, attorneys etc

13.25   When an overpayment was paid to an appointee, attorney or someone else on your behalf (paras 12.5-6) it is recoverable from you or them.

Landlords and agents

13.26   The rules about recovering overpayments from landlords are in paras 13.28-35 and table 13.1. In this chapter, we use 'landlord' to mean either your landlord or your landlord's agent – whichever of them collects your rent.

Overpayments recoverable from more than one person

13.27   When an overpayment is recoverable from more than one person (e.g. you or your landlord in paras 13.29 and 13.33), the DWP can choose which of them to recover from. Changes in their circumstances or the relationship between them may alter the action taken to recover it (BORG 2.22).

Overpayments towards housing costs

13.28   The following rules (paras 13.29-33) are about overpayments of amounts the DWP pays you or your landlord towards your rent (para 12.37). They apply to overpaid rent payments and the DWP treats them as applying to overpaid service charge payments (para 6.23).

Housing costs overpaid due to a move

13.29   An overpayment of UC for housing costs that results from you moving home is recoverable:

(a) from you if it was paid to you (not from your landlord);

(b) from you or your landlord if it was paid to your landlord.

13.30   However, if the housing costs were payable to you on both homes, or to the same landlord on both homes, the DWP can treat the overpayment on the old home as having been correctly paid on the new home. So, an overpayment only remains if the new housing costs are lower than the old ones.

> ### Example: Moving home
>
> Lynda and Saeed are getting UC which includes a housing element of £880 per month towards their rent. The whole of this £880 is paid to their landlord. They move to a cheaper home rented from the same landlord and their housing element is now £800 per month. The DWP delays acting on this.
>
> The DWP decides to treat what they were paid for their old home as having been paid for their new home (para 13.30). This means they have only been overpaid £80 per month. The DWP can recover this from them or their landlord.

13.25   OPR 4(2),(3); NIOPR 4(2),(3)

13.26   OPR 4(3); NIOPR 4(3)

13.28   OPR 2(1) def of 'housing costs', 4(4); NIOPR 2(1), 4(4)

13.29   OPR 4(5); NIOPR 4(5)

13.30   OPR 9; NIOPR 9

Housing costs overpaid due to misrepresentation

13.31   An overpayment of UC for housing costs that was caused by misrepresentation (other than one resulting from a move) is recoverable:

(a) from you if you caused the overpayment (not from your landlord, even if it was paid to them);

(b) from your landlord if they caused the overpayment (not from you, even if it was paid to you).

13.32   A person has 'caused' an overpayment if it occurred because they misrepresented or failed to disclose a material fact (whether fraudulently or not). The DWP gives extensive advice on this (ADM D1133 onwards) and says that a landlord should only be regarded as having caused an overpayment if they had a legal duty to disclose a fact in question (ADM D1170).

Housing costs overpaid for other reasons

13.33   Any other overpayment of UC for housing costs is recoverable:

(a) from you if it was paid to you (not from your landlord);

(b) from you or your landlord if it was paid to them. But if your landlord was paid more than your housing costs, the excess is recoverable only from them.

Overpayments towards rent arrears and other debts

13.34   This rule applies to overpayments of amounts the DWP pays:

(a) your landlord towards rent arrears (para 12.48); or

(b) a third party towards other debts (para 12.55).

13.35   In this case, an overpayment is recoverable from you (not from the landlord or third party). But if the landlord or third party was paid more than the amount calculated in paras 12.54 and/or 12.58, the excess is recoverable from them.

Methods of recovery

13.36   The DWP can recover overpaid UC by any lawful method, but usually uses one of the methods in this section. Table 13.1 summarises the methods for overpayments that are recoverable from you (see (a) to (e)) or from your landlord (see (f)-(i)), and how they affect your rent or rent arrears.

Deductions from your UC when it is payable to you

13.37   The DWP can make deductions from UC that is payable to you:

(a) when an overpayment is recoverable from you;

(b) but not when an overpayment is recoverable from your landlord.

13.31-32   OPR 4(6); NIOPR 4(6)

13.33   OPR 4(7)-(8); NIOPR 4(7)-(8)

13.34-35   OPR 4(2); NIOPR 4(2)

13.36   AA 71ZB(7); NIAA 69ZB(7)

13.37-39   AA 71ZC(1),(2)(b), 71ZF; NIAA s 69ZC(1),(2)(b), 69ZF; OPR 10, 11; NIOPR 10, 11

Table 13.1 **Overpaid UC: recovery methods and rent arrears**

Overpayments that are recoverable from you

Recovery methods

  (a) Deductions from your UC when it is payable to you (para 13.37)

  (b) Deductions from your UC when it is is payable to your landlord (para 13.40)

  (c) Deductions from your other benefits (para 13.43)

  (d) Deductions from your earnings (para 13.44)

  (e) Sending you a bill, making payment arrangements and court action (para 13.49)

Effect on your rent or rent arrears

■   Method (b) creates rent arrears (if you don't pay the shortfall in your rent)

■   Methods (a) and (c) to (e) don't create rent arrears

Overpayments that are recoverable from your landlord

Recovery methods

  (f) Deductions from your UC when it is payable to your landlord (para 13.40)

  (g) Deductions from another (blameless) tenant's UC that is payable to your landlord (para 13.47)

  (h) Deductions from your landlord's own UC or other benefits (para 13.48)

  (i) Sending your landlord a bill, making payment arrangements and court action (para 13.49)

Effect on your rent or rent arrears

■   Method (f) creates rent arrears (if you don't pay the shortfall in your rent) unless your landlord has committed an offence (para 13.42)

■   Methods (g) to (i) don't create rent arrears unless your tenancy agreement expressly allows recovered overpayments to be charged as additional rent

Note

■   In this table a landlord includes an agent (para 13.26).

13.38   When an overpayment is recoverable from you the DWP:

  (a) can make limited deductions (para 13.39) from current payments of UC, including payments that were suspended and then restored (para 11.40);

  (b) doesn't make deductions from arrears of UC when these are 'for a specific reason and are earmarked for a specific purpose or expenditure' (BORG para 5.50) such as rent or childcare costs;

  (c) can make unlimited deductions from other arrears of UC (up to the whole amount).

13.39   Deductions from current payments of your UC:

(a) must not exceed the maximum rate in table 13.2;

(b) can be lower if the maximum rate would cause your family hardship;

(c) must not reduce your UC to below 1p.

Table 13.2 **Recovery of overpayments: maximum deductions from UC (2023-24)**

(a) Fraud cases and earned income cases: 25% of UC standard allowance
(cases in paras 13.52-63 and cases in which your UC was reduced for earned income, para 9.8(b))

▪ single person under 25	£73.03
▪ single person aged 25 or over	£92.19
▪ couple both under 25	£114.63
▪ couple at least one aged 25 or over	£144.71

(b) All other cases: 15% of UC standard allowance

▪ single person under 25	£43.82
▪ single person aged 25 or over	£55.31
▪ couple both under 25	£68.78
▪ couple at least one aged 25 or over	£86.82

Notes

▪ For fraud cases in (a), the law permits the DWP to recover up to 40% of the UC standard allowance, but the DWP policy is to recover only 25% (BORG 5·19-21).

▪ 'Single person' here includes a couple claiming as a single person (para 2.7).

▪ The DWP must consider your personal circumstances rather than automatically deducting the maximum figures (R (Blundell and Others) v SSWP).

▪ The 25% maximum also applies to recovery of advance payments (paras 12.25, 12.29).

Deductions from your UC when it is payable to your landlord

13.40   The DWP can make deductions from the part of your UC that is payable to your landlord:

(a) when an overpayment is recoverable from you; or

(b) when an overpayment is recoverable from your landlord.

In these cases, the DWP can make unlimited deductions (up to the whole amount).

T13.2   OPR 11(2)-(4); NIOPR 11(2)-(4)
         R (Blundell and Others) v SSWP [2021] EWHC 608 (Admin) www.bailii.org/ew/cases/EWHC/Admin/2021/608.html

13.40   AA 71ZC(1),(2)(b), 71ZF; NIAA s 69ZC(1),(2)(b), 69ZF; OPR 10, 11; NIOPR 10, 11

13.41   Except as described in para 13.42, the deductions leave you with more rent to pay. They put you in rent arrears if you don't make up the shortfall in your rent.

13.42   But if your landlord has been found guilty of an offence relating to the overpayment or has agreed to pay a penalty as an alternative to prosecution, the landlord:

(a) must treat you as having paid the amounts that were deducted; and

(b) can't put you into rent arrears for those amounts.

The DWP must notify both you and your landlord when this rule applies and explain (a) and (b) in each notification.

Deductions from your other benefits

13.43   When an overpayment is recoverable from you, the DWP can make deductions from any of the following benefits from you are getting:

(a) PIP, DLA, AA or (in Scotland) adult or child disability payment;

(b) JSA, ESA, SDA;

(c) retirement pension, SPC;

(d) maternity allowance, child's special allowance, guardian's allowance;

(e) widow's pension, widowed mother's allowance, widowed parent's allowance, bereavement pension;

(f) invalid care allowance;

(g) industrial injuries benefit including any amounts for constant attendance, severe disablement or reduced earnings.

Deductions from your earnings

13.44   When an overpayment is recoverable from you, the DWP can require your employer to make deductions from your earnings (without the need for a court order). This is sometimes called making a 'direct earnings attachment' (DEA). The DWP says this method of recovery is useful for people who no longer get benefits and won't come to a voluntary agreement to make payments [www].

13.45   The DWP should send a notice to both you and your employer before deductions are made. The employer should tell the DWP if they are not in fact your employer or if they think they are exempt from the deduction arrangement because they are a new business or a micro-business. This should be done within ten days of the day after the notice was sent.

13.46   Your employer calculates the amount (which can include £1.00 towards administration), informs you of the amount and pays it to the DWP. The employer must also keep records of the amounts deducted and of people for whom such deductions have been made. You must

---

13.42   AA 71ZC(3), OPR 15; NIAA 69ZC(3), NIOP 15

13.43   AA 71ZC(1), 71ZF; NIAA s69ZC(1), 69ZF; OPR 11; NIOPR 11

13.44-46   AA 71ZD; NIAA 69ZD; OPR part 6, sch 2; NIOPR part 6, sch
           DWP Direct Earnings Attachment: an employers' guide (Apr 2022) https://tinyurl.com/EarningsAttachment

tell the DWP within seven days if you leave the employment or when you become employed or re-employed. Your employer should also tell the DWP if you are no longer employed by them. It is a criminal offence to fail to make or pay deductions or to provide information. Guidance for employers is available online [www].

Deductions from a 'blameless' tenant's UC payments

13.47   When an overpayment is recoverable from your landlord, the DWP can recover it by making deductions from payments to that landlord of another tenant's UC. In this guide we call this recovery from a 'blameless' tenant because the tenant had nothing to do with the overpayment. In these cases, the blameless tenant's obligation to the landlord is treated by the law as paid off and the landlord cannot in law put the 'blameless' tenant into rent arrears because of this deduction.

Deductions from your landlord's own benefits

13.48   When an overpayment is recoverable from your landlord, the DWP can recover it from the landlord's personal entitlement to UC or to any of the benefits in para 13.43. This is in practice rare.

Recovery through the courts

13.49   UC overpayments are recoverable through the county court in England and Wales and through the sheriff court in Scotland. The DWP tries to recover court costs when there is a court judgment in its favour. It can add these to the recoverable overpayment and recover them by any method by which overpaid UC can be recovered.

Time limits on recovery

13.50   In England, Wales and Northern Ireland the DWP/DFC can't use the courts to enforce a recovery (para 13.49) more than six years from the date you were first notified of the decision (paras 14.7-8) but this does not stop the DWP/DFC from recovering the overpayment by other means (such as deductions from your future UC payments: para 13.37). In Scotland the time limit for recovery through the courts is five years from the date you were notified or 20 years by any method.

13.47   AA 71ZC(2)(c),(4); NIAA 69ZC(2)(c),(4); OPR 15; NIOPR 15

13.48   AA 71ZC(1),(2)(a); NIAA 69ZC(1),(2)(a)

13.49   AA 71ZE; NIAA 69ZE

13.50   Limitation Act 1980 s9, 38(11) (as amended by WRA 108);
        Prescription and Limitation (Scotland) Act 1973 s6, 7 sch 1 para 1(b);
        Limitation (Northern Ireland) Order 1989 arts 2(11), 6 (as amended by NIWRO 111)

Bankruptcy etc

13.51   An overpayment can't be recovered if:

(a) the DWP made the overpayment decision (para 13.7) before you were granted a bankruptcy order (unless the overpayment was due to fraud); or

(b) the overpayment was included in a debt relief order (DRO) in England and Wales or a sequestration order in Scotland.

While the order is in force and after it ends, the DWP can't recover the overpayment by any method (including by making deductions from your UC or other benefits): SSWP v Payne and Cooper; Re Nortel Companies [www].

Fraud and penalties

13.52   The DWP's Counter Fraud and Compliance Directorate in Great Britain and the DFC's single Fraud Investigation Service in Northern Ireland are responsible for investigating fraud and related offences across all social security benefits, tax credits and HB – but not CTR, which is the responsibility of local authorities. Prosecutions are conducted by the Crown Prosecution Service in England and Wales, the Procurator Fiscal in Scotland and the Public Prosecution Service in Northern Ireland but in some cases you may be offered the chance of paying a penalty rather than face prosecution (paras 13.58-63).

Fraud offences by the claimant

13.53   You (the claimant) can be prosecuted under one of the social security fraud offences if you:

(a) make a false statement; or

(b) produce, provide or supply any document or that is false in a material particular,

with the view to receiving UC (or other DWP benefit). You also commit an offence if you fail to promptly report a change of circumstances that you have a duty to notify (para 11.2) with the knowledge that it affects your award.

13.54   If you are convicted in the magistrates' court you are liable for an unlimited fine or up to three months in prison (or both), or up to six months in prison (and/or a fine) if the offence involved dishonesty. If you are convicted in the crown court for dishonestly making a false statement or failing to report a change the maximum sentence is seven years in prison (and/or a fine). You are dishonest if you knew you were not telling the truth.

13.55   If you are convicted for fraud or agree to pay a penalty (paras 13.58-61) the DWP can reduce your UC (or other benefits) for a fixed period.

13.51   SSWP v Payne & Cooper 14/12/11 UKSC [2011] UKSC 60 www.bailii.org/uk/cases/UKSC/2011/60.html
        Re Nortel Companies 24/07/13 UKSC [2013] UKSC 52 www.bailii.org/uk/cases/UKSC/2013/52.html

13.52   AA 111A, 112, 115A, 115C, 115D; NIAA 105A, 106, 109A

13.53   AA 111A, 112; NIAA 105A, 106

13.54   AA 111A(3), 112(2); NIAA 105A(3), 106(2)

13.55   The Social Security (Loss of Benefit) Regulations 2001 No 4022
        The Social Security (Loss of Benefit) Regulations (Northern Ireland) 2002 No 79

Fraud offences by the landlord

13.56 If you are a landlord/agent you can be prosecuted for fraud (paras 13.53-54) if you assist the claimant by providing false information, etc. You also commit an offence if you (the landlord/agent) receive UC on behalf of one (or more) of your tenants (paras 12.37-47) and you dishonestly (or knowingly) fail to report a change of circumstances promptly that you could reasonably be expected to know affects the claimant's entitlement to UC. You also commit this offence if you dishonestly cause the payee not to report the change (for example, if the landlord withholds relevant information from his/her agent so that the agent continues to be paid).

13.57 If the landlord is a company, the company is liable for any offence (para 13.56) committed as well as any director, manager, secretary or officer of the company who consented to the act or omission from which the offence arose. If a landlord/agent is convicted of an offence or agrees to a pay a penalty (para 13.58) the DWP may decide that it is not in the claimant's interests to pay housing costs to them, or if the claimant is on HB in supported or temporary accommodation (table 5.3) the council may stop paying HB to the landlord.

Administrative penalties

13.58 The DWP may offer you the chance to pay an 'administrative penalty' rather than face prosecution, if:

(a) a UC overpayment was caused by an 'act or omission' on your part; and

(b) there are grounds for bringing a prosecution against you for an offence relating to that overpayment.

The DWP decides whether to offer an administrative penalty and calculates the amount [www]. You do not have to agree to a penalty. You can opt for the possibility of prosecution instead.

13.59 The DWP's offer of a penalty must be in writing, explain that it is a way of avoiding prosecution, and give other information – including the fact that you can change your mind within 14 days (including the date of the agreement), and that the penalty will be repaid if you successfully challenge it by asking for a reconsideration or appeal. The DWP does not normally offer a penalty (but prosecutes instead) if an overpayment is substantial or there are other aggravating factors (such as you being in a position of trust).

13.60 The amount of the penalty is 50% of the recoverable overpayment. This is subject to a minimum of £350 and a maximum of £5,000 where your act or omission causing the overpayment occurred wholly on or after 1st April 2015. The maximum penalty where the relevant act or omission occurred before that date is £2,000. In Northern Ireland the maximum penalty is £2,000.

13.56 AA 111A(1C)-(1E), 112(1C),(1D); NIAA 105A(1C)-(1E), 106(1C),(1D)

13.57 AA 115; NIAA 109

13.58 AA 115A(1)-(1A); NIAA 109A(1)-(1A)
DWP Penalties policy: in respect of social security fraud and error (14 August 2017)
https://tinyurl.com/DWP-penalty-policy

13.59 AA 115A(5)-(6); NIAA 109A(5)-(6)

13.60 AA 115A(3)(a)-(b); art 1(3) of SI 2015/202; NIAA 109A(3)(a)-(b)

13.61   The DWP may also make an offer of a penalty where your act or omission could have resulted in an overpayment and it thinks there are grounds for bringing a prosecution for a related offence. In these cases, the penalty is the fixed amount of £350.

Civil penalties

13.62   In Great Britain the DWP may impose a civil penalty of £50 on you if you:

(a) negligently make an incorrect statement or representation or negligently give incorrect information or evidence relating to a claim or award and fail to take reasonable steps to correct the error; or

(b) without reasonable excuse, fail to provide required information or evidence relating to a claim or award or fail to tell the DWP about a relevant change of circumstance; and

(c) in any of these circumstances this results in the DWP making an overpayment; but

(d) you have not been charged with an offence or cautioned.

The DWP's staff guidance on civil penalties (and when to impose them) is set out in ADM D1271-1302 [www].

13.63   The amount of the civil penalty is added to the amount of the recoverable overpayment. If you have been successfully prosecuted for fraud or offered an administrative penalty or caution, the DWP cannot issue you with a civil penalty for the same offence.

13.61   AA 115A(3A); NIAA 109A(3A)

13.62   AA 115C-115D; SI 2012/1990; NISR 1997/514; NISR 2016/63
         DWP ADM Ch D1; https://tinyurl.com/ADM-D1

Chapter 14 **UC decisions and appeals**

- Decisions: see paras 14.1-16.
- Mandatory reconsiderations: see paras 14.17-24.
- When reconsidered decisions take effect: see paras 14.25-38.
- Appeals to a tribunal: see paras 14.39-54.
- Tribunal hearings and decisions: see paras 14.55-67.
- Further appeals and complaints: see paras 14.68-73.

Decision rights

14.1 This chapter explains the rights that go with UC decisions. The main rights are:

(a) getting the reasons for a decision;

(b) asking the DWP to reconsider;

(c) appealing to a tribunal; and

(d) making a further appeal.

The same rules apply to decisions about SMI (chapter 8), but different rules apply to CTR (chapter 18), rate rebates (paras 19.34-35, 19.56-57) and to rent officer decisions (paras 6.53-55).

Who has decision rights?

14.2 These rights belong to:

(a) you (the claimant) or either of you if you are claiming UC as a couple (para 2.5);

(b) an attorney or appointee who is acting for you (paras 3.8-10), including someone managing your UC after your death;

(c) a landlord/agent about whether UC should be paid to them towards rent arrears (para 12.48) or whether an overpayment is recoverable from them (para 13.33);

(d) a representative acting for you or for a landlord/agent (para 14.43).

Time limits

14.3 Many of the rights in this chapter have a time limit of one month from the date a decision is issued (or corrected: para 14.33). The date of issue is usually taken to mean the day the notice becomes available to view on your online account (para 3.13), or the day it is posted or handed to you. 'One month' means a calendar month counted as follows:

14.2   SSA 12(2),(4); D&A 49(a),(b),(d); NISSO 13(2),(4); NID&A 48(a),(b),(e)

14.3   D&A 3, 4; FTPR 12; UTPR 12(1),(2); C&P 3, sch 2; NID&A 3, 4; NIC&P 3, sch 1; NIDAR99 31(1), 32, 58(1)

(a) if the date of issue is 17th January, the month runs up to and includes 17th February;

(b) if the date of the issue is 31st January, the month runs up to and includes 28th February (29th February in leap years).

For appeals, this means 5pm on the last day, or if that isn't a working day, 5pm on the next working day. For reconsiderations, the DWP always accepts requests on the next day (ADM A3049). For both, up to 13 months can be allowed in special circumstances (paras 14.28, 14.48).

Decisions, notices and reasons

'Decisions' and 'determinations'

14.4   The law about UC and other benefits often distinguishes between these terms. The Upper Tribunal has described them as follows (R(IB) 6/03; [2023] UKUT 9 (AAC)):

(a) 'a decision upon the actual question whether a claimant is entitled to a particular benefit or not'; and

(b) 'a determination of any matter along the way to a decision'.

For example, a UC determination could be that you have a particular amount of income or capital; and a UC decision would then be that you are entitled to a particular amount of UC or not entitled to UC.

Decisions

14.5   The DWP makes a decision about your UC:

(a) when you claim (para 3.17);

(b) when your circumstances change (para 11.9);

(c) when your UC is overpaid (para 13.4); and

(d) when you ask for a reconsideration (para 14.22).

Decision notices

14.6   The DWP sends you a decision notice about each decision it makes. This tells you:

(a) what the decision is;

(b) the reasons for it (in most cases); and

(c) your rights to a written statement, to request a reconsideration and to appeal.

However, when your earnings (employed or self-employed) change from one assessment period to another, the DWP tells you your new entitlement to UC but doesn't have to send you a formal decision notice. You can nonetheless request a written statement, reconsideration or appeal.

14.7   Notices are normally sent to your online account but can alternatively be sent by post or given to you by telephone or in person (paras 3.13-14).

14.5   SSA 8(1)(a),(3)(aa), 9(1), 10(1); D&A 5, 8, 9, 22-24; NISSO 9(1)(a),(3)(aa), 10(1), 11(1); NID&A 5, 8-9, 22-24

14.6   SSA 8, 10, 12(6), D&A 7(1),(3), 51; NISSO 9, 11, 13(6), NID&A 7(1),(3), 51

14.7   D&A 3, 4; C&P 2 definition: 'electronic communication' 3, sch 2; NID&A 3, 4; NIC&P 2, 3, sch 1

14.8 The DWP also notifies:

(a) your partner if you are claiming UC as a couple. It does this even if the notice is about sanctions or fraud, but has said it intends to protect sensitive information about your health and similar matters;

(b) your landlord etc if it decides to pay UC to them (para 12.37). It normally does this by post, saying how much they will receive but not what your personal and financial details are.

Getting a written statement of reasons

14.9 If the reasons for a decision aren't in the decision notice, you can ask the DWP for a written statement of reasons within one month of the notice's date of issue. The DWP provides this within 14 days of your request or as soon as practicable after that. In this case, your time limit for getting arrears of UC is extended: para 14.27(b).

How decisions are made

14.10 When the DWP makes a decision about your UC or the council makes a decision about your CTR, they should:

(a) identify the facts (paras 14.11-13); and

(b) apply the law to those facts (paras 14.14-16).

Deciding the facts

14.11 The DWP/council should only take account of facts that are relevant to your UC/CTR. For example, whether you qualify, how much you qualify for, and who it should be paid to.

Balance of probability

14.12 When there is a disagreement about the facts or the facts are uncertain, the DWP/council should decide taking into account the weight of evidence each way.

Burden of proof

14.13 When there is no evidence about the facts or where the evidence is balanced equally each way, the DWP/council should decide what the evidence is based on and who has to demonstrate what. For example:

(a) when you make a claim, it is up to you to demonstrate you are entitled;

(b) when you are told an overpayment is recoverable from you, it is up to the DWP/council to demonstrate this.

14.8 SSA 12(2),(4); D&A 2 definition: 'claimant', 49(a),(b),(d); NISSO 13(2),(4); NID&A 2, 48(a),(b),(e)

14.9 D&A 5(1), 7(1),(3)(b),(4); NID&A 5(1), 7(1),(3)(b),(4)

Applying the law

14.14   The words of Acts of Parliament, regulations, orders, etc have their ordinary English meaning. But:

(a)   some words or phrases are defined in the law – for example 'child' and 'young person' (paras 3.63-64);

(b)   some law has been interpreted by Upper Tribunals and courts in case law (para 1.28) – for example deciding whether two people are a couple (paras 3.54-57);

(c)   the Supreme Court has decided that the DWP/DFC, council/NIHE or a tribunal may disapply a regulation, order, etc (but not an Act of Parliament) if it breaches the Human Rights Act 1998 (RR (AP) v SSWP (2019)).

The footnotes throughout this guide give the details of relevant law and case law.

Judgment

14.15   The law uses terms like 'reasonable' or 'special circumstances' to show that the DWP/council has to make a judgment. Examples include:

(a)   whether it is 'reasonable' for the DWP to award UC towards housing costs on two homes if you are in fear of violence (para 5.53);

(b)   whether you have 'special circumstances' for a delay in reporting a change that increases your UC (para 11.15).

Discretion

14.16   A discretion differs from a judgment in the sense that the DWP/council may choose what to do. The law usually says that they 'may' do something to show this. Examples include:

(a)   whether to pay part of your UC to your landlord (para 12.30);

(b)   what method to use to recover an overpayment of UC (para 13.36).

Mandatory reconsiderations

14.17   You (or another person in para 14.2) can ask the DWP to reconsider any UC decision it has made. We call this a 'mandatory reconsideration' (because you can't miss this stage out if you want to go on to a tribunal) or just a 'reconsideration'. In the law it is called a 'revision'.

14.18   You usually ask for a reconsideration because you think the DWP has got the facts wrong or applied the law incorrectly. Reconsiderations can be about:

14.14   RR (AP) v SSWP [2019] UKSC 52
https://www.bailii.org/uk/cases/UKSC/2019/52.html

14.18   SSA 9(1), D&A 5, 9; NISSO 10(1), D&A 5, 9

(a) whether you qualify for UC;

(b) the amount of your UC and how it is calculated;

(c) when your UC begins, changes or ends;

(d) whether you have been overpaid; or

(e) any other matter (unlike appeals there are no exceptions).

The DWP can also reconsider a decision without a request, for example because a case is being checked or there are new regulations or new case law (paras 14.34-35).

When to request a reconsideration

14.19 You can request a reconsideration at any time. But you could be worse off if you don't stick to the time limit, because you could get a substantially lower payment of arrears (table 14.2).

How to request a reconsideration

14.20 Requests for a reconsideration should normally be in writing or by telephone, and it is advisable for you to keep a copy or a written record. The DWP says [www] it accepts requests made:

(a) in its appeal form CRMR1 (in Northern Ireland form MR2 (NI)) [www];

(b) in a letter;

(c) via your online account;

(d) by telephone; or

(e) in person.

The address for letters is Freepost DWP (Universal Credit Full Service).

Information and evidence

14.21 When you request a reconsideration, you should provide any new information or evidence you have. If the DWP needs further information or evidence, it should request this, and must take it into account if you provide it within one month.

Reconsideration decisions

14.22 The DWP makes a decision about whether your UC should change, and if so, how and when. This is also called a 'revision' or a 'supersession'. These terms are explained in table 14.1, but you don't have to use them when you contact the DWP.

14.23 The law doesn't set a time limit for dealing with reconsiderations, but the DWP normally does this reasonably quickly unless they are complex.

14.19 D&A 2 definition: 'date of notification', 5(1), 6, 38(4); NID&A 2, 5(1), 6, 38(4)

14.20 D&A 6(1)-(6); NID&A 6(1)-(6)
Explanatory Memorandum to SI 2017/1015 paras 7.28-30 – www.legislation.gov.uk/uksi/2017/1015/memorandum/contents

14.21 D&A 20(2)(3), 33(2),(3); C&P 38(2),(3),(4); NID&A 20(2)(3), 33(2),(3); NIC&P 37(2),(3),(4)

14.22 SSA 9, 10; D&A 5, 8, 20(1), 22, 32, 33(1); NISSO 10, 11; NID&A 5, 8, 20(1), 22, 32, 33(1)

Reconsideration notices

14.24   The DWP sends you a decision notice telling you:

(a)   whether it has altered your UC;

(b)   if it has, what it has altered and when this takes effect; and

(c)   your rights (para 14.1).

Table 14.1 **Decisions, revisions and supersessions**

Decisions: The DWP makes decisions:

(a)   when you claim UC (chapter 3);

(b)   when you report a change of circumstances, or the DWP is aware of a change without you reporting it (para 11.1); and

(c)   when you ask for a decision to be changed because you think it is wrong, or the DWP realises it is wrong without you asking (paras 14.17-18).

The kinds of decision in (b) and (c) are also called revisions and supersessions. Asking for a decision to be changed is often called 'requesting a reconsideration'.

Revisions: A revision is a decision which alters your UC from the same date (in most cases) as the decision it is altering. Revisions are mainly used when a wrong decision is changed. If a revised decision is advantageous to you it usually has a time limit (paras 11.14-15, 14.26-29).

Supersessions: A supersession is a decision which alters your UC from a date later than the decision it is altering. Supersessions are mainly used for changes of circumstances, and sometimes when a wrong decision is changed. If a superseding decision is advantageous to you it often has a time limit (paras 11.14-15 and 14.26-29). A 'closed period supersession' is used when a change of circumstances took place in the past and it has already come to an end. It means your UC is altered, but only for that past fixed period (CH/2595/2003).

When reconsidered decisions take effect

14.25   The DWP can reconsider any decision if you request it, or it can do so on its own initiative (e.g. because it notices an error). When the DWP changes a decision it has reconsidered, the new decision takes effect (alters your UC) from the date in table 14.2.

Time limit for getting your arrears

14.26   If a wrong decision is changed so that it increases or reinstates your UC you may not be paid all your arrears unless the reconsideration was requested (or made by the DWP) within the time limit. But this rule doesn't apply if the wrong decision was due to an official error (para 14.30) – including if the DWP made an error of law (para 14.71) – or a change of circumstance where a separate but similar rule applies instead (paras 11.14-15).

14.25   SSA 10(5),(6); D&A 21, 34; NISSO 11(5),(6); NID&A 21, 34

14.27   Your request is within the time limit if:

(a)   you make it within one month of being notified (para 14.3) of the original decision; or

(b)   you ask for a written statement of reasons (para 14.9) within that month, and you make your reconsideration request within 14 days of:

- the end of that month, or
- the DWP providing the written statement (if later); or

(c)   you make your reconsideration request up to 12 months later than (a) or (b), you ask the DWP to extend the time limit, and the DWP agrees (para 14.28); or

(d)   the DWP makes the change within one month of the decision being issued.

Extending the time limit

14.28   The DWP extends the reconsideration time limit by up to 12 months (para 14.27(c)) if:

(a)   there are special circumstances why you couldn't request it earlier (para 14.29); and

(b)   it is reasonable to allow you extra time – the longer you take the more compelling your reasons need to be.

Table 14.2 **When reconsidered decisions take effect**

Type of reconsideration	When it takes effect
Decisions increasing or reinstating your UC	
(a) Reconsiderations requested or made within the time limit (one month, or in some cases up to 13 months: para 14.27)	The date the original decision took effect (or should have)
(b) All cases correcting an official error at any time (para 14.30)	The date the original decision took effect (or should have)
(c) Other cases	The first day of the assessment period in which the reconsideration is requested, or the DWP first takes action to make it (if this is earlier)
Decisions reducing or ending your UC	
(d) All cases	The date the original decision took effect (or should have)

Notes:

- This table applies to wrongly made decisions; for the equivalent rule for a change of circumstance see table 11.1.
- For rent officer redeterminations, see para 6.53.
- In the law, (a), (b) and (d) are revisions and (c) is a supersession (table 14.1).

14.27   D&A 2 – 'date of notification', 5(1), 6, 38(4); NID&A 2, 5(1), 6, 38(4)

14.28   D&A 6(1)-(6); NID&A 6(1)-(6); Explanatory Memorandum to SI 2017/1015 paras 7.28-30

T14.2   SSA 10(5); D&A 21, 24, 35(2),(4); NISSO 11(5); NID&A 21, 24, 35(2),(4)

14.29   The law doesn't define 'special circumstances'. The DWP interprets this broadly, and usually accepts delays unless there is an exceptional reason not to. The following are some examples of what can be included (ADM A3055):

   (a)   a death or serious illness;

   (b)   not being in the UK;

   (c)   normal postal services being adversely affected;

   (d)   learning or language difficulties;

   (e)   difficulty getting evidence or information to support the application; and

   (f)   ignorance or misunderstanding of the law or time limits.

Official errors

14.30   In the case of official errors (paras 14.31-32), there is no time limit for changes. So your reconsideration request can be made at any time, and (if you are successful) you get arrears of UC back to the date of the original decision took effect or should have taken effect (table 14.2(b)).

Examples: When reconsiderations take effect

1. Capital that should be disregarded

Eva has been getting UC since 9th January and her assessment periods begin on the 9th of each month. She realises that she forgot to tell the DWP that some of her capital comes from an insurance payment in December for flood damage to her home. She asks the DWP to increase her UC and the DWP agrees (table 14.2).

   ■   If she requests the change on (or before) 8th February, she is within the time limit and her UC increases from 9th January.

   ■   If she requests the change on 15th February and doesn't have special circumstances for her delay, her UC increases from 9th February.

2. Undeclared earnings

Frank has been getting UC since 9th January and his assessment periods begin on the 9th of each month. The DWP discovers he has been working since before he claimed UC and reduces his UC (table 14.2).

   ■   Whenever the DWP makes the change, his UC decreases from 9th January.

3. An official error

Gertrude claimed UC on 9th January. She is a full-time student with a low income. Although she told the DWP when she claimed that she was a foster parent and had a foster child placed with her, the DWP said she wasn't entitled to UC. She asks the DWP to change this decision and the DWP agrees because of official error (para 14.30).

   ■   Whenever she requests the change, she is awarded UC from 9th January.

14.29   SSA 9(1); D&A 2 definition: 'appropriate office' 3, 4, 5; NISSO 10(1); NID&A 3-5
       https://tinyurl.com/Form-CRMR1
       https://tinyurl.com/Form-MR2-NI

14.30   D&A 6(7); NID&A 6(7)

14.31   There is an official error when:

(a) the DWP, HMRC or someone acting for them (e.g. a contractor) makes an error; and

(b) neither you nor anyone else (e.g. your landlord) materially contributed to it.

The error could be getting the facts wrong (which you or someone else provided information or evidence about), getting the law or case law wrong (but for changes in the law or case law see paras 14.34-35), or making an accidental error (para 14.33).

14.32   There is also an official error when the DWP uses the wrong figure for any of the following (or uses a figure when none should apply), even if you or someone else did contribute to it:

(a) a local housing allowance (para 6.42),

(b) a housing payment determination (para 6.20),

(c) the benefit cap (para 9.51),

(d) a sanction (para 2.47), or

(e) a penalty (para 13.58).

Accidental errors

14.33   There is an accidental error when the DWP fails to record, or to put into action, its true intentions (e.g. by mis-entering data on a computer) (ADM A3042). The DWP can correct an accidental error at any time. Any resulting change in your UC takes effect from the date the original decision took effect (or should have).

Amendments to regulations and up-ratings

14.34   When an amendment to regulations affects your UC, it takes effect on the first day of your assessment period that begins on or after the date the amendment comes into force. For UC figures that are up-rated in April, this means 6th April; for other amendments, the date is given in the amending regulations.

New case law

14.35   When new case law (in another person's appeal) affects your UC, it takes effect from the date the Upper Tribunal, the Northern Ireland Commissioners or the court gives its judgment in that case (but see para 14.36).

Stayed decisions

14.36   To 'stay' a decision (the legal term) means to defer it (the DWP's term) or to put it on pause. The DWP can 'stay' a decision about your UC if it depends on the outcome of a test case being appealed to the Upper Tribunal, the Northern Ireland Commissioners or a court.

14.31   D&A 2 definition: 'official error', 9, 12, 14, 19; NID&A 2, 9, 12, 14, 19

14.32   D&A 2 definitions: 'official error', 'designated authority'; NID&A 2

14.33   D&A 38; NID&A 38

14.34   D&A 23(1), sch 1 paras 32-33; NID&A 23(1), sch 1 paras 32-33

14.35   SSA 27; D&A 35(5); NISSO 27; NID&A 35(5)

This means that:

(a) for the time being, the DWP makes its decision in your case based on the least favourable outcome of the test case (even if that means you don't get any UC), and explains in the decision notice that the decision has been stayed;

(b) when the judgment is given in the test case, the DWP alters its decision in your case in line with the test case, and this takes effect on the date the original decision in your case took effect (or should have).

After a reconsideration

14.37 If your reconsideration request is unsuccessful or only partly successful, you can:

(a) appeal to a tribunal (paras 14.39-40); or

(b) request another reconsideration (para 14.17).

Usually, (a) is advisable, but (b) can be useful if you have new facts, evidence or arguments.

14.38 However if your reconsideration was unsuccessful because:

(a) it was outside the 13 months allowed by the time limit (paras 14.27-28); and

(b) it was not about official error (para 14.30);

you can't appeal to a tribunal (CSJSA/513/2016 and DWP memo ADM 08/19). You can ask for another reconsideration, or you may be able to make a late appeal (para 14.47(c)) or apply for judicial review (para 14.70).

Appeals to a tribunal

First-tier Tribunal/Appeal Tribunal

14.39 When a UC decision is appealable (para 14.40), you (or another person in para 14.2) can appeal about it to:

(a) a First-tier Tribunal in Great Britain; or

(b) an Appeal Tribunal in Northern Ireland.

These tribunals are independent of the DWP. You can only appeal to them after asking for a mandatory reconsideration (para 14.17). Useful information about appeals is in ADM chapter A5.

Which decisions are appealable

14.40 All UC decisions are appealable to a tribunal except the non-appealable decisions summarised in table 14.3. If a decision is non-appealable, you can ask the DWP to reconsider it (para 14.17), make a complaint (para 14.72), or you may be able to apply for judicial review (para 14.70).

14.37   SSA 27; D&A 35(5); NISSO 27; NID&A 35(5)

14.39   SSA 12(2),(3A); D&A 7(2); NISSO 13(2),(3A); NID&A 7(2)

14.40   SSA 12(1),(2),(3A), sch 2 paras 6, 8A, 9, sch 3 paras 1-6, 6B, 9; D&A 7(2), 50(2), sch 3;
NISSO 13(1),(2),(3A), sch 2 paras 6, 8A, 9, sch 3 paras 1-6, 6B, 9; NID&A 7(2), 49(2), sch 3

Appeal terminology

14.41   When you appeal to a tribunal the following terms are often used:

(a) 'appellant' – you (the person making the appeal);

(b) 'respondent' – the DWP (the maker of the decision you have appealed), also anyone else who has a right of appeal in your case (e.g. your landlord in some overpayment cases: para 14.2);

(c) 'party' – any of the above.

How to appeal

14.42   You can appeal using form SSCS1 in Great Britain or NOA1(SS) in Northern Ireland. These forms are available from many advice agencies or online [www]. Or you can appeal by letter or email. In each case you need to meet the appeal requirements (para 14.45).

Table 14.3 **Non-appealable UC decisions**

(a) Who can claim on your behalf if you are unable to act (paras 3.8-10).

(b) What information or evidence the DWP can require (paras 3.21-26).

(c) The amount of an LHA figure (para 6.42) or housing payment determination (para 6.20) – but the rent officer can redetermine these (para 6.53).

(d) Whether UC amounts should be affected by your age (e.g. para 9.14) or by up-ratings (para 1.22).

(e) Who counts as the carer of a severely disabled person where care is shared (para 9.40).

(f) Whether the DWP should suspend or restore your UC (paras 11.31-35).

(g) How and when your UC is paid (i.e. any matter in paras 12.1-12).

(h) UC advances and budgeting advances (paras 12.19-24, 12.26-28) – but you can appeal about deductions from future UC (paras 12.25, 12.29).

(i) Whether (and/or how much) UC should be paid to your landlord towards your rent (paras 12.37-47) – but you can appeal about payments towards rent arrears (paras 12.48-54).

(j) Whether an overpayment of UC is recoverable and/or the method of recovery (see paras 13.8-9 for further details).

(k) Appeals in which the reconsideration was refused because it was outside the time limit and was not about official error (para 14.38).

(l) Whether the DWP should stay a UC decision or appeal (paras 14.36, 14.54).

(m) Whether a tribunal should correct or set aside a decision it has made (paras 14.66-67).

14.41   FTPR 1(3) definitions: 'appellant', 'respondent', 'party'; NISSO 14(4), 15(3)(a),(b); NIDAR99 1(2) definitions: 'claimant', 'party to proceedings'

14.42   FTPR 13(1), 22(2)(d); NIDAR99 33
https://tinyurl.com/Form-SSCS1
https://tinyurl.com/Form-NOA1SS

T14.3   D&A 50(1),(2), sch 3 paras 1, 3-6, 7, 13-15, 18; NID&A 49(1),(2), sch 3 paras 1, 3-5, 6, 10-12, 15

Representatives

14.43   If you wish, you can ask a representative to appeal (or act in any other way) for you. They could be an advice worker, a solicitor or a friend or family member. Once you have informed the DWP and tribunal in writing about this, your representative can do anything you could do in relation to your appeal (except for signing a witness statement). The DWP and the tribunal should accept this until you or the representative inform them in writing to the contrary.

Where to send your appeal

14.44   In Great Britain you send your appeal to Her Majesty's Courts and Tribunals Service (HMCTS) which sends a copy to the DWP. In Northern Ireland you send it to the DFC which forwards it to the Appeals Service (TAS(NI)). The addresses are:

    (a) in England and Wales, HMCTS, SSCS Appeals Centre, PO Box 1203, Bradford BD1 9WP;

    (b) in Scotland, HMCTS, SSCS Appeals Centre, PO Box 27080, Glasgow G2 9HQ;

    (c) in Northern Ireland, The Appeals Service (NI), PO Box 2202, Belfast, BT1 9YJ.

Appeal requirements

14.45   Your appeal should:

    (a) be written in English or Welsh, and signed by you or your representative;

    (b) say what decision you are appealing about and why you consider it is wrong (this is called your submission: para 14.46);

    (c) give your name and address, and those of your representative if you have one;

    (d) say which address you want documents about your appeal to be sent to;

    (e) give the name and address of any respondent other than the DWP (para 14.41);

    (f) enclose a copy of the DWP's reconsideration notice (para 14.24);

    (g) enclose copies of any statement of reasons (para 14.9) and other relevant documents;

    (h) be within the appeal time limit (paras 14.47-48);

    (i) say whether you want to attend a hearing or have the appeal decided on the papers (para 14.57);

    (j) in the case of a hearing, say which dates you won't be available over the next six months, and whether you have particular needs (e.g. for a signer, interpreter or wheelchair access).

Your submission

14.46   Your submission should say which part of the DWP's decision you disagree with, why you think it is wrong, and what you think it should be. You shouldn't lose out by not using precise legal terms and references, so long as what you say is clear (ADM A5428).

14.43   FTPR 11(2),(5); NIDAR99 49(8)

14.44   FTPR 22(2)(d); NIDAR99 33(1)(b)

14.45   FTPR 22(3),(4); NIDAR99 33(1)(c),(d)

Time limit for appeals

14.47 You are within the appeal time limit in Great Britain if:

(a) your appeal reaches the tribunal within one month of the reconsideration notice being issued (para 14.24); or

(b) your appeal reaches the tribunal up to 12 months later than (a), you ask the tribunal to extend the time limit, and the tribunal also agrees (para 14.48); or

(c) later than (b) if the circumstances are truly exceptional and you have done all you can to obtain a hearing ([2022] UKUT 292 (AAC), [2022] UKUT 340 (AAC)).

In Northern Ireland these time limits relate to when the appeal reaches the DFC.

Extending the time limit

14.48 The tribunal extends the appeal time limit by up to 12 months (para 14.47) if:

(a) neither the DWP nor any other party to the appeal objects; or

(b) they do object, but the tribunal considers the appeal should go ahead. In this case, the tribunal first asks for your comments on the objection.

14.49 If you have one of the following special circumstances, the DWP is unlikely to object to your appeal going ahead (ADM A5081):

(a) you were unable to deal with the reconsideration notice or make an appeal because of illness; mental or physical disability or learning difficulty;

(b) you had difficulty obtaining an appeal form or getting a representative;

(c) you didn't receive the reconsideration notice;

(d) you made your appeal earlier, but it didn't reach the tribunal;

(e) you were wrongly advised by the DWP or an advice worker or a solicitor;

(f) (in some cases) you have a very strong case or there is a lot of money involved.

The DWP's response to your appeal

14.50 After receiving your appeal (para 14.44), the DWP sends a written response to the tribunal within 28 days, or longer if the tribunal agrees. It also sends a copy to you or your representative, and to any other party to the appeal.

14.51 However if the DWP decides it wholly agrees with your appeal, it changes its UC decision in your favour, sends you a decision notice and awards any arrears of UC (in which case your appeal lapses). Or if the DWP only partly agrees with your appeal, it tells the tribunal this in its written response (ADM A5160-61).

14.52 The DWP must deal with your appeal in one of the ways in paras 14.50-51 or 14.54. In particular, it has no power to lapse your appeal in other circumstances.

14.47　FTPR 22(2)(d),(6)(a),(8); NIDAR99 31(a), 32

14.48　FTPR 22(8); NIDAR99 32(4)-(8)

14.50　FTPR 24(1)(c),(5)

14.51　D&A 52; NID&A 51

14.52　D&A 52(1); NIDAR99 51(1)

Further submissions

14.53 After receiving the copy of the DWP's response, you can make a further written submission or provide further evidence to the tribunal within one month, or longer if the tribunal agrees, HMCTS/TAS(NI) sends a copy of this to the DWP and to any other party to the appeal.

Stayed appeals

14.54 To 'stay' an appeal (the legal term) means to defer it (the DWP's term) or put it on pause. The DWP can 'stay' your appeal if it depends on the outcome of a test case being appealed to the Upper Tribunal, the Northern Ireland Commissioners or a court. This means that:

(a) for the time being, your appeal doesn't go ahead;

(b) when the judgment is given in the test case:

- the DWP alters its decision in your case in line with the test case, and this takes effect on the date the original decision in your case took effect (or should have),

- the rules about whether your appeal goes ahead or 'lapses' are the same as in para 14.51.

Tribunal hearings and decisions

14.55 The tribunal that deals with your appeal normally consists of just one judge, or a judge plus a medically or financially qualified person in appropriate cases. The tribunal's role is inquisitorial, not adversarial, so it can look afresh at your whole case, not just the part you have appealed.

Directions

14.56 The tribunal can issue directions to the parties about the conduct of the appeal at any time (see table 14.4 for examples). You or any party can ask the tribunal for directions or the tribunal can make them without a request. And if you fail to comply with a direction, the tribunal could strike out your appeal (so that it doesn't go ahead).

How appeals are dealt with

14.57 Every appeal is considered at a hearing unless you, the DWP, any other party and the tribunal itself all agree that it can be decided on the papers. Research shows that you have a better chance of success if you attend (along with your representative if you have one).

14.53   FTPR 24(6),(7)
        Practice Statement: Record of Proceedings in Social Security and Child Support Cases in the Social Entitlement Chamber, 3 November 2008 https://tinyurl.com/Practice-Statement-Nov-08; NIDAR99 55

14.54   FTPR 53; NIDAR99 52

14.55   TCEA 3(3), 4(3), sch 2 para 2(2); NISSO 8; NIDAR99 36

14.56   FTPR 5, 6, 8; NIDAR99 38

14.57   FTPR 27(1)

Hearings

14.58   Hearings take place at venues throughout the UK [www]. They are theoretically open to the public, but in practice it is rare for any member of the public to attend. You should get at least 14 days' notice of the date, time and venue of your hearing. Before and during the hearing you have the rights in paras 14.59-60 and so do the DWP and any other party.

Before the hearing

14.59   Before the hearing takes place, you can write requesting the tribunal:

(a) to issue directions (table 14.4);

(b) to postpone the hearing (e.g. if you need time to obtain more evidence);

(c) to withdraw (end) your appeal (or withdraw any part of it).

At the hearing

14.60   When the hearing takes place, you have the right:

(a) to attend;

(b) to have a representative with you (para 14.43);

(c) to have a friend or relative with you (for support, or to help you put your case if you don't have a representative);

(d) to put your case;

(e) to question the DWP and any other party about their case;

(f) to ask for the hearing to be adjourned (e.g. if you need to obtain further evidence);

(g to withdraw your appeal if the tribunal gives you permission to do so.

Tribunal decisions

14.61   The tribunal reaches a decision once it has considered all the evidence. In reaching its decision the tribunal should:

(a) consider the relevant law including any applicable case law;

(b) identify the relevant facts based on the available evidence; and

(c) where the facts are in doubt or dispute, establish them (if necessary, on the balance of probability); and

(d) apply the law to the relevant facts to arrive at a reasoned decision.

14.58   FTPR 28, 29(1),(2); NIDAR99 49(2),(3)
         http://sscs.venues.tribunals.gov.uk/Venues/venues.htm
         https://www.communities-ni.gov.uk/topics/appeals-service-and-appealing-decisions

14.59   FTPR 5(3)(h), 6(2),(3), 17

14.60   FTPR 11(5),(7), 17(1)-(3), 28; NIDAR99 49(7),(8),(11)

14.61   TECA 22, 23, sch 5

Tribunal's decision notices

14.62   The tribunal should write to you as soon as practicable after making its decision, saying:

  (a) what its decision is (e.g. whether your UC should change, and if so, how and when);

  (b) how to get a statement of reasons (para 14.64); and

  (c) how and when to make a further appeal (para 14.68).

If you attend a hearing, you may be told the decision on the day.

Table 14.4 **Directions a tribunal can give**

A tribunal can give directions about any UC appeal. For example (ADM A5428) it can:

  (a) Set, extend or shorten any time limit.

  (b) Allow or require the parties to provide or amend documents, information, evidence or submissions, or require a third party to release evidence ([2022] UKUT 77 (AAC)).

  (c) Hold a hearing (or not: para 14.57) and decide how it is run.

  (d) Deal with preliminary matters in advance of a hearing.

  (e) Adjourn or postpone a hearing.

  (f) Join appeals so that they are dealt with together.

  (g) Treat one appeal as a lead case and 'stay' other similar cases until the lead case is decided (para 14.54).

  (h) Transfer proceedings to another court or tribunal in certain circumstances.

Note: The law was amended due to the coronavirus outbreak to make it easier for tribunals in Great Britain to:

  ■ hold video or audio recorded hearings;

  ■ deal with urgent appeals without a hearing; or

  ■ close hearings to the public.

When tribunal decisions take effect

14.63   If the tribunal changes your UC, its decision notice either gives the new amounts and dates they take effect or clearly instructs the DWP how to work these out (ADM A5501). The DWP should action this as soon as practicable unless it knows that a further appeal is pending (para 14.68).

14.62   FTPR 33(1),(2); NIDAR99 53(2),(3)

T14.4   FTPR 5, 5A, 30A; SI 2020/416; NIDAR99 38

14.63   FTPR 5(3)(l); D&A 44(1)-(4); NID&A 43(1)-(4)

Statement of reasons

14.64   You can get a statement of reasons by asking the clerk at the hearing, or by applying to the tribunal up to one month after receiving its decision notice (this can be extended if the tribunal agrees). The statement gives the tribunal's findings of fact as well as its reasons for its decision. It is necessary to have this if you want to make a further appeal (para 14.68).

Record of proceedings

14.65   You can get a copy of the record of proceedings by applying to the tribunal up to 18 months after receiving its decision notice [www]. This means 18 months after the last activity in relation to the decision such as a correction, or from the date the statement of reasons was issued ([2015] UKUT 509 (AAC)). The record gives a summary of the evidence and submissions received by the tribunal. It isn't necessary to have this if you want to make a further appeal, but it is often useful.

Changes to tribunal decisions

14.66   A tribunal decision can be changed if:

(a) the tribunal (after a request from you, the DWP or another party, or without a request):

■   corrects an accidental error (an error that fails to record what the tribunal intended), or

■   sets the decision aside (para 14.67); or

(b) you, the DWP or another party make a further appeal (para 14.68); or

(c) the DWP alters the decision because:

■   your or someone else's circumstances change (para 11.1), or

■   new factual evidence shows the decision was wrong.

The time limit for any request in (a) is one month.

Setting aside

14.67   'Setting aside' a tribunal decision means it is cancelled and the appeal starts again (with a new hearing or a new consideration of the papers). The tribunal can set a decision aside if it is in the interests of justice to do so; and

(a) a document was not sent to, or was not received at any appropriate time by, the tribunal or any party; or

(b) any party or representative was not present at a hearing; or

(c) there has been some other procedural irregularity.

14.64   FTPR 34(2)-(4); NIDAR99 53(4), 54

14.65   www.judiciary.uk/publications/practice-statement-from-the-senior-president-of-tribunals-social-security-and-child-support-cases

14.66   TCEA 9; FTPR 36, 37, 38; D&A 23(1)(a), 31(a); NID&A 23(1)(a), 31(a); NIDAR99 56, 57

14.67   FTPR 37; NIDAR99 57

Further appeals

Upper Tribunal/Northern Ireland Commissioners

14.68   You can write asking for permission to make a further appeal:

(a) to the Upper Tribunal in Great Britain (against a decision of the First-tier Tribunal);

(b) to the Northern Ireland Commissioners in Northern Ireland (against the decision of an Appeal Tribunal).

The DWP or another party can also do this. In all cases the further appeal has to be on the grounds that there was an error of law (not that you just disagree about the facts), and you may well need help from a lawyer or advice worker at this stage. See para 14.71 for the meaning of error of law.

14.69   To begin with, you send your further appeal to the First-tier Tribunal or Appeal Tribunal. They then decide:

(a) to reconsider and alter their own decision; or

(b) to give you permission to appeal, in which case you send your further appeal to the Upper Tribunal or Northern Ireland Commissioners; or

(c) to refuse permission, in which case you can apply directly to the Upper Tribunal or Northern Ireland Commissioners for permission to appeal.

In all cases, you should use form UT1 in Great Britain or form OSSC1 in Northern Ireland [www]. And in each case the time limit is normally one month (which the tribunal can extend in limited circumstances).

The appeal courts and judicial review

14.70   Depending on the situation you may be able to:

(a) Appeal to the Court of Appeal against a decision of the Upper Tribunal or Northern Ireland Commissioners on a point of law of wide-ranging significance. You must apply to the Upper Tribunal for permission to appeal within three months of the date of its decision or, if permission is refused, to the Court of Appeal within 21 days after that (seven days if it is for a judicial review) [www].

(b) Apply for judicial review of a decision you can't appeal (para 14.40) or a decision of the Upper tribunal. For decisions you can't appeal you should apply for permission to proceed to the High Court (Court of Session in Scotland), within 21 days of the decision [www].

In these cases, you will almost certainly need to get professional legal advice and representation.

14.68   FTPR 38(2),(3),(6); NISSO 14, 15; NIDAR99 58

14.69   TCEA 10; FTPR 39(1),(2),(4), 40(2); UTPR 21(4)(a)-(e), 22, 23(2)(a),(4); NIDAR99 58
         https://tinyurl.com/Form-UT1
         https://tinyurl.com/OSSC1
         https://tinyurl.com/OSSC1-guidance

14.70   TCEA 13, 14A-14C; UTPR 44(2),(3), ; SI 2008 No. 2834
         https://www.justice.gov.uk/courts/procedure-rules/civil/rules/part52#52.7
         https://www.justice.gov.uk/courts/procedure-rules/civil/rules/part52#52.9
         https://www.justice.gov.uk/courts/procedure-rules/civil/rules/part52#52.12

What is an error of law?

14.71   An appeal to the Upper Tribunal can only be made on an error of law. An error of law is where the First-tier Tribunal did one or more of the following:

(a)   failed to apply the correct law;

(b)   wrongly interpreted the relevant Acts or regulations;

(c)   followed a procedure that breached the rules of natural justice;

(d)   took irrelevant matters into account, or did not consider relevant matters, or did both of these things;

(e)   did not give adequate reasons in the full statement of reasons;

(f)   gave a decision which was not supported by the evidence;

(g)   decided the facts in such a way that no tribunal properly instructed as to the law, and acting judicially, could have reached that decision.

These are examples, not an exhaustive list (R(IS) 11/99).

Complaints

Making a complaint

14.72   If you want to make a complaint, rather than an appeal, you should first contact the DWP office you are dealing with, explain the matter and give them the opportunity to put things right. It is probably best to do this in writing so that you have a record of the action you have taken. If this is unsuccessful the DWP has a formal complaints procedure that may provide a remedy for your problem [www]. If you remain dissatisfied, you can escalate your complaint by asking the Independent Case Examiner to look at it (this is a free and independent complaint resolution and examination service provided by the DWP) [www]. If you're still dissatisfied, you can ask your MP [www] to send your complaint to the Parliamentary and Health Service Ombudsman (this is also a free and independent service) [www].

The response to your complaint

14.73   The DWP says that if it gets something wrong it will act quickly to put it right. This might include any of the following: an apology; an explanation; putting things right, or a special payment if something the DWP has done (or not done) has caused injustice or hardship (see DWP (2012) *Financial Redress for Maladministration*) [www].

14.72   www.gov.uk/government/organisations/department-for-work-pensions/about/complaints-procedure
        www.gov.uk/government/organisations/independent-case-examiner
        www.parliament.uk/mps-lords-and-offices/mps/
        www.ombudsman.org.uk/

14.73   www.gov.uk/government/publications/compensation-for-poor-service-a-guide-for-dwp-staff

Chapter 15 **Council tax**

- What is council tax and who is liable to pay it: see paras 15.1-21.
- Reducing your council tax bill: see paras 15.22-30.
- Claims, changes and appeals: see paras 15.31-36.

What is council tax

15.1   Council tax is a tax on dwellings that helps to pay for local services. It applies in England, Scotland and Wales.

15.2   Local councils send out the bills for council tax. In most cases:

(a) one or more residents of a dwelling are liable for council tax there, but in some cases the owner/landlord is liable instead;

(b) the amount of your bill depends on which valuation band your dwelling is in and whether you qualify for any reduction.

This chapter gives the details and the exceptions.

Council tax bands

15.3   The amount of council tax depends on what valuation band a dwelling is in:

(a) in England and Scotland there are eight bands, from A to H;

(b) in Wales there are nine, from A to I.

You can find out which band your home is in online [www]. The amounts for each band are always in proportion to band D (table 15.1).

Dwellings

15.4   There is one council tax bill per dwelling. A 'dwelling' is a single domestic property, for example a house, a flat, a mooring with a houseboat or a pitch with a mobile home. (The last two are 'hereditaments', but we use 'dwellings' for all of them in this guide.) Shops, offices, warehouses, factories and other non-domestic property are subject to business rates (not council tax). Non-domestic property includes holiday lets. In England they must have been available for at least 140 days and actually let for at least 70 days in the previous year.

Your home

15.5   Your 'home' is the dwelling where you live or mostly live. The law calls this your 'sole or main residence'.

15.2   LGFA 1

15.3   LGFA 5(1),(2) www.gov.uk/council-tax-bands www.saa.gov.uk

15.4   LGFA 3, 4, 7; Local Government Finance Act 1988, s66(2B); SI 2022/217

15.5-6   LGFA 6(1)(2)(a)-(e),(3),(5) definition: 'resident'

Table 15.1 **Council tax bands**

Band	Proportion: England and Wales	Proportion: Scotland
A	6/9 of band D (67%)	240/360 of band D (67%)
B	7/9 of band D (78%)	280/360 of band D (78%)
C	8/9 of band D (89%)	320/360 of band D (89%)
D	–	–
E	11/9 of band D (122%)	473/360 of band D (131%)
F	13/9 of band D (144%)	585/360 of band D (163%)
G	15/9 of band D (167%)	705/360 of band D (196%)
H	18/9 of band D (200%)	882/360 of band D (245%)
I (Wales only)	21/9 of band D (233%)	
Percentages are rounded.		

Residents and occupiers

15.6   The people living in a dwelling are either:

(a) 'residents' – over 18-year-olds who live there as their sole or main residence, including householders, lodgers and non-dependants (paras 15.7-9); or

(b) other occupiers – under 18-year-olds and people with no sole or main residence or whose sole or main residence is elsewhere.

Only residents can be liable for council tax (para 15.10) but both residents and other occupiers can affect whether you qualify for a reduction (para 15.22).

Householders

15.7   We use 'householders' (not a legal term) for residents of a dwelling who own or rent it. You can be a sole householder, householder couple, or joint householder (paras 15.13-16).

Lodgers

15.8   A lodger is someone over 18 who pays a commercial rent to you (or your partner) to live in part of your home.

Non-dependants

15.9   A non-dependant is someone over 18 who:

(a) lives in your home – for example a son, daughter, other relative or friend or a sponsored Ukrainian (table 15.3); but

(b) isn't your partner, young person (para 3.64), joint householder, or a lodger (table 3.3).

T15.1   LGFA 5(1),(2), 36(1)

Who is liable for council tax

15.10 This section explains when the residents of a dwelling are liable for council tax (paras 15.11-16) and when the owner/landlord is liable instead (paras 15.17-21).

When the residents are liable

15.11 The general rule is that liability for council tax falls on the resident(s) of a dwelling. If there is more than one, it falls on the resident(s) with the highest legal interest which is the first of the following:

(a) the freehold owner;

(b) the leasehold owner;

(c) the tenant;

(d) the licensee;

(e) any other resident(s).

If you are a couple who reside together and you are liable as in (a)-(e), your partner is also liable, even when they have a lesser interest.

'FTS/SMI' and care leavers

15.12 The rules in paras 15.13-16 refer to people who are full-time students (FTS) or severely mentally impaired (SMI) as described in table 15.4(a),(b). In Wales only, these rules also apply to care leavers aged under 25 (table 15.4(d)) in the same way as to people who are FTS/SMI, except that if the only resident is a care leaver (or all the residents are) you aren't exempt.

Sole householders

15.13 If you are a single person (para 3.47) and own or rent your home just in your name:

(a) you are liable for council tax on your home; but

(b) when you are FTS/SMI, your home is exempt from council tax unless other adults live with you who aren't FTS/SMI or in table 15.3(a) or you live in an HMO (para 15.17).

Householder couples who are joint owners/tenants

15.14 If you are a couple (para 3.49) and own or rent your home in both your names:

(a) you are both jointly liable for council tax on your home; but

(b) when one of you is FTS/SMI, only the other is liable; or

(c) when both of you are FTS/SMI, your home is exempt from council tax unless other adults live with you who aren't FTS/SMI or in table 15.3(a) or you live in an HMO (para 15.17).

15.11   LGFA 6(1)(2)(a)-(e), 9(1),(2)

15.12   LGFA 6(4),(4A),(4B), sch 1 paras 2, 4; SI 2022/210

15.13   LGFA 6(1),(2)(a)-(e)

15.14   LGFA 6(1)

Householder couples: only one an owner/tenant

15.15   If you are a couple and one partner owns or rents your home but the other partner doesn't:

    (a)   you are both jointly liable for council tax on your home; or

    (b)   when only the owner/renter partner is FTS/SMI, you are both jointly liable; but

    (c)   when only the non-owner/renter partner is FTS/SMI, only the owner/renter partner is liable; or

    (d)   when both of you are FTS/SMI, your home is exempt from council tax unless other adults live with you who aren't FTS/SMI or in table 15.3(a).

These rules were confirmed in E v Sandwell MBC, which is not binding case law but is widely accepted as correct (CTGM 8.3.8(b)).

Joint householders

15.16   If you are single or a couple and own or rent your home with one or more others (e.g. relatives or friends in a house-share):

    (a)   you are all jointly liable for council tax on your home; but

    (b)   when one or more of you is FTS/SMI, only the other(s) are liable; or

    (c)   when all of you are FTS/SMI, your home is exempt unless other adults live with you who aren't FTS/SMI or in table 15.3(a) or you live in an HMO (para 15.17).

When the owner is liable not the residents

15.17   Non-resident owners are liable if there are no residents in the dwelling (para 15.21). Additionally, in the classes of dwelling in table 15.2, the owner/landlord is liable for the council tax, not the resident(s). This is the case even if all the occupiers are FTS/SMI or under 18, because the council tax exemptions in table 15.3 don't apply.

Houses in multiple occupation

15.18   A house in multiple occupation (HMO) is a building that:

    (a)   has been constructed or adapted for occupation by more than one household; or

    (b)   is inhabited by one or more people each of whom:

        ■   is a tenant of or has a licence to occupy only part of the dwelling, or

        ■   has a licence to occupy but is not solely or jointly liable to pay rent for the whole dwelling.

The adaptation in (a) can be adding locks to rooms, converting the use of a room, etc, depending on the details of the individual case (CTGM 8.3.5).

15.15   LGFA 6(3),(4), 9(1),(2)

15.16   LGFA 6(3),(4)

15.17   LGFA 8, CT(LO) 2

15.18   Table 15.2 Class C as amended by SI 1993/151 and SI 1995/620

Table 15.2 **Owner liable not residents**

(a)   A house in multiple occupation (para 15.18).

(b)   A bail/probation hostel or hostel providing personal care (para 15.20(a),(b)).

(c)   A care home or independent hospital.

(d)   A dwelling occupied by a minister of religion.

(e)   A dwelling occupied by a religious community (table 15.4(l)).

(f)   A second home occupied only by live-in staff and their families.

(g)   A dwelling provided to asylum seekers by the Home Office.

(h)   An empty dwelling (para 15.21).

Note:

- If you live in an HMO or hostel, your rent usually includes an amount towards the landlord's council tax.

15.19   The most familiar example of an HMO is a house where the landlord lets out rooms separately and there is a shared bathroom/WC, kitchen and/or living room. But any dwelling that meets the conditions in para 15.18 is an HMO for council tax purposes, even if it doesn't count as an HMO for Housing Act licensing or other purposes.

Hostels

15.20   A hostel is:

(a) a bail or probation hostel ('approved premises');

(b) a building or part of a building used solely or mainly for residential accommodation that is provided in non-self-contained units, together with personal care for people who are elderly, disabled, have a past or present alcohol or drug dependence or a past, or present mental disorder; or

(c) a dwelling (including a night shelter) that provides non self-contained accommodation:

- for people with no fixed abode or settled way of life; and

- where the individual lettings are licences rather than tenancies.

T15.2(a)-(g)   LGFA 8(1)-(3); CT(LO) 2, Classes A to F

T15.2(a)   CT(LO) 2, Class C substituted by SI 1993/151, amended by SI 1995/620 reg 2

T15.2(b),(c)   CT(LO) 2, Class A as substituted by SI 2003/3125, amended by SI 2015/643

T15.2(d)   CT(LO) 2, Class E amended by SI 1995/620 reg 3

T15.2(e)   CT(LO) 2, Class B

T15.2(f)   CT(LO) 2, Class D

T15.2(g)   CT(LO) 2, Class F added by SI 2000/537

T15.2(h)   LGFA 6(1),(2)(f)

15.20   LGFA sch 1 paras 7, 10; in DDO 6 definition: 'hostel' as substituted by SI 2003/3121 art 4

Empty dwellings

15.21   A dwelling with no occupiers is exempt from the council tax in some cases (table 15.3). Otherwise, the landlord/owner:

(a) qualifies for a 50% discount for the first six months that the dwelling is empty (this six months continues to run even when the dwelling changes hands); but

(b) in England and Wales, may be liable for up to four times the normal amount of council tax if it is empty for longer periods.

National rules prevent the increases in (b) in certain cases, but otherwise local councils decide whether and when to apply them and must publish their rules about this.

Table 15.3 **Council tax exempt dwellings**

(a) A dwelling whose only occupiers are any combination of:

- full time students (table 15.4(a)),
- people who are severely mentally impaired (table 15.4(b)),
- in Wales, young care leavers (table 15.4(d)),
- a Ukrainian who has leave under the Homes for Ukraine scheme, or in Scotland, a person from Ukraine to whom para 20.25(e) applies, or
- under 18-year-olds.

(b) An unoccupied dwelling left empty by a student or someone who became a student within six weeks after leaving.

(c) A hall of residence predominantly for students.

(d) An unoccupied dwelling whose owner/renter (the last person liable for council tax):

- resides elsewhere to receive personal care,
- resides elsewhere to provide personal care,
- is in hospital or long-term care,
- has died within the last six months, or
- is detained in prison or hospital.

(e) An unoccupied dwelling that is owned by a charity and was in use by the charity within the last six months.

15.21   LGFA 11(2), 11A, 11B, as amended by the Rating (Property in Common Occupation) and Council Tax (Empty Dwellings) Act 2018, s2

T15.3(a) CT(ED) Class N substituted by SI 1993/150, amended by SI 1995/619, SI 2005/2865;
          Class S added by SI 1995/619; Class U substituted by SI 1999/536; Classes N, S and U amended by SI 2022/439

T15.3(b) CT(ED) Class K substituted by SI 1993/150

T15.3(c) CT(ED) Class M amended by SI 1993/150 and SI 1994/539

T15.3(d) CT(ED) Class I substituted by SI 2003/3121; Classes D, E, F and J
          amended/substituted by SI 1994/539, Class E amended by SI 2005/2865

T15.3(e) CT(ED) Class B, amended by SI 1994/539

(f) In Wales, an unoccupied dwelling that has been vacant:

- for less than six months, or
- for less than 12 months and which requires major repairs or structural changes to make it habitable.

(g) An unoccupied dwelling awaiting occupation by a minister of religion.

(h) An unoccupied dwelling whose owner/renter (the person who would now be liable for council tax) is bankrupt.

(i) An unoccupied dwelling that has been repossessed by a mortgage lender.

(j) An unoccupied dwelling whose occupation is prohibited by law or by a planning restriction.

(k) UK armed forces accommodation owned by the Secretary of State for Defence.

(l) Visiting forces accommodation.

(m) A dwelling where the liable resident has diplomatic immunity.

(n) An empty houseboat mooring or mobile home pitch.

(o) An unoccupied annex or dwelling, that can't be let separately due to a planning restriction.

(p) An annex or self-contained part of a property occupied by a dependant relative who is over 65, or severely mentally impaired (table 15.4(b)), or substantially and permanently disabled.

Notes:

- A Ukrainian who has leave under the Homes for Ukraine scheme is disregarded when deciding if the dwelling is unoccupied in items (b), (d), (e), (g)-(i) and (o).
- None of the exemptions apply to HMOs, hostels or any dwelling where the owner is liable, not the residents (table 15.2).
- All exemptions apply in England and Wales. In Scotland (a)-(l) apply with some differences, and there are further exemptions including sheltered housing owned by a housing association and a dwelling which is the main residence of an asylum seeker who has been resettled under a UK government programme.

T15.3(f)	CT(ED) Classes A and C abolished in England by SI 2012/2965
T15.3(g)	CT(ED) Class H
T15.3(h)	CT(ED) Class Q added by SI 1993/150, amended by SI 1994/539
T15.3(i)	CT(ED) Class L
T15.3(j)	CT(ED) Class G substituted by SI 2006/2318
T15.3(k)	CT(ED) Class O amended by SI 1992/2941
T15.3(l)	CT(ED) Class P added by SI 1992/2941
T15.3(m)	CT(ED) Class V added by SI 1997/656, definition – 'dependent relative' in class amended by SI 1998/291
T15.3(n)	CT(ED) Class R added by SI 1994/539
T15.3(o)	CT(ED) Class T added SI 1995/619
T15.3(p)	CT(ED) Class W added by SI1997/656, definition – dependent relative in class amended by SI 1998/291
T15.3 notes	CT(ED) 2(1),(3A) – 'relevant Ukrainian person', amended by SI 2022/439

Reducing your council tax bill

15.22   You can get help with council tax if you qualify for:

(a)   an exemption (para 15.23);

(b)   a disability reduction (para 15.24);

(c)   a discount (para 15.26); and/or

(d)   a council tax rebate (chapter 16).

Your council may also offer discounts for prompt payment or for payment by one of its preferred methods.

Council tax exemptions

15.23   When a dwelling is exempt, no one has to pay council tax on it. Your council tax bill should show you have a nothing to pay. Table 15.3 lists all the classes of exempt dwelling.

Council tax disability reductions

15.24   When you qualify for a disability reduction:

(a)   your council tax is reduced to the amount for the next band down – for example, for homes in band D the bill is reduced to the amount for band C;

(b)   if your home is in band A (the lowest band) your bill is reduced by one sixth.

Who gets a disability reduction

15.25   You qualify for a disability reduction if:

(a)   you are disabled, or at least one disabled adult or child has their home with you; and

(b)   your home provides:

   ■   an additional kitchen or bathroom for the disabled person's use; or

   ■   an additional room (not a kitchen, bathroom or toilet) used predominantly to meet their special needs; or

   ■   sufficient floor space to use a wheelchair if they need one; and

(c)   this is of major importance to the disabled person's well-being, taking account of the nature and extent of their disability; and

(d)   you make a written application for it (see also para 15.34).

Your home doesn't need to have been specifically adapted. For example, it could be that the disabled person has to have a separate bedroom or a bedroom downstairs.

Council tax discounts

15.26   When you qualify for a discount, your council tax is reduced by 25% ('single occupancy' discount) or 50% ('empty dwelling' discount) (but see para 15.21).

15.22   LGFA 4, 11, 13, 13A

15.23   LGFA 4(1)-(4)

15.24   LGFA 13(1),(4),(6),(7); CT(RD) 4 as amended by SI 1999/1004

15.25   CT(RD) 3(1),(3)

15.26   LGFA 11(1)-(3), 11A(1)-(4)

Examples: Council tax discounts

1. Single person with discount

June owns her home and is the only person who lives there.

- She qualifies for a 25% discount – because she is the only adult there.

2. Couple with no discount

Jane and John are a couple. They rent their home and are the only people who live there.

- They don't qualify for a discount – because there are two adults and neither are disregarded persons.

3. Couple with discount

Geoff and Gina are a couple. They rent their home and Geoff is severely mentally impaired.

- They qualify for a 25% discount – because there are two adults and one is a disregarded person (table 15.4(b)).

4. Single person plus non-householder

Geri rents her home. Her father lives with her and is on the guarantee credit of SPC.

- Geri can't get a discount – because there are two adults, and neither are disregarded.
- But she can get second adult rebate – because her father is a non-dependant with a low income (para 17.19).

Table 15.4 **Council tax disregarded persons**

The following 'disregarded persons' affect discounts (paras 15.27-30), non-dependant deductions in main CTR (table 17.2) and second adult rebate (paras 17.18-23). Definitions (a) and (b) also apply for exemptions (table 15.3). Details for Scotland and Wales may differ in some cases.

(a) Full-time students

Anyone who:

- is on a one-year or longer UK or EU course at level 3 or above (A levels, degrees etc) and is expected to study at least 21 hours per week, for at least 24 weeks per year; or
- is under 20 and is on a three-month or longer UK or EU course and is expected to study for at least 12 hours per week during term times; or
- is studying to be included for the first time in the nursing register; or
- is a foreign language assistant registered with the British Council; or
- is under 20 and left one of these courses during May to October – this applies until 31st October in the year they leave.

T15.4(a)-(m) LGFA 11(5), sch 1

T15.4(a)   LGFA sch 1 paras 4, 5; DDO 4, sch 1 paras 2-7; DDR 3 Class C; SI 1993/149; SI 1994/543; SI 2006/3396 art 2(2)(b)

(b) People who are severely mentally impaired

Anyone who has a medical certificate confirming they have a severe impairment of intelligence and social functioning, and receives (or would receive but for being over 66):

- the daily living component of PIP or (in Scotland) the standard or enhanced rate of the daily living component of adult disability payment; or
- the middle or highest rate of the care component of DLA or (in Scotland) child disability payment; or
- attendance allowance or an equivalent benefit (para 10.54); or
- JSA(IB) or IS on the grounds of incapacity for work; or
- SDA; or
- the LCW or LCWRA element of UC or in Scotland ESA.

(c) Under 20-year olds for whom child benefit is payable

Anyone aged under 20 for whom child benefit could be paid (para 3.64).

(d) Care leavers under 25/26 (Wales and Scotland only)

Anyone who:

- is under 25 (Wales) or 26 (Scotland); and
- was in local authority care at any time after age 16, but has since left care; and
- in Wales only, was in care between the ages of 14 and 16 for one or more periods totalling at least three months (but ignoring any short-term placements intended to last less than four weeks).

Many English councils offer a similar reduction using CTR (paras 16.14, 16.20).

(e) Youth trainees under 25

Anyone under 25 who is undertaking government funded youth training.

(f) Apprentices

Anyone who is studying for an accredited qualification as part of their employment and is paid no more than £195 per week.

(g) Carers

Any carer who provides care for at least 35 hours per week to someone in your home, if the person they care for gets or could get:

- the daily living component of PIP or (in Scotland) adult disability payment; or
- the middle or highest rate of the care component of DLA; or
- attendance allowance or an equivalent benefit (para 10.54).

T15.4(b)   LGFA sch 1 para 2; DDO 3; SI 1994/543; SI 2013/388 sch para 12; SI 2013/591 sch para 5; SI 2013/630 reg 55

T15.4(c)   LGFA sch 1 para 3

T15.4(d)   See Appendix 4

T15.4(e)   LGFA sch 1 para 4(1); DDO 4, sch 1 para 8; SI 2006/3396 art 2(2)(c)

T15.4(f)   LGFA sch 1 para 4(1); DDO 4, sch 1 para 1; SI 2006/3396 art 2(2)(a)

But in Scotland in each case, the award must be at the enhanced/highest/higher rate. The carer can be a relative or friend of the person they care for; but not their partner, nor (in the case of a child/young person under 18) their parent.

(h) Live-in care workers

Any carer who:

- provides care to someone in your home; and
- was introduced by a local council, government department or charity; and
- is paid no more than £44 per week.

(i) Night shelter and homeless hostel residents

Anyone who, on any day has his/her sole or main residence under a licence agreement in a resettlement/homeless hostel or night shelter (para 15.20(c)) that mainly provides non-self-contained accommodation.

(j) Care home and hospital residents

Anyone whose sole or main residence is an NHS hospital, independent hospital or care home, or hostel that provides personal care for people who require it due to old age, disability, mental disorder or past or present alcohol or drug dependence (para 15.20(b)).

(k) Prisoners, bail hostel residents and hospital detainees

For details about who is a prisoner or hospital detainee see paras 2.22 and 2.27.

(l) Members of religious communities

Any member who is maintained by the community and has no money of their own (apart from an occupational pension).

(m) Non-British partners of students

Any spouse or civil partner who is not permitted to work or claim benefits.

(n) Diplomats etc

Anyone who has diplomatic immunity or is a member of visiting forces, and in some cases their spouse, civil partner or dependants.

(o) Persons evacuated from Ukraine and other resettled asylum seekers

A person who has leave under the Homes for Ukraine sponsorship scheme, or in Scotland a person seeking asylum who entered the UK under a relocation or resettlement scheme.

T15.4(g)   LGFA sch 1 para 9(1)(b),(g); DDR 2; sch paras 3, 4; SI 1994/540; SI 1996/637; SI 2013/388 sch para 3; SI 2013/591 sch para 6; SI 2013/725

T15.4(h)   LGFA sch 1 para 9(1),(2)(a)-(g); DDR 2; sch paras 1, 2; SI 2006/3395 reg 4

T15.4(i)   LGFA sch 1 para 10

T15.4(j)   LGFA sch 1 paras 6, 7; DDO 6(b) definition: 'hostel' as substituted by SI 2003/3121 art 4

T15.4(k)   LGFA sch 1 paras 1, 7; DDO 2, 6(a) definition: 'hostel' as substituted by SI 2003/3121 art 4

T15.4(l)   LGFA sch 1 para 11; DDR 3 Class B

T15.4(m)   LGFA sch 1 para 11; DDR 3 Class A, Class E; SI 1995/620 reg 4

T15.4(n)   LGFA sch 1 para 11; DDR 3 Class A, Class D, Class F; SI 1992/2942 reg 2; SI 1995/620 reg 4; SI 1997/657

T15.4(o)   LGFA sch 1 para 11; DDR3 Class G added by SI 2022/439 reg 2

Who gets a discount

15.27   Discounts depend on how many adults there are in your home (this means people over 18) and how many of them are 'disregarded persons' (table 15.4).

15.28   When you are the only adult in your home, you qualify for:

(a) a 25% discount; or

(b) a 50% discount if you are a disregarded person (table 15.4)

15.29   When there are two adults in your home (including you), you qualify for :

(a) a 25% discount if one of you is a disregarded person; or

(b) a 50% discount if you both are.

15.30   When there are three or more adults in your home, you qualify for:

(a) a 25% discount if all but one of you are disregarded persons; or

(b) a 50% discount if you all are.

Claims, awards and appeals

Claims and awards

15.31   The council uses information you provide, or that it already holds, to decide:

(a) who is liable for council tax; and

(b) who qualifies for exemptions, disability reductions or discounts.

When your liability increases, you have 21 days to inform the council, otherwise you can incur a penalty. When it reduces there is no time limit (para 15.34) but the longer you leave it, the more difficult it may be to provide any evidence the council needs.

Changes to your council tax bill

15.32   When your circumstances change, your council tax starts, changes or ends on the exact day. For example, when you move:

(a) your council tax on the new home starts on the day of your move;

(b) your council tax on the old home ends on the day before (or later in some cases if you leave it empty).

Council tax reconsiderations

15.33   You can ask the council to reconsider decisions it makes about council tax liability, exemptions, disability reductions and discounts. The time limit is usually two months. (For reconsiderations about council tax rebates, see paras 18.8-10.)

15.27-30   LGFA 11(1)-(3)

15.31   CT(A&E) 11, 16; CT(RD) 5

15.32   LGFA 2

15.33   LGFA 15, 16

Mistakes about liability

15.34 When there has been a mistake about whether or when you are liable for council tax, or qualify for an exemption or discount, there is no time limit on how far back the council can go. If you make an appeal the Limitation Act 1980 sets a six-year time limit from the date on which 'the cause of action accrued' but the Valuation Tribunal has interpreted this phrase fairly widely (CTGM 10.3.7(b)-(c)). For example, your council must take reasonable steps to find out if you qualify for a discount or an exemption and the tribunal may decide the time limit starts from the date they do this. But if your appeal relates to a disability reduction the time limit runs back from the date you first apply for it (Arca v Carlisle CC).

15.35 A dispute about liability, a discount etc (para 15.34) is not a defence against the council getting a liability order in the magistrates court for unpaid council tax. This is because only a tribunal can decide these disputes (Lone v LB Hounslow).

Council tax appeals

15.36 You can then appeal to a valuation tribunal in England and Wales or a first-tier tribunal in Scotland. For the rules and time limits, see paras 18.11-31.

15.34   CT(A&E) 8, 14; Arca v Carlisle [2013] RA 248

15.35   Lone v LB Hounslow [2019] EWCA Civ 2206
        www.bailii.org/ew/cases/EWCA/Civ/2019/2206.html

Chapter 16 **Council tax rebates**

- ■ Who can get CTR: see paras 16.1-12.
- ■ Local CTR/CTR classes: see paras 16.13-19.
- ■ Discretionary CTR: see paras 16.20-23.
- ■ Exclusions from CTR: see paras 16.24-31.
- ■ CTR claims and changes: see paras 16.32-48.

Who can get CTR

16.1 Council tax rebates (CTR) apply in England, Scotland and Wales. This chapter and chapter 17 describe the different kinds of council tax rebate you can get and these are summarised in table 16.1. The law calls them 'council tax reductions' and some councils in England call them council tax support.

Table 16.1 **Kinds of CTR**

(a) Main CTR

Main CTR has national rules that apply in England for pension age claims, and in Wales and Scotland for all claims. It is for when you have a low income, and if you have a non-dependant they may be expected to contribute towards your council tax (paras 17.6-16).

(b) Second adult rebate

SAR has national rules that apply in England for pension age claims and in Scotland for all claims. It is for when you have a non-dependant who stops you getting a discount (para 15.26) but has a low income (paras 17.18-25).

(c) Local CTR /CTR classes

Councils in England must have a local CTR scheme for working age claims, and this is made up of CTR classes (para 16.11). Councils can also have CTR classes for pension age claims in England and all claims in Wales (paras 16.7-9). Local CTR classes have local rules (para 16.13).

(d) Discretionary CTR

Discretionary CTR applies in England and Wales. Councils can award it whether or not you qualify for any of the above (para 16.20).

T16.1   LGFA 13A(1)(c),(2) sch 1A para 2(1)-(4),(9); CTP sch 1 paras 1-4; CTR 13-18

Residents

16.2   To get any of the kinds of CTR you must be a resident who is liable for council tax (paras 15.6, 15.11). If you are jointly liable with one or more others (apart from just your partner in a couple) the figures used in the main CTR and SAR calculations are shared between you (paras 17.16, 17.25).

Your family and non-dependants

16.3   Your CTR takes account of you and your family; this means the members of your household who are in your benefit unit (para 3.46). Non-dependants are usually adult sons, daughters, other relatives or friends who live with you (para 3.70). They can't get CTR themselves but may affect your CTR (para 17.6).

Working age and pension age

16.4   Working age means under 66 and pension age means 66 or over. Table 16.2 shows whether you can get working age or pension age CTR.

Table 16.2 **Pension age or working age CTR**

Single person

(a)	Over 66	Pension age CTR
(b)	Under 66	Working age CTR

Couple

(c)	Both over 66	Pension age CTR
(d)	Both under 66	Working age CTR
(e)	Mixed ages (one over, one under 66):	
	■ Applicant is over 66	Pension age CTR
	■ Applicant is under 66	Working age CTR

National variations

16.5   Paras 16.6-12 summarise the CTR variations between Scotland, Wales and England. The most notable is that:

(a) CTR for all ages in Scotland and Wales and for pension age claims in England have mainly national rules; but

(b) CTR for working age claims in England has mainly local rules.

16.2   LGFA sch 1A para 2(2)(a),(b); CTP sch 1 paras 1(1), 2(a), 3(a), 4(1)(a); CTR 13(a), 14(a), 15(1)(a), 16(a), 17(a), 18(1)(a)

16.3   LGFA sch 1A para 2(2)(c); CTP 9; CTR 9

16.4   Pensions Act 1995, sch 4 para 1(6); CTP 2(1) definitions: 'pensioner', pensionable age, 'qualifying age for state pension credit'; CTR 2(1)

T16.2   CTP 3, sch 1 para 2(f), 3(f), 4(e), sch 8 paras 3, 4(1); CTR 3, 13(f), 14(g), 15(1)(e), 16(f), 17(g), 18(1)(e), 109(1)

16.5   LGFA sch 1A para 2(1),(3),(8),(9); CTP 11(1), 14(1), sch 1 paras 1-4

CTR in Scotland

16.6   Every council in Scotland operates the national CTR rules. The council:

(a)   must have main CTR and SAR for both pension age and working age claims (chapter 17);

(b)   must include the alternative main CTR calculation for dwellings in bands E to H (para 17.17); and

(c)   must fully disregard war pensions (table 17.3).

Discretionary CTR doesn't apply.

CTR in Wales

16.7   Every council in Wales must have a CTR scheme. This scheme:

(a)   must include main CTR for both pension age and working age claims (chapter 17);

(b)   may lengthen the backdating period (para 16.42) and/or the period of extended CTR (para 17.36);

(c)   may increase the disregard for war pensions (table 17.3); and

(d)   may have additional CTR classes that supplement main CTR (para 16.8).

The council must also provide for discretionary CTR.

16.8   CTR classes must follow the rules in paras 16.13-16. They are in practice uncommon. Those that exist are like SAR or council tax discounts, where a flat rate is awarded to people who meet the conditions set by the council.

Pension age CTR in England

16.9   Every council in England must have a CTR scheme for pension age claims, made up of CTR classes. This scheme:

(a)   must include main CTR (para 17.4) – this counts as two classes (class A for claimants without excess income and class B for those with excess income);

(b)   must include SAR (para 17.18) – this counts as one class (class C);

(c)   may increase the disregard for war pensions (table 17.3); and

(d)   may have additional CTR classes that supplement main CTR and/or SAR (para 16.10).

The council must also provide for discretionary CTR.

16.10   CTR classes must follow the rules in paras 16.13-16. They are in practice rare.

16.6   LGFA 80(1),(2); CTS 3, 13(1), 14(1), 57(1); CTS66+ 12, 14(1), 14A(1), sch 3 paras 1-2

16.7   LGFA 13(1)(b),(c),(4),(5), sch 1B paras 2(1), 3, 4; CTPW 14, 21-24, 32, 33, 34(4),(5)

16.8   LGFA 13A(1)(b),(4),(5), sch 1B paras 3-5; CTPW 3-10, 12, 14-18, 27-29

16.9   LGFA sch 1A para 2(1)-(4),(8),(9); CTP 11(1), 14(1), sch 1 paras 1-4

16.10   LGFA 13A(2), sch 1A paras 2, 3, 5; SI 2017/1305, reg 2

Working age CTR in England

16.11   Every council in England must have a CTR scheme for working age claimants made up of CTR classes. This scheme:

(a) must include one or more CTR classes giving the council's primary rules for working age CTR – this is sometimes called 'local CTR' (para 16.12);

(b) may increase the disregard for war pensions (table 17.3); and

(c) may have additional CTR classes that supplement local CTR (para 16.12).

The council must also provide for discretionary CTR.

16.12   All CTR classes must follow the rules in paras 16.13-16. For examples of local CTR, see paras 16.17-19.

Example: Working age CTR in England

Joyce is a care leaver aged 23. She has lost her job and claims UC and CTR. The DWP awards her UC. Her local council has two CTR classes that apply to her:

■ a reduced form of main CTR based on 80% of the council tax (para 16.17) – the council calls this class D;

■ a flat rate 25% reduction for care leavers under 25 (para 16.19) – the council calls this class G;

and people who qualify for both get whichever is the most.

Joyce's CTR claim covers both classes, and she is awarded the council's class D.

Local CTR/CTR classes

16.13   When councils set CTR classes, there are requirements (in paras 16.14-16) about:

(a) basing classes on financial need;

(b) following national rules; and

(c) setting and changing classes.

Those requirements apply to the CTR classes that make up working age CTR in England (local CTR) and all other CTR classes in England and Wales.

Financial need

16.14   CTR classes must be based on financial need, not on other factors such as length of residence (R (Winder) v Sandwell MBC). This means your or your family's:

(a) own financial circumstances; or

(b) membership of a group that is generally at higher risk of being in financial need than the wider population, such as people with disabilities, carers, young care leavers and others.

16.11   LGFA 13A((1)(a),(c),(2),(3), sch 1A para 2(1)-(4)

16.12   LGFA 13A(2), sch 1A paras 2, 3, 5; SI 2017/1305, reg 2

16.13   LGFA sch 1A paras 2(1),(3),(5)-(7),(9), 3(1)-(3), 5; SI 2017/1305, reg 2; CTP 11-15, sch 1 paras 1-5

16.14   LGFA 13A(2), sch 1B para 3(4)-(7)
         R (Winder) v Sandwell MBC [2014] www.bailii.org/ew/cases/EWHC/Admin/2014/2617.html

Following national rules

16.15   And all local CTR classes must follow the national CTR rules about:

(a) what is a 'working age' claim;

(b) who is included in your household;

(c) which migrants and recent arrivals are excluded;

(d) certain minimum standards relating to claims, decision notices and appeals.

Setting and changing CTR classes

16.16   All CTR classes apply and can be changed from 1st April each year. Councils must:

(a) consult with local residents about classes and changes to them – this must be done in a 'meaningful way' (R (Moseley) v Haringey LBC);

(b) include transitional rules when changes to schemes end or reduce your entitlement; and

(c) publish details of their classes and how you can apply (which most councils do on their website).

Any changes in CTR classes must be confirmed by 11th March (in Wales, 31st January) in time for the new financial year starting on 1st April.

Local CTR: classes based on national CTR

16.17   Some councils have CTR classes for working age claims that adopt the national CTR rules in full (the 'default scheme'). Many more have variations on national CTR that do one or more of the following:

(a) reduce the amount of council tax that can be met by CTR (this is often the only variation);

(b) set a minimum award;

(c) reduce the upper capital limit;

(d) increase or restructure the non-dependant contributions and the income bands;

(e) vary the assessment of different kinds of income;

(f) increase the excess income taper above 20%;

(g) limit or remove entitlement to backdated CTR;

(h) limit or remove entitlement to SAR; or

(i) set their own rates for some or all of the allowances, premiums and components in the calculation of the applicable amount.

These schemes have the advantages of sensitivity to changes in income and being similar to other benefits, but the disadvantages of requiring frequent changes in the award.

16.15   LGFA sch 1A para 2(9); CTP 3-15, sch 7, sch 8
         R (Moseley) v Haringey LBC [2014] www.bailii.org/uk/cases/UKSC/2014/56.html
16.16   LGFA sch 1A paras 3(1),(3),(5), 5(1)-(6); SI 2017/1305 reg 2
16.17   LGFA 13A(2), sch 1A para 2(2),(4)

Local CTR: classes based on income bands

16.18   Some councils have CTR classes for working age claims that are based on income bands. Usually your CTR equals a high percentage of your council tax if you are in the lowest income band, and the percentage reduces for higher income bands. These classes have the advantage of simplicity and less frequent changes in your CTR, but the disadvantage of sudden jumps from one amount of CTR to another (or to nil) when your income crosses between bands.

Local CTR: other kinds of classes

16.19   CTR classes can also be designed in other ways. Some councils have CTR classes that are like SAR or council tax discounts, where a flat rate is awarded to people who meet conditions set by the council, for example, for young care leavers.

Discretionary CTR

16.20   Discretionary CTR applies in England and Wales, not Scotland. Councils can award it based on the individual merits of your claim or on the basis of your membership of a group at risk of financial need.

16.21   You can get discretionary CTR:

(a)   to top up your main CTR, SAR or local CTR; or

(b)   even when you don't qualify for these (e.g. because your income is too high or you are excluded: para 16.24).

This could reduce the amount of council tax you have to pay to a lower figure or to nil.

16.22   The council can treat any claim for CTR as a request for discretionary CTR. But in practice you need to make it clear in writing that you are asking for discretionary CTR, and if the council requires you to request it in a particular way (e.g. on a form) it must tell you.

16.23   You can appeal almost any decision about discretionary CTR to a tribunal (para 18.20).

Exclusions from CTR

16.24   You may be excluded from:

(a)   main CTR and SAR if you are absent from home (paras 16.25-29);

(b)   main CTR and SAR if you are a migrant (para 16.30);

(c)   main CTR (not SAR) if you are a full-time student (para 16.31);

(d)   main CTR (not SAR) if you have capital over £16,000 (paras 17.5, 17.32).

16.18   LGFA 13A(2), sch 1A para 2(2),(4)

16.19   LGFA 13A(2),(3), sch 1A para 2(1)-(4)

16.20   LGFA 13A(1)(c),(6),(7)

16.21   LGFA 13A(1)(c),(6), sch 1A para 2(2),(4)

16.22   LGFA 13A(1)(c),(6),(7); CTP sch 7 para 9(2)

16.23   SC v East Riding of Yorkshire Council [2014]) EW Misc B46 (UT) www.bailii.org/ew/cases/2014/Misc/B46.html

In the case of local CTR/CTR classes, councils must apply exclusion (b) to working age and pension age claims and (d) to pension age claims. They can choose whether to apply any of the other exclusions. None of the exclusions apply to discretionary CTR.

Absences from home

16.25   You are excluded from main CTR and SAR while you (the claimant) are absent from your home unless you meet one of the conditions in paras 16.26-29.

Temporary absences within Great Britain

16.26   You can get CTR during an absence within Great Britain:

(a) for up to 52 weeks if it is due to you receiving medically approved treatment or convalescence or to accompany a family member who is; or

(b) for up to 52 weeks if you are a hospital patient or it is due to domestic violence, studying, attending training or imprisonment; or

(c) for up to 13 weeks if you are in a care home for a trial period; or

(d) for up to 13 weeks for any other absence.

Temporary absences outside Great Britain

16.27   In England, you can get CTR during an absence outside Great Britain:

(a) for up to 26 weeks if it is due to your employment as a mariner, offshore worker, Crown servant or in the armed forces;

(b) for up to 26 weeks if it is due to receiving or providing care or to domestic violence; or

(c) for up to eight weeks if it is due to a death in your family; or

(d) for up to four weeks in any other case.

The details are the same as HB (volume 2 chapter 3).

16.28   In Scotland, you can get CTR during an absence outside Great Britain:

(a) without time limit if it is due to your employment as an aircraft worker, mariner, offshore worker, Crown servant or in the armed forces;

(b) for up to six months if it is due to receiving or providing care;

(c) for up to two months if it is due to a death in your family; or

(d) for up to one month in any other case, but in pension age claims only if you haven't had more than two absences outside Great Britain in the past 12 months, or in working age claims only if you were on CTR before you left home.

16.29   In Wales, you can only get CTR during absences outside Great Britain and Northern Ireland for up to 52 weeks to attend a training course or for the conditions in para 16.26(a).

16.24   LGFA sch 1A para 2(9); CTP 11-13; sch 1 paras 2(b),(d), 3(b),(d), 4(1)(b),(d), 5; CTR 13-24, 75(1),(2)

16.25   CTP 12(2),(6),(7), sch 1 paras 2(b), 3(b), 4(1)(b), 5; CTR 13(b), 14(b), 15(1)(b), 16(b), 17(b), 18(1)(a), 19, 21(2),(6),(7)

16.26   CTP sch 1 para 5; CTR 19

16.27   CTP sch 1 para 5(2)(c),(d),(2A)-(2F),(3B)-(3G)

Migrants

16.30   You are excluded from main CTR, SAR and local CTR/CTR classes if you (the claimant) are a migrant or have recently arrived in the UK, unless you are on UC, SPC, JSA(IB), ESA(IR) or IS, or in one of the eligible groups in table 20.1.

Full-time students

16.31   You are excluded from main CTR (but not SAR) if you (the claimant) are a working age full-time student in Scotland or Wales, unless you are on SPC, JSA(IB), ESA(IR) or IS (or in Scotland, UC), or are in one of the eligible groups. These are normally the same as in UC (table 2.3) and the full details are as in HB (volume 2 chapter 2). But note that the rules can differ for local CTR/CTR classes, and also that students can be exempt or a disregarded person for council tax purposes (tables 15.3, 15.4) whether or not eligible for benefits.

CTR claims and changes

16.32   The rules in this section apply to main CTR and SAR. In England and Wales councils can have their own rules for local CTR/CTR classes and discretionary CTR.

Claims

16.33   To get CTR you have to make a claim to the council that sends your council tax bill:

   (a)   in England and Wales, you have to make a separate CTR claim to the council even if you are claiming UC or SPC at the same time;

   (b)   in Scotland, when you claim UC, the DWP tells the council and the council treats this as if you had made a CTR claim; but when you claim SPC and in all other situations, you have to make a separate CTR claim to the council.

(In CTR law, claims are called 'applications' and claimants are called 'applicants'.)

Advance claims

16.34   You can make an advance claim for CTR:

   (a)   up to 17 weeks (in Wales, 13 weeks) before your 66th birthday; or

   (b)   up to 17 weeks (in Wales, 13 weeks) before you expect to qualify for pension age CTR;

   (c)   up to 13 weeks before you expect to qualify for working age CTR; or

   (d)   in England and Scotland, up to eight weeks before you expect to become liable for council tax.

In (a)-(c) for example, this could be because you know your income will go down.

16.30   CTP 12, 13; CTR 21, 22

16.31   CTR 20, 24, 75(1),(2)

16.33   CTP sch 1 paras 2(f), 3(g), 4(1)(e), sch 7 paras 2, 3, 9, sch 8 paras 3, 4
          CTR 13(f), 14(g), 15(1)(e), 16(f), 17(g), 18(1)(e), 109, sch 1 paras 2, 3, 11

16.34   CTP sch 8 para 5(6),(7); CTR 110(6),(7)

How to claim

16.35   You can claim CTR on your council's claim form or in most areas by telephone or online [www]. If you are in a couple, one of you ('the claimant') makes the claim for you both.

Help with claiming

16.36   You can ask the council or an advice organisation to help with your claim, or you can ask a family member or friend. If you can't manage your financial affairs, an attorney can claim for you, or the council can appoint someone to do this.

Information and evidence

16.37   You should provide the information and evidence the council reasonably needs, including personal, family and household details and your (and your partner's) capital, income and (except in Scotland) national insurance number. The council can request this when you claim or at any time during your CTR award, and should allow you at least one month to provide it.

Decisions about your CTR

16.38   Chapter 18 gives the rules about decision notices, reconsiderations and appeals.

The date your CTR starts

16.39   Your CTR starts:

(a) in England and Scotland, on the Monday following your date of claim or backdated date of claim (paras 16.41-43); or

(b) in Wales, on your exact date of claim or backdated date of claim.

16.40   But your CTR starts on the day your council tax starts if that is in the same benefit week (para 17.2) as your date of claim or backdated date of claim.

Date of claim

16.41   Your date of claim is the earliest of the following dates:

(a) the day the council received your CTR claim;

(b) the day you told the council you want to claim CTR, so long as the council received your CTR claim within one month;

(c) the day your partner died or you separated from them (if they were previously the CTR claimant), so long as the council received your CTR claim within one month;

16.35   CTP sch 7 paras 2, 3, sch 8 para 4(1); CTR 109(1), sch 1 paras 2, 3 www.gov.uk/apply-council-tax-reduction

16.36   CTP sch 8 para 4; CTR 109

16.37   CTP sch 8 para 7; CTR 113

16.39   CTP sch 1 para 45(1); CTR 106(1)

16.40   CTP sch 1 para 45(2); CTR 106(2)

(d) the day your UC or guarantee credit of SPC began, as long as the council received your CTR claim within one month of the DWP receiving your UC/SPC claim;

(e) the day your council tax started if you are on UC or guarantee credit of SPC, so long as the council received your CTR claim within one month of that.

Backdating

16.42   For pension age CTR claims, your date of claim (para 16.41) is backdated for three months in all cases. For working age CTR claims, it is backdated for up to six months in Scotland or three months in Wales (or longer: para 16.7), but only if you have 'good cause'. In England, some councils include similar working age rules in their local CTR scheme.

16.43   'Good cause' is decided in the same way as in HB (volume 2 chapter 16). You may qualify if you were too ill to claim, were wrongly advised, or had some other good reason for not claiming CTR earlier.

The date your CTR changes or ends

16.44   You should tell the council about any change that could affect your CTR. Your CTR changes when there is a change in your income, capital, family, household, or other circumstances. It only ends when:

(a) your liability for council tax ends;

(b) you move out of the council's area;

(c) you stop meeting the conditions for CTR (e.g. you are excluded: para 16.24); or

(d) the CTR calculations give a figure of nil or a negative figure.

16.45   In most cases, your CTR changes or ends:

(a) in England and Scotland, on the Monday following the change;

(b) in Wales, on the exact day of the change.

But changes in your council tax take effect the exact day, and some changes relating to non-dependant deductions or finding a job are delayed (paras 17.14, 17.36).

Payments of CTR

16.46   Your CTR is awarded (or 'paid') by crediting it to your council tax account – so you have less council tax to pay. If you are jointly liable for council tax the council can pay you instead if it considers it would be 'inappropriate' to credit it to your account. If you have already paid your council tax bill in full, a payment is made to you.

16.41   CTP sch 7 paras 2-7, sch 8 para 5; CTR 110, sch 1 paras 2-7

16.42   CTP sch 8 para 6; CTR 111, 112

16.44   CTP sch 1 para 46(1); CTR 107(1)

16.45   CTP sch 1 para 46(1),(3),(4); CTR 107(1),(3),(4)

16.46-47   LGFA 13A(1)(a); CTP sch 8 para 14; CTR 118
           CT(A&E) 1(2) definition: 'discount', 20, 24(2); SI 2013/3086

Shortfalls and excess CTR

16.47   If your CTR was calculated incorrectly in the past (for example because the wrong facts were used) it must be recalculated. There are two possibilities:

(a) if you were awarded too little CTR, the shortfall (or 'underpayment') is awarded as in para 16.46;

(b) if you were awarded too much CTR, the excess (or 'overpayment') is recovered by increasing your council tax bill or by sending you an invoice.

Official error overpayments in Scotland

16.48   In Scotland, if you were overpaid CTR due to an official error and you could not have reasonably been expected to realise that you were being overpaid at the time it arose, or when you were notified of your award, the overpayment is not recoverable. An 'official error' means a mistake by the council, or someone acting for the council or providing services to the council. It is not an official error however if you, or someone acting for you, caused or materially contributed to the mistake.

16.48   CTS 21; CTS66+ 19A

Chapter 17 **Main CTR and SAR**

- Main CTR: see paras 17.4-17.
- Second adult rebate: see paras 17.18-25.
- Capital and income for main CTR: see paras 17.26-36.

17.1   This chapter explains who can get main CTR and SAR and how they are calculated. It gives the national rules (table 16.1). But for working age claims in England, local CTR often has different rules (paras 16.11-12).

Benefit weeks

17.2   Main CTR and SAR are awarded for benefit weeks which always start on a Monday, or on a daily basis if you only qualify for part of a benefit week.

Conversion to weekly amounts

17.3   To obtain weekly figures to use in CTR:

(a) divide annual council tax by 365 (or 366 in a leap year) and multiply by 7;

(b) multiply calendar monthly earnings or other income by 12 and divide by 52.

Main CTR

17.4   Main CTR applies:

(a) in Scotland and Wales whether you are working age or pension age;

(b) in England if you are pension age.

Working age claims in England have local CTR rules (paras 16.11-12).

Who can get main CTR

17.5   You can get main CTR if:

(a) you are a resident who is liable for council tax (para 15.6);

(b) you aren't excluded due to an absence (para 16.25);

(c) you aren't an excluded migrant or student (paras 16.30-31);

(d) you don't have capital over £16,000 (paras 17.31-32); and

(e) your income is low enough (para 17.6).

17.2   CTP 2(1) definition: 'reduction week'; CTR 2(1)

17.3   CTP sch 1 paras 7(1), 17(1); CTR 29(1), 40(1), 49(1), 50(1),(2)

17.4   CTP 11(1), 14, sch 1 paras 1-4; CTR 13, 14, 16, 17

17.5   CTP 14(2), sch 1 paras 2, 3; CTR 13, 14, 16, 17

Amount of main CTR

17.6   To calculate your weekly main CTR:

(a) start with your weekly council tax (para 17.7);

(b) if you have one or more non-dependants, deduct the amounts they are expected to contribute (para 17.13); and

(c) if you have excess income (paras 17.8-11), deduct 20% of it.

See also para 17.16 if you are jointly liable for council tax and para 17.17 for council tax bands E to H in Scotland.

Weekly council tax for main CTR

17.7   For main CTR, your weekly council tax means the amount due on your home in the current benefit week (para 17.2) after any disability reduction or discount that applies.

Excess income

17.8   'Excess income' can be described as income beyond what you need for your basic living needs. Paras 17.9-11 give the details. You don't have excess income if you are on the guarantee credit of SPC, or on JSA(IB), ESA(IR) or IS.

Excess income for people who aren't on UC

17.9   In England, Wales and Scotland, if you aren't on UC, your excess income equals:

(a) your weekly net income as assessed by the council (para 17.26);

(b) minus your applicable amount as assessed by the council (para 17.12).

But in England if you have a working age claim, your CTR is worked out under the council's local scheme (para 16.11).

Excess income for people who are on UC

17.10   In Wales for all claims, and in England for pension age claims and for councils that use the default scheme for working age claims (para 16.17), your excess income equals:

(a) your weekly net income as assessed by the DWP in your UC claim (chapter 10);

(b) minus the DWP's maximum UC figure (para 9.4).

In each case the DWP's figures are converted into a weekly figure by multiplying by 12 and dividing by 52. In England other councils have their own CTR scheme which may be a variant on this or may be completely different (paras 16.17-19).

17.6   CTP sch 1 paras 2(c),(e), 3(c),(e),(f), 7, 10(2),(3); CTR 13(c),(e), 14(c),(e),(f), 16(c),(e), 17(c),(e),(f), 29, 32(2),(3)

17.7   CTP sch 1 para 7(1),(2); CTR 29(1),(2)

17.8   CTP sch 1 paras 3(e),(f), 10(3); 13; CTR 14(e),(f), 17(e),(f), 32(3), 35, sch 7 para 14, sch 8 para 9

17.9   CTP sch 1 paras 10(3), 13-15; CTR 32(3), 35, 36, 38, 52-54

17.10   CTR 28, 32(3), 37

17.11 In Scotland, if you are on UC (no matter how much UC), your excess income equals:

(a) your weekly net income as assessed by the council (paras 17.26-29);

(b) minus your applicable amount as assessed by the council (para 17.12).

Before 1st April 2022 councils in Scotland used a method similar to councils in Wales, but with adjustments to the maximum UC figure for households with children.

Applicable amounts

17.12 Your applicable amount is used in the calculation of main CTR (paras 17.9-11). It represents your weekly living needs and those of your family (para 16.3). It is made up of personal allowances plus additions for disability, carers and people with limited capability for work. Appendix 2 gives the figures. The detailed rules are the same as in HB (volume 2 chapter 12) except that:

(a) in Scotland for all claims, and in Wales for claims where you or your partner don't get UC, there is no limit on how many additions you get for a child or young person, and in Scotland these additions are 25% higher than the rates used for HB (appendix 2)

(b) in England if you have a working age claim, your CTR is worked out under the council's local scheme, and this may not use applicable amounts (para 16.9 and 16.11). But councils which use the default scheme (or a modified version of it) still use applicable amounts.

Non-dependant deductions

17.13 Non-dependants are adult sons, daughters, other relatives, or friends who live with you (para 15.9). They are expected to contribute towards your council tax (which means an amount is deducted from your CTR) unless one of the exceptions applies. Table 17.1 gives the current figures and table 17.2 lists the exceptions.

Delayed non-dependant deductions

17.14 If you or your partner are 66 or over in England (or 65 or over in Scotland), new deductions or increases in deductions during your award of CTR are delayed for 26 weeks.

Non-dependant's gross weekly income

17.15 A non-dependant's gross weekly income includes all types of earned and unearned income, with only the following being disregarded:

(a) SPC;

(b) JSA(IB), ESA(IR) and IS;

(c) PIP, DLA, child disability payment, adult disability payment, attendance allowance and equivalent benefits (para 10.54); and

(d) payments from government sponsored trusts and funds etc (para 10.85).

No deductions are made for tax, national insurance or pension contributions.

17.11 CTS 34, 42, 49, 57(1)(p),(2)(d)

17.12 CTP sch 1 para 6, sch 2; CTR 25, 26, sch 2, sch 3; Policy note to SSI 2016/253

17.13 CTP 9, sch 1 para 7(1), 8; CTR 9, 29(1), 30

17.14 CTP sch 1 para 46(10)-(13); CTR 107(10)-(13)

17.15 CTP sch 1 para 8(8)(a),(c),(9),(10); CTR 30(9)

Examples: Main CTR

1. A single person on SPC with a non-dependant

Darra lives in England and is on SPC. His council tax is £30 per week. He has one non-dependant, his daughter. She works full-time and has gross income of £550 pw, so her non-dependant contribution is £14.15 pw (table 17.1).

- ■ Weekly council tax   £30.00
- ■ Minus non-dependant deduction   − £14.15
- ■ Equals weekly main CTR   £15.85

2. A band H home in Scotland

Dolores and Diane live in a band H home in Scotland. Their council tax is £45 per week. They have net income of £500 pw. For the ordinary main CTR calculation, this is too high for them to qualify (para 17.6). But for the alternative calculation, it is £21 above the threshold of £479 (para 17.17).

- ■ 22½% of weekly council tax   £10.13
- ■ Minus 20% of £21   − £4.20
- ■ Equals weekly main CTR   £5.93

Table 17.1 Main CTR: weekly non-dependant deductions

(a) Non-dependants working at least 16 hours per week

Deductions are based on gross weekly income (para 17.15)

England		Scotland		Wales	
Income	*Deduction*	*Income*	*Deduction*	*Income*	*Deduction*
At least £511.00	£14.15	At least £517.00	£14.65	At least £511.00	£16.40
At least £410.00	£11.80	At least £418.00	£12.30	At least £410.00	£13.70
At least £236.00	£9.40	At least £241.00	£9.70	At least £236.00	£10.90
Under £236.00	£4.60	Under £241.00	£4.90	Under £236.00	£5.45

(b) Other non-dependants

England		Scotland		Wales	
England	£4.60	**Scotland**	£4.90	**Wales**	£5.45

(c) Non-dependant couples

There is one deduction per couple: (a) applies to combined gross weekly income if one or both work at least 16 hours pw; (b) applies otherwise.

T17.1   CTP sch 1 para 8(1),(2); CTR 30(1),(2)
        England: SI 2023/16 reg 6
        Scotland SSI 2023/38 regs 18, 26
        Wales SI 2023/47 regs 6, 8

Table 17.2 **Main CTR: no non-dependant deductions**

Your circumstances

No deductions apply for any non-dependants in your home if you or your partner are:

(a) on the daily living component of PIP or (in Scotland) adult disability payment;

(b) the care component of DLA or (in Scotland) child disability payment;

(c) on attendance allowance or an equivalent benefit (para 10.54);

(d) on an armed forces independence payment (AFIP);

(e) entitled to (a), (b), (c) or (d) but not receiving it because of being in hospital; or

(f) certified as severely sight impaired or blind by an ophthalmologist or have regained your sight in the last 28 weeks.

Non-dependant's circumstances

No deduction applies for any single non-dependant who is, or any non-dependant couple who both are:

(g) under 18;

(h) on UC without any earned income;

(i) on SPC;

(j) on JSA(IB), ESA(IR), or IS;

(k) a youth trainee getting a training allowance;

(l) a full-time student;

(m) a disregarded person in table 15.4 (other than a student, youth trainee or an apprentice) – this includes education leavers, care leavers and people who are severely mentally impaired;

(n) a hospital in-patient for 52 weeks (including two or more periods in hospital separated by 28 days or less);

(o) in England and Scotland, a member of the armed forces who is away on operations;

(p) in Scotland, a person who was residing in Ukraine to whom para 20.39(c) applies who left due to the Russian invasion.

Note:

- There is no non-dependant deduction for someone who doesn't 'normally live' with you even if they eventually return (paras 3.71-72).

T17.2   CTP 3, sch 1 para 8(6)-(8),(11),(12); CTR 3, 30(6)-(8)

Main CTR if you are jointly liable

17.16   If you are jointly liable for council tax with someone other than your partner (para 15.16), the main CTR calculation (para 17.6) uses your share of the weekly council tax and of any non-dependant deductions:

(a)   the weekly council tax on your house is shared equally between the jointly liable people except for any who are excluded students (para 16.31) – e.g. if there are three this is one third each, or if one is an excluded student it is half each for the other two;

(b)   each non-dependant deduction is shared equally between whichever of you the non-dependant lives with – if they live only with you it applies wholly to you.

Main CTR for bands E to H in Scotland

17.17   If your home is in Scotland and in council tax band E to H, the following calculation is used (instead of the calculation in para 17.6) when it would give you more main CTR:

(a)   start with:

  ■   7½% of your weekly council tax (para 17.7) if your home is in band E,

  ■   12½% if it is in band F,

  ■   17½% if it is in band G, or

  ■   22½% if it is in band H;

(b)   if you have one or more non-dependants, deduct the amounts they are expected to contribute (para 17.13); and

(c)   if your net weekly income (para 17.34) is above the threshold of:

  ■   £321 (single people with no children of young persons), or

  ■   £479 (others),

  subtract 20% of the excess.

Scotland has this rule because its council tax proportions are higher for these bands (table 15.1).

Second adult rebate

17.18   SAR applies:

(a)   in Scotland whether you are working age or pension age;

(b)   in England if you are pension age.

It doesn't apply in Wales (para 16.8) and working age CTR in England usually has different rules (paras 16.9-12).

17.16   CTP sch 1 paras 7(1),(3)-(5); CTR 29(1),(3)-(5)

17.17   CTS 4(1) – 'appropriate maximum council tax reduction', 14(4),(5), 79(2),(3); CTS66+ 2(1), 14A(4),(5), 47(1A),(1B)

17.18   CTP 14(2), sch 1 para 4; CTR 15, 18

Who can get SAR

17.19   You can get SAR if:

(a) you meet the liability condition (para 17.20);

(b) you have at least one second adult with a low enough income (paras 17.21-23);

(c) you don't have any lodgers who pay a commercial rent to live in part of your home;

(d) you aren't excluded due to an absence (para 16.25);

(e) you aren't an excluded migrant (para 16.30).

For SAR, your own income is completely ignored and so is your capital, even if it is over £16,000. If you qualify for both main CTR and SAR, you get whichever of them is worth more.

SAR liability condition

17.20   You meet the SAR liability condition if:

(a) you are a sole householder (para 15.13); or

(b) you are a householder couple or two joint householders (paras 15.14-16) and:

  ■ one of you is a disregarded person (table 15.4), or

  ■ both of you are; or

(c) you are three or more joint householders (para 15.16) and:

  ■ all but one of you are disregarded persons, or

  ■ all of you are.

Second adults

17.21   A second adult is an adult (over 18) in your home who:

(a) is a non-dependant (para 15.9); but

(b) isn't a disregarded person (table 15.4).

Amount of SAR

17.22   If your second adult is on SPC, JSA(IB), ESA(IR), IS or in Scotland, UC with no earned income, your SAR is:

(a) 25% of your weekly council tax (para 17.24); or

(b) 100% of your weekly council tax if you (the claimant) are an excluded student (para 16.31).

When you have more than one second adult, they must all be on the benefits mentioned.

17.19   CTP sch 1 paras 4(1),(2), 9(1), sch 6 para 27; CTR 15(1),(2), 18(1),(2), 31(1), sch 9 para 27, sch 10 para 49

17.20   CTP sch 1 paras 4(2),(3), 9(2),(3); CTR 15(2),(3), 18(2),(3), 31(2),(3)

17.21   CTP sch 1 para 4(2),(3), sch 3 para 1(1); CTR 15(2),(3), 18(2),(3), sch 4 para 1(1)

17.22   CTP sch 1 paras 9(1), 10(4), sch 3 paras 1, 3; CTR 31(1), 32(4), sch 4 paras 1, 3

17.23   Otherwise, your SAR is:

(a)   7½% of your weekly council tax if your second adult's gross weekly income is below £317 pw in England or £308 pw in Scotland; or

(b)   15% of your weekly council tax if it is below £244 pw in England or £237 pw in Scotland.

A second adult's gross weekly income is worked out in the same way as in para 17.15. When your second adult is in a couple, both their incomes are combined. And when you have more than one second adult, all their gross weekly incomes are combined.

Weekly council tax for SAR

17.24   For SAR, your weekly council tax means the amount due on your home in the current benefit week (para 17.2) after any disability reduction but before any discount. (This ensures that discounts and SAR calculations are based on the same amount.)

SAR if you are jointly liable

17.25   If you are jointly liable for council tax with someone other than your partner (para 15.16), the result of the SAR calculation (paras 17.22-23) is shared equally between all of you. So, if there are three jointly liable people and two are a couple, the couple's share is two thirds.

Examples: Second adult rebate

1. A single person with one second adult

Dorinder has too much capital to qualify for main CTR. Her council tax is £36 per week. She has one second adult, her son, who works full-time and has gross income of £240 pw.

▪ Weekly SAR of 7½% of council tax	£2.70

2. Discount plus SAR

Dan is a carer (table 15.4(g)). He cares for his mother who is a second adult and is on SPC. His council tax is £30 per week.

▪ Weekly discount of 25% of council tax	£7.50
▪ Plus weekly SAR of 25% of council tax	£7.50

17.23   CTP sch 3 paras 1, 3; CTR sch 4 paras 1, 3; SI 2023/16 reg 8; SSI 2023/38 regs 21, 28

17.24   CTP sch 3 para 1(2); CTR sch 4 para 1(2)

17.25   CTP sch 1 para 9(2),(3) ; CTR 31(2),(3)

Capital and income for main CTR

17.26　　This section summarises how your capital and income are assessed for main CTR. For SAR, see instead para 17.15. The rules about income and capital vary between England, Wales and Scotland and also between working age and pension age CTR (paras 17.28-30). In Scotland the rules changed on 1st April 2022 (para 17.11).

Whose capital and income counts

17.27　　If you are a single person, your own income and capital are taken into account. If you are a couple, your partner's capital and income are included with yours. But if you are on a guarantee credit of SPC, JSA(IB), ESA(IR) or IS all of your income and capital is disregarded so you don't have any excess income (para 17.8).

Working age CTR

17.28　　For working age CTR, your capital and income are assessed as follows:

(a) in England for councils that use the default scheme for its local CTR (paras 16.9-12 and 17.10), the rules are summarized in paras 17.31-36;

(b) in Wales, the council uses the rules summarized in paras 17.31-36;

(c) in Scotland, the council uses rules that are similar to those in paras 17.31-36, but:

- if you are on UC, part of your UC can be included as income (para 17.29),

- most other kinds of unearned income in working age claims is disregarded (table 17.3),

- if you have earned income the council assesses it in a way that is similar to how it would be for income tax purposes, and

- 100% of your pension contributions are deducted from your gross earnings instead of 50% (table 17.3).

17.29　　In Scotland, the following part of your UC is included as your income:

(a) if you have at least one child or young person:

- the total of your UC child elements, disabled child elements, childcare costs element and transitional element (paras 9.15, 9.16, 9.42 and 4.36); or

- if lower, the actual amount of your UC, after any deductions due to the benefit cap (para 9.51) but before any deductions for payments to your landlord or a third party (paras 12.30-59);

(b) in any other case:

- the amount of your transitional element, or

- if you don't get a transitional element, nil.

17.27　　CTP sch 1 paras 11, 13; CTR 33, 35, sch 7 para 14, sch 8 paras 8, 9, sch 10 paras 8, 9

17.28　　CTS 49(6)

17.29　　CTS 57(1)(p),(2)(d)

Pension age CTR

17.30 For pension age CTR throughout the UK, your capital and income are assessed as follows:

(a) if you are on the savings credit of SPC, the council uses the DWP's figures for your capital and income, but adjusts these to take account of the higher income disregards in CTR (volume 2 chapter 13);

(b) in any other case, the council assesses your capital and income as described in paras 17.31-.36.

Your capital

17.31 Capital means savings, investments, and other holdings. Some kinds are disregarded and in most cases, these are as in UC (table 10.6). The full details are the same as in HB (volume 2 chapter 15 and appendix 3).

17.32 If your capital is over £16,000 (the capital limit), you can't get main CTR.

17.33 If your capital is £16,000 or less, it is treated as giving you an assumed weekly income (tariff income) as follows:

(a) for working age main CTR, deduct £6,000 and divide the remainder by 250;

(b) for pension age main CTR, deduct £10,000 and divide the remainder by 500;

(c) if the result of (a) or (b) isn't a multiple of £1, round it up to the next whole £1.

Your net weekly income

17.34 Your net weekly income is made up of:

(a) earned income from employment or self-employment;

(b) state, occupational and private pensions;

(c) the savings credit of SPC;

(d) new-style JSA/ESA and WTC;

(e) CTC in working age claims;

(f) in Scotland, part of your UC (para 17.29); and

(g) any other unearned income you have.

The amounts in table 17.3 are then disregarded.

Changes in income and capital

17.35 Changes in your income and capital are usually taken into account:

(a) in England and Scotland, from the Monday following the change;

(b) in Wales, from the exact day of the change.

17.30   CTP sch 1 paras 14, 15; CTR 36, 38

17.32   CTP 11(2),(3), sch 1 paras 2(d), 3(d), 4(d), sch 6 para 27; CTR 13(d), 14(d), 15(1)(d), 16(d), 17(d), 18(1)(d), 20, 23, sch 9 para 27, sch 10 para 49

17.33   CTP sch 1 para 37; CTR 71, 72

17.34   CTP sch 1 paras 14(2)(a), 16(1)(a)-(d),(j), 17(11),(13); CTR 36(2)(a), 39(1)(a)-(d),(j), 40(11),(13), 49(1), 54(1),(2)

17.35   CTP sch 1 para 46(1); CTR 107(1)

Starting work and extended CTR

17.36 But in Scotland and Wales, you get four weeks' extended CTR if:

(c) you have been on JSA(IB), ESA or IS (not UC or SPC) for at least 26 weeks; and

(d) this ends because you start work or increase your hours or earnings.

During those four weeks, your main CTR continues at the level it was beforehand.

Table 17.3 **Main income disregards in main CTR**

Earned income

Your earned income is taken into account after deductions for tax, national insurance and 50% of any pension contributions you pay. The following amounts are then disregarded.

(a) A standard amount of:
- £5 for single people;
- £10 for couples;
- £20 for many disabled people; or
- £25 for lone parents.

(b) An amount for childcare costs of up to:
- £175 for one child; or
- £300 for two or more.

(c) An additional amount of £17.10 if:
- you work at least 30 hours a week; or
- you have one or more children/young persons or are disabled, and work at least 16 hours a week.

Unearned income

Your pensions, benefits and other unearned income are taken into account after any tax you pay on them. The following amounts are then disregarded.

(d) The guarantee credit of SPC.

(e) JSA(IB), ESA(IR) and IS.

(f) PIP, DLA, attendance allowance and equivalent benefits (para 10.54) and (in Scotland) child and adult disability payment.

17.36　　CTR 95-98

T17.3(a)-(c)　CTP sch 1 paras 19(2), 24(1)(c),(3), 29(2), 30(3), sch 4 paras 1-5, 8, 10;
　　　　　　CTR 42(2), 52(3), 57(1)(c),(3), 61(3), 62(3), sch 5 paras 1-5, 8, 10, sch 7 paras 4, 5, 11, 18

T17.3(d)-(n)　CTP sch 1 para 17(13), CTR 40(13), sch 8 para 4

T17.3(d)-(h)　CTP sch 1 paras 13, 16(1)(j)(i)-(vii); CTR 35, 39(1)(j)(i)-(vii), sch 8 paras 8, 9, 11, 14, 21, 52, 66

(g) CTC in pension age claims.

(h) Child benefit, guardian's allowance and widowed parent's allowance.

(i) HB and most other council payments.

(j) in Scotland, all war disablement and war bereavement pensions; in England and Wales, £10 of these and many councils disregard part or all of the remainder.

(k) bereavement support payments or £15 of widowed mother's/parent's allowance.

(l) if you have children/young persons:

   ■ all maintenance you receive for the children/young persons

   ■ in England and Wales, £15 of maintenance you receive for you/your partner;

   ■ in Scotland, all maintenance you receive for you/your partner unless it is paid under a court order.

(m) if you receive rent from a lodger in your home:

   ■ in England and Wales, £20 of the rent, plus 50% of the remainder if you provide meals;

   ■ in Scotland, all the rent.

(n) Compensation payments for personal injury, charitable payments, and expenses payments for charitable or voluntary work.

(o) Payments from government sponsored trusts and funds relating to certain diseases, independent living for disabled people, the London and Manchester bombings and government compensation from the Windrush scheme or for historical institutional child abuse.

(p) In England and Scotland any payments made in connection with the Homes for Ukraine sponsorship scheme are disregarded as income and capital in both working age and pension age claims.

Note:

   ■ For further details, see volume 2 chapters 13, 14.

   ■ If you are on the guarantee credit of SPC, JSA(IB), ESA(IR) or IS the whole of your income and capital is disregarded (para 17.27).

T17.3(i)   CTP sch 1 para 16(1)(j)(ix)-(xi); CTR 39(1)(j)(ix)-(xi), sch 8 paras 30-34, 37, 42, 64, 65

T17.3(j)   CTP sch 1 para 16(1)(e),(f),(l),(m), sch 5 paras 1-5, 13; CTR 39(1)(e),(f),(l),(m), sch 6 paras 1-5, 13, sch 8 para 20, 53-56

T 17.3(k) CTP sch 1 para 16(1)(j)(xiii); sch 5 paras 7,8; CTR 39(1)(j)(xiii), sch 6 paras 7,8, sch 8 para 21

T17.3(l)   CTP sch 1 para 16(1)(o), sch 5 para 20; CTR 39(1)(o), sch 6 para 20, sch 8 paras 49, 50

T17.3(m) CTP sch 1 para 16(1)(p),(v), sch 5 paras 9, 10; CTR 39(1)(p),(v), sch 6 paras 9, 10, sch 8 paras 26, 27

T17.3(n)   CTP sch 1 paras 16(1)(s), 18(2)(f), sch 6 paras 12, 14, 15; CTR 39(1)(s), 41(2)(f), 51(2)(d), sch 6 paras 12, 14, 15, sch 8 paras 5, 6, 19

T17.3(o)   CTP sch 1 para 16(1), sch 6 para 16(1); CTR 39(1), sch 8 para 41, sch 9 para 16, sch 10 para 29

T17.3(p)   CTP 17 as inserted by SI 2023/16 reg 5

Chapter 18 **CTR decisions and appeals**

- CTR decisions and reconsiderations: see paras 18.1-10.
- Council tax and CTR appeals: see paras 18.11-31.

Decisions and reconsiderations

Decision notices

18.1   The council must make decisions about your CTR:

(a) when you make your claim;

(b) when your circumstances change; and

(c) when your CTR is overpaid.

In England and Wales, the council notifies you of each decision it makes and in Wales the notice must tell you how your CTR has been calculated (like the HB notice rules). In Scotland, the council normally also does this (para 18.6).

Decision rights

18.2   When the council makes a decision about your CTR, you have the right to:

(a) get a statement of reasons for the decision (para 18.7);

(b) ask the council to reconsider the decision (para 18.8); and

(c) appeal to a tribunal (para 18.11).

These rights belong to you (the claimant) or someone acting for you. When you request a reconsideration or appeal, the law calls you an 'aggrieved' person.

18.3   As this chapter explains there are some differences between the law in England, Scotland and Wales. For guidance see para 18.15.

Time limits for decisions and notices

18.4   In England and Wales when you make a claim for CTR, the council must:

(a) make a decision within 14 days of getting the information and evidence it requires (para 16.37), or as soon as reasonably practicable;

(b) send you a decision notice on the day it makes the decision or as soon as reasonably practicable.

18.1   CTP sch 8 paras 11, 12(1); CTPW sch 13 paras 8, 9(1),(4), sch 14

18.2   CTP sch 7 para 8; sch 8 para 12(5)-(8); CTPW sch 12 paras 8-10, sch 13 para 9(5)-(8); CTS 93(2),(4), 94(1); CTS66+ 70A(2),(4), 70B(1)

18.4   CTP sch 8 paras 11, 12(1)(a); CTPW sch 13 paras 8, 9(1)(a)

18.5   When the council makes any other CTR decision, it must send you a decision notice within 14 days or as soon as reasonably practicable. Every decision notice must tell you about your appeal rights including any local scheme rules (para 18.9) and in Wales it must tell you how your CTR has been calculated or why you don't qualify (similar to the HB notice rules).

18.6   Scottish CTR law doesn't set a time limit for making or notifying decisions, but in practice councils normally follow the HB rules when making decisions (which are the same as for CTR in England and Wales).

Getting a statement of reasons

18.7   If the council's decision notice doesn't give reasons, you can write requesting these within one month. The council must send a written statement of reasons within 14 days or as soon as reasonably practicable after that. Scottish CTR law does not require this, but it is good practice, and it may be unreasonable to refuse [www].

Requesting a reconsideration

18.8   You can ask the council to reconsider any CTR decision (paras 18.17-20 apply to reconsiderations in the same way as to appeals). Your reconsideration request should:

    (a) be sent in writing to the council;

    (b) say what CTR matter you are asking the council to reconsider;

    (c) give your grounds; and

    (d) be within the time limit if there is one (para 18.9).

In England and Wales, it is advisable to state that your email or letter is a 'notice of appeal under section 16 of the Local Government Finance Act 1992'. A reconsideration is often called a 'mandatory reconsideration' because you have to request one before you appeal (para 18.12). A request for discretionary CTR counts as a notice of appeal because a person requesting it is aggrieved at the calculation of council tax he has otherwise been found liable to pay (CTGM para 17.4.2).

Time limit for reconsiderations

18.9   In England, each council decides its own time limit for requesting a reconsideration or can decide not to have a time limit. In Wales, your request for a reconsideration should reach the council within one month, or in Scotland within two months, of:

    (a) the date the council issued its decision notice; or

    (b) the date the council issued a statement of reasons, if later.

18.5   CTP sch 8 para 12(1)(b),(4); CTPW sch 13 para 9(1)(b),(4), sch 14

18.7   CTP sch 8 para 12(5),(6); CTPW sch 13 para 9(5),(6)
       Right First Time, Scottish Government (2021) https://tinyurl.com/SG-Right-1st-Time-2021

18.8   CTP sch 7 para 8(1); CTPW sch 12 para 8(1); CTS 93(2),(3); CTS66+ 70A(2),(3)

18.9   LGFA sch 1A para 2(6); CTPW sch 7 para 8(2); CTS 93(3); CTS66+ 70A(3)

The council's response to your reconsideration request

18.10   The council must write telling you the outcome of your request:

(a)   if it accepts your request, it must say how this changes your CTR entitlement; or

(b)   if it refuses your request, it must give reasons and explain how to appeal to a tribunal and the time limit.

In Scotland, the council must do this within two months of receiving your request. In England and Wales, the council should normally meet the same time limit.

Council tax and CTR appeals

18.11   You can appeal about council tax and CTR decisions to:

(a)   a valuation tribunal in England and Wales; or

(b)   a first-tier tribunal in Scotland.

Before 1st April 2023 in Scotland, appeals went to the Valuation Appeal Committee in the case of council tax, and the Council Tax Reduction Review Panel in the case of CTR.

When you can appeal

18.12   You can appeal if:

(a)   you asked for a reconsideration and the council has responded to it (para 18.10); or

(b)   you asked for a reconsideration at least two months ago and the council hasn't responded to it.

The time limit for appealing is explained in table 18.1

Making an appeal

18.13   You make your appeal (para 18.11):

(a)   in England, to the Valuation Tribunal by completing the online form [www];

(b)   in Wales, to the Valuation Tribunal for Wales by downloading the online form [www] and emailing it to correspondence@valuationtribunal.wales (or posting it to the regional office); or

(c)   in Scotland, to the First-tier Tribunal for Scotland, Local Taxation Chamber, by writing to the Glasgow Tribunals Centre, 20 York Street, Glasgow, G2 8GT.

In England and Wales there are separate forms for liability and CTR appeals.

18.10   CTP sch 7 para 8(2),(3), sch 8 para 12(4); CTPW sch 12 paras 9, 10, sch 13 para 9(4), sch 14 para 3; CTS 93(4); CTS66+ 70A(4)

18.11   England and Wales: LGFA 16; CTP sch 7 para 8(3); CTPW sch 12 para 10
Scotland: LGFA 81; CTS 94(1); CTS66+ 70B(1)
The First-tier Tribunal for Scotland (Transfer of Functions of Valuation Appeals Committees) Regulations 2023, No 45
The First-tier Tribunal for Scotland (Transfer of Functions of the Council Tax Reduction Review Panel) Regulations 2023, No 46

18.12   LGFA 16; CTP sch 7 para 8(3); VTRE 21; CTPW sch 12 para 10; VTRW 29; CTS 94(1),(2); CTS66+ 70B(1),(2); FTSLT sch paras 35, 41(4),(5)

18.13   England (CTR): www.appeals.valuationtribunal.gov.uk/Appeal/CTR
England (liability): www.appeals.valuationtribunal.gov.uk/Appeal/CTL
Wales (CTR): www.valuationtribunal.wales/council-tax-reduction.html
Wales (liability): www.valuationtribunal.wales/council-tax-liability.html

Table 18.1 **Appeals time limits**

Situation	England and Wales	Scotland
(a) You receive a reply from the council to your request for a reconsideration (para 18.10).	Send your appeal to the valuation tribunal within two months of the council's reply	Send your appeal to the first-tier tribunal within six weeks of the council's reply
(b) You don't receive a reply from the council within two months of the date you requested a reconsideration	Send your appeal to the valuation tribunal within two months of those two months elapsing	Send your appeal to the first-tier tribunal within six weeks of those two months elapsing

Note:

The tribunal can allow a later appeal if you fail to meet the time limits due to circumstances beyond your control.

18.14   Your appeal request should:

(a)   be in writing (or on the online form);

(b)   give your name and address, the name and address/email of your representative and the address of the dwelling you are appealing about if different;

(c)   give the name of your council and the date you requested a reconsideration and enclose a copy of it (para 18.8);

(d)   if the council responded to that request, give the date of the response and enclose a copy of it (para 18.10); and

(e)   give the grounds of your appeal and brief reasons for them.

You should inform the tribunal if you have also made an HB appeal on similar grounds, and in Wales enclose a copy of your HB appeal letter.

Law, guidance, and appeal forms

18.15   The law about CTR appeals is in appendix 1 and is supplemented by practice statements and protocols [www]. General guidance and contact details are available online [www].

T18.1   LGFA 16; CTP sch 7 para 8(3); VTRE 21; CTPW sch 12 para 10; VTRW 29; CTS 94(1),(2); CTS66+ 70B(1),(2); FTSLT sch paras 35, 41(4),(5)

18.14   England and Wales: LGFA 16; VTRE 20A; VTRW 30(2),(2A)
          Scotland: LGFA 81; CTS 94(2); CTS66+ 70B(2); FTSLT sch paras 35, 41(3), 47

18.15   https://valuationtribunal.gov.uk/guidance-booklets (Council Tax Guidance Manual – England)
          https://valuationtribunal.gov.uk/vtc-guidance (Consolidated Practice Statement April 2022 – England)
          https://tinyurl.com/VT-Wales-BPP (Best Practice Protocols – Wales)
          https://tinyurl.com/VT-Wales-CTR-Forms (CTR appeal forms/guidance – Wales)

Appeals about council tax

18.16 Your council tax appeal can be about whether you are liable for council tax, and/or whether you qualify for an exemption, disability reduction or discount (paras 15.10-30).

Appeals about CTR

18.17 Your CTR appeal can be about most matters (paras 18.18-21). For example, your grounds of appeal can be that the council:

(a) has got the facts or the calculation wrong;

(b) has wrongly applied national CTR law or the rules of its local CTR scheme;

(c) has wrongly exercised its discretion; or

(d) a combination of the above.

Appeals about national CTR

18.18 You can appeal about national CTR law (table 16.1(a)-(b)). If you aren't awarded CTR (or a particular kind of CTR), you can appeal about that. If you are awarded CTR, you can appeal about the amount. Your appeal can be about your capital, income, applicable amount, residence or any other matter that affects your CTR.

Appeals about local CTR

18.19 In England and Wales you can appeal about local CTR (table 16.1(c)) – for example, about how your income was assessed (if the scheme is income based) or whether a particular description applies to you (if the scheme is category based). But you can't appeal about whether the scheme the council has chosen is reasonable or lawful – this can only be challenged by judicial review (para 14.70).

Appeals about discretionary CTR

18.20 You can appeal about discretionary CTR (table 16.1(d)) so long as you requested this when you asked for a reconsideration (para 18.8) (DG v Liverpool City Council). The tribunal can consider whether the council has exercised its discretion in a reasonable way (para 14.16) or it can substitute its own discretion if this is 'soundly and solidly based' (SC v East Riding of Yorkshire Council). Even if the council's decision complies with its own published policy, this doesn't stop the tribunal allowing the appeal, although it does make it less likely.

8.16   LGFA 15, 16; 81, 82; SSI sch 2 para 8

18.17-18 England and Wales: LGFA 16; CTP sch 7 para 8(1),(3); CTPW sch 12 paras 8(1), 10
          Scotland: LGFA 81; CTS 94; CTS66+ 70B

18.19   LGFA 66(2)(ba)

18.20   Consolidated Practice Statement, PS10; CTGM paras 17.3.1, 17.4.1 (see footnote to 18.15)
         DG v Liverpool City Council Appeal No 4310M140277/CTR
         https://hbinfo.org/caselaw/dg-v-liverpool-city-council
         SC v East Riding of Yorkshire Council [2014] EW Misc B46 (VT)
         https://www.bailii.org/ew/cases/Misc/2014/B46.html

Appeals about excess CTR (overpayments)

18.21   If the council says you have been awarded excess CTR (an 'overpayment') (para 16.47):

(a) you can appeal about the new calculation of your CTR – on any of the grounds in para 18.17; but

(b) you can't appeal about whether the excess CTR (the 'overpayment') is recoverable or about the method of recovery – for example, you can't appeal on the grounds that it shouldn't be added to your council tax bill. But you could appeal the decision not to award discretionary CTR to offset the debt (para 18.20).

For (b), see DG v Liverpool City Council, a valuation tribunal decision that is not binding (para 1.28) but is widely accepted.

What happens when you appeal

18.22   The tribunal writes to you acknowledging receipt of your appeal. It also writes to the council inviting it to send a submission to the tribunal and to you. In either case, it must do this within two weeks.

Appeal hearings

18.23   Your appeal can be decided on the paperwork if you, the council and the tribunal all agree to this. Otherwise, the tribunal holds an appeal hearing. You usually get 14 days notice of the hearing in England, four weeks in Wales, or 31 days in Scotland.

18.24   The tribunal decides how the hearing is conducted and in England and Scotland its procedures are based on practice statements/guidance issued by the tribunal president.

18.25   An appeal hearing is open to the public unless the tribunal decides it should be in private. In practice the only people likely to attend are you, your representative (and/or a friend/helper if you have one), the council's representative, the tribunal member(s) and their clerk. The tribunal tells you what to expect from the hearing and what order the hearing will be in.

Appeal decision notices

18.26   The tribunal sends you a decision notice as soon as reasonably practicable. If you have a hearing, you may also be told the decision (and in some cases the reasons) when the hearing ends.

18.22   VTRE 28(2); VTRW 30(5); FTSLT sch paras 36, 42

18.23   VTRE 29, 30; VTRW 33, 34; ; FTSLT sch paras 11, 46(1)

18.24   England and Wales: Local Government Finance Act 1988, sch 11 paras A17, 1(2); VTRE 6; VTRW 37
         Scotland: LGFA 82; FTSLT sch paras 4(1), 12-15

18.25   VTRE 5-19, 31; VTRW 27-46; FTSLT sch para 12(1),(2)

18.26   VTRE 36, 37(3); VTRW 40; FTSLT sch para 17(2)-(4)

Reasons for appeal decisions

18.27 In Wales and Scotland, the appeal decision notice always includes a statement of reasons. In England, it may or may not do so. If it doesn't provide its reasons in writing (para 18.26), you can request a statement within 14 days of the date of the decision notice and the tribunal must provide them within 14 days or as soon as reasonably practicable.

Setting aside appeal decisions

18.28 The tribunal can review and set aside a decision it has made in the interests of justice. You should normally request this in 28 days in England and Wales, or in 14 days in Scotland. If the tribunal sets the decision aside, the appeal must be decided at a hearing again (or on the paperwork if the parties agree).

Split decisions

18.29 In England, if a two-member tribunal are unable to agree the outcome your appeal is reheard by a different tribunal. In Scotland if here is a tie the chairing member has the casting vote.

Correcting appeal decisions

18.30 The tribunal can correct clerical mistakes and accidental slips and omissions in its decisions and notices. The law does not set a time limit for requesting this.

Further appeals to the courts

18.31 In England and Wales, you can make a further appeal to the High Court, but only if you consider the valuation tribunal made an error of law (para 14.71). The time limit is four weeks from the date of the tribunal's decision notice. Or in England it is two weeks from the date a statement of reasons was issued (para 18.27) if this would be later. In Scotland, you can make a further appeal to the Upper Tribunal (para 14.68). You must normally do this within 30 days.

18.27   VTRE 36, 37(4)-(7); VTRW 40(3); CTS 96(6)(f); CTS66+ 70C(6)(f); Review Panel Guidance, part 10; FTSLT sch para 17(4)

18.28   VTRE 40; VTRW 42(1)(a),(5); Tribunals (Scotland) Act 2014, s43; FTSLT sch para 19

18.29   Consolidated Practice Statement, Part 1; FTSLT sch para 17(2)

18.30   VTRE 39; VTRW 43(7); FTSLT sch para 21

18.31   VTRE 43(1),(2); VTRW 43, 44; Tribunals (Scotland) Act 2014, s46; FTSLT sch paras 39, 50; SSI 2016/231 regs 2, 3

Chapter 19 **Rate rebates**

- Rates, exemptions and disability reductions: see paras 19.1-10.
- Rate rebates general rules: see paras 19.11-17.
- UC rate rebates: see paras 19.18-35.
- HB rate rebates: see paras 19.36-57.

Rates

19.1   This chapter describes who is liable for domestic rates and the different ways your rates bill can be reduced. Rates only apply in Northern Ireland and are administered by Land and Property Services (LPS).

Dwellings

19.2   There is one rates bill per dwelling. A dwelling means a single residential property, for example a house, flat, a houseboat or a mobile home.

Who is liable to pay rates

19.3   The rates bill for your home goes to:

(a) you if you are an occupier or shared owner;

(b) your landlord if you are an NIHE or housing association tenant;

(c) your landlord if you are a private tenant and the dwelling you live in:

- is a house in multiple occupation (HMO), or
- is let as separate lodgings or apartments, or
- has a capital value less than (or equal to) £150,000;

(d) you if you are a private tenant in any other case.

19.4   If you are a tenant and the rates bill goes to your landlord, your rent is treated as including rates even if your landlord hasn't said this.

The amount of your rates bill

19.5   Rates bills are issued by LPS and run from 1st April to 31st March. The bill for your home is calculated using:

(a) its rateable value if you are an owner occupier, shared owner or private tenant – this is based on its purchase price in January 2005, capped at £400,000; or

(b) its social sector value if you are an NIHE or housing association tenant – this is assessed by DFC based on the rent you pay.

19.2   RO 4, sch 5 para 1
19.3   RO 20, 25 sch 8
19.4   RO 23A, 24, 25

The annual amount equals (a) or (b) multiplied by the rate poundage for the district you live in [www]. Or if you are only liable for part of a year this is calculated on a daily basis. Your rates bill shows these figures along with any reduction or rebate you qualify for.

Reducing your rates

19.6   You can get help with your rates if you qualify for:

(a) an exemption (para 19.8);

(b) a disability reduction (para 19.9)

(c) a rate rebate (para 19.11).

19.7   All these apply whether you are an owner occupier, shared owner or tenant (paras 19.3-4). If you are a tenant, you can get a rate rebate towards your rates as well as UC or HB towards your rent.

Exemptions

19.8   The main kinds of exemptions are for:

(a) dwellings occupied and owned by a registered charity;

(b) some unoccupied dwellings.

In these cases, no-one has to pay rates on the dwelling. An unoccupied dwelling is exempt in similar circumstances to those in table 15.3(d),(h),(j) for council tax (and some other situations). In any other case the rates payable are half for unoccupied dwellings.

Disability reductions

19.9   You qualify for disability reduction equal to 25% of your rates bill if:

(a) you are disabled, or at least one disabled adult or child has their home with you; and

(b) your home provides:

   ■   an additional kitchen or bathroom for the disabled person's use; or

   ■   an additional room (not a kitchen, bathroom or toilet) used predominantly to meet their special needs; or

   ■   sufficient floor space to use a wheelchair if they need one; and

(c) this is of major importance to them, taking account of the nature and extent of their disability.

Your home doesn't need to have been specifically adapted. For example, it could be that the disabled person has to have a separate bedroom or a bedroom downstairs.

19.5   RO 6(1),(3), 17(1)(b), 18(2), 23A, 39(1A)-(1C), sch 12 paras 7-12, 16
           The Rates (Social Sector Value) Regulations (Northern Ireland) 2007 No. 86
           The Rates (Maximum Capital Value) Regulations (Northern Ireland) 2007 No. 184; NISR 2009/77
           Rateable value: https://lpsni.gov.uk/vListDCV/search.asp?submit=form
           https://valuationservice.finance-ni.gov.uk/Property/Search

19.6   RO 30A, 31A, sch 7 paras 1(b), 2(2)

19.8   RO 25A, 41 sch 7 paras 1(b), 2(2), 3, sch 8A paras 1(1)-(3), 2(2)
           The Rates (Unoccupied Hereditaments) Regulations (Northern Ireland) 2011 S.R. 2011 No. 36, reg 3, sch paras 6, 10, 11, 12, 17

19.9   RO 31A(2),(3),(10)

Reconsiderations and appeals

19.10   You can ask LPS to reconsider any decision it has made about your rates, e.g. whether you are liable and whether you qualify for a disability reduction. You normally have 28 days to do this. After that you can appeal to a valuation tribunal about most decisions and should normally do this within one month.

Rate rebates

19.11   Rate rebates are divided into:

(a) UC rate rebate; and

(b) three kinds of HB rate rebate:

  ■ standard rate rebate,

  ■ supplementary rate rebate, and

  ■ lone pensioner rate rebate.

The law refers to some of these as different types of 'rate relief'.

Who can get a rate rebate

19.12   The main rules are:

(a) if you have a working age claim and are on UC, you can get a UC rate rebate (para 19.18); or

(b) if you have a working age claim and aren't on UC, you can't get any kind of rate rebate unless you have an old claim (para 19.46);

(c) if you have a pension age claim, you can get one or more of the HB rate rebates (para 19.36).

The detailed conditions are in the rest of this chapter.

Working age and pension age claims

19.13   You have a working age claim if you are under 66 or are in a couple and at least one of you is. You have a pension age claim if you are aged 66 or over, or in a couple and both of you are.

19.10   RO 31A(11A),(12),(12A),(12B)
        The Valuation Tribunal Rules (Northern Ireland) 2007 No 182, Reg 5(b)

19.11   RO 30A, NICBA 129

19.12   RO 9(1)(b),(2), NICBA 129, RR 10, NIUC 3, NIUCTP 3-6, NIHB 12, NIHB66+ 12; RRLPA 3(1),(3)

19.13   State Pension Credit Act (Northern Ireland) 2002, 1(6); NIHB 5(1); NIHB66+ 5(1)

Your home

19.14   You can only get a rate rebate on:

(a)   your home – this means the dwelling where you live or mainly live (paras 5.45, 5.48 for UC rate rebates; volume 2 chapter 3 for HB rate rebates); or

(b)   two homes if you have a large family and rent from a social landlord or in other limited situations (para 5.60 for UC rate rebates; volume 2 chapter 3 for HB rate rebates). But you can only get a lone pensioner allowance on one home.

However, only (a) applies in the case of lone pensioner rate rebate.

Your monthly/weekly rates

19.15   Rate rebates are based on:

(a)   the monthly or weekly rates on your home (para 19.16) after any disability reduction that applies; or

(b)   your share of (a) if you are a joint householder or have a resident landlord or tenant – this is decided by the number of people, how much each pays and other relevant factors; or

(c)   the domestic share of (a) if your rates bill also includes business premises (e.g. if you live over your shop) – this is decided by floor areas.

19.16   For UC rate rebates your monthly rates equal the annual amount divided by 12. For HB rate rebates, your weekly rates equal:

(a)   the annual amount divided by 365 and multiplied by seven; or

(b)   if your landlord gets the rates bill (para 19.3), the annual amount divided by 52.

Example: Annual and weekly rates

A dwelling has a capital value of £135,000 in an area where the rate poundage is £0.0057777 per £1 of capital value. Capping does not apply so the annual rates (paras 19.5, 19.16) are:

$$£135,000 \times 0.0057777 = £780.00$$

The weekly eligible rates (to the nearest 1p) are therefore:

£780.00 ÷ 365 × 7	£14.96 if paid separately from rent or
£780.00 ÷ 52	£15.00 if paid along with rent

Excluded groups

19.17   Except for a lone pensioner allowance you can't get a rate rebate if:

(a)   you are an excluded migrant (para 20.2); or

(b)   you are an excluded student (para 2.19 for UC rate rebates; volume 2 chapter 2 for HB rate rebates); or

---

(c) you are absent from home or from Northern Ireland for longer than the time limits – these range from one to 12 months for UC rate rebates (paras 2.29-35, 5.47-54) or from 13 to 52 weeks for HB rate rebates (volume 2 chapter 3); or

(d) you are a tenant and have a resident landlord who is your close relative (para 5.38): terminology); or

(e) your rates liability was contrived to obtain an increase in your rate rebate; or

(f) your home is a care home or independent hospital.

However, none of these apply in the case of lone pensioner rate rebate.

UC rate rebates

19.18   UC rate rebates are for people on UC. They are awarded for monthly assessment periods (para 19.29) and are based on UC law.

Who can get UC rate rebate

19.19   You can get a UC rate rebate if:

(a) you are on UC;

(b) you are liable for rates on your home (but not in supported accommodation); and

(c) you aren't in an excluded group (para 19.17).

How much UC rate rebate

19.20   To calculate your monthly UC rate rebate:

(a) start with the monthly rates on your home, or your share of them (para 19.15);

(b) if you have excess income (para 19.21) subtract 15% of it.

No deductions are made for non-dependants.

Excess income for UC rate rebates

19.21   You only have excess income if you have earnings. Your excess income equals:

(a) 45% of your earnings, after deducting a work allowance if you qualify for one (table 10.1);

(b) plus 50% of your work allowance if you qualify for one;

(c) minus any payment in lieu of notice or holiday pay (i.e. when notice is not worked or holidays not taken).

LPS always uses the DFC's figures for (a) and (b), but you need to tell LPS about (c).

19.17   IAA99 115; NIWRO 8-10; NICBA 129; RR 10(1),11(4), 28-35; NIHB 7, 9, 10, 53; RRHB 11-13, 21; NIHB66+ 7, 9, 10; RRHB66+ 11-13

19.19   RO 30A(3)(a); RR 10(1)-(3), 28(1)

19.20   RR 10(3)(b)

19.21   RR 10(7); NISR 2020/308

Examples: UC rate rebates

1. A single person on UC with no other income

Leon is on UC and has no other income. His rates are £780.00 for the year.

■	Monthly rates	£65.00
■	Equals monthly rate rebate	£65.00

2. A couple on UC with unearned income

Eleanor and James are on UC and Eleanor receives a private pension. The pension is ignored for UC rate rebate (19.22). Their rates are £840.00 for the year.

■	Monthly rates	£70.00
■	Equals monthly rate rebate	£70.00

3. A couple on UC with earnings (no work allowance)

Vijay and Kelly are on UC and have earnings. They don't qualify for a UC work allowance. Their earnings are £600 per month, and their rates are £1020.00 for the year.

■	45% of earnings (para 19.21)	£270.00
■	Equals excess income	£270.00
■	Monthly rates	£85.00
■	Minus 15% of excess income	−£40.50
■	Equals monthly rate rebate	£44.50

4. A single person on UC with earnings (and work allowance)

Cherelle is on UC and has earnings. She has two children so qualifies for a UC work allowance of £379. Her earnings are £779 per month (too low for tax or national insurance), leaving £400 after the work allowance is deducted. Her rates are £720.00 for the year.

■	45% of earnings above the work allowance (para 19.21)	£180.00
■	Plus 50% of work allowance (para 19.22)	£189.50
■	Equals excess income	£369.50
■	Monthly rates	£60.00
■	Minus 15% of excess income	− £55.43
■	Equals monthly rate rebate	£4.57

19.22   The excess income calculation in para 19.21:

(a) uses 45% of your earnings because the other 55% is used in your UC (para 9.8);

(b) adds back 50% of the work allowance because all of it is allowed in UC but only half is allowed in UC rate rebates;

(c) doesn't use any of your unearned income because all of it is used in your UC (para 9.8).

19.23 Rate rebate law expresses this in a more complicated way, saying your excess income equals:

(a) your earnings (after the work allowance), unearned income and UC; minus

(b) your maximum UC.

But because of how UC and maximum UC are calculated (paras 9.8, 9.4), the calculation method in para 19.21 gives the same result with fewer steps.

Claims

19.24 To get a UC rate rebate you have to make a claim to Land and Property Services (LPS). This is the case even if you are claiming UC at the same time. If your entitlement to rebate changes before LPS decides your claim you are treated as having made multiple claims.

19.25 You make your claim by creating an online rate rebate account [www], giving your name and address and agreeing LPS can obtain your earnings and other information from DFC. If you are a couple, one of you makes the claim on behalf of you both.

19.26 If there are breaks in your UC, your rate rebate claim covers each period you are on UC, but only until LPS confirms your rate rebate award. After that you have to reclaim rate rebate each time you go back on UC.

Information and evidence

19.27 If LPS needs any further information and evidence, it can request this when you claim or at any time during your rate rebate award. You have one month to provide it or longer if LPS agrees.

Help with claiming

19.28 You can ask LPS or an advice organisation to help with your claim or ask a family member or friend [www]. If LPS believes you need support it must arrange to assist you. If you can't manage your financial affairs an attorney can claim for you.

Assessment periods

19.29 UC rate rebates are calculated and paid for monthly assessment periods (in rate rebate law called 'attribution periods'). The first one begins on the day your rebate starts, so UC and UC rate rebate assessment periods are often the same (para 19.30(a)).

19.24   RO 30A(2); RR 2(1) – ' the Department', 3(1)

19.25   RR 3(2), 36
        https://www.nidirect.gov.uk/services/create-or-log-in-to-a-rate-rebate-account

19.26   RR 5(6), sch para 2(6)

19.26   RR 5(12)

19.27   RR 3(3), 4

19.28   RR 5(1), 6, 12
        https://www.nidirect.gov.uk/articles/getting-help-your-rate-rebate-claim

The date your rate rebate starts

19.30   Your UC rate rebate starts:

(a) on the same day your UC starts, if you make your rebate claim:

- within three months of your first payment of UC, or
- within 48 hours of the LPS computer system becoming available after a failure, if it wasn't available on the last day of the three months;

(b) on the first day of a new rates bill that follows the death of your partner, if you make your rebate claim within one month of it being issued;

(c) on the day you make your rebate claim in any other case.

The date your rebate changes or ends

19.31   Table 19.1 shows when your UC rate rebate changes or ends. This can be at the beginning of an assessment period or it can be part way through, in which case it is calculated daily both up to and after the change occurs (see examples).

Examples: UC rate rebate changes and revised awards

1. Increase in earnings

A single claimant with earned income is awarded a UC rate rebate from 14th June 2023. Based on the DFC's income figures, she is awarded a rebate of £30.00 per month. On 22nd September her earnings increase; based on the new DFC income figures her rebate would be £15.00 per month. Her UC rate rebate does not change until the next assessment period following the anniversary date of her claim: 14th July 2024.

2. Award of HB

A single claimant claims and is awarded a UC rate rebate on 1st April 2023 when she claims UC. Her rates are £840 per year. On 10th November she reaches pension age and claims SPC and HB rate rebate. Her HB rate rebate starts on Monday 14th November. Her UC rate rebate ends on 13th November and for the assessment period 1st-30th November is

£70 x 13/30 = £30.33.

Table 19.1 **When UC rate rebates change**

Specific change (increase or decrease)	
(a) A change in earned income	The start of the assessment period that immediately follows the anniversary date of claim
(b) UC award ends	The day after your last day of entitlement to UC

(c) Change in rateable value notified within three months of the revaluation	The date the new rateable value applies from
Other changes resulting in a higher award	
(d) Official error or the wrong UC figures	Date of the original decision
(e) Error due to a mistaken fact notified within three months or which the authority already had sufficient information to identify it	Date of the original decision
(f) Other changes in your circumstances (except as in (g))	Date the change occurs
(g) Other changes that are notified later than three months or that you fail to notify	Date you notify LPS of the change or the date it is first identified
Any other change resulting in a lower award	
(h) Error due to mistaken fact	Date of the original decision
(i) Any other change of circumstance (i.e. reduced award)	Date the change occurs

Payments and overpayments

19.32   Your UC rate rebate is awarded (or 'paid') by crediting it to your rates account if you get the rates bill, or your landlord's if your landlord does (para 19.3) [www]. LPS normally corrects any errors by:

(a) crediting that rates account if you've been paid too little rebate; or

(b) deducting rebate from that rates account if you have been paid too much – so you have more rates to pay.

Decision notices

19.33   LPS provides an online decision when your circumstances change. This says how much you qualify for (or that you don't qualify).

Reconsiderations and appeals

19.34   You can ask LPS to reconsider any decision it has made about your UC rate rebate, e.g. whether you qualify and how much for. You normally have three months to do this.

T19.1   RR 14

19.32   RR 21-27 https://tinyurl.com/UC-rate-rebates

19.33   RR 17(1)

19.34   RR 17(2)

19.35　　After that you can appeal to a valuation tribunal and should do this within three months. But your appeal can only be about whether you occupy somewhere as your home in the situations in paras 5.50-52, 5.59-60. This is because other UC rate rebate matters (e.g. your earnings) are decided as part of your UC, so you need to use the UC appeal procedure about them (para 14.39).

HB rate rebates

19.36　　HB rate rebates are for people who have a pension age claim (para 19.13) or an old working age claim (para 19.46). They are awarded for benefit weeks (para 19.52) and are based on HB law.

Kinds of HB rate rebate

19.37　　HB rate rebates are made up of:

(a)　standard rate rebates (para 19.38);

(b)　supplementary rate rebates (para 19.41); and

(c)　lone pensioner rate rebates (para 19.44).

Some people qualify for one or two of these and some people qualify for all three. They are calculated in the order shown and your HB rate rebate is the total of (a), (b) and/or (c).

Who can get standard rate rebate

19.38　　You can get a standard rate rebate if:

(a)　you have a pension age claim (para 19.13) or an old working age claim (para 19.46);

(b)　you are liable for rates on your home (paras 19.3-4);

(c)　you aren't in an excluded group (para 19.17); and

(d)　your capital isn't over £16,000.

How much standard rate rebate

19.39　　To calculate your weekly standard rate rebate:

(a)　start with the weekly rates on your home, or your share of them (para 19.15);

(b)　if you have one or more non-dependants, subtract the appropriate amount for each (para 19.47); and

(c)　if you have excess income (para 19.40) subtract 20% of it.

19.35　　RR 18

19.36-37　　NICBA 129; RO 30A; NIUCTP 3-6; NIHB 12; RRHB 7, 14; NIHB66+ 12; RRHB66+ 7, 14; RRLPA 3(1),(3)

19.38　　IAA99 115; NICBA 129(1),(3), 130; NIHB 7, 9, 10, 12, 40, 53; NIHB66+ 7, 9, 10, 12, 41

19.39　　NIHB 12, 68, 69, 78, 79; NIHB66+ 12, 48, 49, 59, 60

19.40 For standard rate rebates, your excess income equals:

(a) your weekly income;

(b) minus your weekly applicable amount.

Your applicable amount, income and capital are assessed in the same way as for HB (volume 2 chapters 12-15).

Who can get supplementary rate rebate

19.41 You can get a supplementary rate rebate if:

(a) you have a pension age claim (para 19.13) or an old working age claim (para 19.46);

(b) you are liable for rates on your home (paras 19.3-4);

(c) you aren't in an excluded group (para 19.17); and

(d) your capital isn't over £50,000 (pension age claims) or £16,000 (old working age claims).

How much supplementary rate rebate

19.42 To calculate your weekly supplementary rate rebate:

(a) start with the weekly rates on your home, or your share of them (para 19.15);

(b) if you qualify for standard rate rebate (para 19.39) subtract that;

(c) if you have one or more non-dependants, subtract the appropriate amount for each one (para 19.47);

(d) if you have excess income (para 19.43) subtract 12% of it.

19.43 For supplementary rate rebates, your excess income equals:

(a) your weekly income;

(b) minus your weekly applicable amount adjusted as follows:

- if you are single and reached age 66 before 1st April 2021, the personal allowance is £249.55,

- if you are single and reached age 66 on or after 1st April 2021, the personal allowance is £231.21,

- if you are a couple (or polygamous marriage) and you both (or all members) reached age 66 before 1st April 2021, the personal allowance is £357.17, plus £118.47 for each additional spouse,

- if you are a couple (or polygamous marriage) and you both (or all members) reached age 66 on or after 1st April 2021, the personal allowance is £337.54, plus £116.38 for each additional spouse,

- the carer premium is £51.30 (for working age and pension age claims).

Apart from the adjustments in (b), your applicable amount, income and capital are assessed in the same way as for HB (volume 2 chapters 12-15).

19.40 NICBA 129(3)(b)

19.41 IAA99 115; RO 30A; NISR 2008/68; RRHB 7, 9-13, 19(1)(q); RRHB66+ 7, 9-13, 19(1)(o)

19.42 RRHB 22, 23; RRHB66+ 21, 22

19.43 NISR 2011/43 regs 2(3)(b), 3(3)(b); RRHB 17(2)(g), 23; RRHB66+ 17(2)(c),(e), 22; NISR 2007/244 reg 2; NISR 2021/70; NISR 2022/92

Who can get a lone pensioner rate rebate

19.44   You can get a lone pensioner rate rebate if:

(a) you are aged 70 or over;

(b) you live alone, apart from anyone:

- who is aged under 18, or

- who is a young person aged 18-20 years (para 3.64), or

- who has a medical certificate confirming they have a severe impairment of intelligence and social functioning, or

- other than your partner who is providing you with care or who is receiving care from you and you both meet the conditions in table 15.4(g) as for Scotland;

(c) you are liable for rates on your home (paras 19.3-4);

(d) you make a claim for it; and

(e) you still have some rates to pay after deducting any standard and/or supplementary rate rebate you qualify for (para 19.45).

There is no capital limit; your income and capital are ignored.

How much lone pensioner rate rebate

19.45   To calculate your weekly lone pensioner rate rebate:

(a) start with the weekly rates on your home, or your share of them (para 19.15);

(b) if you qualify for standard and/or supplementary rate rebate (paras 19.39, 19.42) subtract them;

(c) multiply the remainder by 20%.

Examples: HB rate rebates

1. Standard rate rebate

Charlie and Miriam are on SPC. Their rates are £18.00 per week. They have one non-dependant, their son, who works full time and has gross income of £250.00 per week.

- Weekly rates   £18.00
- Minus non-dependant deduction (para 19.47)   −£6.55
- Equals weekly standard rate rebate   £11.45

Charlie and Miriam are on a 'full rebate', so they don't get a supplementary rate rebate.

2. Standard and supplementary rate rebate

Josef is a single person who works part time during his retirement. His rates are £22.00 per week. He has one non-dependant, his sister, who has a private pension and doesn't work. Josef's excess income is assessed as being £27.00 per week. First, he is considered for a standard rate rebate:

19.44   RO 30A; RRLPA 3(1),(3), sch paras 1-7

19.45   RRLPA 8

▪	Weekly rates	£22.00
▪	Minus non-dependant contribution	−£3.30
▪	Minus 20% of excess income	−£5.40
▪	Equals weekly HB rate rebate	£13.30

Then he is considered for a supplementary rate rebate:

▪	Weekly rates	£22.00
▪	Minus standard rate rebate	−£13.30
▪	Minus non-dependant deduction (para 19.47)	−£3.30
▪	Minus 12% of excess income	−£3.24
▪	Equals supplementary rate rebate	£2.16

Josef's total weekly HB rate rebate is:

▪	£13.30 + £2.16	£15.46

3. Lone pensioner rate rebate

Enda is aged 70 and lives alone. Her rates are £17.00 per week. She has capital of over £50,000 so can't get a standard or supplementary rate rebate.

▪	20% of weekly rates	£3.40
▪	Equals lone pensioner rebate	£3.40

Old working age claims

19.46   Until 5th December 2018, people of any age could get HB rate rebates. If you are working age and claimed before that date:

(a) you continue to be eligible for any of the kinds of HB rate rebate for as long as you are getting at least one of them;

(b) you stop being eligible for all of them if:

- ▪ they all end, or
- ▪ you are awarded UC, or
- ▪ you claim UC and meet its basic conditions (table 2.1) but don't qualify due to the level of your income.

Non-dependant deductions

19.47   Any non-dependants who live with you (para 19.48) are assumed to contribute to your rates unless one of the exceptions applies. Their assumed contribution is deducted from your maximum standard or supplementary rebate (paras 19.39, 19.42). Table 19.2 gives the current figures and table 19.3 lists the exceptions. A non-dependant's gross weekly income is assessed the same way as as in para 17.15.

19.46   NIUCTP 3-6; RR 38; RRHB 7; RRHB66+ 7; NISR 2018/138 reg 3

19.47   NIHB 68(b); RRHB 22(1)(e); NIHB66+ 48(b); RRHB66+ 21(1)(e)

19.48 A non-dependant is an adult who:

(a) lives in your home (para 3.71) – for example a daughter, son, other relative or friend; but

(b) isn't a member of your benefit unit (para 3.46), a joint householder, a lodger or your landlord.

Table 19.2 **HB rate rebates: weekly non-dependant deductions**

(a) Non-dependants working at least 16 hours per week

Gross weekly income	Deduction
At least £394.00	£9.90
At least £316.00	£8.25
At least £183.00	£6.55
Under £183.00	£3.30

(b) Other non-dependants

Regardless of income	£3.30

(c) Non-dependant couples

There is one deduction per couple: (a) applies to combined gross weekly income if one or both work at least 16 hours per week; (b) applies otherwise.

Table 19.3 **HB rate rebates: no non-dependant deductions**

Your circumstances

No deduction is made for any non-dependants in your home if you or your partner are:

(a) on the daily living component of PIP or adult disability payment;

(b) on the middle or highest rate of the care component of DLA;

(c) on an armed forces independence payment

(d) on attendance allowance or an equivalent benefit (para 10.54);

(e) entitled to (a), (b) or (c) but not receiving it because of being in hospital; or

(f) certified as severely sight impaired or blind by an ophthalmologist or you have regained your sight in the last 28 weeks.

19.48   NIHB 3; RRHB 3(a); NIHB66+ 3; RRHB66+ 3(a)

T19.2   NIHB 72(1)(a)(ii),(b)(ii),(2)(f)-(h),(3); RRHB 22(1)(i); NIHB66+ 53(1)(a)(ii),(b)(ii),(2)(f)-(h),(3); RRHB 21(1)(j)

T19.3   NIHB 72(6)-(10); RRHB 22(1)(i); NIHB66+ 53(6)-(9); RRHB 21(1)(j)

> **Non-dependant's circumstances**
>
> No deduction is made for any single non-dependant who is, or any non-dependant couple who both are:
>
> (g) on SPC;
>
> (h) on UC with no earnings;
>
> (i) on JSA(IB), the assessment phase of ESA(IR), or IS;
>
> (j) aged under 25 on a training allowance;
>
> (k) a full-time student (except during the summer vacation if the student is working at least 16 hours per week and the claimant and their partner are both aged under 65); or
>
> (l) a member of the armed forces away on operations.

Who administers HB rate rebates

19.49   HB rate rebates are administered by:

(a) the Northern Ireland Housing executive (NIHE) if you are a social or private tenant, or have a life interest or are in a co-ownership or rental purchase scheme;

(b) Land and Property Services (LPS) if you are an owner occupier, or the owner's partner, former partner or former non-dependant (but from June 2022 the administration is transferred to the NIHE).

Claims

19.50   To get an HB rate rebate you must make a claim to LPS/NIHE (para 19.49). You can do this online, by telephone or on a written application form, and in each case you have to give your personal, financial and household details. You are considered for all three kinds of HB rate rebate (para 19.37) unless you say otherwise.

19.51   If you are a couple, one of you makes the claim on behalf of you both. If you are a tenant, you can usually claim an HB rate rebate and HB for rent at the same time. The rules about information and help with claiming are the same as in paras 19.27-28 and apply to both LPS and NIHE.

Benefit weeks

19.52   HB rate rebates are calculated and paid for benefit weeks that always run from Monday to Sunday.

19.49   NIAA 126(3); RRHB 6; RRHB66+ 6; RRLPA 4; NISR 2022/27
https://www.legislation.gov.uk/nisr/2022/27/memorandum/contents

19.50   NIHB 81; RRHB 26(1), 27; NIHB66+ 62; RRHB66+ 25(1), 26; RRLPA 5

19.51   NIHB 80; RRHB 26(1); NIHB66+ 61, 25(1)

19.52   NIHB 2(1) – definition 'benefit week', RRHB 2(2) – definition 'rate relief week'; NIHB66+ 2(1); RRHB66+ 2(2)

The date your rate rebate starts

19.53   Your HB rate rebate normally starts on the Monday following the date of your claim. But it starts when your HB starts if you claim your UC rate rebate within one month of receiving the decision on your HB claim. And it is backdated for up to three months automatically if you have a pension age claim.

Payments, overpayments and decision notices

19.54   The rules about payments (except as in para 19.55), corrections and decision notices are the same as in paras 19.32-33 and apply to both LPS and NIHE.

Paying HB rate rebates with HB for rent

19.55   If you are a tenant and your HB for rent is paid as a rent allowance, your standard rate rebate can be added to it. So you or your landlord receive a single payment, usually four weekly or monthly, covering both. Further details are the same as in HB (volume 2 chapter 18). But this rule doesn't apply to supplementary rate rebate and lone pensioner rate rebate, which are always paid separately.

Reconsiderations and appeals

19.56   You can ask LPS/NIHE (para 19.49) to reconsider any decision about your standard rate rebate and supplementary rate rebate. You normally have one month to do this. After that you can appeal to an appeal tribunal about most decisions and you should normally do so within one month. You make your appeal to LPS/NIHE who forward it to the appeal tribunal if they still disagree with any part of your appeal. The procedures, including how to appeal and when the time limit can be extended, are the same as HB for rent: see volume 2 chapter 20 for further details.

19.57   You can ask LPS/NIHE (para 19.49) to reconsider any decision about your lone pensioner rate rebate. You must do this within 28 days of the decision notice issued by LPS/NIHE. After that you can appeal to the valuation tribunal: you must do this within 28 days using Form 5.

19.53   NIHB 74, 81(12); RRHB 25, 41-44; NIHB66+ 55, 62(1); RRHB66+ 24

19.54   NIHB 86, sch 10; RRHB 30, ; NIHB66+ 67, sch 9; RRHB66+ 29, 40-43; RRLPA 9

19.55   NIHB 88; RRHB 31(e); NIHB66+ 69; RRHB66+ 30(e); RRLPA 7

19.56   RRHB 41-43; RRHB66+ 40-42; The Housing Benefit (Decisions and Appeals) Regulations (Northern Ireland) 2001, No 213, regs 4, 20

19.57   RRLPA 9, 10(1); The Valuation Tribunal Rules (Northern Ireland) 2007, No 182, reg 5(e), sch Form 5; NISR 2008/153 regs 4, 7, sch

Chapter 20 **Migrants and recent arrivals**

- The rules that apply to migrants: see paras 20.1-11.
- How the decision is made: see paras 20.12-19.
- The immigration control test, asylum seekers and refugees: see paras 20.20-37.
- Habitual residence and the right to reside: see paras 20.38-52.

20.1　This chapter is about when you are eligible for UC, housing benefit (HB) or CTR if you have recently arrived in the UK. It covers everyone, whether you are from the British Isles, Europe or the rest of the world, and whether you are arriving in the UK for the first time or returning after a time abroad.

Which rules apply

20.2　If you are not a British citizen and/or you have recently arrived in the UK, there are three main rules which affect whether you are eligible for UC/HB/CTR:

(a) the immigration control test;

(b) the right to reside test; and

(c) the habitual residence test.

We avoid using the term 'person from abroad' because it means a claimant who fails (b) or (c) in HB law only.

20.3　You must pass all three tests to be entitled to UC/HB/CTR, but in practice if you pass the immigration control test you also have a right to reside (and before 1st January 2021 the reverse was also true). In the law the right to reside test is part of the habitual residence test and this is reflected in the way the DWP notifies its decisions (para 20.40).

Eligibility of nationals of different parts of the world

20.4　This section identifies which rules apply to you depending on your nationality, followed by a straightforward example of each. Table 20.1 summarises how the three tests apply to all new claims from 1st January 2021.

Nationals of the British Isles (the Common Travel Area)

20.5　The 'British Isles' (a geographical term, roughly meaning all the islands off the North-West of the continent) is also called the 'Common Travel Area'. Both terms mean:

(a) the United Kingdom (England, Wales, Scotland and Northern Ireland);

(b) the Republic of Ireland;

(c) the Isle of Man; and

(d) the Channel Islands (all of them).

20.2　IAA 115(1),(3); UC 9(1),(2); HB 10(1)-(3); HB66+ 10(1),(3); NIUC 9(1),(2); NIHB 10(1)-(3); NIHB66+ 10(1)-(3)

20.6   In this guide you are national of the British Isles if you:

(a)   are a British citizen;

(b)   are a Commonwealth citizen with the 'right of abode' (table 20.2); or

(c)   are an Irish citizen.

If (a)-(c) apply, you are entitled to UC/HB/CTR if you are habitually resident (paras 20.38-52).

20.7   If you are a member of a couple and para 20.6 only applies to your partner, your entitlement depends on who makes the claim. The outcome depends on which of the three tests (para 20.2) applies to you and whether you are claiming UC or HB/CTR (paras 20.15-16).

Nationals of the European Economic Area

20.8   Table 21.1 lists all the countries in the European Economic Area (EEA) plus Switzerland which for UC/HB/CTR purposes UK law treats as being part of the EEA. The EEA includes all the EU states plus some others.

20.9   If you are an EEA national (or family member) the rules in this chapter apply to you in the same way as a national of the rest of the world if:

(a)   you first entered the UK after 31st December 2020;

(b)   you entered the UK before 1st January 2021, applied to the EU settlement scheme and have been granted EU settled status; or

(c)   you entered the UK before 1st January 2021, and either:

■   you applied to the EU settlement scheme and were refused EU settled or pre-settled status, or

■   you did not apply to the EU settlement scheme by the 30th June 2021 deadline, or you made a late application which was refused.

In the case of (c) you are likely to be an overstayer (table 20.2) and you are advised to seek advice from a registered immigration adviser [www].

20.10   If you applied to the EU settlement scheme and have not yet received a decision – including if you made a late application which has been accepted – or you have been granted EU pre-settled status, then the rules in chapter 21 apply to you instead.

Nationals of the rest of the world

20.11   In this guide you are a national of the rest of the world if you are not a national of the British Isles (paras 20.5-6) or an EEA national to whom chapter 21 applies (para 20.10). Nationals of the rest of the world must satisfy the immigration control test (paras 20.20-37) and the habitual residence test (paras 20.38-52) to be entitled to UC/HB/CTR.

20.6   IAA 115(9); Immigration Act 1971, s.1(1), 2, 3ZA

20.6   Immigration and Social Security Co-ordination (EU Withdrawal) Act 2020, s5; SI 2020 No. 1209 regs 3, 11, 12(1)(i); SI 2020 No. 1309, regs 12(7), 83, sch 4 paras 1-3

20.9   IAA 115(9); Immigration Act 1988, s.7; Immigration and Social Security Co-ordination (EU Withdrawal) Act 2020, s.1, sch 1 paras 1, 2(2); SI 2020/1209 regs 3(3), 11; SI 2020/1309 reg 83, sch 4 paras 1-4 https://home.oisc.gov.uk/adviser_finder/finder.aspx

20.10   SI 2020/1209 regs 4, 11; SI 2020/1309 reg 83, sch 4 paras 1-4

20.11   IAA 115(9); Immigration Act 1971, s.2, 3ZA; Immigration and Social Security Co-ordination (EU Withdrawal) Act 2020, s.1, sch 1 paras 1, 2(2)

Table 20.1 **Migrants: who can get UC/HB/CTR**

Nationality/date of entry	Test	Expires
British and Irish citizens		
Any date	Habitual residence	No limit while met
EEA and EEA family members		
Entered UK after 31 December 2020	Immigration control and habitual residence	No limit while met
Entered UK before 1 January 2021 and granted EU settled status	Habitual residence	No limit while met
Entered UK before 1 January 2021 and granted EU pre-settled status	Right to reside and habitual residence	When granted EU settled status
Entered UK before 1 January 2021, applied to EUSS, await decision	Right to reside and habitual residence	When leave is finally determined
ECSMA/ESC nationals		
Entered UK after 31 December 2020	Immigration control and habitual residence	No limit while met
Entered UK and claimed UC before 1 January 2021	Right to reside and habitual residence	When UC ends
Claimed HB before 3 May 2022	Right to reside and habitual residence	When HB ends
Claimed CTR in Scotland	Right to reside and habitual residence	No limit while met
Rest of the world		
On entry to the UK	Immigration control and habitual residence	No limit while met

Notes

- For EEA member states see table 21.1. For ECSMA/ESC member states see para 20.29.
- In law the claimant must pass all three tests but in practice it is either one or two (paras 20.38, 20.41).
- 'Applied to EUSS' means your application was made in time or your late application has been accepted (paras 21.19-20).
- For EEA family members the entry date applies to the person they accompany (para 21.15).
- Different rules apply to claimants who have applied for asylum (para 20.30).

Decision-making

20.12   This section covers general matters relevant to this chapter and chapter 21, including decision-making and claims, and how the law and terminology work.

DWP and council decisions

20.13   If you are claiming UC the DWP decides whether you satisfy each of the three tests (para 20.2) and can get UC. If you are claiming HB and/or CTR your council decides this, but the law says you pass the habitual residence and right to reside test if you get one of the following DWP benefits:

(a)   income-based jobseeker's allowance (but see para 21.34 for exceptions);

(b)   income-related employment and support allowance;

(c)   income support;

(d)   state pension credit (guarantee credit or savings credit).

(And in practice your council will also accept that you pass the immigration control test (HBGM para C4.33).)

20.14   The rule in para 20.13 about HB/CTR only applies if the DWP has decided (in full possession of the facts) that you can get JSA(IB)/ESA(IR)/IS/SPC and not, say, where you wrongly continue to get it. If the DWP has decided that you cannot get one of these benefits, your council is not compelled to make the same decision – but a considered decision by the DWP carries weight.

Examples: Eligibility for UC

1. A British citizen

A British citizen has been living abroad for 12 years. During that time, she gave up all her connections in the UK. She has now just come 'home' and has rented a flat here.

The only test that applies to a UK national is the habitual residence test. It is unlikely that she satisfies that test to begin with but she probably will after (say) three months or possibly a shorter period (para 20.47). So, for the time being she can't get UC.

2. National of the EEA who entered the UK before 1 January 2021

An Italian national has been working in the UK for several years. He applied to the EU settlement scheme before 1st July 2021 and has EU pre-settled status. He has recently taken a more poorly paid job. He passes the right to reside test because he is working. So he can get UC.

3. National of the rest of the world

An Indian national arrived in the UK six months ago to be with her family. She was given leave to enter by the Home Office without a 'no public funds' condition, so she is able to claim benefits. She now claims UC.

The two tests that apply to a national of the rest of the world are the immigration control test and the habitual residence test. She passes both tests. So she can get UC.

20.13   HB 10(3B)(k),(l); HB66+ 10(4A)(k); NIHB 10(5)(l),(m); NIHB66+ 10(5)(l); CTP 12(4)(h),(ha)

Claims and couples

20.15 If you are a couple you usually claim UC jointly (para 3.3), but if only one of you is eligible that person can get UC as a single person (paras 2.7-8). You are eligible if you (or you and your partner if you are a joint-claim couple) pass each of the three tests (para 20.2).

20.16 If you are a couple and claiming HB/CTR it can matter which partner makes the claim (because only one of you can be the claimant). The rules in this chapter apply to each partner individually. If partner A is eligible, but partner B is not, partner A must be the claimant to get benefit. In these cases:

(a) if the 'wrong' partner claims the council must give you a 'not entitled' decision (but it is good practice to explain this and invite a claim from the other partner);

(b) if the claim is made by the 'correct' partner, it is assessed (e.g. income, applicable amount, etc) in the usual way, so you get a couple personal allowance even though only one of you is entitled (HBGM para C4·218). But if your partner is subject to immigration control, they should get advice before you make a claim, because it may affect their immigration status (para 20.18).

National insurance numbers

20.17 If you are claiming UC you must provide your national insurance number (or have applied for one) to complete your claim (para 3.28). If you have applied for a national insurance number, the DWP can refuse to issue you with one if you are not a UK resident [2022] UKUT 189 (AAC). If you are a couple this applies to both of you (unless you are claiming as a single person (para 20.15).

20.18 If you are claiming HB/CTR and you:

(a) are single or a lone parent, you must provide your national insurance number (or have applied for one) to complete your claim;

(b) are a couple, the rule in (a) applies to both of you except that:

- if only one of you needs 'leave' from the Home Office (table 20.2) to be in the UK but does not have it (for example, if you have not applied for it or if it has expired) then the requirement does not apply to that person and the DWP advises councils to assign a dummy number (GM D1·284-286);

- it is not a legal requirement if you (or your partner) are claiming CTR in Scotland (para 16.37).

This rule (and the rule in para 20.16) is only about who can get HB/CTR. It does not mean that it is safe for your partner in terms of their immigration status to be part of your HB/CTR claim (the higher couple personal allowance counts as 'public funds'). The council may inform the Home Office, although it is not obliged to do so (HBGM para C4·219).

20.15   UC 3(1),(3); NIUC 3(2)

20.16   HB 8(1)(b), 10(1); HB66+ 8(1)(b), 10(1); NIHB 8(1)(b), 10(1); NIHB66+ 8(1)(b), 10(1); CTP sch 8 para 4(1)

20.17   AA (1),(1A),(1B),(4)(za); NIAA (1),(1A),(1B),(4)(za)

20.18   AA (1),(1A),(1B),(4)(b); HB 4(c); HB66+ 4(c); NIHB 4(c); NIAA 1(1),(1A),(18),(4)(b); NIHB66+ 4(c); CTP 15, sch 8 para 7(2)-(3)
        Immigration rules, rule 6.2 – 'public funds'

Making a claim

20.19   Your online UC claim asks you:

(a) if you are British, Irish or a citizen of a different country; and

(b) if you have been out of the UK or Ireland in the past two years.

Most HB/CTR claim forms ask similar questions. Both questions are intended to act as a trigger for further investigation. If you are British/Irish and have not been out of the UK/Ireland in the past two years, the DWP/council will normally assume you pass all three tests (para 20.2).

The immigration control test

20.20   If you are from a country other than the UK or Ireland (para 20.11) you must pass the immigration control test to get UC/HB/CTR. (You must also pass the habitual residence test: paras 20.38-52.) A basic understanding of immigration law terminology is useful to understanding UC/HB/CTR decisions. Table 20.2 explains the key terms.

Table 20.2 **Simplified immigration law terminology**

EU settled and pre-settled status

EU settled status is a form of indefinite leave for EEA nationals with five years residence. Those with less than five years get pre-settled status (a form of limited leave) until then. Both are granted without a 'no public funds' condition. See paras 21.13-20 for more details.

Immigration rules

The legal rules approved by parliament which UKIV officers use to decide whether a person should be given permission ('leave') to enter or remain in the UK.

UK Immigration and Visas (UKIV)

The Home Office agency responsible for immigration control and determining asylum claims (including asylum support).

Leave and settled status

Leave is legal permission to be in the UK. Leave can be for a fixed period (limited leave) or open ended (indefinite leave). Both can be granted with a 'no public funds' condition, which is usually the case for limited leave. Leave can be varied, provided an application is made before it has expired (para 20.26). Indefinite leave to enter or remain without conditions is also known as 'settled status'. Partners of British/ settled persons usually get leave in two blocks of 30 months each after which they can apply for settled status.

Temporary admission and temporary permission to stay

Temporary admission is a period of grace given at UKIV's discretion that allows you time to do something – such as apply for leave – without falling foul of the law. Since it isn't 'leave', it does not confer a right to reside (para 20.41).

T20.2   www.gov.uk/right-of-abode/apply-for-a-certificate-of-entitlement

Temporary permission to stay (TPS) is a form of limited leave. It is granted to survivors of trafficking or slavery who do not qualify for any other form of leave where it is necessary to help that person recover from physical or psychological harm, to seek compensation, or to help police investigate who exploited them. TPS replaces discretionary leave for survivors of trafficking or slavery. TPS is granted for 30 months, or 12 months if pursuing compensation, and in either case without a 'no public funds' condition.

Public funds

Nearly all tax credits and non-contributory benefits (including UC/HB/CTR and legacy benefits) count as public funds. So does a local authority homelessness duty or acceptance on its housing waiting list.

Sponsorship and maintenance undertaking

A sponsored migrant is someone (typically a partner or elderly relative) who is granted leave to join a family member (a 'sponsor') on the understanding that their maintenance and accommodation will be provided by their sponsor. If the sponsor signs a written agreement (a 'maintenance undertaking') to this effect the person granted leave is usually excluded from UC/HB/CTR for five years (paras 20.21, 20.27).

Illegal entrant and overstayer

These refer to a person who needs leave to enter or remain in the UK but does not have it nor temporary admission. An illegal entrant is someone who entered the UK without leave. An overstayer is someone who entered with leave but which has since expired.

Right of abode and right to reside

'Right of abode' is a term that describes someone who is entirely free of immigration control. It applies to all British citizens and some citizens of Commonwealth countries, but not necessarily to other forms of British nationality. Non-British citizens can apply for a certificate in their passport to confirm this [www].

'Right to reside' is a wider term that describes any legal authority to reside in the UK. It includes the right of abode, any form of leave (table 20.2) and use of EU free movement rights up to the end of implementation period (paras. 21.6-9). EU free movement rights are now only used to determine rights to UC/HB/CTR (and other public services) for people with EU pre-settled status (paras 21.2, 21.31).

20.21   The immigration control test stops you getting UC/HB/CTR if:

(a) you require 'leave' but do not have it – e.g. you are an illegal entrant or overstayer (table 20.2); or

(b) you have been granted leave but with a 'no public funds' condition (but see paras 20.27-28 for exceptions); or

(c) you have been granted leave as a result of a maintenance undertaking (i.e. you are a sponsored immigrant, but see paras 20.27-28 for exceptions); or

(d) you have been granted temporary admission (table 20.2) while your application to the Home Office is being decided – for example if you are an asylum seeker.

20.21   IAA99 115(9); CTP 13(2)

People who pass the immigration control test

20.22 You pass the immigration control test regardless of your nationality if:

(a) you hold a passport containing a certificate of entitlement to the 'right of abode' (table 20.2) in the UK;

(b) you have 'indefinite leave to remain' (also called settled status), including EU settled status;

(c) you have EU pre-settled status (but in this case you must have a qualifying right to reside or be exempt from the habitual residence test to be entitled to UC/HB/CTR);

(d) you fall within one of the exceptions described in paras 20.27-28);

(e) you applied for asylum and you have been granted refugee status, humanitarian protection or discretionary leave (paras 20.33-34).

The DWP/council normally needs to see your passport or other Home Office documentation to confirm the above.

People with limited leave

20.23 Having limited leave does not of itself exclude you from UC/HB/CTR but rather the fact that limited leave is usually granted with a 'no public funds' condition (para 20.21(b)). For example, under the immigration rules (table 20.2) most work permit holders and students get leave but with a 'no public funds' condition.

20.24 In certain uncommon situations, UKIV officers can grant limited leave without conditions under the immigration rules or in exceptional circumstances 'outside the immigration rules' using their discretion. If you have limited leave without conditions, you are entitled to UC/HB/CTR provided you are habitually resident (paras 20.38-52).

20.25 Limited leave without conditions can be granted:

(a) to a person who has established a 'right to family life' due to their long residence (immigration rules, 'appendix FM');

(b) to a person who was refused settled status due to minor criminal offences or because they failed the 'life in the UK' test (immigration rules, 276DG);

(c) to a person from Hong Kong with a British National (Overseas) visa and who has successfully applied to have their no public funds condition lifted;

(d) to a stateless person for that reason (para 20.35);

(e) to Ukrainian national (or family member) who has leave under the Ukraine Sponsorship Scheme (Homes for Ukraine), the Ukraine Extension Scheme (extending and/or varying existing leave) or the Ukraine Family Scheme (Ukrainians with UK-based immediate family members) [www];

(f) to a person from Afghanistan who was employed by the UK armed forces under the Afghan Relocations and Assistance Policy (ARAP) or the Afghan Locally Employed Staff ex-gratia scheme (ALES);

20.23   IAA 115(1)-(3),(9)(b)

20.25   https://tinyurl.com/Ukraine-visas

(g) to an Afghan citizen at risk of persecution under the Afghan Citizens Resettlement Scheme (ACRS);

(h) to a person who is the partner of a British citizen or a settled person who has applied under the domestic violence concession (para 20.36); or

(i) to a survivor of trafficking or slavery (as 'temporary permission to stay': table 20.2).

This list is not exhaustive and limited leave without conditions may be granted for other reasons. Leave granted under (g) and (h) is outside the immigration rules. If you have leave under (e) to (h) you are exempt from the habitual residence test (para 20.39).

Entitlement when leave starts and ends

20.26 Your entitlement to UC/HB/CTR doesn't always coincide with the date of your leave:

(a) your UC/HB/CTR starts from the date you receive your Home Office confirmation letter or the date your passport is endorsed, and not from the date the Immigration Appeal Tribunal allowed your appeal, even though that means confirmation of your leave will inevitably follow: [2011] UKUT 373 (AAC);

(b) if your leave was granted for a set period you can apply for it to be extended before it expires. Provided your application is made in time and in the correct form, you are still treated as having leave until 28 days after the decision is made on your application, and so you pass the immigration control test until then; but

(c) if your application for leave was refused or the leave you are applying to extend didn't allow you to claim benefit (e.g. if it had a 'no public funds' condition), you aren't entitled to UC/HB/CTR while you appeal the Home Office decision, even if that appeal was made in time: [2018] UKUT 418 (AAC).

Exceptions to the immigration control test

20.27 The law allows the DWP to set out in regulations exceptions to the general rule that if you fail the immigration control test you are excluded from benefit (para 20.21). The only exceptions are in para 20.28.

20.28 You are not affected by the general rule (para 20.27) and pass the immigration control test if:

(a) you are a national of a European Convention on Social and Medical Assistance (ECSMA)/ European Social Charter (ESC) treaty member state with any kind of leave and you meet the conditions in para 20.29;

(b) you were admitted to the UK as a result of a maintenance undertaking (a 'sponsored immigrant'), but you have been resident for at least five years beginning with the date of your entry or date the undertaking was signed, whichever is the later;

(c) you were admitted to the UK as a 'sponsored immigrant' and have been resident for less than five years and your sponsor (or all your sponsors if there is more than one) has died.

20.26 Immigration Act 1971 s3C

20.27 IAA99 115(4); Immigration rules, rule 6.2 – 'public funds'

20.28 SI 2000 No. 636 reg 2(1),(1A), sch part 1, paras 2-4; NISR 2000 No. 71 reg 2(1),(1A), sch part 1, paras 2-4; CTP 13(1A)

Nationals of ECSMA or ESC treaty member states

20.29   If you are a national of an ECSMA/ESC member state and have leave you are entitled to:

(a) CTR, in Scotland (but not England or Wales after 31st March 2023);

(b) HB, if you claimed it before 3rd May 2022 (in Northern Ireland,15th September 2022);

(c) UC, if you claimed it before 1st January 2021 (in Northern Ireland, 28th October 2021).

You must also satisfy stage two of the habitual residence test (para 20.43). The ECSMA/ESC member states are: North Macedonia, Turkey and the EEA member states (table 21.1) other than Bulgaria, Liechtenstein, Lithuania, Romania, Slovenia and Switzerland.

Asylum seekers

20.30   You are an asylum seeker if you have made a claim to be recognised as a refugee (para 20.33) under the United Nations Convention because of fear of persecution in your country of origin (typically on political or ethnic grounds).

20.31   While your asylum claim is being processed you fail the immigration control test and are disqualified from UC/HB/CTR and most other benefits (para 20.21), although there are some limited exceptions (para 20.32). If you are disqualified, you may be able to get help with your maintenance and accommodation from the Home Office asylum support scheme [www].

20.32   The exceptions to the general rule in para 20.31 apply if:

(a) you are a couple, and your partner is eligible (paras 20.15-16) (and in this case if you are claiming HB/CTR any payment you get from the Home Office for support counts as income: HBGM para C4.128); or

(b) you have been granted discretionary leave (para 20.33) (e.g. if you are aged under 18 and unaccompanied by an adult: but see para 2.10 for UC).

Refugees and others granted leave on humanitarian grounds

20.33   Following your claim for asylum the Home Office may:

(a) recognise you as a refugee (i.e. accept your claim for asylum) and grant leave; or

(b) refuse asylum but grant humanitarian protection (which is a form of leave) or discretionary leave (which is made outside the immigration rules); or

(c) refuse asylum and not grant leave.

Discretionary leave is usually only granted to unaccompanied children. For survivors of trafficking or slavery, see para 20.25(i).

20.29   SI 2000/636 reg 2(1),(1A), sch part 1, para 4; SI 2022/449 reg 1; SI 2023/47 reg 5;
           NISR 2000/71 reg 2(1),(1A), sch part 1, para 4; NISR 2022/202 reg 1

20.31   www.gov.uk/asylum-support

20.34   If leave is granted it is normally for an initial period of 30 months, and then one further period of 30 months, after which you can normally apply for settled status (table 20.2). Refugee status, humanitarian protection and discretionary leave are usually granted without a 'no public funds' condition and in each case you are exempt from the habitual residence test (para 20.39) so you are entitled to UC/HB/CTR from the date your status is confirmed (para 20.26(a)). If you are granted refugee status (but not in other cases) then your dependants are granted leave as well, so they are also entitled to UC/HB/CTR.

Stateless persons

20.35   You are a stateless person if you are not recognised as a citizen by the law of any country. A stateless person can be granted leave in the same way as any other non-UK national (e.g. as a student, worker permit holder, etc) but can also apply for leave for that reason. The Home Office says it only grants stateless leave if the applicant does not meet the criteria for asylum or qualify for leave under any other category – although the law does not strictly require this. Stateless leave is for five years without a public funds condition [www] so if you get it you are entitled to UC/HB/CTR provided you are habitually resident (paras 20.38-52).

Destitution domestic violence concession

20.36   If you are the partner of a British citizen or a person with settled status (table 20.2) who is experiencing domestic violence you can apply for the destitution domestic violence concession (DDVC) [www]. DDVC is leave without a 'no public funds' condition granted outside the immigration rules for up to three months (ADM C1674-76; HB circular U2/2012 [www]). It allows you time to make an application to UKIV to settle in the UK. You are entitled to UC/HB/CTR until your application to settle is decided (para 20.39).

20.37   You should always get specialist immigration advice from a OISC registered adviser [www] before you apply for DDVC. Getting DDVC does not mean that your application to settle will succeed and if it fails you could lose your right to remain in the UK.

20.34   UC 9(4)(d),(e)(i),(f); NIUC 9(4)(d),(e)(i),(f); HB 10(1),(3B)(g),(h)(i),(hh); HB66+ 10(1),(4A)(g),(h)(i),(hh);
         NIHB 10(1),(5)(g),(h)(i),(i); NIHB66+ 10(1),(5)(g),(h)(i),(i); CTP 12(5)(d),(e)(i),(f)

20.35   IAA 115(4); SI 2000/636 reg 2(1),(1A), sch part 1 para 4; SI 2020/1505 regs 1(2), 2(2)(a);
         NISR 2000/71 reg 2(1),(1A), sch part 1 para 4; NISR 2021/281 regs 1(3), 2(2)

20.35   IAA 115(1)-(3),(9)(b); UC 9(1); HB 10(1),(2); HB66+ 10(1),(2); NIUC 9(1); NIHB 10(1),(2); NIHB66+ 10(1),(2)
         www.gov.uk/guidance/immigration-rules/immigration-rules-part-14-stateless-persons

20.36   UC 9(4)(e)(ii); NIUC 9(4)(e)(ii); 10(3B)(h)(ii); HB66+ 10(4A)(h)(ii);
         NIHB 10(5)(h)(ii); NIHB66+ 10(5)(h)(ii); CTP 12(5)(e)(ii);
         www.gov.uk/government/publications/application-for-benefits-for-visa-holder-domestic-violence
         See Home Office Guidance (2018), DDV concession, page 5 https://tinyurl.com/DDVC-Feb-2018
         https://tinyurl.com/U2-2012

20.37   https://home.oisc.gov.uk/adviser_finder/finder.aspx

The habitual residence test

What is the habitual residence test

20.38   In law the habitual residence test has two parts:

(a) you aren't entitled to UC/HB/CTR unless you are 'habitually resident' in the British Isles – this is decided according to the particular facts in your case (paras 20.43-52); and

(b) you cannot be treated as being habitually resident unless you have a 'right to reside' there – this is decided according to immigration status (e.g. British citizen, paras 20.40-42).

It applies to you regardless of your nationality (including if you are British) – but people with certain kinds of status are exempt (para 20.39). Its purpose is to ensure that someone with the right to take up residence here cannot receive benefit immediately or shortly after their arrival.

Who is exempt from habitual residence test

20.39   You are exempt from both parts of the test – and so entitled to UC/HB/CTR – if:

(a) you applied for asylum and have been granted:

- refugee status,

- humanitarian protection, or

- discretionary leave (paras 20.22 and 20.33);

(b) you have been granted leave under the Afghan Citizens Resettlement Scheme (ACRS), the Afghan Relocations and Assistance Policy or the Afghan Locally Employed Staff ex-gratia scheme (ALES) for former British forces staff, or you left Afghanistan due to the collapse of the Afghan Government on 15th August 2021;

(c) you were resident in Ukraine before 1st January 2022, you left due to the Russian invasion and either:

- you have been granted leave (para 20.25(e)), or

- you are a British citizen, Irish citizen, or a Commonwealth citizen with the right of abode (table 20.2);

(d) you have been granted leave outside the immigration rules (such as the destitution domestic violence concession) (para 20.36);

(e) you are an EEA national to whom chapter 21 applies (para 21.2) and you are exempt from the habitual residence test because you are an EEA worker or self-employed person etc (para 21.33);

(f) you are a British citizen, a Commonwealth citizen with the right of abode or a person with settled status (table 20.2) and you have been deported to the UK from another country; or

(g) for HB/CTR only, you get one of the DWP benefits in para 20.13.

20.38   UC 9(1),(2); HB 10(2),(3); HB66+ 10(2),(3); NIUC 9(1),(2); NIHB 10(2),(3); NIHB66+ 10(2),(3); CTP 12(2),(3)

20.39   UC 9(4)(za)-(zc),(a)-(c),(ca)-(cc),(d)-(g);
HB 10(3B)(zza)-(zzc),(za)-(zf),(g),(h),(hh),(i),(k),(l); HB66+ 10(4A)(zza)-(zzc),(za)-(zf),(g),(h),(hh),(i),(k);
NIUC 9(4)(za)-(zc),(a)-(c),(ca)-(cc),(d)-(g); NIHB 10(5)(zza)-(zzc),(za)-(zf),(g),(h),(i),(j),(l),(m);
NIHB66+ 10(5)(zza)-(zzc),(za)-(zf),(g),(h),(i),(j),(l); CTP 12(5)(za),(zb),(a)-(c),(g),(h),(ha)

How habitual residence (HR) decisions are made and notified

20.40   When the DWP considers the habitual residence test it decides if you have a right to reside as the first stage (para 20.38(b)). If you fail this stage your decision notice usually just says that you are not entitled because you aren't habitually resident. Decisions about the right to reside for EEA nationals with pre-settled status are often very complex (paras 21.36 onwards); if this applies to you it may be helpful to ask for a statement of reasons before you ask for a reconsideration or appeal (para 14.9).

Habitual residence stage one: the right to reside

20.41   You must have a right to reside in the UK, Ireland, the Channel Islands or the Isle of Man. This is straightforward if you are a British Citizen, Irish Citizen or a Commonwealth Citizen with the 'right of abode' (table 20.2). You also have a right to reside if you have indefinite leave to remain (including EU settled status: para 21.16) and (presumably) limited leave provided you comply with any conditions: R(IS) 8/07. But if you have temporary admission (table 20.2) this isn't enough to be a right to reside: R(H) 7/09.

20.42   If you are a person to whom chapter 21 applies (EEA nationals and EEA family members with pre-settled status) you have a right to reside so long as:

   (a) you are a worker or self-employed person, or you have retained your worker/self-employed status while temporarily out of work (para 21.36-50);

   (b) you have a right of permanent residence (para 21.53-61, 21.64);

   (c) you are a student (para 21.83);

   (d) you are a 'self-sufficient person' (para 21.85);

   (e) you are the family member of someone above;

   (f) you have a 'derivative' right to reside (paras 21.25, 21.72-77); or

   (g) you are a jobseeker or the family member of jobseeker (para 21.51).

But in the case of (f) and (g) you aren't entitled to UC/HB/CTR if the right you are using is excluded (para 21.34). Although EU pre-settled status is a 'right to reside' (para 20.41) it isn't sufficient on its own (or together with an excluded right) to get UC/HB/CTR (para 21.35).

Habitual residence stage two: based on your facts

20.43   What counts as habitual residence is a 'question of fact'. It is decided by looking at all the facts in your case; no list of considerations can be drawn up to govern all cases. The DWP gives general guidance on this (ADM C1946-70; HBGM paras C4.87-106).

20.41-42   R(IS) 8/07 is Abdirahman v SSWP [2007] EWCA Civ 657
           R(H) 7/09 is Yesiloz v Camden LBC [2009] EWCA Civ 415

What is habitual residence

20.44   There are two elements to 'habitual residence':

(a) 'Residence': you must actually be resident, a mere intention to reside is insufficient; and mere physical presence is not residence.

(b) 'Habitual': there must also be a degree of permanence in your residence in the British Isles (HBGM para C4.80), the word 'habitual' implying a more settled state in which you are making your home here. There is no requirement that it must be your only home, or that it is permanent, provided it is your genuine home for the time being.

Losing and gaining habitual residence

20.45   Habitual residence can be lost in a single day: for example, if you leave the UK intending to take up long-term residence in another country. But if you have recently entered the UK from another country with the intention to settle here you don't become habitually resident immediately on arrival. Instead, there are two main requirements (R(IS) 6/96):

(a) your residence must be for an 'appreciable period of time'; and

(b) you must have a 'settled intention' to live in the UK.

'Appreciable period of time' and 'intention to settle'

20.46   There is no fixed period that amounts to an appreciable period (R(IS) 2/00). It varies according to the circumstances of your case and takes account of the 'length, continuity and nature' of your residence (R(IS) 6/96).

20.47   Case law (CIS 4474/2003) suggests that, in general, the period lies between one and three months, and a decision maker needs 'powerful reasons to justify a significantly longer period'. But that time must be spent making a home here, rather than merely studying or on a temporary visit.

20.48   As suggested by the DWP (ADM C1965-69 HBGM C4.85-86), factors likely to be relevant in deciding what is an appreciable period of time include:

(a) the length and continuity of your residence;

(b) your reasons for coming to the UK;

(c) your future intentions;

(d) your employment prospects (para 20.49); and

(e) your centre of interest (para 20.50).

The relative weighting given to each will depend on the facts in your case but no one factor is ever decisive.

20.49   In considering your employment prospects, your education and qualifications are likely to be significant (CIS 5136/2007). An offer of work is also good evidence of an intention to settle. If you have stable employment it is presumed that you reside here, even if your family lives abroad (ADM C1969).

Centre of interest

20.50   Your centre of interest is concerned with the strength of your ties to this country and your intention to settle. As suggested by the DWP (ADM C1966; HBGM C4.105), this can be shown by:

(a) the presence of close relatives;

(b) decisions made about the location of your family's personal possessions (e.g. clothing, furniture, transport);

(c) substantial purchases, such as furnishings, which indicate a long-term commitment; and

(d) the membership of any clubs or organisations in connection with your hobbies or recreations.

Temporary absence and returning residents

20.51   Once your habitual residence has been established, it resumes immediately on your return from a single short absence (such as a holiday or visiting relatives).

20.52   In considering whether you regain your habitual residence following a longer absence, or repeated absences, the following points need to be considered:

(a) the circumstances in which your habitual residence was lost;

(b) your intentions – if your absence was always intended to be temporary (even in the case of longer absences) you are less likely to lose your habitual residence than someone who originally never had an intention to return;

(c) your continuing links with the UK while abroad;

(d) the circumstances of your return. If you slot straight back into the life you had before you left, you are likely to resume habitual residence more quickly.

Chapter 21 **EEA nationals**

- ■ When this chapter applies: see paras 21.1-5.
- ■ The UK's exit from the EU: see paras 21.6-12
- ■ The EU settlement scheme, time limits and who can apply: see paras 21.13-29
- ■ EEA nationals etc, who can get UC/HB/CTR: see paras 21.30-35
- ■ EEA self-employed and worker status: see paras 21.36-52.
- ■ The right of permanent residence: see paras 21.53-61.
- ■ EEA family member rights: see paras 21.62-70.
- ■ Other EEA rights to reside (derivative rights, students and self-sufficient persons: see paras 21.71-88.

21.1   This chapter describes your right to UC/HB/CTR if you are an EEA national or an EEA family member and you exercised your European Union (EU) free movement rights on or before 31st December 2020.

When this chapter applies

21.2   This chapter only applies to you if:

(a) you are a person who was entitled to apply to the EU settlement scheme (paras 21.22-29); and

(b) you applied within the time limit or your late application was accepted (para 21.19); and

(b) either:

- ■ you have been granted EU pre-settled status; or
- ■ your application has been accepted (whether in time or late) but has not yet been decided.

You can make an application to the EU settlement scheme if you are an EEA national, an EEA family member, or in certain circumstances, the family member of a British citizen. But in each case your right to do so depends on the date you, or the EEA national/British citizen you accompany, first entered the UK (para 21.15).

21.3   You can't apply to the EU settlement scheme if you first entered the UK after the implementation period (para 21.7). Your rights to UC/HB/CTR are described in chapter 20.

21.4   Once you get EU settled status your EEA rights are extinguished (for all time) and your rights to UC/HB/CTR are described in chapter 20.

21.3   European Union (Withdrawal Agreement) Act 2020, s.7

21.4   Immigration and Social Security Co-ordination (EU Withdrawal) Act 2020, sch 1 para 2(2);
SI 2020/1209 regs 4(2),(4),(6), 11; SI 2020/1309 reg 83, sch 4 paras 1, 2

21.5   If you have any other kind of leave (table 20.2) other than EU pre-settled status your rights are also described in chapter 20. For example, you might have been granted indefinite leave to remain before your country joined the EU or before EU free movement rights began (table 21.1).

The UK's exit from the EU (Brexit)

21.6   The UK left the European Union (EU) at 11pm on 31st January 2020.

The implementation period

21.7   The implementation period started immediately after the UK left the EU and ended at 11pm on 31st December 2020.

21.8   As part of the UK's withdrawal agreement with the EU, the same EU free movement rights to enter the UK, live, work, and to access UK benefits and services continued to apply to EEA nationals/EEA family members during the implementation period. Anyone doing so could also apply to the EU settlement scheme (para 21.13).

21.9   EEA nationals (and their family members) who entered the UK for the first time after the implementation period are subject to UK immigration control and can't apply to the EU settlement scheme. See chapter 20 for their rights to UC/HB/CTR.

The grace period

21.10   The grace period started immediately after the implementation period (para 21.7) and ended at midnight on 30th June 2021.

21.11   The grace period gave EEA nationals/family members who qualified for the EU settlement scheme extra time to apply. During the grace period EEA nationals/family members could continue to use their EU free movement rights in the same way as during the implementation period even if they had not yet submitted their application.

21.12   EEA rights to reside ended on 1st July 2021 for anyone didn't apply to the EU settlement scheme (para 21.13) before then. If you didn't apply you may be an overstayer (table 20.2) and resident in the UK unlawfully. You should get advice immediately from a OISC registered adviser [www] about making a late application.

21.6   European Union (Withdrawal Agreement) Act 2020, s.1, s.20(1) – 'exit day'; Immigration Rules, Appendix EU, Annex1 – 'date and time of withdrawal'

21.7-8   European Union (Withdrawal Agreement) Act 2020, s.1A(1)-(3),(6) – 'implementation period', 'IP completion day'

21.10   European Union (Withdrawal Agreement) Act 2020, s.7; SI 2020/1209 reg 3(5)(a)

21.11   SI 2020/1209 regs 3(3), 11

21.12   European Union (Withdrawal Agreement) Act 2020, s.7; SI 2020/1209 regs 82, 83, sch 3 paras 4, 6, sch 4 paras 1-4
        https://home.oisc.gov.uk/adviser_finder/finder.aspx

The EU Settlement Scheme (EUSS)

21.13   This section (paras 21.14-29) describes the main features of the EU settlement scheme. It tells you:

(a) what the EU settlement scheme does and how it relates to UK immigration control (paras 21.16-18);

(b) who can apply (paras 21.22-29); and

(c) the time limits for making an application (paras 21.19-21).

21.14   The EUSS is part of the UK's withdrawal agreement with the EU. It provides a simple route for EEA nationals to legally settle in the UK so that they can continue to live, work, and get access to UK benefits and services after the UK has left the EU. The scheme is free of charge and is part of the UK's immigration rules ('Appendix EU'). The scheme also applies to EEA family members and to certain family members of British citizens. A separate application is required by each family member and must be made within the time limit.

21.15   The scheme is only open to EEA nationals who first entered the UK before 11pm on 31st December 2020 (paras 21.7-9). In the case of EEA family members, the entry cut-off date applies to the EEA national they accompanied (not the date the family member entered the UK) and certain other rules apply such as when the relationship with the EEA national began.

EU settled status and pre-settled status

21.16   If your application is successful you will be given:

(a) indefinite leave to enter/remain ('settled status'); or

(b) limited leave to enter/remain ('pre-settled status');

EU settled and pre-settled are kinds of indefinite and limited leave granted under the immigration rules (table 20.2), and both are granted without a public funds condition. You can use the online service to view, prove and share your settled or pre-settled status with others (e.g., with the DWP) [www].

21.17   You are eligible for settled status if you have completed a continuous qualifying period of five years lawful residence and certain other conditions are met. This is not dependent upon you having met any EEA right of residence conditions (paras 21.36 onwards).

21.18   You are eligible for pre-settled status if you would be eligible for settled status but for the fact that you have not yet completed the five-year qualification period. Once you have completed your five years you can reapply to get settled status.

Time limit for applications

21.19   The scheme opened for applications on 30th March 2019. Your application is within the time limit if it was made on or before 30th June 2021 (the end of the grace period).

21.15   European Union (Withdrawal) Act 2018, s.4

20.16   www.gov.uk/view-prove-immigration-status

21.17   Immigration Rules, Appendix EU11, EU11A

21.18   Immigration Rules, Appendix EU14, EU14A

21.19   SI 2020/1209 reg 3; Immigration Rules, Appendix EU, Annex 1 – 'relevant EEA citizen'

Late applications

21.20   You can make a late application if you have 'reasonable grounds' for missing the deadline [www]. The government has published 'caseworker guidance' [www] which sets out a wide range of circumstances that would constitute reasonable grounds. These include but are not limited to:

(a) you are a child/young person and the person responsible for you failed to apply on your behalf;

(b) you had a serious medical condition, which meant you were unable to apply by the deadline;

(c) you were in an abusive relationship or a victim of modern slavery;

(d) you are isolated, vulnerable or did not have the digital skills to make the application;

(e) you were unable to apply by the relevant deadline for compelling practical or compassionate reasons – including considering the coronavirus pandemic.

Late applications and claims for UC/HB/CTR

21.21   DWP guidance says that you are entitled to UC/HB once you have confirmation that your late application has been accepted (ADM memo 30/20 paras 12-13, HB circular A10/2021). But until you get your settlement decision you must show you have a right to reside and pass the habitual residence test (para 21.32).

Who can apply to the EUSS: EEA nationals and EEA family members

21.22   You are an EEA national if you are a citizen of an EEA member state or Switzerland (table 21.1).

21.23   You are an EEA family member if:

(a) you are accompanying an EEA national who exercised his/her EU right to live, work or study in the UK before the end of the implementation period (para 21.7);

(b) you are related to that person in one of the ways described in table 21.2); and

(c) you arrived to join them in the UK before 1st July 2021 (the end of the 'grace period').

You do not need to be a citizen of an EEA country yourself (although you can be). In certain circumstances you can retain your EEA family member rights after your relationship ends (paras 21.65-70).

21.20   SI 2020/1209 reg 4(2),(4),(6)
         www.gov.uk/government/publications/eu-settlement-scheme-information-for-late-applicants
         www.gov.uk/government/publications/eu-settlement-scheme-caseworker-guidance

21.22   EEA 2(1) – 'EEA national', 'EEA State'

21.23   EEA 7, 8

Who can apply to the EUSS: Family members of British/Irish citizens

21.24   Certain family members of a British or Irish citizens could also apply to the EUSS:

(a)   a non-EEA parent of a British child ('Zambrano carer') (para 21.25);

(b)   a family member of a British citizen who exercised his/her free movement rights in another EEA member state before 1 February 2020 ('Surinder Singh' rights); or

(c)   a family member of a relevant person of Northern Ireland (paras 21.28-29).

Non-EEA parent of British child ('Zambrano' carer)

21.25   You had a right to reside under the EEA regulations if:

(a)   you are a non-EEA national who is the primary carer (para 21.78) of a British child; and

(b)   that child was resident in the UK before the end of the implementation period (para 21.7); and

(c)   that child would have been unable to continue living in the UK or another EEA state if you left the UK for an indefinite period.

This right is sometimes referred to as a 'Zambrano' right after the case that established it (and is another kind of 'derivative right to reside': para 21.73). If you had this right to reside before implementation period ended, you could apply the EUSS for settled status.

Family members of British citizens with 'Surinder Singh' rights

21.26   A British citizen who exercised their EU free movement rights in another member state before 1st February 2020 can in certain circumstances, bring his/her family members back to the UK to live here. These are sometimes called 'Surinder Singh' rights after the case that established it. The British citizen you accompany must have returned to the UK on or before 31st December 2020.

21.27   If you were a 'Surinder Singh' family member you could enter the UK and apply to the EUSS. But the time limits vary depending on when your relationship with the British citizen began:

(a)   if you are the partner (or the partner's dependent child) and the relationship began before 1st February 2020 (the date the UK left the EU), you could apply to the EUSS at any time up to and including 29th March 2022;

(b)   if you are the UK national's dependent child, parent or grandparent (or of his/her spouse/civil partner) and that relationship continued to exist when applied, you could apply up to and including 29th March 2022; but

(c)   if your relationship began between 1st February 2020 and 31st December 2020 (during the 'implementation period'), you must have entered the UK before that period ended and applied to the EUSS on or before 30th June 2021.

21.25   EEA 16(5); Zambrano v Office national de l'emploi [2010] ECJ C-34/09
www.bailii.org/eu/cases/EUECJ/2010/C3409_0.html

21.26   Singh v SSHD [1992] EUECJ C-370/90; www.bailii.org/eu/cases/EUECJ/1992/C37090.html

21.27   Immigration Rules, Appendix EU, EU12, Annex 1 – 'family member of a qualifying British citizen', 'specified date'

Table 21.1 **The European Economic Area (EEA)**

This table shows the EEA members from 20th July 1994 (when the EEA free movement rights began), the dates member states joined and any transitional period of worker registration/authorisation. For the rules about worker registration/authorisation, see previous editions of this guide.

Member states/date of joining	Transitional period/description
(a) Member states joining before 20th July 1994	
Belgium, Denmark, France, Germany, Greece, Hungary, Iceland, Ireland, Italy, Luxembourg, Netherlands, Norway, Portugal, Spain	**No**
(b) 1st January 1995	
Austria, Finland, Sweden	**No**
(c) 1st May 1995	
Liechtenstein	**No**
(d) 1st June 2002	
Switzerland (treated as an EEA state)	**No**
(e) 1st May 2004	
Cyprus, Malta	**No**
Czech Republic, Estonia, Hungary, Latvia, Lithuania, Poland, Slovakia, Slovenia	**Yes** – 1st May 2004-30th April 2009 (see note): Worker Registration Scheme
(f) 1st January 2007	
Bulgaria, Romania	**Yes** – 1st January 2007-31st December 2013: Worker Authorisation Scheme
(g) 1st July 2013	
Croatia	**Yes** – 1st July 2013-30th June 2018: Worker Authorisation Scheme

Note: The extension of the worker registration scheme in (e) between 1st May 2009 and 30th April 2011 was ruled unlawful by the Supreme Court (SSWP v Gubeladze).

T21.1(a)-(f) **The Immigration (European Economic Area) Regulations:**
20/07/1994 - 01/10/2000: SI 1994/1895
02/10/2000 - 29/04/2006: SI 2000/2326
30/04/2006 - 31/01/2017: SI 2006/1003
01/02/2017 onwards: SI 2016/1052

T21.1(d) SI 2002/1241; EEA 2(1) – 'EEA state'

T21.1 note   SSWP v Gubeladze [2019] UKSC 31 https://www.bailii.org/uk/cases/UKSC/2019/31.html

Worker Registration/Authorisation Regulations
T21.1(e) SI 2004/1219
T21.1(f) SI 2006/3317
T21.1(g) SI 2013/1460

Family members of people born in Northern Ireland

21.28   If you are not a British or an EEA citizen you can apply to the EU settlement scheme if you are the 'family member' (para 21.29) of a 'relevant person of Northern Ireland'. A relevant person of Northern Ireland is a person who was born in Northern Ireland to a mother or father who was (at that time):

   (a)   a British citizen;

   (b)   an Irish citizen; or

   (c)   a person with settled status.

21.29   You are the 'family member' of a relevant person of Northern Ireland if you are:

   (a)   his/her spouse or civil partner;

   (b)   aged under 21 and you are the child, grandchild or great grandchild of that person or of his/her spouse or civil partner; or

   (c)   his/her child, grandchild, great grandchild, parent or grandparent or that of his/her spouse/civil partner and you are dependent on that person's support for your essential living needs.

EEA nationals etc can get UC/HB/CTR

21.30   This section (paras 21.31-35) tells you when you are entitled to UC/HB/CTR from 1st July 2021 onwards:

   (a)   if you have EU pre-settled status; or

   (b)   if you applied to the EU settlement scheme but have not received a decision.

If you have been granted EU settled status or refused EU pre-settled status, then chapter 20 applies to you instead.

How the law works from 1st January 2021

21.31   The Immigration (European Economic Area) Regulations 2016 (the 'EEA regulations') are revoked from 1st January 2021 but are saved in modified form for UC/HB/CTR purposes:

   (a)   during the grace period (para 21.10) (whether you applied to the EU settlement scheme or not);

   (b)   during any period while you are waiting for a decision from the EU settlement scheme about your settled status provided you applied in time, or your late application was accepted. If the decision is not to grant you leave (para 21.16) your right to reside continues while you appeal until that appeal is finally determined;

   (c)   while you have EU pre-settled status (paras 21.16-18)

The rights to reside described in this chapter are based on the EEA regulations in their modified form.

21.28   Immigration rules, Appendix EU, EU12, Annex 1 – 'EEA citizen', 'family member of a relevant EEA citizen', 'relevant person of Northern Ireland'

21.31   SI 2020/1209 regs 3, 4(4),(6), 11; SI 2020/1309 sch 4 paras 1-4

EEA rights and entitlement to UC/HB/CTR

21.32   You are entitled to UC/HB/CTR using one of your EEA rights if:

(a) you are a person who is entitled to apply to the EU settlement scheme; and

(b) you made an application in time, or your late application has been accepted; and

(c) either:

■   your application has not been decided, or

■   you have been granted pre-settled status; and

(d) either:

■   you are exempt from the habitual residence test, or

■   you have some other right to reside that isn't excluded from UC/HB/CTR and you are habitually resident (on the facts) (paras 20.43-52).

If you are a couple, see paras 20.15-16 for how all these rules apply to you.

Who is exempt from the habitual residence test

21.33   You are exempt from the habitual residence test if your EEA right to reside is:

(a) as a worker, frontier worker or self-employed person (paras 21.37-50);

(b) a right of permanent residence acquired through retirement (para 21.59);

(c) as a 'family member', as defined in table 21.2(a)-(c), of a worker or self-employed person;

(d) a right of permanent residence as a family member which you acquired because the EEA national you accompanied:

■   retired or ceased working due to incapacity (paras 21.59-60), or

■   died (para 21.70); or

(e) as a family member of a 'relevant person of Northern Ireland' (paras 21.28-29).

EEA rights to reside excluded from UC/HB/CTR

21.34   You aren't entitled to UC/HB/CTR if your only EEA right to reside is:

(a) your first three months residence in the UK;

(b) as a jobseeker or as a family member of a jobseeker (para 21.51);

(c) as 'Zambrano' carer (para 21.25); or

(d) EU pre-settled status either on its own (para 21.35) or with one of (a)-(c) above.

Although you can't get UC/HB/CTR these rights to reside can help you qualify for EU settled status (paras 21.17-18). If your partner has a right to reside, see paras 20.15-16. If you are a Zambrano carer you may qualify for other financial support from social services: Sanneh v SSWP, Yekini v LB Southwark.

21.32   SI 2020/1209 regs 4(4), 11; SI 2020/1309 sch 4 paras 1-4

21.33   UC 9(4)(a)-(c),(ca)-(cc); HB 10(3B)(za)-(zf); HB66+ 10(4A)(za)-(zf); NIUC 9(4)(a)-(c),(ca)-(cc); NIHB 10(3B)(za)-(zf); NIHB66+ 10(4A)(za)-(zf)

21.34   UC 9(3); HB 10(3),(3AA); HB66+ 10(4),(4ZA); NIUC 9(3); NIHB 10(3),(3AA); NIHB66+ 10(4),(4ZA)
         Sanneh v SSWP [2015] EWCA Civ 49; www.bailii.org/ew/cases/EWCA/2015/49.html
         Yekini v LB Southwark [2014] EWHC 2096 (Admin) www.bailii.org/ew/cases/EWHC/Admin/2014/2096.html

People with EU pre-settled status without a right to reside

21.35   In most cases if you have EU pre-settled status you must also have a right to reside to be entitled to UC/HB/CTR. The fact you need both does not constitute discrimination against EEA nationals who exercise their EU free movement rights (Fratila and another v SSWP). However, if you do not have a right to reside before UC/HB/CTR is refused the decision maker must be satisfied that refusal would not prevent you from living in dignity. If not satisfied the decision maker must waive the requirement to have a right to reside: [2022] UKUT 330 (AAC). The DWP has been granted permission to appeal the upper tribunal's decision but in the meantime, you can ask the DWP to apply the same approach as in that case.

EEA self-employed and worker status

21.36   This section (paras 21.37-52) describes who has the right to reside as a self-employed person or a worker and how that status can be retained during temporary periods of sickness or unemployment, etc.

Self-employed people

21.37   You have the right to reside if you are an EEA national engaged in self-employed business in the UK. Your self-employment must be 'real', and have actually begun, but the ten-hour threshold (para 21.43) does not apply and your self-employed status can continue even where there is no current work, provided you continue to look for it: [2010] UKUT 451 (AAC). A seller of *The Big Issue* who buys the magazine at half price and sells it has been found to be in self-employment: [2011] UKUT 494 (AAC). But your self-employed income must provide a real contribution to your required income: [2017] UKUT 155 (AAC).

21.38   You have a legal duty to register with HMRC within three months of starting your business – even if you think you won't earn enough to pay tax/national insurance. However, the mere fact of being registered does not determine your self-employed status nor does it necessarily mean that HMRC accepts you are self-employed. On the other hand, the fact that you have not registered doesn't mean that you aren't self-employed: CIS/3213/2007.

Workers

21.39   You have the right to reside as a 'worker' if you are an EEA national in paid employment in the UK provided your work meets the minimum requirements (paras 21.41-44).

Frontier workers

21.40   You are a frontier worker if you are a worker or self-employed in the UK, but you are not 'predominantly resident' here. You can retain your frontier worker status in a similar way to a worker while you are temporarily out of work.

21.35   SI 2020/1309 sch 4 paras 2-4
        UC 9(3)(c); HB 10(3AA); HB66+ 10(4ZA); CTP 12(4A); NIUC 9(3)(c); NIHB 10(3AA); NIHB66+ 10(4ZA)
        Fratila and another v SSWP [2021] UKSC 23; www.bailii.org/uk/cases/UKSC/2021/23.html
21.37   EEA 6(1)(c), 14(1)
21.39   EEA 6(1)(b), 14(1)
21.40   SI 2020/1213, regs 3, 4
        UC 9(4)(cb),(cc); HB 10(3B)(ze),(zf); HB66+ 10(4A)(ze),(zf); NIUC 9(4)(cb),(cc); NIHB 10(3B)(ze),(zf); NIHB 66+ 10(4A)(ze),(zf)

Deciding worker status

21.41   To decide whether you are a worker the DWP applies a two-tier test:

(a) you are 'automatically' considered to be a worker/self-employed (ADM C1487) if your average gross earnings from employment/self-employment:

  ■ are at least equal to the national insurance primary threshold (£1,048 per month/ £242 per week in 2023-24), and

  ■ were at least that level for a continuous period of three months immediately before you claimed UC; or

(b) if the above criteria aren't met the DWP decides the matter according to your individual circumstances by considering:

  ■ whether you are exercising your EU free movement rights (ADM C1495-96), and

  ■ if you are, whether you are engaged in 'remunerative' work which is 'effective and genuine' (para 21.42) and not 'on such a small scale to be purely marginal and ancillary'.

Test (a) has no basis in law, so if you fail it the DWP must properly consider part (b) before concluding that you aren't a worker: [2019] UKUT 52 (AAC).

21.42   'Remunerative' has its ordinary English meaning: broadly payment for services you provide. The following are relevant to whether your work is 'effective and genuine' (ADM para C1499):

(a) the period of employment;

(b) the number of hours worked;

(c) the level of earnings; and

(d) whether the work is regular or erratic.

21.43   The number of hours worked is not conclusive of your worker status, but it is relevant: CH/3733/2007. The European Commission considers ten hours to be enough [www] although this may not be enough when the other factors here are considered – and not doing ten hours does not automatically exclude you. The factors must always be considered together. DWP guidance notes that work that is part-time or low paid is not necessarily always marginal or ancillary – and gives the example of working three hours a day, five days a week for the last four months as being enough (ADM C1501 and example 4). But if you work full time (other than a fixed-term contract) you could acquire worker status in as little as two weeks: Tarola v Minister for Social Protection.

21.44   The fact that your job is poorly paid or the fact that you need to claim UC, is not enough on its own to stop you from qualifying as a worker. You can be a 'worker' even if your work is paid 'cash in hand': [2012] UKUT 112 (AAC).

21.43   European Commission Communications COM (2002) 694, p5 https://tinyurl.com/EC-COM-2002-694
         Tarola v Minister for Social Protection Case C-483/17 www.bailii.org/eu/cases/EUECJ/2019/C48317.html

Retained worker/self-employed status: temporary incapacity for work

21.45   You retain your EEA worker or self-employed status if you are temporarily unable to work due to sickness or injury. What counts as being temporary isn't defined and there is no set maximum period. Provided your incapacity isn't permanent and there is a realistic prospect of you being able to return to work within the foreseeable future you retain your worker status ([2016] UKUT 389 (AAC), De Brito v SSHD). You do not have to show you have 'limited capability for work' (para 2.43) – the test is whether you would be able to do the work you were doing (CIS/4304/2007, [2017] UKUT 421 (AAC)). If your incapacity is permanent see para 21.60.

Retained worker/self-employed status: pregnancy and childbirth

21.46   If you are a worker and stop working because of pregnancy or recent childbirth you retain your worker/self-employed) status as follows:

(a) (as a worker) while you are still under contract, such as on maternity leave even if it isn't paid (CIS/4237/2007);

(b) (as self-employed) if you stop work for maternity leave provided you intend to resume your business (CIS/1042/2008);

(c) (as a worker) if you gave up work or seeking work due to the physical constraints of the late stages of pregnancy or the aftermath of childbirth, provided you start work/seeking work again within a 'reasonable period' after the birth – this usually means up to 52 weeks, starting with 11 weeks before your due date: Saint Prix v SSWP and [2016] AACR 16.

Retained worker status: vocational training

21.47   You retain your worker status or self-employed status while you are undertaking vocational training that is related to your previous employment (or any work if there is no work available that is reasonably equivalent to your last job).

Retained worker status: registered unemployed

21.48   You retain your worker status or self-employed status during a period of registered unemployment:

(a) for up to six months if you were employed (in the UK) for less than a year (which could have been for as little as two weeks: para 21.43); or

(b) without time limit if you were employed for at least a year.

21.49   The one year's employment need not be continuous: [2015] UKUT 128 (AAC). Small gaps (probably no longer than three months) between leaving your employment and registering as a jobseeker can be ignored: [2013] UKUT 163 (AAC).

21.45   EEA 6(2)(a),(4)(a); De Brito v SSHD [2012] www.bailii.org/ew/cases/EWCA/Civ/2012/709.htm

21.46   Saint Prix v SSWP [2014] AACR 18; www.bailii.org/eu/cases/EUECJ/2014/C50712.html
         [2016] AACR 16 is [2015] UKUT 502 (AAC)

21.47   EEA 6(2)(d),(e),(4)(d),(e)

21.48   EEA 6(2)(b),(c),(3),(4)(b),(c),(4A); SI 2020/1309, sch 4 para 4(e)

21.50   The easiest way to register as unemployed is to make a claim for UC, JSA(C) or national insurance credits (although it is not strictly necessary that you qualify for these (CIS 184/2008)). Even if you don't qualify for UC/JSA/HB for the time being you should keep 'signing on' because it can help you qualify for a right of permanent residence (para 21.56) until you get EU settled status.

Who is an EEA jobseeker

21.51   You are an 'EEA jobseeker' if you have a period of registered unemployment that started immediately after:

(a)   you entered the UK (without work); or

(b)   you have worked in the UK for less than a year before becoming unemployed and your retained worker status ended after six months registered unemployment.

Your jobseeker status continues if you can show you have 'genuine prospects of work' (ADM C1403-50) for a maximum period of 91 days. But if you have EU pre-settled status (para 21.16) you can continue to live in the UK lawfully after your right to reside as a jobseeker has expired.

The genuine prospects of work test

21.52   The DWP used to apply the 'genuine prospects of work test' (GPoW) (para 21.51) to everyone after six months registered unemployment but now only does this if you have worked in the UK for less than one year (paras 21.48, 21.51). The DWP now accepts that if you have worked in the UK for at least one year you can retain your worker status for long as you are registered unemployed and the GPoW should not be applied to you ([2020] UKUT 50 (AAC), ADM memo 31/20). This change is confirmed in the modified EEA regulations (para 21.31).

The right of permanent residence

21.53   This section (paras 21.54-61) describes who has an EEA right of permanent residence. A different set of rules applies to EEA family members (para 21.64).

21.54   Even though it is called 'permanent' you lose it if you failed to apply to the EU settlement scheme by the deadline (para 21.19) or when you get EU settled status.

21.55   Apart from that, once you have acquired a permanent right of residence (paras 21.56-61 and 21.64) you only lose it after an absence from the UK of more than two years.

21.51   EEA 6 as modified by SI 2020/1309, sch 4 para 4(e)

21.54   Immigration and Social Security Co-ordination (EU Withdrawal) Act 2020, sch 1 para 2(2); SI 2020/1309, reg 83, sch 4 paras 1, 2

21.55   EEA 15(3)

Right of permanent residence: the five-year rule

21.56 If you have lived in the UK continuously for five years while using your free movement rights you have a permanent right to reside and you are entitled to UC/HB/CTR provided you are also habitually resident (para 21.32). You are using your free movement rights during any time in which you had the right to reside as a 'qualified person'. This means you are:

(a) a worker or a retained worker (paras 21.39-49);

(b) a self-employed person (paras 21.37-38);

(c) a jobseeker (whether you receive JSA or not) (para 21.51);

(d) a student (para 21.83); or

(e) a self-sufficient person (para 21.85).

You can also count your first three months residence in the UK towards the qualifying period if none of the above applied.

21.57 A period of residence counts as 'continuous' despite a period of absence from the UK if:

(a) in any one year, the total length of your absence(s) is no more than six months, and this can be longer if your absence is due to compulsory military service; or

(b) the total period of absence is not more than 12 months – so long as the reason is pregnancy, childbirth, serious illness, study, vocational training, a posting in another country, or some other important reason.

Right of permanent residence: retired workers

21.58 You get the right of permanent residence without having to complete five years residence if you qualify as a retired worker/self-employed person (paras 21.59-61). You are exempt from the habitual residence test and entitled to UC/HB/CTR (para 21.33). If you are the family member of a retired worker see para 21.64.

Retirement due to old age

21.59 You have a right of permanent residence due to old age (ADM C1799-1802) if:

(a) you have retired as a worker before or after reaching pension age, or as a self-employed person after reaching pension age: and

- you worked in the UK as a worker or self-employed person for at least 12 months before you retired; and

- you had been continuously resident in the UK for more than three years before you retired; or

(b) you have retired after reaching pension age (whether you have worked or not) and your spouse or civil partner is a British citizen.

21.56   EEA 6(1) – definition: 'qualified person', 13, 14(1), 15(1)(a)

21.57   EEA 3(2)

21.58   EEA 5(1), 15(1)(c); UC 9(4)(c); HB 10(3B)(zc); HB66+ 10(4A)(zc); CTP 12(5)(c)
NIUC 9(4)(c); NIHB 10(3B)(zc); NIHB66+ 10(4A)(zc)

21.59   EEA 5(2),(6)

Retirement due to permanent incapacity

21.60 You have a right of permanent residence due to incapacity (ADM C1799-1802) if:

(a) you have ceased working because of permanent incapacity; and

(b) either:

- your incapacity is the result of an accident at work or an occupational disease which entitles you to ESA, incapacity benefit, industrial injuries benefit or some other pension payable by a UK institution (private company or the DWP); or

- you had resided continuously in the UK for more than two years immediately before you stopped working; or

- your spouse or civil partner is a British citizen.

Retired workers: qualifying periods of work and UK residence

21.61 In deciding whether you meet employment condition (para 21.59(a)) a period of inactivity in which you are unable to work due to illness, accident or some other reason 'not of [your] own making' is counted as a period of employment/self-employment. If you are a worker, any period of inactivity in which you retained your worker status while unemployed (paras 21.48-50) is also counted as a period of employment. Qualification for the residence conditions (paras 21.59-60) is counted in the same way as para 21.57.

EEA family member rights

21.62 This section describes who has the right to reside as an EEA family member (paras 21.63-64) and who can retain their family member rights when the relationship ends (paras 21.65-70).

21.63 You are an EEA family member if you satisfy the conditions in table 21.2. You do not need to be an EEA national yourself (although you can be). Your right to reside lasts for as long as you remain a family member, so if you aren't married or in a civil partnership it usually ends when you separate unless you have a permanent right to reside or you meet the conditions to retain your family member rights (para 21.65).

Right of permanent residence: family members

21.64 You get a right of permanent residence as a family member if:

(a) you are a non-EEA national who has resided in the UK for a continuous period of five years as an EEA family member;

(b) you have resided in the UK for a continuous period of five years as a qualified person or as an EEA family member and at the end of that period you were a family member who had a retained right of residence (para 21.65);

21.60　EEA 5(3),(6)

21.61　EEA 3(2), 5(7)

21.63　EEA 14(3)

21.64　EEA 15(1)(b),(d)-(f)

(c) the EEA national you accompany has the right of permanent residence through retirement or incapacity (paras 21.59-61) and:

- you were his/her family member at the point s/he stopped working, and

- at that point you enjoyed the right to reside on the basis that you were his/her family member;

(d) the family member you accompany is a worker or self-employed person who has died, and:

- you were living with them immediately before their death, and

- s/he had lived continuously in the UK for at least the two years immediately before their death or s/he died as a result of an accident at work or occupational disease.

Former EEA family members with retained rights

21.65 If you are a former EEA family member (FM) you retain your family member rights if you satisfy any of the conditions in paras 21.66-70.

Table 21.2 **Who is an EEA family member**

You are an EEA family member if you accompany an EEA national who is self-employed, a worker, a student or a self-sufficient person and you are:

(a) their spouse or civil partner (until divorce/dissolution, not mere separation or estrangement);

(b) a direct descendant of that person (e.g. a child or grandchild) or of their spouse or civil partner, and you are

- aged under 21; or

- dependent on them or their spouse or civil partner (for example, because you are studying or disabled);

(c) a dependent direct relative in ascending line (e.g. a parent or grandparent) or of their spouse or civil partner;

(d) some other family member (an 'extended family member') who has been admitted to the UK on the basis that you are:

- their partner (in the benefit sense, instead of being their spouse or civil partner),

- a dependent household member of that person in their country of origin, or

- a relative who is so ill that you strictly require personal care from that person.

Note: If the EEA national you accompany is a student without any other right to reside you are only treated as their family member if you are their spouse/civil partner or dependent child (i.e. under 18 or dependent in other ways).

Retained FM: termination of marriage or civil partnership

21.66   You retain your family member status if:

(a) your marriage or civil partnership to the EEA national is terminated; and

(b) s/he had the right to reside at least until the termination proceedings began; and

(c) either:

- before the termination started (which must occur while the EEA national is in the UK), the marriage/civil partnership must have lasted for at least three years with both of you residing in the UK for at least one of those, or

- you have custody of the EEA national's child, or

- your continued right of residence is warranted by particularly difficult circumstances, for example if you or another family member were the victim of domestic violence during the marriage/civil partnership; and

(d) either:

- you are not an EEA national yourself, but if you were you would be a worker, a self-employed person or a self-sufficient person, or

- you are the family member of such a person (in the bullet above).

Retained FM: a child in education

21.67   You retain your family member status if:

(a) you are the EEA national's child or grandchild (or the child or grandchild of his/her spouse or civil partner);

(b) the EEA national you accompanied was a 'qualified person' (para 21.56);

(c) you were attending a course of education in the UK when s/he left the UK; and

(d) you are still attending that course.

21.68   You also retain your family member status as in para 21.67 above if condition (b) is read as if it said a 'qualified person' or a person with a right of permanent residence; and condition (c) is read as if it said you were attending a course of education when the family member you accompanied died.

Retained FM: parent of a child in education

21.69   You retain your family member status if you are the parent with custody of a child who satisfies either of the two paras above.

21.66   EEA 10(5),(6)

21.67-68   EEA 10(3)

21.69   EEA 10(4)

Retained FM: bereavement

21.70   You retain your family member status if:

  (a)   the EEA national you accompanied was a worker, self-employed, self-sufficient, a student or a person with a right of permanent residence;

  (b)   you had resided in the UK for at least a year immediately before s/he (the person in (a)) died; and

  (c)   either:

- you are not an EEA national yourself, but if you were you would be a worker, a self-employed person or a self-sufficient person, or

- you are the family member of such a person (in the sub-bullet above).

Other EEA rights to reside

21.71   This section describes other EEA rights to reside you may have other than those acquired through being economically active (e.g. worker, jobseeker etc) or as an EEA family member.

Primary carer of an EEA worker's child in education ('Ibrahim/Teixeira' rights)

21.72   You have a right to reside if:

  (a)   you are the 'primary carer' (para 21.78) of a child/young person; and

  (b)   that child (now or at any time in the past) has resided with either one of his/her parents at the same time during which that parent was a 'worker' (para 21.74); and

  (c)   that child is in 'education' in the UK (para 21.81); and

  (d)   that child would be unable to continue their education here if you left the UK; and

  (e)   you and the child you care for don't possess any other 'right to reside' (para 21.79).

21.73   This right to reside is sometimes called an 'Ibrahim/Teixeira' after the case that established it or (in the EEA regulations) a 'derivative right to reside'. To be entitled to UC/HB/CTR you must also be habitually resident (paras 20.38-52). For guidance see ADM C1827-39 and HB Circular A10/2010 [www].

21.74   This right to reside can't be established through being self-employed ([2018] UKUT 401 (AAC)): one of the child's parents must be/have been a worker who was exercising their EU freedom of movement right to work in the UK (paras 21.39-50). A person can't be a worker during a period of employment before his/her country joined the EU (table 21.1), but employment during the worker registration/authorisation scheme does count, whether s/he completed 12 months in continuous employment or not (ADM para C1837).

21.70   EEA 10(2),(6)

21.72   EEA 16(1),(3),(4)

21.73   https://tinyurl.com/HB-A10-2010

21.75 Your right to reside continues until the child completes their education. The guidance states that your right to reside normally ends when the child reaches 18 but 'it can continue beyond that age if the child continues to need [your] presence and care [...] in order to be able to complete their education' (ADM para C1835).

Primary carer of an EEA national child ('Chen' rights)

21.76 You have the right to reside if:

(a) you are the primary carer of an EEA national child aged under 18; and

(b) the EEA national child resides in the UK as a self-sufficient person (para 21.85);

(c) the EEA national child would be unable to continue to live in the UK if you (the primary carer) were to leave for an indefinite period; and

(d) you (the primary carer) don't possess any other EEA right to reside (para 21.79).

21.77 This right to reside is often referred to as a 'Chen right' after the case that established it. Until as recently as September 2021 it was thought that few qualified because the child required (private) comprehensive sickness insurance. But following VI v HMRC (para 21.87) it is now known that this requirement is met if the child is registered for NHS treatment. It follows that many of these cases will also now have acquired a right of permanent residence under the five-year rule (para 21.56) and also have EU settled status (para 21.17).

Primary carer

21.78 You are the child's 'primary carer' if:

(a) you are their 'direct relative' or legal guardian; and

(b) either

  ▪ you have primary responsibility for their care, or

  ▪ you share responsibility equally with one other person. In this case the rule in para 21.72(d) is read as if it said the child couldn't continue their education if both of you left the UK. But if that person's only right to reside in UK is as a primary carer and they acquired it before you became a joint carer, the rule is read in the normal way.

The issue as to who is the child's primary carer mustn't be decided solely on the basis of the financial contribution a person makes towards the child's care.

Primary carers with other EEA rights

21.79 Although the EEA regulations state that a primary carer cannot benefit from a derivative right to reside (paras 21.72(e), 21.76(d)) if they possess any other EEA right to reside, they cannot be excluded from using those rights if their other right to reside is as a jobseeker (para 21.51): [2022] UKUT 123 (AAC). The DWP accepts that this is the correct interpretation.

21.76   EEA 16(1)(a),(2)

21.77   Chen and others v Home Secretary [2004] EUECJ C-200/02 www.bailii.org/eu/cases/EUECJ/2004/C20002_0.html

21.78   EEA 16(8)-(11)

21.79   EEA 16(1)(a),(7)(c)(i)

Direct relative

21.80   The law doesn't define 'direct relative' but it probably means parent, grandparent, etc. DWP guidance (ADM C1832) states that a 'direct relative' can only be the parent and not a grandparent, but the law doesn't say this.

Being in education

21.81   Nursery education doesn't count as 'being in education' but being in a reception class or any education received before compulsory school age that 'is equivalent to' compulsory education does (ADM para C1835). It doesn't matter that the child started their education after the EEA national parent finished work – only that the child lived with that parent during a time when they were a worker (ADM para C1833.2).

Students and self-sufficient persons

21.82   If you aren't engaged in the labour market (including if you are a student) you have a right to reside as an EEA national if you entered the UK on the basis that you were 'self-sufficient' – in other words you had your own resources: [2014] UKUT 32 (AAC).

21.83   You have the right to reside as a student if:

(a)   you are currently studying on a course in the UK;

(b)   you signed a declaration at the beginning of the course that you were able to support yourself without social assistance (which means UC and any legacy benefit); and

(c)   the declaration was true at the time it was signed and for the foreseeable future; and

(d)   you have comprehensive sickness insurance for the UK (para 21.87).

21.84   In practice, this means that if you are an EEA student you are unlikely to get UC/HB/CTR. However, it is possible to get UC/HB/CTR if your circumstances have changed since you started your course (e.g. your source of funds has unexpectedly dried up) – provided you satisfy the other student entitlement rules (table 2.3, para 16.31).

21.85   You have the right to reside as a self-sufficient person if you:

(a)   have enough resources not to be an 'unreasonable burden' on the benefits system; and

(b)   have comprehensive sickness insurance (para 21.87).

21.86   The fact that your income is so low that you qualify for UC does not automatically mean you are not self-sufficient (although in most cases you will be) and the DWP has discretion to decide otherwise given your circumstances (ADM C1729.2). The fact that you have been able to manage without claiming UC until now is a relevant consideration in deciding whether you are an 'unreasonable burden' as is the length of time you are likely to be claiming (HBGM para C4.123). For example, if your funds have been temporarily disrupted the decision maker may decide you are self-sufficient.

21.81   EEA 16(3)(b),(7)(a)

21.82   EEA 6(1)(d),(e), 14(1)

21.83   EEA 4(1)(d),(3)

21.85   EEA 4(1)(c),(3)

21.86   EEA 4(4)(b)

Comprehensive sickness insurance

21.87   Until as recently as September 2021, it was thought that the requirement for comprehensive sickness insurance to be self-sufficient was only satisfied by private cover so very few qualified. But following VI v HMRC it is now known that this requirement is met if you were registered for NHS treatment. Due to the terms of the UK/EU withdrawal agreement this case is binding on the UK and overturns the long standing Court of Appeal decision in Ahmad v Home Secretary.

21.88   If you aren't/weren't registered for NHS treatment you are likely to satisfy this condition if you receive a pension or invalidity benefit from your own country (provided it is an EEA member state) (ADM C1730).

21.87   VI v Commissioners for HMRC [2021] EUECJ C-247/20; www.bailii.org/eu/cases/EUECJ/2022/C24720_0.html
          Ahmad v Home Secretary [2014] EWCA Civ 988

Appendix 1 **UC/SMI/CTR legislation**

UC/SMI: England, Scotland and Wales

Main primary legislation (Acts)

The Social Security Administration Act 1992
The Welfare Reform Act 2012
The Welfare Reform and Work Act 2016

Main secondary legislation (regulations and orders)

SI 2013/376	The Universal Credit Regulations 2013
SI 2013/380	The Universal Credit, Personal independence Payment, Jobseeker's Allowance and Employment and Support Allowance (Claims and Payments) Regulations 2013
SI 2013/381	The Universal Credit, Personal Independence Payment, Jobseeker's Allowance and Employment and Support Allowance (Decisions and Appeals) Regulations 2013
SI 2013/382	The Rent Officers (Universal Credit Functions) Order 2013
SI 2013/383	The Social Security (Payments on Account of Benefit) Regulations 2013
SI 2013/384	The Social Security (Overpayments and Recovery) Regulations 2013
SI 2013/386	The Universal Credit (Transitional Provisions) Order 2013
SI 2014/1230	The Universal Credit (Transitional Provisions) Regulations 2014
SI 2012/1483	Social Security (Information-sharing in relation to Welfare Services etc) Regulations 2012
SI 2017/725	The Loans for Mortgage Interest Regulations 2017

Recent amending regulations and orders

SI 2022/448	The Universal Credit (Local Welfare Provision Disregard) (Amendment) Regulations 2022
SI 2022/449	The Social Security and Council Tax Reduction Schemes (Amendment) Regulations 2022
SI 2022/886	The Universal Credit (Administrative Earnings Threshold) (Amendment) Regulations 2022
SI 2022/907	The Renting Homes (Wales) Act 2016 (Consequential Amendments to Secondary Legislation) Regulations 2022
SI 2022/942	The Housing Benefit and Universal Credit (Victims of Domestic Abuse and Victims of Modern Slavery) (Amendment) Regulations 2022
SI 2022/990	The Social Security (Habitual Residence and Past Presence) (Amendment) (No. 2) Regulations 2022
SI 2023/7	The Universal Credit (Administrative Earnings Threshold) (Amendment) Regulations 2023
SI 2023/6	The Rent Officers (Housing Benefit and Universal Credit Functions) (Modification) Order 2023
SI 2023/134	The Bereavement Benefits (Remedial) Order 2023
SI 2023/157	The Universal Credit (Work-Related Requirements) In Work Pilot Scheme (Extension) Order 2023
SI 2023/226	The Loans for Mortgage Interest (Amendment) Regulations 2023
SI 2023/316	The Social Security Benefits Up-Rating Order 2023
SI 2023/335	The Benefit Cap (Annual Limit) (Amendment) Regulations 2023

Recent transitional regulations: universal credit

SI 2022/752	The Universal Credit (Transitional Provisions) Amendment Regulations 2022
SI 2023/340	The Social Security Benefits Up-rating Regulations 2023

CTR: England, Scotland and Wales

Main primary legislation (Acts)

The Local Government Finance Act 1992

The Local Government Finance Act 2012

Main secondary legislation England

SI 2012/2885	The Council Tax Reduction Schemes (Prescribed Requirements) (England) Regulations 2012
SI 2012/2886	The Council Tax Reduction Schemes (Default Scheme) (England) Regulations 2012
SI 2013/215	Council Tax Reduction Schemes (Transitional Provision) (England) Regulations 2013
SI 2013/501	Council Tax Reduction Schemes (Detection of Fraud and Enforcement) (England) Regulations 2013
SI 1996/1880	Local Authorities (Contracting Out of Tax Billing, Collection and Enforcement Functions) Order 1996
SI 2013/502	Local Authorities (Contracting Out of Tax Billing, Collection and Enforcement Functions) (Amendment) (England) Order 2013
SI 2009/2269	Valuation Tribunal for England (Council Tax and Rating Appeals) (Procedure) Regulations 2009
SI 2013/465	The Valuation Tribunal for England (Council Tax and Rating Appeals) (Procedure) (Amendment) Regulations 2013

Recent amending secondary legislation England: council tax and CTR

SI 2022/439	The Council Tax (Discount Disregards and Exempt Dwellings) (Amendment) (England) Regulations 2022
SI 2022/449	The Social Security and Council Tax Reduction Schemes (Amendment) Regulations 2022
SI 2023/16	The Council Tax Reduction Schemes (Prescribed Requirements) (England) (Amendment) Regulations 2023

Main secondary legislation Scotland

SSI 2021/249	The Council Tax Reduction (Scotland) Regulations 2021
SSI 2012/319	The Council Tax Reduction (State Pension Credit) (Scotland) Regulations 2012
SSI 2013/87	Council Tax (Information-sharing in relation to Council Tax Reduction) (Scotland) Regulations 2013

Recent amending secondary legislation Scotland: council tax and CTR

SSI 2022/161	The Council Tax Reduction (Scotland) Amendment (No. 3) Regulations 2022
SSI 2022/271	The Council Tax Reduction and Council Tax (Discounts) (Miscellaneous Amendment) (No. 2) (Scotland) Regulations 2022
SSI 2022/272	The Council Tax (Exempt Dwellings) (Scotland) Amendment (No. 2) Order 2022
SSI 2022/364	The First-tier Tribunal for Scotland Local Taxation Chamber (Rules of Procedure) Regulations 2022
SSI 2023/38	The Council Tax Reduction and Council Tax (Discounts) (Scotland) (Miscellaneous Amendment) Regulations 2023
SSI 2023/45	The First-tier Tribunal for Scotland (Transfer of Functions of Valuation Appeals Committees) Regulations 2023
SSI 2023/46	The First-tier Tribunal for Scotland (Transfer of Functions of the Council Tax Reduction Review Panel) Regulations 2023

Main secondary legislation Wales

SI 2013/3029	The Council Tax Reduction Schemes and Prescribed Requirements (Wales) Regulations 2013
SI 2013/3035	The Council Tax Reduction Schemes (Default Scheme) (Wales) Regulations 2013
SI 1993/255	Council Tax (Demand Notices) (Wales) Regulations 1993
SI 2013/63	Council Tax (Demand Notices) (Wales) (Amendment) Regulations 2013
SI 1996/1880	Local Authorities (Contracting Out of Tax Billing, Collection and Enforcement Functions) Order 1996
SI 2013/695	Local Authorities (Contracting Out of Tax Billing, Collection and Enforcement Functions) (Amendment) (Wales) Order 2013
SI 2013/588	Council Tax Reduction Schemes (Detection of Fraud and Enforcement) (Wales) Regulations 2013
SI 2013/111	Council Tax Reduction Schemes (Transitional Provisions) (Wales) Regulations 2013
SI 2010/713	The Valuation Tribunal for Wales Regulations 2010
SI 2013/547	The Valuation Tribunal for Wales (Wales) (Amendment) Regulations 2013

Recent amending secondary legislation Wales: council tax and CTR

SI 2022/722	The Council Tax (Amendments Relating to Discount Disregards and Exempt Dwellings) (Wales) Regulations 2022
SI 2023/47	The Council Tax Reduction Schemes (Prescribed Requirements and Default Scheme) (Wales) (Amendment) Regulations 2023

UC/SMI: Northern Ireland

Main primary legislation (Acts and Orders)

Northern Ireland (Welfare Reform) Act 2015

The Welfare Reform (Northern Ireland) Order 2015 SI 2015 No 2006 (N.I. 1)

The Welfare Reform and Work (Northern Ireland) Order 2016 SI 2016 No 999 (N.I. 1)

Main secondary legislation (statutory rules)

NISR 2016/216   The Universal Credit Regulations (Northern Ireland) 2016

NISR 2016/220   The Universal Credit, Personal Independence Payment, Jobseeker's Allowance and Employment and Support Allowance (Claims and Payments) Regulations (Northern Ireland) 2016

NISR 2016/221   The Universal Credit, Personal Independence Payment, Jobseeker's Allowance and Employment and Support Allowance (Decisions and Appeals) Regulations (Northern Ireland) 2016

NISR 2016/222   The Universal Credit Housing Costs (Executive Determinations) Regulations (Northern Ireland) 2016

NISR 2016/226   The Universal Credit (Transitional Provisions) Regulations (Northern Ireland) 2016

NISR 2016/178   The Welfare Supplementary Payments Regulations (Northern Ireland) 2016

NISR 2016/56   The Social Security (Information-sharing in relation to Welfare Services etc) Regulations (Northern Ireland) 2016

NISR 2017/176   The Loans for Mortgage Interest Regulations (Northern Ireland) 2017

Recent amending regulations and orders

NISR 2022/172   The Income-Related Benefits (Local Welfare Provision Disregard) (Amendment) Regulations (Northern Ireland) 2022

NISR 2022/202   The Social Security (Amendment) Regulations (Northern Ireland) 2022

NISR 2022/211   The Housing Benefit and Universal Credit (Victims of Domestic Abuse and Victims of Modern Slavery) (Amendment) Regulations (Northern Ireland) 2022

NISR 2022/223   The Universal Credit (Administrative Earnings Threshold) (Amendment) Regulations (Northern Ireland) 2022

NISR 2022/230   The Social Security (Habitual Residence and Past Presence) (Amendment No. 2) Regulations (Northern Ireland) 2022

NISR 2023/3   The Universal Credit (Administrative Earnings Threshold) (Amendment) Regulations (Northern Ireland) 2023

NISR 2023/4   The Housing Benefit and Universal Credit Housing Costs (Executive Determinations) (Modification) Regulations (Northern Ireland) 2023

NISR 2023/31   The Loans for Mortgage Interest (Amendment) Regulations (Northern Ireland) 2023

NISR 2023/42   The Benefit Cap (Annual Limit) (Amendment) Regulations (Northern Ireland) 2023

NISR 2023/43   The Social Security Benefits Up-rating Order (Northern Ireland) 2023

Recent transitional regulations: universal credit

NISR 2022/194   The Universal Credit (Transitional Provisions) (Amendment) Regulations (Northern Ireland) 2022

NISR 2023/45   The Social Security Benefits Up-rating Regulations (Northern Ireland) 2023

Rate rebates: Northern Ireland

Main primary legislation (Acts and Acts of Northern Ireland Assembly)

The Social Security Contributions and Benefits (Northern Ireland) Act 1992

The Social Security Administration (Northern Ireland) Act 1992

The Rates (Northern Ireland) Order 1977 SI 1977/2157

The Rates (Amendment) (Northern Ireland) Order 2006 SI 2006/2954

The Welfare Reform (Northern Ireland) Order SI 2015/2006

The Welfare Reform and Work (Northern Ireland) Order 2016 SI 2016/999

Main secondary legislation (Statutory Rules and Orders)

NISR 2006/405   The Housing Benefit Regulations (Northern Ireland) 2006

NISR 2006/406   The Housing Benefit (Persons who have attained the qualifying age for state pension credit) Regulations (Northern Ireland) 2006

NISR 2007/203   The Rate Relief (Qualifying Age) Regulations (Northern Ireland) 2007

NISR 2007/204   The Rate Relief (General) Regulations (Northern Ireland) 2007

NISR 2008/124   The Rate Relief (Lone Pensioner Allowance) Regulations (Northern Ireland) 2008

NISR 2017/184   The Rate Relief Regulations (Northern Ireland) 2017

Main amending regulations: rate relief

The following is a list of amendments to the main rate relief regulations from 1st April 2007.

NISR 2007/244   The Rate Relief (Qualifying Age) (Amendment) Regulations (Northern Ireland) 2007

NISR 2022/92   The Rate Relief (Qualifying Age) (Amendment) Regulations (Northern Ireland) 2022

NISR 2011/43   The Rate Relief (Amendment) Regulations (Northern Ireland) 2011

NISR 2018/109   The Rate Relief (Amendment) Regulations (Northern Ireland) 2018

NISR 2023/39   The Rate Relief (Amendment) Regulations (Northern Ireland) 2023

Appendix 2 **Weekly CTR applicable amounts: 2023-24**

Personal allowances

Single person	pension age rate	£217.10
	working age rate	£84.80
	working age rate (Wales)	£90.40
	lower rate	£67.20
	lower rate (Wales)	£71.55
Couple	pension age rate	£324.70
	working age rate	£133.30
	working age rate (Wales)	£141.95
Polygamous spouse	pension age rate	£107.70
	working age/lower rate	£48.50
	working age/lower rate (Wales)	£51.55
Child or young person	each (in England up to two only)	£77.78
	each (Scotland)	£97.23

Additional amounts: any age

Family premium (transitional) element		£18.53
Disabled child premium	each child/young person	£74.69
Enhanced disability premium (child)	each child/young person	£30.17
Severe disability premium	single rate	£76.40
	double rate	£152.80
Carer premium	claimant/partner/each	£42.75

Additional amounts: working age only

Disability premium	single person	£39.85
	couple	£56.80
Enhanced disability premium (adult)	single person	£19.55
	couple	£27.90
Support component	single person/couple	£44.70
WRA component	single person/couple	£33.70

Appendix 3 **Selected weekly benefit rates from April 2023**

Attendance allowance

Higher rate	£101.75
Lower rate	£68.10

Bereavement benefits

Widowed parent's allowance (standard rate)	£139.10
Bereavement allowance (standard rate)	£139.10
Bereavement support payment (higher rate)	£80.77
Bereavement support payment (lower rate)	£23.08

Child benefit

Eldest/only child	£24.00
Each other child	£15.90

Carer's allowance

Claimant	£76.75

Disability living allowance

Care component

Highest rate	£101.75
Middle rate	£68.10
Lowest rate	£26.90

Mobility component

Higher rate	£71.00
Lower rate	£26.90

Employment and support allowance (new style)

Under 25	£67.20
25 or over	£84.80
Work-related component	£33.70
Support component	£44.70

Guardian's allowance £20.40

Housing benefit applicable amounts

Personal allowance for child/young person	£77.78

All other HB figures are the same as in main CTR (appendix 2), but using the Scotland personal allowances throughout the UK.

Industrial injuries disablement benefit

20% disabled	£41.52
For each further 10% disability up to 100%	£20.76
100% disabled	£207.60

Jobseeker's allowance (new style)

Single under 25	£67.20
Single over 25	£84.80

Maternity and paternity pay and allowance

Statutory maternity, paternity and adoption pay	£172.48
Maternity allowance	£172.48

Personal independence payment

Daily living component

Enhanced	£101.75
Standard	£68.10

Mobility component

Enhanced	£71.00
Standard	£26.90

Retirement pension

New state pension (full rate)	£203.85
Old state pension single (basic rate)	£156.20
Old state pension spouse or civil partner's insurance (basic pension)	£93.60

Severe disablement allowance

Basic rate	£92.20

Age-related addition

Higher rate	£13.80
Middle rate and lower rate	£7.65

Statutory sick pay

Standard rate	£109.40

Appendix 4: **Equivalent footnote references for Scotland and Wales**

Council tax and council tax rebates

This table shows the equivalent footnote references in chapters 15 to 17 for the law on council tax and council tax rebates in Scotland and Wales. 'Not Scotland' means there is no equivalent law in Scotland. For abbreviations see the key to footnotes at the front of this guide.

	Wales	**Scotland**
15.2	LGFA 1(1),(2)(b)	LGFA 70
15.3	LGFA 5(1A),(3)	LGFA 74(1),(2); SSI 2016/368
15.4	See text	LGFA 72
15.5-6	See text	LGFA 99(1) – definition – 'resident'
T15.1	LGFA 5(1A),(3),36(1)	LGFA 74(1),(2),93(1); SSI 2016/368
15.11	See text	LGFA 75(2)(a)-(e)
15.13	See text	LGFA 75(4), sch 1 paras 2, 4
15.14	See text	LGFA 75(1),(2)(a)-(e)
15.15	See text	LGFA 75(3),(4), 77
15.16	See text	LGFA 75(3),(4)
15.17	LGFA 8, The Council Tax (Liability for Owners) Regulations 1992, No 551	LGFA 76, The Council Tax (Liability of Owners) (Scotland) Regulations 1992, No 1331
15.18	Table 15.2 Class C as amended by SI 1993/151 and SI 1995/620	SI 1992/1331, sch para 3 as substituted by SSI 2003/137
T15.2(a)-(g)	LGFA 8(1),(3),(6); The Council Tax (Liability for Owners) Regulations 1992, No 551, reg 2, Classes A to F	LGFA 76(1)-(3), The Council Tax (Liability of Owners) (Scotland) Regulations 1992, No 1331, sch paras 1-7
T15.2(a)	Class C substituted by SI 1993/151, amended by SI 1995/620 reg 2	para 3 substituted by SSI 2003/137
T15.2(b),(c)	Class A substituted by SI 2004/2920	para 1
T15.2(d)	Class E amended by SI 1995/620 reg 3	para 5
T15.2(e)	Class B	para 2
T15.2(f)	Class D	para 4
T15.2(g)	Class F added by SI 2000/1024	para 7 added by SI 2000/715
T15.2(h)	LGFA 6(1),(2)(f)	LGFA 75(1),(2)(f)(iii)
15.20	Table 15.2 Class A; definition 'hostel', in DDO 6 as substituted by SI 2004/2921 art 4	LGFA sch 1 para 8, definition of 'hostel' repealed by Regulation of Care (Scotland) Act 2001, sch 3 para 18
15.21	LGFA 11(2), 12, 12A, 12B, The Council Tax (Exceptions to Higher Amounts) (Wales) Regulations 2015, No 2068; 2019/1458; 2023/253	Local Government in Scotland Act 2003, s33; The Council Tax (Variation for Unoccupied Dwellings) (Scotland) Regulations 2013, No 45, regs 2-4
T15.3	The Council Tax (Exempt Dwellings) Order 1992, SI 1992/558, reg 3, Classes A to X	The Council Tax (Exempt Dwellings) (Scotland) Order 1997, No 728, reg 3, sch 1 paras 1-25

T15.3(a)	Class N substituted by SI 1993/150, amended by SI 1995/619, SI 2004/2865; Class U substituted by SI 1999/536; Class S added by SI 1995/619; Class X added by SI 2019/432; amended by 2022/722	sch 1 paras 10, 18, 23; SI 1999/757; SSI 2018/45; SSI 2022/124
T15.3(b)	Class K substituted by SI 1993/150	sch 1 paras 11-12; SI 1998/561
T15.3(c)	Class M amended by SI 1993/150 and SI 1994/539	sch 1 para 16
T15.3(d)	Class I substituted by SI 2004/2921	sch 1 para 5
T15.3(e)	Class B, amended by SI 1994/539; SI 2003/673, regs 3, 4	sch 1 para 3
T15.3(f)	Class A substituted by SI 2000/1025; Class C substituted by SI 1993/150	sch 1 paras 2, 4; SSI 1999/140; SSI 2012/339
T15.3(g)	Class H	sch 1 para 9
T15.3(h)	Class Q added by SI 1993/150, amended by SI 1994/539	sch 1 para 21
T15.3(i)	Class L	sch 1 para 13
T15.3(j)	Class G	sch 1 para 7
T15.3(k)	Class O amended by SI 1992/2941	sch 1 para 17
T15.3(l)	Class P added by SI 1992/2941	sch 1 para 22
T15.3(m)	Class V added by SI1997/656, definition of dependent relative in class amended by SI 1998/291	Not Scotland
T15.3(n)	Class R added by SI 1994/539	Not Scotland
T15.3(o)	Class T added SI 1995/619	Not Scotland
T15.3(p)	Class W added by SI 1997/656, definition of dependent relative in class amended by SI 1998/291	Not Scotland
T 15.3 (notes)	—	sch 1 paras 15, 26-29; SSI 2022/124; SSI 2022/272; SSI 2023/36
15.22	LGFA 4, 11, 13, 13A	LGFA 72, 79, 80
15.23	LGFA 4(1)-(4)	LGFA 72(1),(6)
15.24	LGFA 13(1),(4),(6),(7); The Council Tax (Reductions for Disabilities) Regulations 1992 No 554, reg 4 as amended by SI 1999/1004	The Council Tax (Reductions for Disabilities) (Scotland) Regulations 1992 No 1335, reg 4 as amended by SI 1999/756
15.25	The Council Tax (Reductions for Disabilities) Regulations 1992 No 554, reg 3(1),(3)	The Council Tax (Reductions for Disabilities) (Scotland) Regulations 1992 No 1335, reg 3(1),(3)
15.26	LGFA 11(1)-(3),12	LGFA 79(3); The Council Tax (Variation for Unoccupied Dwellings) (Scotland) Regulations 2013, No 45, reg 2
T15.4(a)-(m)	LGFA 11(5), sch 1	LGFA 79(5), sch 1
T15.4(a)	LGFA sch 1 paras 4, 5, 11; DDO art 4, sch 1 paras 2-7; DDR reg 5, class C; SI 2019/431	LGFA sch 1 paras 4, 5, 11; SI 1992/1409, reg 3, sch para 3; SSI 2003/176 art 6, 7; SSI 2011/5; SSI 2014/37
T15.4(b)	LGFA sch 1 para 2, DDO art 3; SI 2013/638; SI 2013/1048	LGFA sch 1 para 2; SSI 2003/176 art 4; SSI 2008/1879 reg 39; SSI 2013/65; SSI 2013/137 reg 14; SSI 2013/142 reg 8; SSI 2022/31 reg 9
T15.4(c)	LGFA sch 1 para 3	LGFA sch 1 para 3
T15.4(d)	LGFA sch 1 para 11; DDR reg 5, class G; SI 2019/431	LGFA sch 1 para 11; SI 1992/1409 reg 3, sch para 6; SSI 2018/39
T15.4(e)	LGFA sch 1 para 4; SI 2003/673 art 3	LGFA sch 1 para 4; SSI 2003/176 art 8
T15.4(f)	LGFA sch 1 para 4; DDO art 4, sch 1 para 1; SI 2007/580	LGFA sch 1 para 4; SSI 2003/176 art 5; SSI 2007/214

	Wales	**Scotland**
T15.4(g)	LGFA sch 1 para 9; DDR reg 2, sch paras 3, 4; SI 2013/639; SI 2013/1049	LGFA sch 1 para 9; SI 1992/1409 reg 2(3); SSI 2013/65; SSI 2013/142 reg 2; SSI 2022/31 reg 2
T15.4(h)	LGFA sch 1 para 9; DDR reg 2, sch paras 1, 2; SI 2007/581	LGFA sch 1 para 9; SI 1992/1409 reg 2(2); SSI 2007/213 reg 2
T15.4(i)	LGFA sch 1 para 10	LGFA sch 1 para 10
T15.4(j)	LGFA sch 1 paras 6, 7; DDO 6(b); SI 2004/2921 art 4	LGFA sch 1 para 8, as amended by Regulation of Care (Scotland) Act 2001, sch 3 para 18
T15.4(k)	LGFA sch 1 para 1; DDO arts 2,5; SI 2009/2054, sch 1 para 13; SI 2004/2921 art 4	LGFA sch 1 para 1; SSI 2003/176 art 3; SI 2009/2054, sch 1 para 23
T15.4(l)	LGFA sch 1 para 11; DDR reg 5, Class B; SI 2019/431	LGFA sch 1 para 11; SI 1992/1409 reg 3, sch para 2
T15.4(m)	LGFA sch 1 para 11; DDR reg 5, Class E; SI 2019/431	LGFA sch 1 para 11; SI 1992/1409 reg 3, sch para 1
T15.4(n)	LGFA sch 1 para 11; DDR reg 5, Class A, D, F; SI 2019/431	LGFA sch 1 para 11; SI 1992/1409 reg 3, sch para 1
T15.4(o)	LGFA sch 1 para 11; DDR reg 5 Class H; SI 2023/722	LGFA sch 1 para 11; SI 1992/1409 reg 3, sch paras 7,8; SSI 2022/125 reg 2; SSI 2023/38 reg 29
15.27-30	LGFA 11(1)-(3)	LGFA 79(1)-(3)
15.31	See text	CT(A&E)S 10, 15
15.32	See text	LGFA 71
15.33	See text	LGFA 81, 82
15.34	See text	CT(A&E)S 7, 12
15.35	See text	See text
T16.1	LGFA 13A(1)(c),(2), sch 1B paras 3(1)-(3), 4; CTPW 21-25; CTRW 13-16	LGFA 80; CTS 13(1),(3)-(7), 14; CTS66+ 14(1),(3)-(6), 14A
16.2	LGFA sch 1B para 3(7)(a)-(c); CTPW 22(a), 23(a), 24(a), 25(a); CTRW 13(a), 14(a), 15(a), 16(a)	LGFA 80(1); CTS 13(3)(a), 14(3)(a); CTS66+ 14(3)(a), 14A(3)(a)
16.3	LGFA sch 1B para 3(7)(e); CTPW 9; CTRW 9	CTS 8; CTS66+ 3
16.4	CTPW 2(1); CTRW 2(1) – 'qualifying age for state pension credit'	CTS 4(1) definition – 'pensionable age'; CTS66+ 2(1)
T16.2	CTPW 3, 22(f), 23(g), 24(f), 25(g), sch 13 para 1; CTRW 3, 13(f), 14(g), 15(f), 16(g), 107(1)	CTS 3, 11, 13(3)(c), 14(3)(c); CTS66+ 7, 12, 14(3)(c), 14A(3)(c), 61
16.5	LGFA 13A(4),(5), sch 1B paras 1-4; CTPW 11, 12, 14, 15, 32, 33	LGFA 80; CTS 13, 14; CTS66+ 14, 14A
16.6	Not Wales	LGFA 80(1),(2); CTS 3, 13(1), 14(1), 57(1); CTS66+ 12, 14(1), 14A(1), sch 3 paras 1-2
16.7	LGFA 13(1)(b),(c),(4),(5), sch 1B paras 2(1), 3, 4; CTPW 14, 21-24, 32, 33, 34(4),(5)	Not Scotland
16.8	LGFA 13A(1)(b),(4),(5), sch 1B paras 3-5; CTPW 3-10, 12, 14-18, 27-29	Not Scotland
16.9-12	Not Wales	Not Scotland
16.13	LGFA sch 1B para 3(5),(7)(a),(b),(e); CTPW 12(1), 14(b), 15(2),(3)	Not Scotland
16.14	See text	Not Scotland
16.15	LGFA sch 1B paras 3-5; CTPW 3-10, 27-31, 34(1)-(3)	Not Scotland
16.16	LGFA sch 1B paras 2, 6; CTPW 13, 17, 18	Not Scotland
16.17	Not Wales	Not Scotland
16.18	Not Wales	Not Scotland
16.19	LGFA sch 1B para 4(4),(5)	Not Scotland
16.20	LGFA 13A(1)(c),(6),(7)	Not Scotland

16.21	LGFA 13A(1)(c),(6), sch 1B para 4(1),(2)	Not Scotland
16.22	LGFA 13A(1)(c),(6); CTPW sch 12 para 11(2)	Not Scotland
16.23	Not Wales	Not Scotland
16.24	LGFA sch 1B para 3(1)(b); CTPW 21-31, sch 11 para 3(1),(2); CTRW 13-22, 72(1),(2)	CTS 13(3)(b), 14(3)(b), 15-20, 66; CTS66+ 14(3)(b), 14A(3)(b), 15-19, 40
16.25	CTPW 22(b), 23(b), 24(b), 25(b), 26, 28(2),(6),(7); CTRW 13(b), 14(b), 15(b), 16(b), 17, 19(2),(6),(7)	CTS 15, 16(1), 17; CTS66+ 15, 16(1), 17
16.26	CTPW 26; CTRW 17	CTS 15; CTS66+ 15
16.27	Not Wales	Not Scotland
16.28	Not Wales	CTS 16(1), 17; CTS66+ 16(1), 17
16.29	CTPW 26(1),(3),(3)(c)-(e),(g); CTRW 17(1),(3),(3)(c)-(e),(g)	Not Scotland
16.30	CTPW 28, 29; CTRW 19, 20	CTS 16, 19; CTS66+ 16, 19
16.31	CTPW 31, sch 11 para 3(1),(2); CTRW 18, 22, 72(1),(2)	CTS 20(1)-(3)
16.33	CTPW 22(f), 23(g), 24(f), 25(g), sch 12 paras 2, 3, 11, sch 13 para 1; CTRW 13(f), 14(g), 15(f), 16(g), 107, sch 1 paras 2, 3, 11	CTS 11, 13(3)(c), 14(3)(c), 23-25, 30; CTS66+ 7, 14(3)(c), 14A(3)(c), 63, 64, 71
16.34	CTPW sch 13 para 2(7); CTRW 108(7)	CTS 26(5),(6); CTS66+ 65(2),(3)
16.35	CTPW sch 12 paras 2, 3, sch 13 para 1(1); CTRW 107(1), sch 1 paras 2, 3	CTS 11, 22-25, 30; CTS66+ 7, 61, 63, 64, 71
16.36	CTPW sch 13 para 1; CTRW 107	––
16.37	CTPW sch 13 para 5; CTRW 111	CTS 27; CTS66+ 66
16.39	CTPW sch 1 para 39, sch 6 para 45; CTRW 104(1)	CTS 33(1); CTS66+ 58(1)
16.40	CTPW sch 1 para 39, sch 6 para 45; CTRW 104(2)	CTS 33(2); CTS66+ 58(2)
16.41	CTPW sch 12 paras 2-7, sch 13 para 2; CTRW 108, sch 1 paras 2-7	CTS 26, 30; CTS66+ 65, 71
16.42	CTPW sch 13 paras 3, 4; CTRW 109, 110	CTS 26(7),(8); CTS66+ 62
16.44	CTPW sch 1 para 40(1), sch 6 para 46(1); CTRW 105(1)	CTS 34(1); CTS66+ 59(1)
16.45	CTPW sch 1 para 40(1),(3),(4), sch 6 para 46(1),(3),(4); CTRW 105(1),(3),(4)	CTS 34(1)-(4); CTS66+ 59(1)-(3)
16.46	LGFA 13A(1)(b); CTPW sch 13 para 10; CTRW 116; CT(A&E) 1(2) definition – 'discount', 20 as amended by SI 2013/62	CTS 21, sch 5; CTS66+ 19A, sch 7
17.2	CTPW 2(1) definition – 'reduction week'; CTRW 2(1)	CTS 4(1) definition – 'reduction week'; CTS66+ 2(1)
17.3	CTPW sch 1 paras 2(1), 11(1) sch 6 paras 4(1), 13(1),(2); CTRW 27(1), 37(1), 46(1), 47(1),(2)	CTS 41(1), 43(1),(2); CTS66+ 31(1), 47(1)
17.4	CTPW 22-25; CTRW 13, 14, 15, 16	CTS 13(1)(a); CTS66+ 14(1)(a)
17.5	CTPW 22-25; CTRW 13, 14, 15, 16	CTS 13(1)(a),(3),(5); CTS66+ 14(1)(a),(3),(5)
17.6	CTPW 22(c),(e), 23(c),(e),(f), 24(c),(e), 25(c),(e),(f), sch 1 paras 2, 4(2),(3), sch 6 paras 4, 6(2),(3); CTRW 13(c),(e), 14(c),(e),(f), 15(c),(e), 16(c),(e),(f), 27, 29(2),(3)	CTS 13(5),(6),(9)(a),(b), 79(1),(4); CTS66+ 14(4),(5),(8)(a),(b), 47(1),(2)
17.7	CTPW sch 1 para 2(1),(2), sch 6 para 4(1),(2); CTRW 27(1),(2)	CTS 79(1); CTS66+ 47(1)
17.8	CTPW 24(e), 25(e),(f), sch 6 paras 3, 6(2),(3), 9; CTRW 15(e), 16(e),(f), 26, 29(2),(3), 34	CTS 13(6), 35(b), 42(2), 49, sch 1 para 2; SSI 2022/52 reg 25(b)
17.9	CTPW sch 6 para 9(1)-(4); CTRW 34(1)-(4)	CTS 49(13)-(3),(6)

	Wales	**Scotland**
17.10	CTPW 22(e), 23(e),(f), 24(e), 25(e),(f), sch 1 paras 4(2),(3), 5(1), 7, 9, sch 6 paras 6(2),(3), 7(1), sch 8 para 14, sch 9 paras 8, 9; CTRW 13(e), 14(e),(f), 15(e), 16(e),(f), 29(2),(3), 30(1), 32, 35, sch 6 para 14, sch 7 paras 8, 9	CTS 13(5),(6),(9)(a),(b), 79(1) CTS66+ 14(5),(8)(a),(b), 47(1)
17.11	CTPW sch 1 para 5(1), sch 6 para 7(1); CTRW 30(1)	CTS 38(2),(50), CTS66+ 21(1),(2)
17.12	CTPW sch 1 para 1, sch 2, sch 6 para 1, sch 7; CTRW 23, 24, sch 2, sch 3	CTS 35, sch 1; CTS66+ 20, sch 1
17.13	CTPW 9, sch 1 paras 2(1), 3 sch 6 paras 4(1), 5; CTRW 9, 27(1), 28	CTS 8,79(1), 90; CTS66+ 3, 47(1), 48
17.14	Not Wales	CTS66+ 59(10)-(13)
17.15	CTPW sch 1 para 3(9) sch 6 para 5(9); CTRW 28(9)	CTS 90(9); CTS66+ 48(9)
T17.1	CTPW sch 1 para 3(1),(2) sch 6 para 5(1),(2); CTRW 28(1),(2)	CTS 90(1),(2); CTS66+ 48(1),(2)
T17.2	CTPW 9, sch 1 para 3(6)-(8) sch 6 para 5(6)-(8); CTRW 3, 28(6)-(8)	CTS 8, 90(6)-(8); CTS66+ 3, 48(6)-(8)
17.16	CTPW sch 1 para 2(1),(3)-(5), sch 6 para 4(1),(3)-(5); CTRW 27(1),(3)-(5)	CTS 90(1),(2); CTS66+ 47(1),(2)
17.17	Not Wales	See text
17.18	Not Wales	CTS 13(1)(b),(3),(7); CTS66+ 14(1)(b),(3),(6)
17.19	Not Wales	CTS 13(1)(b),(3),(7),(9)(c); CTS66+ 14(1)(b),(3),(6),(8)(c), sch 4 para 27
17.20	Not Wales	CTS 13(1)(b),(3),(7),(8), 91(2),(3); CTS66+ 14(1)(b),(3),(6),(7), 56(2),(3)
17.21	Not Wales	CTS 13(1)(b),(7),(8), 91(2),(3), sch 2 para 1(1); CTS66+ 14(1)(b),(3),(6),(7), 56(2),(3), sch 5 para 1(1)
17.22	Not Wales	CTS 13(9)(c), 91(2),(3), sch 2 paras 1, 3; CTS66+ 14(8)(c), 56(2),(3), sch 5 paras 1, 3
17.23	Not Wales	CTS sch 2 paras 1, 3; CTS66+ sch 5 paras 1, 3
17.24	Not Wales	CTS sch 2 para 1(2); CTS66+ sch 5 para 1(2)
17.25	Not Wales	CTS 91(2),(3); CTS66+ 56(2),(3)
17.27	CTPW sch 1 para 5, sch 6 para 7; CTRW 30	CTS 36; CTS66+ 21
17.28	—	See text
17.29	Not Wales	See text
17.30	CTPW sch 1 para 5(1), sch 6 para 7(1); CTRW 30(1)	CTS 36(1), 38(2), 42(2); CTS66+ 21(1), 26
17.31	CTPW sch 1 para 25(1),(2), sch 5, sch 6 para 26(1),(2), sch 10; CTRW 60(1),(2), sch 8, sch 9	CTS 67(1),(2), 69(1), sch 4; CTS66+ 41(1),(2), sch 4
17.32	CTPW 22(d), 23(d), 24(d), 25(d), 27, 30; CTRW 13(d), 14(d), 15(d), 16(d), 18, 21, sch 8 para 27	CTS 66; CTS66+ 40
17.33	CTPW sch 1 para 31, sch 6 para 33; CTRW 68, 69	CTS 63(1); CTS66+ 27(2)
17.34	CTPW sch 1 paras 8(2)(a), 10(1)(b)-(d),(j), 11(11),(13), sch 6 paras 12(1), 17(1),(2), sch 9 para 4; CTRW 33(2)(a), 36(1)(b)-(d),(j), 37(11),(13), 46(1), 51(1),(2), sch 7 para 4	CTS 38(2); 41(1), 42(2), 57(1)(a),(b),(p)-(r) CTS66+ 25(2)(a), 27(1)(b)-(d),(j), 31(10),(12)
17.35	CTPW sch 1 para 40(1), sch 6 para 46(1); CTRW 105(1)	CTS 34(1); CTS66+ 59(1)
17.36	CTPW sch 6 paras 34-37; CTRW 93-96	CTS 80-88

T17.3(a)-(c)	CTPW sch 1 para 18(1)(c),(3), sch 3 paras 1-5, 8, 10, sch 6 para 20(1)(c),(3), sch 8 paras 4, 5, 11, 18; CTRW 54(1)(c),(3), sch 4 paras 1-5, 8, 10, sch 6 paras 4, 5, 11, 18	CTS 38(2)(c),(4), 49(6)(d), 50(3)(i), sch 4 paras 8, 11, 15; CTS66+ 28(1)(c),(3), sch 2 paras 1-5, 8, 10
T17.3(d)-(h)	CTPW sch 1 paras 7, 10(1)(j)(i)-(vii), sch 9 paras 8, 9, 11, 14, 21, 52, 66; CTRW 32, 36(1)(j)(i)-(vii), sch 7 paras 8, 9, 11, 14, 21, 52, 66	CTS 4(1) – 'qualifying income-related benefit claimant', 57(1)(b),(r) CTS66+ 24, 27(1)(j)(i)-(viii)
T17.3(i)	CTPW sch 1 para 10(1)(j)(ix),(xi), sch 8 paras 30-34, 37, 42, 64, 65; CTRW 36(1)(j)(ix),(xi), sch 7 paras 30-34, 37, 42, 64, 65	CTS 57(1); CTS66+ 27(1)(j)(xi),(xiii)
T17.3(j)	CTPW sch 1 para 10(1)(e),(f),(l),(m), sch 4 paras 1-5, 13, sch 9 para 20, 53-56; CTRW 36(1)(e),(f),(l),(m), sch 5 paras 1-5, 13, sch 7 para 20, 53-56	CTS 57(1); CTS66+ 27(1)(e),(f),(l),(m), sch 3 paras 1-4, 12
T17.3(k)	CTPW sch 1 para 10(1)(j)(xiii), sch 4 paras 7,8, sch 9 paras 21, 67 CTRW 36(1)(j)(xiii), sch 5 paras 7,8, sch 7 paras 21, 67	CTS 57(1)(b)(v),(vi),(4) CTS66+ 27(1)(j)(xva), sch 3 paras 6,7
T17.3(l)	CTPW sch 1 para 10(1)(o), sch 4 para 20, sch 9 paras 49, 50; CTRW 36(1)(o), sch 5 para 20, sch 7 paras 49, 50	CTS 57(1)(d); CTS66+ 27(1)(o), sch 3 para 19
T17.3(m)	CTPW sch 1 para 10(1)(p),(v), sch 4 paras 9, 10, sch 9 paras 26, 27; CTRW 36(1)(p),(v), sch 5 paras 9, 10, sch 7 paras 26, 27	CTS 57(1); CTS66+ 27(1)(p),(v), sch 3 paras 8, 9
T17.3(n)	CTPW sch 1 paras 10(1)(s), 12(2)(f), sch 4 paras 12, 14, 15, sch 6 paras 14(2)(d), sch 9 paras 5, 6, 19; CTRW 36(1)(s), 38(2)(f), 49(2)(d), sch 5 paras 12, 14, 15, sch 7 paras 5, 6, 19	CTS 57(1)(j),(k),74; CTS66+ 27(1)(s), 32(2)(f), sch 3 paras 11, 13, 14
T17.3(o)	CTPW sch 1 para 10(1), sch 9 para 41; CTRW 36(1), sch 7 para 41	CTS 57(1)(k), 75 CTS66+ 27(1)
T17.3(p)	—	CTS 57(1), sch 4 para 43 CTS66+ 27(1), sch 4 para 30J

Index

References in the index are to paragraph numbers (not page numbers), except that 'A' refers to appendices, 'T' refers to tables in the text and 'Ch' refers to a chapter.

A

Adoption 9.23
Advance payments of UC, 12.22-25
Alternative payment arrangements 12.16-17, T12.1
Amount of UC/CTR *see* Calculating UC/CTR
Appeals CTR
    Appealable decisions 18.17-21
    Correcting decisions 18.30
    Decision notice 18.1, 18.5-6, 18.26
    Further appeals 18.31
    Hearings/Procedure 18.23-25
    How to appeal 18.8, 18.13-14
    Overpayments 16.48, 18.21
    Reconsiderations 18.8
    Setting aside 18.28-29
    Statement of reasons 18.7, 18.27
    Time limits 18.4-6, 18.12, T18.1
    Tribunals 18.11
Appeals UC
    Accidental error 14.33, 14.66
    Appeal to first tier tribunal 14.39
    Appeal to Upper Tribunal 14.68-69
    Decision of FTT 14.61-65
    Decision statement of reasons 14.8, 14.64
    Decisions that cannot be appealed 14.40, T14.3
    Disputes about FTT decision 14.66-70
    DWP decision 14.4-9
    Error of law, 14.71
    Generally, and complaints 14.1-3, 14.72-73
    Late application 14.28-30
    Mandatory reconsideration 14.17, 14.25
    Official error 14.30-32
    Reconsideration 14.9-16
    Reconsideration, effective date, 14.17-24
    Setting aside 14.66-67
    Time limits 14.3, 14.26-29, 14.30, 14.47-49, 14.66, 14.69, 14.70
    Who can appeal 14.2
Applicable amount, *see* Calculating CTR
Assessment period 3.38-45, 10.13-14, 10.17, 10.23-27, 10.31, 10.41, 10.49

B

Bedroom (additional) 7.19-28
Bedroom (definition) 7.6-7
Bedroom (number) 7.5
Bedroom tax, *see* Size cirteria
Benefit cap UC 9.51-63, T9.4, T9.5
Benefit rates (other DWP benefits), A3
Benefit unit UC
    Children 3.62-69
    Couples 3.49-51
    Household members 3.52-53
    Living together 3.54-59
    Polygamous marriages 3.60-61
    Single people 3.47-48
Benefit income, *see* Social security
Bereavement run-on UC 11.27-28
Budgeting advance UC, 12.26-29
Burden of proof 14.13

C

Calculating CTR
    Applicable amount 17.12, A2
    Conversion to weekly figures 17.3
    Excess income and taper 17.6, 17.8-10
    Maximum CTR 17.6-7
    Non-dependant deductions 17.13-15, T17.1, T17.2
    Passport benefit (SPC, IS etc) 17.8, T17.2, 17.22, T17.3
    Personal allowances 17.12, A2
    Premiums and components, 17.12, A2
    Polygamous marriages A2
    Savings credit 17.30
    Second adult rebate 17.18-25
    Scotland (Bands E-H) 17.17
    Universal credit 17.8-9, T17.2(h)
Calculating UC
    Amount of UC 9.1-11, T9.1
    Benefit cap 9.51-63, T9.4, T9.5
    Capital limit 9.6
    Carer element T9.2, 9.39-41, T9.3
    Childcare costs element T9.2, 9.42-50
    Child element (and two child limit) 9.15, T9.2, 9.17-28
    Disabled child element 9.16, T9.2

Hardship payments 2.49-54
Housing cost contributions 6.59-65, T6.6
Housing costs element 6.9-10, 6.36-37
Income (taper etc) 9.7-8
Maximum UC 9.4, 9.7
Minimum UC 9.9
Non-dependants 6.59-65, T6.6
Rounding 9.10
UC allowances T9.2, 9.14-28
Work allowance 10.11-12, T10.1
Work capability elements 9.29-38, 9.41
Capital CTR *see* Income and capital CTR
Capital UC 10.4-6, 10.71-90, T10.6
Capital limit 9.6, 10.73, 16.24, 17.32
Carer 9.39-41, T9.3, T15.4(g),(h), A2
Changes CTR 16.44-45

Changes UC
Advantageous changes 11.13-14, T11.1
Appeal about 11.8, 11.41
Assessment period T11.1
Benefits (*see* Social security)
Bereavement run on 11.27-28
Capability for work 11.24-25
Changes of circumstance 11.1-15, T11.1
Duty to report 11.2-4
Earnings 11.19-20
Effective date 11.11-12, T11.1
Ending UC T11.1, 11.36-37
General rule 11.12
Information and evidence 11.8
Moving home T11.1
Notification 11.10
Other DWP benefits 11.21-23
Rent increase/decrease 11.16-17
Rent officer/DFC redeterminations 6.53-55
Social security benefits 11.21-23
State pension credit age, reaching 11.26
Supersessions T14.1
Suspending and restoring UC 11.31-35, 11.38-40
Time limits for reporting 11.13-15
Childcare costs 9.42-50
Child element and two child limit 9.15, 9.17-28

Claimant commitment UC
Generally 2.36-37
Work related requirements 2.38-39, 2.40-46, T2.4, T2.5

Claims UC
Advance 3.30
Amending 3.18
Appointee 3.8-11
Assessment period 3.38-45, T3.2
Award length 3.27, 3.45
Backdating 3.34-37, T3.1
Couples 3.3-7, 3.11

Date of claim 3.28-29
Defective 3.15-16
How to claim 3.12-18
Information and evidence 3.21-22
Making a claim 3.1-11
National Insurance numbers 3.25
Online 3.13
Reclaims within six months 3.43-45
Start of entitlement 3.27-29
Telephone 3.14
Unable to act 3.8-11
Withdrawing 3.18
Components *see* Calculating CTR

Council tax (liability, discounts etc)
Bands, 15.3, T15.1
Calculating liability 15.3
Care leaver aged under 26 15.12, T15.3(a), T15.4(d)
Disability reductions 15.24-25
Discounts 15.8, 15.26-30, T15.4
Disregarded persons T15.4
Exemptions 15.12-16, 15.23, T15.3
Hostel, T 15.2, 15.20
House in multiple occupation, T15.2, 15.18-19
Joint liability 15.16
Liability, 15.10-17, T15.2
Owner liable, T15.2
Severe mental impairment 15.12-16, T15.3(a),(p), T15.4(b)
Students 15.12-16, T15.3(a), T15.4(a)
Unoccupied dwellings 15.17, T15.2(h), 15.21
Valuation bands 15.3, T15.1

Council tax rebate
Absence from Great Britain 16.27-28
Absence from home 16.25-26
Amount of CTR *see* Calculating CTR
Couples 16.35
Discretionary CTR, T16.1, 16.20-23, 18.20
Eligibility, basic conditions 16.13-14, 16.24-31, 17.4-5, 17.19-20
England, CTR schemes T16.1, 16.11-19
Great Britain, variations T16.1, 16.5-11
Habitual residence 16.30, 20.38-52
Household members and occupiers 17.5
Income and capital limits 16.24, 17.5, 17.8-10, 17.26-34, T17.3
Joint occupiers 17.16, 17.25
Local schemes, T16.1, 16.7, 16.9, 16.11, 16.13-19
Lodgers 17.19, T17.3(l)
Migrants and recent arrivals 16.24, 16.30, 17.5, 17.19, Ch 20
Non-dependants 15.9, 16.3, 17.6, 17.13-16, T17.1, T17.2
Overpayments 16.46-48

Pension age/Working age 16.4, T16.2, 16.9-11
Prisoner 16.26
Scotland CTR scheme T16.1, 16.6, 17.4, 17.17
Second adult rebate T16.1, 17.18-25
Students 16.24, 16.31, T17.2, 17.22
Wales, CTR schemes T16.1, 16.7-8
Couples 16.2, 16.35, 17.20, 17.27

CTR claims
Backdating 16.42-43
Complete applications 16.37
Couples 16.2
Date of claim 16.41
End of award 16.45
How to apply 16.35
Information and evidence 16.37
National insurance numbers 16.37
On passport benefit 17.8
Payment 16.46
Start of award 16.39-40
Time limit for 16.42-43
Who can apply 16.2, 16.33

D

Death 3.45, 11.27-28, 11.29, 12.11, 16.44
Decisions (generally) 14.2, 14.4-5, 14.10-13
Disability adaptations 5.57-58, 8.21, T8.2, 8.42, 15.25
Disability reductions 15.24-25
Disabled child 7.25, 7.27-28, 9.16, T9.2, A2
Discounts (council tax) 15.8, 15.26-30, T15.4
Discretion 14.16
Domestic violence T5.3, 5.11, 5.50, 5.53-55, 5.60, 6.16, 9.26, 20.36-37, 20.39, 21.66

E

Earnings, *see* Income
Earnings disregards (work allowance) 10.11-12, T10.1, T17.3
Earnings thresholds 2.39-42
EEA national *see* Migrants

Eligible rent
Actual rent 6.37
Bedroom tax *see* Under-occupation
Cap rent – private renter 6.41
Core rent – private renter 6.41
Eligible rent T6.2, 6.9-14, T6.3, 6.36-41
Joint tenants 6.11-13, 6.38-40, 7.18
Local housing allowance 6.42-47, T6.4, T6.5
Private renter 6.34-54, T6.4, T6.5
Service charges 6.23-33, T6.3
Social renter 6.7-33, T6.1, T6.2, T6.3
Supported housing T5.2, T5.3, 5.10-13
Temporary accommodation T5.2, T5.3, 5.10-13

Under-occupation 6.15-18, Ch 7
Unreasonably high 6.19-22
Existing benefits *see* Legacy benefits
EU pre-settled status 20.9, 21.18, 21.35
European national *see* Migrants
EU settled status 20.9, 21.16-17

F

Fear of violence 5.53-55
First tier tribunal (UC)
Decision and notice 14.61-62
Directions by 14.56
Disputed decision of 14.66-70
Generally (membership, functions) 14.55-58
Hearing (conduct etc) 14.55-58
Postponement 14.59
Record of proceedings 14.65
Setting aside 14.67
Statement of reasons 14.64
Foster care 9.24
Fraud and penalties 13.52-58, 16.46
Fuel T6.3, 12.55, T12.4

G

Genuine prospects of work (GPoW) test 21.51, 21.52
Guidance 1.24-25, 1.26-27, 1.29

H

Habitual residence 2.31, 16.30, 20.2, 20.6, 20.11, 20.38-52, 21.32-33, *see also* Migrants
Hardship payments 2.49-54
HB run-on (transitional payment) 4.5-7
Homeless, *see* Temporary accommodation
Home loan, *see* Owner occupier
Housing costs element UC
Basic conditions 5.4
Calculating 6.9-10, 6.36-37, 6.56-58
Excluded liabilities 5.31-42, T5.6, T5.7
Excluded payments T5.2, T6.3, 6.29-30, 6.32-33
Housing cost contributions 6.59-65, T6.6
Housing costs UC can meet, 5.2, T5.2, 6.7-8, T6.2, 6.28-33, T6.3
Liability for rent etc. 5.14-30, T5.5
Moving and two homes 5.56-63
Night shelters (short-term) 5.46
Normal home 5.45
Occupying your home 5.43
Payments it can meet 5.2, T5.1, T5.2
Rent payments 5.2, 5.16-21, T5.5, T6.2
Service charge payments T5.1, T5.2, 6.23-33, T6.3
Temporary absence 5.47-55
Young people (16-21s) 2.10-13, T2.2

I

Immigration control, *see* Migrants

Income and capital CTR
Additional earnings disregard T17.3
Assessment period (earned income) 17.34
Childcare disregard T17.3
Deductions from earnings (tax etc) T17.3
Earned income T17.3
Lodgers T17.3
Maintenance T17.3
Non-passport generally 17.34
Passport benefit (IS etc) and CTR 17.8, T17.3
Savings credit 17.30
Social security benefits disregarded T17.3
Tariff income from capital 17.33
Tax credits (CTC and WTC) 17.34, T17.3
Universal credit 17.28
Valuing items of capital/property 17.31
War pensions T17.3(j)

Income and capital UC
Annuity 10.65, 10.81-82
Assessment periods (earned income) 10.17, 10.23-27, 10.31, 10.41
Assumed income from capital (tariff) 10.74
Business assets T10.6
Business expenses (self-employed) 10.35-39, T10.3
Business start up 10.46-47
Capital disregarded (your home etc) T10.6
Capital limit 10.73
Distinguishing income from capital 10.4
Earned income 10.7-15
Earnings disregard 10.11-12, T10.1
Earnings review period (six months) 10.13-14
Employed earnings 10.16-10.29
Expenses (business) 10.35-39, T10.3
Expenses (service user group member) 10.53
Foreign currency 10.79
Generally 10.1-6
Independent living fund 10.85
Insurance 10.64
Life insurance, pensions etc T10.6
Local authority benefits 10.53, T10.6
Macfarlane trust etc 10.85
Maintenance T10.4, 10.55
Minimum income floor T2.4, T2.5, 2.42, 10.42-47
Notional capital 10.91-97
Notional income (inc notional earnings) 10.29, 10.42-45, 10.70
Personal injury payments 10.65, 10.83-84
Rent (lodgers etc) 10.68, 10.89-90
Retirement pension income 10.51
Self-employed earnings 10.30-41, T10.3, 10.42-47
Social security benefits T10.4, 10.52-53
Student and trainee income 10.56-63, T10.5
Surplus earnings 10.15, T10.2
Tax/national insurance deductions 10.18, 10.20, 10.32, 10.34
Trusts 10.65, 10.81-85
Unearned income 10.48-69, T10.4, T10.5
Work allowance (earnings disregard) 10.11-12, T10.1
Islamic mortgages, *see* Owner occupier

J

Judgment, 14.15

L

Law 1.24-29, T1.3, A1
LCW/LCWRA *see* Limited capability for work
Leaving care/hospital 5.59
Legacy benefits 1.12, 4.3, 4.5-8, 4.15-16, 4.19-21, 4.22, 4.27, 4.35, 4.40, T4.2
Limited capability for work, T2.5(c), 2.43-45, T2.7, 9.29-38, 9.41
Loan payments for mortgage interest etc
see Owner occupiers
Local CTR schemes, 16.7, 16.9, 16.11, 16.13-19

M

Managed migration 4.2, T4.1, 4.24-35
Maximum UC 9.4, 9.7-8

Migrants and recent arrivals
Afghans 20.25, 20.39
Asylum seekers 20.30-32
Brexit 20.9, 21.6-12
Child of migrant worker in education 21.72-74
Couples 20.15-16, 20.18
ECSMA/ESC nationals T20.1, 20.28-29
EEA national 20.8, 21.2-3, T21.1
EU settlement scheme 21.13-29
Excluded from UC/HB/CTR 2.20-21, 16.24, 16.30, 20.2-3, 21.34
Comprehensive sickness insurance 21.87
'Chen' rights 21.76-79
Domestic violence 20.36-37, 21.66
Family member (EEA) 21.2, T21.2, 21.62-70, 21.72, 21.76
Family members of British citizens 21.24-29
Frontier worker 21.40
Habitual residence 20.38-52
'Ibrahim' / 'Teixeira rights' 21.72-75
Incapacity for work 21.45, 21.60
Immigration terminology 20.20, T20.2
Immigration control 20.21-37
Jobseeker (EEA national) 21.51

National insurance number 20.17-18
No public funds 20.21, 20.23, 20.28-29
Refugees, humanitarian protection etc. 20.33-34
Retained worker (unemployed) 21.45-50
Retired worker/self-employed 21.59-61
Right to reside 20.38, 20.41-42, 21.36-70, 21.72, 21.76, 21.82-86
Self-employed 21.33, 21.37-38, 21.45-50
Self-sufficient/student 21.82-86
Stateless person 20.35
Ukrainians 20.25, 20.39
Worker (including retained worker) 21.33, 21.39-50

Migration to UC
Advance payment (benefit transfer), 12.22, 12.24
Better off 4.11-12
Couples T4.1, 4.22-23, 4.35
Deadline day 4.28-33
End of legacy benefits 4.3, 4.19-21
Final deadline 4.29-30, 4.33-34
Generally 4.2
HB run-on (transitional HB) 4.5-7
Indicative UC 4.39-40, T4.3
JSA(IB)/ESA(IR)/IS run on 4.8
Managed migration 4.2, T4.1, 4.10, 4.24-35
Migration day 4.32
Migration notice 4.3, 4.27
Natural migration 4.2, 4.18-23, 4.43
Managed migration pilot 4.25
Severe disability T4.1, 4.9, 4.43-49
Students 4.10
Time limit 4.32-34
Transitional capital disregard 4.53-56
Transitional element 4.3, T4.1, 4.39-55, T4.1, T4.2, T4.3
Transitional SDP T4.1, 4.9, 4.43-49,
Transitional protection T4.1, 4.9-10, 4.36, 4.38, 4.43
Voluntary migration 4.13-17
Minimum earnings 2.39-42
Minimum income floor T2.4, T2.5, 2.42, 10.42-47
Minimum UC 9.9
Minimum wage 2.40, T2.6, 2.41, 10.45
Mortgage interest, *see* Owner occupiers
Moving home and two homes 5.56-63, 13.9, 13.29-30, 16.44
Multiple births (twins etc) 9.25

N

National minimum wage, *see* Minimum wage#
Natural migration, 4.2, T4.1, 4.18-23
Non-consensual conception 9.26-27

Non-dependants
Contributions in UC 6.59-65, T6.6
Council tax rebate 17.6, 17.13-15, T17.1, T17.2

No deduction 6.64-65, T6.6, 15.9, T17.2
Rate rebate/relief 19.20, 19.42, 19.47-48, T19.2, T19.3
Who is a 3.70-77, T3.3, 17.13

O

Occupying the home
Generally 5.4, 5.43-46
Moving home 5.56-59
Prisoner 2.22-26
Temporary absence 5.47-55
Two homes 5.60-63

Overpayments
Generally 13.1-9
Calculating 13.15-21
Court action 13.49
CTR 16.46
Deductions from earnings 13.44-46
Deductions from other benefits T13.2, 13.43
Deductions from UC 13.37-42
Fraud and penalties 13.52-58, 16.46
Maximum rate of recovery T13.41-42, T13.1
Method of recovery 13.36-51
Rate rebates 19.32, 19.54
Recoverability 13.10-21
Recovery from landlord 13.19, 13.31, T13.1, 13.48
Time limits 13.50
Who they can be recovered from 13.22-35

Owner occupiers
Amount of loan 8.18, 8.20, 8.40-42
Amount of SMI 8.18-26, 8.43
Calculation of SMI 8.18-19
Charge on home 8.29, 8.36-37
Disability adaptations 8.21-22, T8.2, 8.42
Eligible payments UC 6.2-4, 6.5, 6.23-33, T6.3
Entitled to SMI 8.3, 8.40
How to apply for SMI 8.27-28
Income 8.5, 8.18, 8.19, 8.43
Islamic mortgages 8.10, T8.1
Legacy benefits/SPC and SMI 8.39-44
Mortgage interest 8.9, 8.40
New loans while on SMI 8.23, 8.41-42
Payment of SMI 8.31-32
Pension credit 8.39-44
Rate of interest (SMI payments) 8.18, 8.25-26
Rate of interest (SMI repayments) 8.35
Repairs and improvements, 8.40, T8.2
Repayment of SMI 8.35-37
Service charges 5.2, 5.5-8, 6.23-33, T6.3
Shared owners 8.11-13
Waiting period for HCE/SMI, 6.5, 8.3, 8.14-17, 8.44

P

Payments on account 12.22-25
Payment of SMI 8.31-32

Payment UC/CTR
Advance payments (*see* Payments on account)
Alternative payment arrangements 12.16-17
Appointee 12.5
Budgeting support UC 12.15
Council tax arrears 12.55
Couples 12.3-4, 12.16
CTR 16.46
Date of payment UC 12.10
Method 12.1
Northern Ireland 12.45-47
Payment to landlord/agent 12.30-36
Payments on account 12.22-25, T12.1
Rent arrears 12.30-44, 12.48-54
Scotland 12.45-47
Third party debts (fuel, water etc) 12.55-59, T12.4
Premiums *see* Calculating CTR
Presence in UK 2.29-35
Prisoner T2.1, 2.7, 2.22-26, T2.5(q), 16.26

Private renter
Landlord is relative T5.5, T5.6, 5.36-40
Liability for rent 5.14-30, T5.5, T5.6
Local housing allowance 6.42-47, T6.4, T6.5
Rent payments eligible/not eligible 5.4, T5.2, 5.31, T5.6, 6.2, 6.34-41
Service charges T5.1, 5.5-8, T5.2, 6.37
Size of accommodation 6.44-47, T6.4, T6.5, Ch 7
Supported accommodation 5.10-13, T5.3
Treated as liable 5.23-30
Treated as not liable 5.31-42, T5.6, T5.7

R

Rape, *see* Non-consensual conception

Rates and rate rebates/rate relief (Northern Ireland)
Appeals rates (liability etc) 19.10
Appeals rate rebates 19.33-35, 19.56-57
Basic conditions rate rebate 19.17, 19.19, 19.38, 19.41, 19.44
Calculation of rates 19.5
Calculation of rate rebate 19.15, 19.20-21, 19.39, 19.42-43, 19.45
Changes rate rebates 19.31, T19.1
Claims for rate rebate 19.24-26, 19.50
Disability reductions 19.9
Eligible rates 19.15-16, 19.20, 19.39
HB rate rebates (and rate relief) 19.36-43
Joint occupiers 19.15
Liability for rates 19.3

Lone pensioner allowance 19.44-45
Non-dependants and rate rebates 19.20, 19.42, 19.47-48, T19.2, T19.3
Overpayments of rate rebate 19.32-33, 19.54
Reconsiderations (revisions) *see* Appeals UC
Reconsiderations (supersessions) *see* Changes UC

Rent and other housing costs
Rent discounts/incentives 6.14
Eligible rent private renter 6.34-54
Eligible rent social renter 5.2, T5.1, 5.5, T5.2, T5.5, T5.6, T5.7, 6.7-33, T6.3
Excluded (social rent) 6.29-33
Liability for rent 5.4, 5.14-21, T5.5, T5.6
Local housing allowance 6.42-47, T6.4, T6.5
Owner occupiers 5.3, 5.6, 5.8, 6.2-4, 6.23-33, T6.3, Ch 8
Service charges 5.2, T5.1, 5.5-8, T5.2, 6.3, 6.6, 6.23-33, T6.3
Treated as liable for HC 5.23-30
Treated as not liable for HC 5.14, 5.31-42, T5.6, T5.7
Payments UC can meet 5.2, T.5.1, 5.5-8, T5.2, T6.3
Unreasonably high rents 6.19-22, T6.3, 6.33
Rent arrears 12.30-47, 12.48-54
Right to Reside *see* Migrants

S

Sanctuary scheme 6.16
Second adult rebate T16.1, 16.6, 16.9, 17.18-26
Secured loan *see* Owner occupier
Service charges 5.2, T5.1, 5.5-8, T5.2, 6.19, 6.23-33, T6.3, 6.37
Severe disability premium 4.43-49, A2
Shared owner T5.1, 5.6-7, 6.2-4

Size criteria
Additional bedrooms 7.19-28
Bedroom (definition) 7.6-7, T7.2
Claimant aged under 35 6.46, T6.4
Disabled who can't share 7.25-28
Fostering/kinship 7.21
Generally 6.17, 6.44, 7.2-4, T7.1
Homeless hostels 6.47
How many bedrooms 6.17, 6.44-46, T6.4, 7.5, T7.1
Joint tenants 6.11-13, 6.38-40, 7.18
Private renters 6.44-46, T6.4, 7.3, 7.5, T7.1
Occupiers counted 7.8-18
Overnight carers 7.22-24
Social renters – reduction 6.18
SMI *see* Owner occupier

Social renter
Eligible rent T6.2, 6.9-14
General rules HC in UC 6.3
Joint tenants 6.11-13
Rent discounts 6.14

Service charges 6.23-33, T6.3
Size criteria reductions 6.15-20, Ch 7
Supported housing 5.10-13, T5.3, T5.4
Temporary accommodation T5.2, 5.10-13, T5.3
Unreasonably high rents 6.19-22, 6.33
Who is a social renter 6.3, T6.1
Social security benefits T10.4, 10.52-53, 11.21-23
Scotland, CTR 16.6, 16.33, 16.42, 16.48, 17.12, T17.1, 17.17, 17.23,
17.36, T17.3, A3, A4

Students
Council tax liability and discounts 15.12-16,
    T15.3(a), T15.4(a)
CTR eligibility 16.24, 16.31, 17.22
EEA nationals 21.82-84
Eligible for UC 2.14-18, T2.3, T2.5(k), 4.10(d)
Income 10.56-60, T10.5
Supported housing 5.10-13, T5.3, T5.4
Support for mortgage interest, *see* Owner occupier
Surplus earnings 10.15, T10.2

Suspending UC
Appeals about 11.41
Grounds 11.32, 11.38
Information and evidence 11.33
Restoring payment 11.34-35
Termination of award following 11.36-37

T

Temporary absence 2.32-35, 5.47-55, 16.25-28
Temporary accommodation T5.2, 5.10-13, T5.3, 6.47
Temporary admission T20.2, 20.41
Temporary permission to stay T20.2, 20.25
Trafficking/slavery 20.25
Transfer to UC *see* Migration to UC
Transitional housing payment (migration to UC) 4.5-7
Transitional protection 4.9-10, 4.36-42, 4.43-49
Twins, *see* Multiple births
Two-child limit, *see* Child element
Two homes 5.60-63

U

UC allowances T9.2

UC entitlement to
Absence from Great Britain 2.29-35
Age limits 2.9-13, T2.2
Basic conditions 2.1, T2.1
Benefit unit 3.46-69
Couples 2.4-8
Financial conditions 2.1, 9.3-11
Hospital T2.1, 2.7, 2.27, T2.7
Migrants 2.20-21, Ch 20, Ch 21
Migration onto from legacy benefits 4.2, T4.1, 4.13,
    4.18, 4.24
Single people 2.2-3, 2.7-8
Students 2.14-19, T2.3, 4.10
Work requirements 2.38-46, T2.4, T2.5, T2.7
Ukraine, person from *see* Migrant
Unearned income 10.48-69, T10.4, T10.5
Under-occupation *see* Size criteria

Upper Tribunal (UC)
Appeals against 14.70.
Appeals to 14.68-69
Time limit 14.69
Utility bills (fuel, water) 12.55-59, T12.4

V

Voluntary migration, 4.2, T4.1, 4.13-17

W

Wales CTR, 16.7-8, 16.13, 16.20,16.33-34, 16.39, 16.42,
17.12, T17.1, 17.36, T17.3, A3, A4
Water T6.3, 6.37, 12.55-59, T12.4
Work allowance 10.11-12, T10.1

Y

Young care leavers 2.11-12
Young people (16-21s) 2.10-13, T2.2, 2.18, T2.3(f), T6.4